Wayland

A PRACTICAL GRAMMAR FOR CLASSICAL HEBREW

A PRACTICAL GRAMMAR FOR CLASSICAL HEBREW

BY

J. WEINGREEN, M.A., PH.D.

EMERITUS FELLOW OF TRINITY COLLEGE, DUBLIN
EMERITUS PROFESSOR OF HEBREW
UNIVERSITY OF DUBLIN

SECOND EDITION

CLARENDON PRESS • OXFORD
OXFORD UNIVERSITY PRESS NEW YORK

Oxford University Press, Walton Street, Oxford OX2 6 DP

LONDON GLASGOW NEW YORK TORONTO
DELHI BOMBAY CALCUTTA MADRAS KARACHI
KUALA LUMPUR SINGAPORE HONG KONG TOKYO
NAIROBI DAR ES SALAAM CAPE TOWN
MELBOURNE AUCKLAND
and associate companies in
BEIRUT BERLIN IBADAN MEXICO CITY

ISBN 0 19 815422 4

First edition 1939
Second edition 1959

Printed in the United States of America

FOREWORD

By PROFESSOR R. M. GWYNN, M.A., B.D., S.F., T.C.D.

MY friend and colleague, Professor Weingreen, has invited me to say something by way of Foreword to his grammar.

In our work for Dublin University, where each year we have large classes of Divinity students beginning Hebrew from the very outset, we have for many years past felt the need of a grammar written on the simplest possible lines, and yet enabling students to begin the actual study of the Old Testament without unnecessary delay. Dr. Weingreen is eminently qualified for the task of producing such a work, for besides possessing exact and accomplished scholarship in advanced Hebrew studies, he has many years' experience of teaching elementary classes as well as more proficient pupils. He has been remarkably successful in arousing interest among his students, and his grammar is based on the methods he has actually followed. I believe that he has achieved a book which will be found really valuable both by the beginner and by those who gradually acquire a greater familiarity with the actual text of the Hebrew Scriptures.

PREFACE

THE aim of this book is to render the teaching and study of Classical Hebrew simple and interesting. While there are a number of Hebrew grammars in English used by teachers and students, my experience in teaching the language has made it clear to me that a more simple, direct, and reasonable system could be devised than is at present available. From conversations with other teachers of Hebrew it has become evident to me that there was a real need for a grammar which would make the study of the language more attractive. It was to satisfy this need that I undertook to prepare a practical grammar and throughout the entire work I have been guided by the following main ideas:

1. Hebrew grammar is essentially schematic and, starting from simple primary rules, it is possible to *work out*, almost mathematically, the main groups of word-building. In this grammar when the reader is confronted with a new point he is usually referred to already known principles which, when applied to the problem, produce the required result. A typical example is the case of 'Weak Verbs': these are explained rationally by the simple method of applying to these verbs the ordinary rules governing 'peculiar' letters and thus *working out* the forms which they, respectively, assume.

2. It is not practicable to attempt to teach Hebrew grammar in all its details to beginners. It is more profitable to deal with the main principles and usages which should rather form the basis for more advanced study later. On this account I have endeavoured to avoid, as far as it is possible and practicable, references to the minute and manifold exceptions which appear in advanced Hebrew grammars.

3. In the interests of true translation I have indicated, wherever necessary, the line of thinking inherent in the Hebrew language. In the exercises words are often put in brackets to show that they are not in the English but must be supplied in the Hebrew, as, for example: 'The man took the book from (upon) the

table.' Attention is frequently called to the advisability of first translating the English sentence into terms of Hebrew thinking and then giving the appropriate Hebrew words.

4. Because of the inflexional capacity of Hebrew words I have found it possible to arrange extensive exercises based on a comparatively small but useful vocabulary. I feel that while the student is engaged in the task of acquiring the essentials of grammar he should not be expected to accumulate an extensive vocabulary. Once he has gained a sound working knowledge of grammar and is ready to study a Biblical text in Hebrew, he can enlarge his stock of words by referring to a lexicon.

5. The exercises are planned not merely to illustrate the points of grammar immediately under consideration but also to include a great deal of the earlier grammar and words, in order that the student may receive as much practice as possible in inflecting Hebrew words. Like the grammatical material itself, the exercises are progressive and each may be regarded as containing much of its predecessors. At the same time, the sentences in the exercises have been designed to maintain interest in the work of translation, for they consist mainly of references to Biblical personalities and events. In the latter half of the book the exercises contain small but complete narratives and some poetry; in this way the student is being prepared gradually for the reading of Biblical texts in Hebrew.

6. For the purposes of revision and reference useful summaries of the elements of Hebrew grammar will be found in the earlier portions of the book.

7. The tables and vocabularies at the end of the book have been extensively illustrated and, in themselves, constitute a skeleton grammar. The advantage of fully illustrated tables and vocabularies is that the student will be able conveniently to find any information he is seeking.

These are the main ideas which I have endeavoured to incorporate into the planning of the book and I venture to hope that the requirements of both teachers and students of Hebrew will thus be met. I am extremely grateful for the encouragement and help I have received while I was engaged in this work.

I wish to thank Professor R. M. Gwynn, M.A., B.D., Senior Fellow, Trinity College, Dublin, for his continued interest in this work, for his careful reading of the manuscript and for his generous introductory note. To Professor G. R. Driver, M.A., M.C., Fellow of Magdalen College, Oxford, I am especially indebted. Professor Driver has been particularly kind in giving me the benefit of his expert help in reading the manuscript, correcting the proofs, offering valuable criticisms and suggestions, and supplying a note in the Appendix on the 'Waw Consecutive'. To the readers of the Clarendon Press my thanks are due for their valuable help in ensuring accuracy.

J. W.

TRINITY COLLEGE,
DUBLIN
June 1939

PREFACE TO THE SECOND (REVISED) EDITION

IN this revised edition no changes have been made in the presentation of the grammar, the tables of verbs, nouns, and adjectives, or the exercises. However, apart from some minor corrections, the following modifications and additions have been introduced. The transliteration of the spirant letters with the additional 'h' (e.g. bh, gh, kh, &c.) has been abandoned and the more convenient method of transliteration by underlining the letter (e.g. ḇ, g̱, ḵ, &c.) has been adopted. It is hoped thus to remove any possible confusion in transliteration, particularly in the early stages of study. In order further to assist the student, fresh footnotes have been added and some existing ones expanded. To clarify and complete the rule governing the construct–genitive relation of nouns involving an adjectival idea, a brief note has been added in the Appendix.

The wide adoption of this Hebrew Grammar as a textbook is a matter of deep gratification to me. I trust that the improvements embodied in this revised edition will contribute further towards the realization of the aims of the book.

J. W.

TRINITY COLLEGE,
DUBLIN
August 1957

CONTENTS

A. THE HEBREW ALPHABET

THE Hebrew alphabet consists of 22 consonants. They are:

Form	Finals	*Name*[a]	*Transliteration*[b]	*Numerical Value*
א		ʼÁlep̱	ʼ	1
בּ ב		Bêṯ, Ḇêṯ	b, ḇ (bh)	2
גּ ג		Gímel, G̱ímel	g, g̱ (gh)	3
דּ ד		Dáleṯ, Ḏáleṯ	d, ḏ (dh)	4
ה		Hē	h	5
ו		Wāw	w	6
ז		Záyin	z	7
ח		Ḥêṯ	ḥ	8
ט		Ṭêṯ	ṭ	9
י		Yôḏ	y	10
כּ כ	ך	Kap̱, Ḵap̱	k, ḵ (kh)	20
ל		Lámeḏ	l	30
מ	ם	Mêm	m	40
נ	ן	Nûn	n	50
ס		Sámeḵ	s	60
ע		ʻÁyin	ʻ	70
פּ פ	ף	Pē, P̱ē	p, p̱ (ph)	80
צ	ץ	Ṣáḏê	ṣ	90
ק		Qôp̱ or Ḳôp̱	q or ḳ	100
ר		Rêš	r	200
שׂ שׁ		Śîn, Šîn	ś, š	300
תּ ת		Tāw, Ṯāw	t, ṯ (th)	400

[a] A spirant letter (ph, th, &c.) is represented by a single underlined letter (p̱, ṯ, &c.).

[b] The phonetic values are given on p. 3.

The foregoing Table shows that:

(*a*) Six consonants have alternate forms, namely:

ת פ כ ד ג ב without a dot, when they are soft or spirant,
b g d k p t

and תּ פּ כּ דּ גּ בּ with a dot, which hardens them.
b g d k p t

(A full account is given on p. 14.)

(*b*) Five consonants assume special forms at the end of words. In the beginning or middle of a word their forms are צ פ נ מ כ, but at the end of a word their forms are ץ ף ן ם ך[a].

(*c*) The consonants are also numerical signs.[b] The units are represented by א to ט, the tens by י to צ, and the hundreds by ק to ת.

Compound numbers are represented thus: 11 יא (1 + 10, *since Hebrew is written from right to left*, see p. 4), 12 יב (2 + 10), 13 יג (3 + 10) &c., 21 כא (1 + 20), 31 לא (1 + 30), 32 לב (2 + 30), 33 לג (3 + 30) &c., 101 קא (1 + 100), 111 קיא (1 + 10 + 100), 121 קכא (1 + 20 + 100) &c., 201 רא (1 + 200), 211 ריא (1 + 10 + 200), 221 רכא (1 + 20 + 200) &c., 500 תק (100 + 400), 600 תר (200 + 400), 1000 תתר (200 + 400 + 400).

Note: In the compounds of tens and units there are two exceptions to the above system. Nos. 15 and 16 are *not* denoted by יה and יו since these combinations represent forms of the divine name (YH and YW representing YAH and YO). No. 15 is therefore designated by טו (6 + 9) and 16 by טז (7 + 9).

B. PHONETIC VALUES OF LETTERS

It is essential to know the correct phonetic value of every Hebrew consonant, since a great deal of Hebrew grammar results directly from the peculiar pronunciation of certain consonants.

[a] This final letter, when vowelless, has two dots in it, thus: ךְ

[b] This usage is not Biblical; the first traces of it are found on Maccabean coins.

Since some consonants have no equivalents in the English alphabet, it was not possible to give their true phonetic value in the foregoing Table. Below is given the pronunciation of each consonant:

א (represented by the light breathing ʾ) is a cutting off of the breath; its consonantal value being apparent when it has a vowel. It is analogous to the silent 'h' in a word like 'honest'.

בּ is simply 'b' and ב (ḇ) is pronounced as 'v'.

גּ is hard 'g' as in 'go' and ג (ḡ) is almost like a guttural 'r'.

דּ is simply 'd' and ד (ḏ) is the same as 'th' in the word 'the'.

ה is 'h'.

ו is 'w'.

ז is 'z'.

ח ('ḥ' with the dot underneath to distinguish it from ה 'h') is like the 'ch' in the Scots word 'loch'.

ט (ṭ with the dot underneath) is a dull 't' produced by placing the tongue against the palate.

י is 'y'.

כּ is 'k' and כ (ḵ) is practically a harsh 'ch' as above.

ל is 'l'.

מ is 'm'.

נ is 'n'.

ס is dull 's'.

ע (represented by the rough breathing ʿ) is very difficult to pronounce, being produced at the back of the throat, almost like a gulping sound.

פּ is 'p' and פ (p̄) is pronounced like 'f'.

צ (represented by ṣ with dot under it) is a hissing 's'.

ק (represented by 'q' or 'ḳ') is a 'k' at the back of the throat, like the cawing of a crow.

ר is 'r'.

שׂ (with a dot over *left-hand* corner) is 's'—conventionally transcribed ś. שׁ (with dot over *right-hand* corner, represented by š) is pronounced as 'sh'.

שׂ and שׁ were originally one letter, and they are still both represented by the one sign ש (without a dot) in vowelless texts.

תּ is 't' and ת (ṯ) is 'th' as in the word 'think'.

DISTINGUISH carefully between consonants of similar form, as below:

ב and כ	ג and נ	ר, ד, and final ך
ה and ח	ט and מ	י, ו, and final ן
final ם and ס		ע, צ, and final ץ

C. VOWEL-SIGNS

Short	*Long*
ַ PATHAḤ[a] -a- as in 'had'	ָ QĀMEṢ -ā- as in 'yard'
ֶ SEGHÔL -e- as in 'bed'	ֵ ṢĒRÊ -ē- as in 'they' ֵי -ê
ִ short ḤÎREQ -i- as in 'lid'	ִי long ḤÎREQ -î- as in 'machine'
ֻ QIBBÛṢ -u- as in 'bull'	וּ ŠÛREQ -û- as in 'flute'
ָ QĀMEṢ-ḤĀṬÛPH -o- as in 'top'	וֹ ḤŌLEM -ô- as in 'hole' ֹ -ō-

NOTE: (*a*) The vowels ā and ŏ are both represented by the sign ָ. No. 7 (page 12) explains how to determine which vowel this sign represents when it occurs in a word, but for the time being (i.e. till we reach no. 7) it may be taken as Qāmeṣ-ā.

(*b*) Most vowel-signs appear below the consonant (בָּ bā, בֻּ bu, בֶּ be) but Šûreq and full Ḥōlem are placed after it (בּוּ bû, בּוֹ bô), while the other form of Ḥōlem is a dot placed over the letter (בֹּ bō).[b]

(*c*) CAUTION must be exercised in giving each vowel its *true phonetic sound.* The student *must not think of* Hebrew vowel-signs in terms of *English vowels.* The sound of Qāmeṣ is 'aa', of Šûreq 'oo', of Ṣērê 'ay', &c.

D. EXPLANATION OF WRITING

HEBREW IS WRITTEN FROM RIGHT TO LEFT, so that a word having, for example, the consonants *l*, *m*, *d̲* is written למד; the vowels being placed under or after the consonant, e.g. lā-mad̲ לָמַד, lā-mûd̲ לָמוּד.

[a] The transliteration of spirant letters in the names of vowel-signs and of grammatical terms follows the older system (bh, kh, &c.), since it is widely used for this purpose.

[b] When this dot follows שׁ or precedes שׂ it coalesces with the dot which marks the letter.

Once the consonants and vowels are known, syllables are easily formed. A syllable (regarded as open) consists of a consonant and a vowel, as בָּ bā, בֵּ bē, בּוּ bû, בּוֹ bô; or (said to be closed when it consists of) a consonant and a vowel followed by another consonant, as בָּר bār, בֵּר bēr, בּוּר bûr, בּוֹר bôr.

It is IMPORTANT to remember that *a syllable* begins with a consonant and *cannot begin with a vowel*,[a] so that, for example, the two-syllabled word בָּרָד is bā-rāḏ (and cannot be bār-āḏ). It follows, too, that a vowel must be preceded by a consonant (רָדָ being impossible).

When reading a word which has more than one syllable, it is best for beginners to treat each syllable separately, thus: בָּ רָד bā-rāḏ.

The following reading exercise is transliterated to facilitate the work of the beginner:

בָּמוֹת	בָּמוֹ	בָּם[b]	בָּזוּז	בָּזַז	בַּז	בָּדָד	בָּד	בָּ	
bā-môṯ	bā-mô	bām	bā-zûz	bā-zaz	baz	bā-ḏāḏ	bāḏ	bā	
בֵּ	בָּהָר	בָּרָד	בָּר	בָּנוֹת	בָּנִים[b]	בָּנוּ	בָּן[b]	בָּמוֹתָם[b]	
bē	bā-hār	bā-rāḏ	bār	bā-nôṯ	bā-nîm	bā-nû	bān	bā-mô-ṯām	
גַּג	גַּ	בֶּהָרִים[b]	בָּבֶל	בֵּיתוֹ	בֵּית	בֵּינָם[b]	בֵּינִי	בֵּין[b]	בֵּן[b]
gag	ga	be-hā-rîm	bā-ḇel	bê-ṯô	bêṯ	bê-nām	bê-nî	bên	bēn
דֶּבֶר	דָּבָר	גֵּבִים[b]	גָּזַל	גֵּזֶל	גָּדוֹל	גַּן[b]	גַּם[b]	גַּל	
de-ḇer	dā-ḇār	gē-ḇîm	gā-zal	gē-zel	gā-ḏôl	gan	gam	gal	
דּוֹרוֹתָם	דּוֹרוֹת	דּוֹר	דִּין	דָּמִים	דַּל	דּוֹדִים	דֶּגֶל	דֹּבֵר	
dô-rô-ṯām	dô-rôṯ	dôr	dîn	dā-mîm	dal	dô-ḏîm	de-gel	dōḇēr	
הַס	הָמוּ	הֹלֵם	הָדָר	הָבוּ	בָּדַק	גָּדַל	בֶּגֶד	דָּשׁוּ	
has	hā-mû	hō-lēm	hā-ḏār	hā-ḇû	bā-ḏaq	gā-ḏal	be-geḏ	dā-šû	
וִיהוֹשָׁפָט	וֶרֶד	וָדֹר	וָבֹהוּ	בָּהֶם	הֵרִים	הֵסֵב			
wî-hô-šā-pāṭ	we-reḏ	wā-ḏōr	wā-ḇō-hû	bā-hem	hē-rîm	hē-sēḇ			
עָז	בָּטַח	חָבֵר	גֶּזֶר	זֶרַע	זָמַם	זֹכֵר	מָוֶת	דָּוִד	
ʿāz	bā-ṭaḥ	ḥā-ḇēr	ge-zer	ze-raʿ	zā-mam	zō-ḵēr	mā-weṯ	dā-wîḏ	
								חָכָם	
								ḥā-ḵām	

[a] The only exception is the conjunction ('and') which sometimes is וּ (see p. 40. 2).

[b] Final forms, at the end of the word. p. 2 (*b*).

The consonant **א** is silent, so that only its vowel is heard; yet in transcription it must be represented by the smooth breathing sign (**אָ** 'ā).[a]

אָ אָב אָבִי אָבִינוּ אֵ אֵל אֵלִי אִישׁ אֶבֶן אֶת אֶלֶף

'e-lep̱ 'eṯ 'e-ḇen 'îš 'ē-lî 'ēl 'ē 'ā-ḇî-nû 'ā-ḇî 'āḇ 'ā

אוֹר אוֹרוֹת הָאָב מָאוֹר מֵהָאָדָם

mē-hā-'ā-ḏām mā-'ôr hā-'āḇ 'ô-rôṯ 'ôr

Read and transcribe:

שָׁמַיִם וָאָרֶץ וִיהִי כּוֹכָב מִינֵהוּ יָמִים רֹמֶשֶׂת כָּנָף עֵזֶר[b]

קֵץ בָּשָׂר תֵּבַת חָמָס קֶדֶם חָמֵשׁ שָׁנִים וָעֶשֶׂר תֵּלֵד זָכָר

יָקֻם עָשׂוּ מוֹעֵד בֶּץ חָדַל יַחַר עֶרֶב בֹּקֶר הוֹצִיאָם

דֶּלֶת שָׁפוּט אוֹכֵל יַיִן מֵתַי רָאִיתָ מָקוֹם יַעֲשׂוּ אֶשֶׁת

בַּעַל יִירַשׁ תַּחַת אַיִל יֹאמַר יֵשׁ מִחוּץ לָעִיר שָׂדֵהוּ

גָּמָל לָבָן

Transcribe into Hebrew:

môṯ mô-ṯî lā-mûṯ śām yôm hēn 'al ʿal gaḏ
pā-rîm lî lûz kēn wā-nāḏ qûm ṭal śîm nā-zîḏ
tôr yô-sēp̱ 'ā-nō-ḵî rā-ḥēl pa-ʿam lā-ḵem ʿam
hā-'ā-ḏām lē-wî bôr pe-reṣ qô-lî pā-rôṯ wā-'ō-mar
nā-ḇôn še-ḇer hā-šîḇ lô yā-ḏî kē-nîm ḥā-lam
hā-rag yā-ḏām ke-sep̱ ʿe-ḇeḏ 'ō-ṯô ʿe-śer ne-peš
hā-ḇû nā-ṯan qā-nî-ṯî le-ḥem sû-sîm tam

1. VOWEL-LETTERS

The original Hebrew alphabet consisted of consonants only; vowels were not represented in writing.[c] Even to-day, the Hebrew Scrolls of the Law which are read in the Synagogues are unpointed, i.e. without vowel-signs.[d]

However, long before the introduction of the vowel-signs it

[a] See p. 3.

[b] 'ē-zer.

[c] The system of vowel-signs was introduced, most probably, about the seventh century of this era.

[d] When one refers to the 'letters' of the Hebrew alphabet, it is the consonants, *and not the vowels*, which are meant.

was felt that the main vowel-sounds should be indicated in writing, and so the three letters הוי were used to represent the long vowels, thus:

ה represents â, so that מה reads mâ.

י represents î and ê, so that מי reads mî or mê.

ו represents û and ô, so that מו reads mû or mô.

Because these three letters—הוי—represent both vowels and letters they are known as VOWEL-LETTERS.

2. OPEN AND CLOSED SYLLABLES

Taking as our example the two-syllabled word קָטַל[a] (qā-ṭál) the syllable קָ (qā) ends in a vowel and is said to be open, whereas the syllable טַל (ṭal) ends in a consonant and is said to be closed.

DEFINITION: An open syllable is one which ends in a vowel, and a closed syllable is one which ends in a consonant.

So that in חֶסֶד (ḥé-seḏ) חֶ is open and סֶד is closed, and in מֵאָדָם (mē-'ā-ḏấm) מֵ אָ are open and דָם is closed.

Usually an open syllable has a long vowel but, if accented,[a] may have a short vowel. Conversely, a closed syllable usually has a short vowel but, if accented, may have a long vowel.[b]

The importance of this section may be expressed in one rule (which is of special significance, e.g. pp. 12 and 13), namely: *A syllable which is* CLOSED *and* UNACCENTED *must have a* SHORT VOWEL.[c]

3. METHEGH[d]

In the word הֶעָרִים (heʿārîm) the vowel Sᵉghol ֶ has a short vertical stroke to the left of it. This vertical stroke is called

[a] An arrow-head is conventionally used to mark the accented syllable, thus: קָטַל qā-ṭál, חֶסֶד ḥé-seḏ.

[b] In קָטַל the open syllable קָ has a long vowel, but in חֶסֶד the open syllable חֶ is accented and therefore can have a short vowel. In חֶסֶד the closed syllable סֶד has a short vowel, but in מֵאָדָם the closed syllable דָם is accented and therefore can have a long vowel.

[c] In the example חֶסֶד the last syllable סֶד is *closed and unaccented*; therefore its vowel *must be short* (the pointing חֶסֵד is impossible).

[d] See p. 4, footnote *a*.

Methegh (מֶֽתֶג 'bridle') and it indicates that the reader must pause, so that the word above is to be read הֶֽעָרִים he'ārîm; similarly הָֽאָדָם hā'āḏām.

Definition: Methegh is a short vertical stroke placed at the left of a vowel. Its effect is to make the reader pause after it. That is to say: when a natural pause occurs within a spoken word, that pause is indicated in writing by a Methegh.

Note: The uses of Methegh are illustrated in the following chapters. It will be seen that, acting as a check, it serves as a kind of half-accent (see 4 below), determines whether a syllable is closed or open (see 5 below), and whether the vowel-sign ָ represents ā or o (p. 12. 7).

4. MILRA' AND MIL'EL

In the word דָּבָר (dāḇár) the accent is on the last (i.e. ultimate) syllable, and is said to be *Milra'* (מִלְרַע 'from below'; i.e. last syllable).

In the word הַחֶסֶד (haḥéseḏ) the accent is on the last but one (i.e. the penultimate) syllable, and is said to be *Mil'êl* (מִלְעֵיל 'from above'; i.e. the syllable before the last).

The accent on דָּבָר (dāḇár) is Milra', and on הַחֶסֶד (haḥéseḏ) is Mil'êl.
,, שָׁמַר (šāmár) ,, ,, שָׁמָרוּ (šāmárû) ,,
,, הָֽאָדָם (hā'āḏám) ,, ,, עֶבֶד ('éḇeḏ) ,,

Most Hebrew words are accented Milra', but there are, of course, many Mil'êl words. In a word of more than two syllables the accent may be either on the last or next but last syllable, but it *never* occurs on the syllable second before the last (the antepenultimate).[a] A methegh often appears two places before the accent, thus: הֶֽעָרִים (he'ārîm), מֵֽהָאָרֶץ (mēhā'áreṣ) and serves as a kind of half-accent.

5. ŠEWA

When, in a pointed text, there is a vowelless letter at the beginning or in the middle of a word, then the sign ְ—called

[a] Except when a long word has two accents, in which case it is treated virtually as two words.

Š^e^wâ (שְׁוָא) fills the gap under it. Thus, instead of writing לשׁמוֹ, בּיַד, one writes לִשְׁמוֹ, בְּיַד.

Šewa is of two kinds: (*a*) SIMPLE and (*b*) COMPOSITE.

(*a*) SIMPLE ŠEWA.

(i) The shewa[a] in שְׁמוֹ (š^e^mô) and שׁוֹ|מְרִים (šô-m^e^rîm) begins the syllable with a quick vowel-like sound.[b] This is *vocal shewa.* The shewa in יִשְׁ|מֹר (yiš-mōr) and אַפְ|קִיד ('ap̱-qîḏ) closes the syllable and is silent. This is *silent shewa.* Hence we see that shewa is *vocal when it begins a syllable*—at the beginning or middle of a word, and *silent when it ends (or closes) a syllable*—in the middle of a word.[c]

(ii) It will also be observed from the above examples that when *shewa* occurs in the middle of a word then, *after a long vowel* it *is vocal* (as שׁוֹ|מְרִים šô-m^e^rîm) and *after a short vowel* it *is silent* (as יִשְׁ|מֹר yiš-mōr).[d]

(iii) *When two shewas occur together* in the middle of a word as in יִשְׁ|מְרוּ (yiš-m^e^rû), *the first* shewa closes the one syllable and *is* therefore *silent*, while *the second* begins the next syllable and *is* therefore *vocal.* Similarly אֶקְטְלָה ('eq-ṭ^e^lâ).

(iv) We shall see later (p. 15) that a dot (called Dagheš Forte) placed in a letter shows that that letter is doubled, so that a word like קִטְּלוּ is really the same as קִטְטְלוּ (qiṭ-ṭ^e^lû); this, then, is a condensed form of the preceding case. Thus, *a shewa under a letter which* is doubled (and *has a Dagheš Forte* in it) *is vocal.*

[a] For the sake of convenience it may be thus spelt—shewa.

[b] The shewa is not a vowel. The quick vowel-like sound is like the 'e' in 'because', and שְׁמוֹ is regarded as one syllable, שׁוֹ|מְרִים as a two-syllabled word.

[c] The vowelless letter at the end of a word has no shewa written, as יִשְׁמֹר. Exceptions to this are some words, such as אַתְּ ('at)—'thou' (f.), נֵרְדְּ (nērd)—'nard'.

[d] Since a long vowel is usually in an open syllable, the shewa following it begins the next syllable. Conversely, since a short vowel is usually in a closed syllable, the shewa following it closes that syllable. A word like וַֽיְהִי (wa-y^e^hî) is an exception. The Methegh after the short vowel makes the reader pause and the syllable is thus left open. The shewa then begins the next syllable and is therefore vocal, see p. 18, Note.

(*b*) Composite Shewa. The guttural letters (אהחע) exhibit many peculiarities (pp. 19 f.). One is that when a guttural stands vowelless at the beginning of a syllable, the shewa-sound is practically a half-vowel. There are three such half-vowels called Ḥāṭēph[a]-vowels (חָטֵף ‘hurried’): ◌ֲ Ḥaṭeph-Pathaḥ [$^{\breve{a}}$], ◌ֱ Ḥaṭeph-Seghol [$^{\breve{e}}$], ◌ֳ Ḥaṭeph-Qameṣ [$^{\breve{o}}$].

The composite representation by shewa and short vowel together gave rise to the term composite shewa, and the ordinary shewa, in contradistinction, is called Simple Shewa.

To illustrate how a composite shewa appears under a guttural instead of a simple vocal shewa, we may take an ordinary verb like שָׁבַר (šāḇar—‘he broke’) the imperative of which is שְׁבֹר (š^{e}ḇōr—‘break’), but of a corresponding verb whose first letter is a guttural like עָבַר (‘āḇar—‘he passed’) the imperative is עֲבֹר (‘$^{\breve{a}}$ḇōr[b]—‘pass’) with composite shewa under the guttural (instead of עְבֹר ‘^{e}ḇōr). Similarly the plural of יָשָׁר (yāšār—‘upright’) is יְשָׁרִים (y^{e}šārîm), but the plural of a corresponding adjective whose first letter is a guttural, such as חָכָם (ḥāḵām—‘wise’), is חֲכָמִים (ḥ$^{\breve{a}}$ḵāmîm: instead of חְכָמִים ḥ^{e}ḵāmîm).

Note: A syllable cannot begin with two vowelless letters, i.e. with two vocal shewas. If, however, conditions are such that a letter with a vocal shewa be placed immediately before another letter with vocal shewa, then the first vocal shewa becomes the nearest short vowel (in sound), namely short Ḥireq (.). For example, the preposition ‘to’ is a prefixed (vowelless) לְ, so that when it is prefixed to the word שְׁמוּאֵל (š^{e}mû’ēl—‘Samuel’) the combination לְשְׁמוּאֵל (l^{e}š^{e}mû’ēl) cannot be articulated, and the first vocal shewa becomes the short vowel Ḥireq לִשְׁמוּאֵל (liš^{e}mûēl—‘to Samuel’). The second shewa remains vocal, as it was before the preposition was attached. (An exception to this will be found later, p. 80, footnote *b*.) When a simple vocal shewa is placed immediately before a composite shewa it becomes, under the influence of the latter, the corresponding short vowel, e.g. ‘To Edom’ is (not לְאֱדוֹם but) לֶאֱדוֹם (cf. p. 27. 4, p. 41. 4).

[a] See p. 4, footnote *a*. [b] The vowel-like sound is like the ‘a’ in ‘about’.

SUMMARY: Shewa fills the empty space under a vowelless letter. It is of two kinds: (*a*) Simple and (*b*) Composite.

(*a*) i. Simple shewa (ְ) is vocal when it begins a syllable (at the beginning or middle of a word) and silent when it closes a syllable (in the middle of a word).

ii. After a long vowel it is vocal: after a short silent.

iii. When two shewas occur together in the middle of a word, the first is silent and the second vocal.

iv. Shewa under a letter doubled by a dot (Dagheš Forte, pp. 15–16) is vocal.

(*b*) Composite shewa ֲ ֳ ֱ replaces vocal shewa simple under the guttural letters (אהחע).

NOTE: When two simple shewas occur together at the beginning of a word, the first becomes the short vowel Ḥireq (ִ); before a composite shewa the simple vocal shewa becomes the corresponding short vowel.

Read and transcribe:

דְּבַר דִּבְרֵי יַרְדֵּן אִשְׁתּוֹ מַמְלֶכֶת בְּרוּךְ מִדְבָּר עֲבָדִים

אֱלֹהִים אֲבִי מוֹשְׁבוֹת מִצְרַיִם יִשְׁבְּרוּ עַבְדְּךָ[a] מַהֲרוּ

בְּרִיתְךָ[a] אַבְרָהָם יִצְחָק יַעֲקֹב הַלְּבָנוֹן[b] יִלְּדוּ[b] כֹּהֲנִים מְלֹךְ

עִמְּךָ[b] הִשְׁחִית אֶפְרַיִם עִנְּבֵי[b] מַלְכְּכֶם וְאָמַרְתָּ אֲלֵיהֶם

בְּתוֹךְ לַעֲבֹר אֶצְלְךָ[a] אֲנַחְנוּ חַרְבּוֹ חֲסָדִים מִשְּׁמוּאֵל[b]

גֻּלְגֹּלֶת מְיַלְּדוֹת[b] עֶלְיוֹן חֲלוֹם נְשֵׁיהֶם אֱדוֹם שַׂמְתִּי

פְּלִשְׁתִּים תּוֹלְדוֹת

Transcribe into Hebrew:

b^{e}nôṯ d^{e}ḇārîm ḥeḇrōn binyāmîn ʼ^{ă}ḏāmôṯ n^{e}ḇîʼîm
nišm^{e}rû hiškîm q^{e}ṭaltem ʼ^{ĕ}mōr ta^{ʻă}ḇōḏ dark^{e}ḵā[a]
miṣrîm zōḇ^{e}ḥê beʼ^{ĕ}meṯ yaḇdēl mōṯ^{e}rôṯ napšî
ʼumlal l^{e}malkî yiṯhall^{e}ḵûn[b] tišm^{e}rēm mišp^{e}ṭê yiḵr^{eʼ}û
baqq^{e}šû[b] mišʼ^{ă}lôṯ

[a] The vowel is placed *in* the final ך.   [b] The doubling dot.

6. MAQQEPH[a]

When two or more short words are closely associated in meaning they are often joined together by a hyphen-like line called Maqqēph (מַקֵּף, 'binding'). For example אִם טוֹב אֲנִי ('im ṭôḇ 'ªnî, 'if good [am] I') may be united by Maqqeph, thus אִם־טוֹב־אֲנִי ('im-ṭôḇ-'ªnî), and then, for grammatical purposes, they are considered as being virtually one word. That is to say:—as separate words not connected by Maqqeph they have each an accent, but once they have been joined together by Maqqeph (and have thereby become one word) it is only the last of the group which retains its accent, while the accent on the word before the Maqqeph is dropped—as above.

The loss of an accent before a Maqqeph may often lead to adjustment in pointing (i.e. in vowels). When, for example, the words אֵת קוֹלִי ('ēṯ qôlî, 'my voice') are joined by Maqqeph, the word אֵת loses its accent and, being a closed syllable, it is now a *closed unaccented syllable*; therefore (see p. 7) it *must have* a *short vowel*, and so the long vowel Ṣere ֵ is shortened to its short vowel Seghol ֶ thus: אֶת־קוֹלִי ('eṯ-qôlî).

DEFINITION: Maqqeph is a short horizontal line connecting words together. Its effect is to deprive those words preceding it of their accents.

7. QAMEṢ-ḤAṬUPH[a]

Since the vowel-sign ָ is used to represent both Qameṣ 'ā' and Qameṣ-Ḥaṭuph 'o', we have to determine when it is (long) 'ā' and when (short) 'o'. The rule enunciated on p. 7 is here applied thus:—If the *vowel*-sign ָ occurs *in* a *closed unaccented syllable* it *must be short* and is therefore (short) 'o' = Qameṣ-Ḥaṭuph. If, on the other hand, it occurs in an *open* syllable, or in a syllable which, though *closed*, is *accented*, then it is long and therefore (long) 'ā' = Qameṣ.[b] Examples:

[a] See p. 4, footnote *a*.

[b] There are some exceptions, e.g. לָחֳלִי (loḥºlî); in this case the vowel under the first letter is 'o', since an original simple vocal shewa under the prefixed ל has become, under the influence of the composite shewa, the corresponding short vowel (see p. 10, Note).

1. וַיָּ֫קָם (wayyắqom). This word is accented Milʿel (p. 8). The vowel ָ in the *open* syllable יָ is 'ā', but in the *closed unaccented syllable* קָם it is 'o'. Similarly וַתָּ֫נָס (wattắnos). However, in the word לֵ֫בָב (lēḇāḇ), the vowel ָ is in a syllable which, though closed, is *accented*; and so it is 'ā'.

2. חָכְמָה (ḥoḵ|mâ). This word is accented Milraʿ (p. 8). The syllable חָכְ is *closed and unaccented*; therefore the vowel ָ in it is 'o'. The vowel ָ in the open syllable מָה is 'ā'.

Note: This type of noun (meaning 'wisdom') can be easily distinguished from the verb חָֽכְמָה (ḥā|kᵉmâ, 'she was wise') by the Methegh in the first syllable of the word. The Methegh makes the reader pause (pp. 7 f.) and leave the syllable open, so that the vowel ָ is in an open syllable and therefore 'ā'. Similarly we distinguish between the noun אָכְלָה ('oḵ|lâ, 'food') and the verb אָֽכְלָה ('ā|kᵉlâ, 'she ate').

3. חָנֵּנִי has the doubling dot (Dagheš Forte, pp. 15–16) in the first נ and is on that account really חָנְ|נֵ֫נִי (ḥon|nēnî). The vowel ָ is in a *closed unaccented syllable* and is therefore 'o'. But in the word לָ֫מָּה = לָ֫מְ|מָה (lắm|mâ) the vowel ָ is in a syllable which, though closed, is *accented*, and it is therefore 'ā'.

N.B. The word בָּתִּים ('houses') is found with Methegh—בָּֽתִּים, which would seem to indicate that it was read as 'bātîm' and not 'bottîm'.

4. כָּל־אִישׁ (kol-'îš). The Maqqeph after כָּל־ has deprived it of its accent (p. 12), so that its vowel ָ is in a *closed unaccented syllable* and is 'o'.[a]

Summary: The vowel-sign ָ is Qameṣ—'ā'—in an open syllable or in a syllable which is closed but accented.
It is Qameṣ-Ḥaṭuph—'o'—in a *closed syllable* which is *unaccented* (i.e. apart from ordinarily recognizable closed syllables, when followed by a silent shewa, by the doubling dot, or by Maqqeph—and the syllable is *unaccented*).

Read and transcribe:

וַיָּ֫מָת[b] עָרְמָה אֱמָר־נָא חָכְמָתוֹ דְּרָכְךָ קָדְקֹד שָׁמָ֫רְתִּי בָּקָר

[a] Without Maqqeph the word is כֹּל ('all', 'every'). When linked by Maqqeph the syllable becomes *un*accented, as well as being closed, so that its vowel is reduced from Ḥolem (ō) to Qameṣ-Ḥaṭuph, see p. 12. 6.

[b] Only words which have the accent Milʿel (i.e. on the syllable before the last) will be marked by the arrow-head over the accented syllable. Words over which there is no arrow-head are Milraʿ (accent on last syllable).

עָנְיֵךְ שְׁמַרְתָּם שָׁמְעוּ יָרָבְעָם מָתְנַיִם נָפְלָה כְּדָרְלָעֹמֶר דָּמְךְ
לַ֫יְלָה גָּדְלְךָ מָרְיָם יִכְתָּב־שָׁם אָזְנֵיהֶם יְבָרְכוּ מִדְבָּר לָרְאוּבֵנִי
כְּתָפְשְׂכֶם רָעָב גָּפְרִית כָּל־הָאָ֫רֶץ שְׁמָר־לִי פָּרַיִם כָּתְנוֹת
הֶחָכָם

8. DĀGHĒŠ[a]

Dāghēš (דָּגֵשׁ, 'piercing') *is a dot in the heart of a letter.* It is of two kinds: (*a*) Dagheš Lene or weak[b] and (*b*) Dagheš Forte or strong.

(*a*) DAGHEŠ LENE. There are six letters which have each a hard and a soft pronunciation—indicated in writing with and without a dot. They are:

ב ḇ	ג g̱	ד ḏ	כ ḵ	פ p̱	ת ṯ
בּ b	גּ g	דּ d	כּ k	פּ p	תּ t

These six letters without the dot are soft, i.e. pronounced as spirants; when the dot is inserted they become hard. This dot is called *Dagheš Lene*. Dagheš Lene, then, applies to the six letters בגדכפת (which are known mnemonically as בְּגַד כְּפַת B[e]gaḏ K[e]paṯ) and, when inserted in them, hardens them.

Below are examples of these letters with and without Dagheš Lene:

	ב		ג	
(i)	בָּטַח (bāṭaḥ)	יִקְבֹּר (yiq bōr)	גָּזַל (gāzal)	לִנְגֹּף (lin gōp̱)
(ii)	יִבְטַח (yiḇ ṭaḥ)	קָבַר (qā ḇar)	יִגְזֹל (yig̱ zōl)	נָגַף (nā gap̱)
	ד		**כ**	
(i)	דָּרוֹם (dārôm)	הִצְדִּיק (hiṣ dîq)	כֹּל (kōl)	אֶזְכֹּר ('ez kōr)
(ii)	וְדָרוֹם (w[e]ḏārôm)	צָדַק (ṣā ḏaq)	וְכֹל (w[e]ḵōl)	זָכַר (zā ḵar)
	פ		**ת**	
(i)	פָּרָה (pārâ)	יִסְפֹּר (yis pōr)	תָּלָה (tālâ)	לַחְתֹּם (laḥ tōm)
(ii)	וּפָרָה (û p̱ārâ)	סָפַר (sā p̱ar)	וְתָלָה (w[e]ṯālâ)	חָתַם (ḥā ṯam)

last) will be marked by the arrow-head over the accented syllable. Words over which there is no arrow-head are Milra' (accent on last syllable).

[a] See p. 4, footnote *a*.

[b] Weak Dagheš may have been so called in contradistinction to the other type of Dagheš which, denoting that a letter is doubled, is considered strong.

Examples in lines (i) show that *Dagheš Lene appears in a letter* (בגדכפת) *when that letter commences a syllable* in the beginning or middle of a word *providing that there is no vowel immediately before that letter.*

Conversely, the examples in lines (ii) show that *Dagheš Lene is absent when the letter* (בגדכפת) *does not commence a syllable or when*, at the beginning of a syllable, *it is immediately preceded by a vowel.*

(*b*) When Dagheš Forte appears in a letter it shows that, for some reason, that letter is doubled: קִטֵּל = קִטְטֵל ; הַשָּׁר = הַשְׁשָׁר : מִשָּׁר = מִשְׁשָׁר. *Dagheš Forte can appear in all letters* (including the six letters בגדכפת), *with the exception of the guttural letters* (אהחע) *and the letter* ר. The gutturals, being throat-letters, cannot be doubled in pronunciation, nor can ר, so that Dagheš Forte cannot apply to these five letters (see p. 16, Note (*b*)).

A letter in a word may have to be doubled—and the doubling represented by a Dagheš Forte—for several reasons. Here are some main types of Dagheš Forte:

(i) *Dagheš Forte Compensative*, e.g.: The preposition מִן (min) —'from'—is often joined to the word it governs, so that the phrase 'from Saul' מִן שָׁאוּל (min šā'ûl) may become one word (a hypothetical) מִנְשָׁאוּל (minšā'ûl); but the vowelless נ between the two vowelled consonants (is scarcely audible and, in fact) disappears—מִנְ שָׁאוּל—causing the following letter to be doubled (in pronunciation) and so represented (in writing) by a Dagheš Forte in it—מִשָּׁאוּל (miššā'ûl). Since the loss of the נ is *compensated* for by the doubling of the following letter, we have an example of *Dagheš Forte Compensative*. The same process is observed in some English words taken directly from Latin, e.g.: 'inlegal' becomes 'illegal', 'inmune' becomes 'immune'.

(ii) *Dagheš Forte Characteristic.* There are conjugations of the Hebrew verb (pp. 105 f.) called 'intensive', because the second root-letter is doubled, e.g. בִּקֵּשׁ (biqqēš, 'to seek'). Since this doubling is *characteristic* of the conjugation, the Dagheš Forte which denotes the doubling is known as *Dagheš Forte Characteristic.*

(iii) *Dagheš Forte Euphonic.* Sometimes, for the sake of clearer or smoother pronunciation, a letter in a word is doubled. The Dagheš which denotes this doubling is called *Dagheš Forte Euphonic.*

NOTE: (*a*) If, for example, the preposition מִן ('from') is joined with a word beginning with one of the six letters בגדכפת, such as כֹּל (kōl, 'all'), and the combination becomes (hypothetically מִנְכֹּל, minkōl, and then) מִכֹּל = מִכְּכֹל (mikkōl), the Dagheš in the כ acts both as Lene (since it shows that the letter is hardened) and Forte (since it shows that the letter is doubled).

(*b*) If the letter to be doubled happens to be a guttural or ר then, since these cannot be doubled (and so cannot receive Dagheš Forte), certain adjustments take place. An example will best illustrate. When the preposition מִן is joined to the noun אִישׁ ('îš, 'a man'), the resulting combination cannot be מִאִּישׁ (mi''îš), so the vowel (here Ḥireq ִ) preceding the guttural (here א) is prolonged (into Ṣere ֵ) producing the form מֵאִישׁ (mē'îš, 'from a man'). The (first) syllable, which would normally be closed by the doubling of the next letter, has become open and, since an open syllable usually has a long vowel (p. 7), the vowel in it is lengthened. Similarly 'from evil' is (not the impossible מִרָּע, mirrā', but) מֵרָע (mērā'). (Ḥireq is lengthened to Ṣere because they are in the same class of vowels.)

SUMMARY: Dagheš—a dot in the heart of a letter—is of two kinds:

(*a*) Dagheš Lene applies to the six letters בגדכפת and, when inserted in them, hardens them by changing the sound from spirant to momentary. Dagheš Lene occurs in these letters at the beginning of a syllable, provided that no vowel immediately precedes.

(*b*) Dagheš Forte denotes that a letter is doubled. It applies to all letters except the gutturals (אהחע) and ר. It may be

(i) *Compensative.* When, for some reason, a letter is assimilated, the following one is doubled (with Dagheš Forte in it) to compensate for its loss.

(ii) *Characteristic.* The characteristic of certain conjugations of the verb is the doubling of the second root-letter, which receives a Dagheš Forte.

(iii) *Euphonic.* A letter in a word is sometimes doubled for clearer pronunciation.

NOTE: When the letter to be doubled is a guttural or ר then, since these cannot be doubled (i.e. receive Dagheš Forte) the preceding vowel is lengthened.

9. MAPPIQ

When the letter ה stands vowelless at the end of a syllable it is usually silent, as מָה (mâ). There are cases, however, where, standing vowelless at the end of a syllable, it is (not meant to be a silent or vowel-letter but) to have the full status of a consonant and be pronounced as a sharp 'h'. To illustrate: the fem. of the noun סוּס (sûs, 'horse') is סוּסָה (sûsâ, 'mare'), but סוּס with the fem. sing. possessive ('her horse') is סוּסָהּ (sûsāh).

The הּ in the first case is silent, but in the second it is audible and sharp—as denoted by the dot in it, called מַפִּיק—Mappîq ('bringing out'). The ה in the verb גָּבַהּ (gābah) is likewise an ordinary letter, sharply audible.

10. RAPHE[a]

We have seen (on p. 16) that a letter is sometimes doubled for smoother pronunciation, in which case it has a Dagheš Forte Euphonic. Conversely, for the same reason, the doubling of a letter is sometimes omitted and Dagheš Forte is dropped, in which case a short horizontal line, called רָפֶה Rāphe[a] ('soft') appears over the letter. For example, the plural verb 'they sought' should be בִּקְּשׁוּ (biqqᵉšû) with a Dagheš Forte Characteristic in the ק (p. 15), but it is often found without the doubling of the second root-letter as בִּקְֿשׁוּ (biqᵉšû) with a Raphe over that

[a] See p. 4, footnote *a*.

letter, indicating that, for smoother pronunciation, the doubling (i.e. the Dagheš Forte) has been omitted.

NOTE: Often, especially in words of very frequent use, even Raphe does not appear over the letter which has been deprived of its (doubling, i.e. its) Dagheš Forte. The expression 'and he was' should strictly be וַיְּהִי (wayy^{e}hî) but is found either as וַֽיְהִי (wa y^{e}hî) (without a Raphe over the י, but) with Methegh after the Pathaḥ showing that the shewa following it is vocal (pp. 7 f., and p. 9, footnote *d*), or simply as וַיְהִי.[a]

DEFINITION: RAPHE is a short horizontal line placed over a letter to indicate that the doubling of that letter, i.e. Dagheš Forte, is omitted.

11. QUIESCENT LETTERS

The letters אהוי are so feeble (in pronunciation) that, under certain conditions, they lose their consonantal character and *quiesce*, i.e. they become silent. Hence they are called *Quiescent Letters*.

The examples below illustrate how they quiesce:

1. The word for 'God' is אֱלֹהִים ('^{ĕ}lōhîm) but in the combination 'to God' (first לֶאֱלֹהִים (le'^{ĕ}lōhîm)[b]) the א *quiesces* and loses it consonantal character, and the word becomes לֵאלֹהִים (lē'lōhîm)—see p. 28. 5.

2. When the preposition לְ ('to') is prefixed to the word יְהוּדָה (y^{e}hûḏâ, 'Judah'), the combination (לְיְהוּדָה, l^{e}y^{e}hûḏâ) first becomes לִיְהוּדָה[b] (liy^{e}hûḏâ), but the י *quiesces* and loses its consonantal status, the word becoming לִיהוּדָה (lîhûḏâ)—see p. 27. 3.

3. The word for 'death' is מָ֫וֶת (má̄weṯ) which, when taken together with a following word (e.g. 'death-of Moses') is spoken hurriedly and (becomes first a hypothetical מָוְת māwṯ and then) the ו *quiesces*, producing the form מוֹת־מֹשֶׁה (môṯ-mōšeh).

[a] וַיְהִי is actually the normal form, but when this expression is attached by Maqqeph to a monosyllable, or a two-syllabled word accented Mil'el, then וַ becomes two places back from the accented syllable and receives Methegh. Thus וַיְהִי מֹשֶׁה, וַיְהִי לָהֶם but וַֽיְהִי־עֶ֫רֶב, וַֽיְהִי־כֵן.

[b] See p. 10, Note.

NOTE: When, at the end of a syllable, the letters י and ו are preceded by vowels which are not homogeneous to them, they retain their consonantal character, e.g.:

[מִי mî and מֵי mê, but] דַּי day, גּוֹי gôy, קָנוּי qānúy.

[לוּ lû and לוֹ lô, but] צַו ṣaw, פִּיו pîw, קַו qaw.

12. THE GUTTURALS—אהחע

The gutturals, אהחע, being throat-letters, have the following peculiarities:

1. As explained on p. 16, Note (*b*), they cannot be doubled and therefore never receive Dagheš Forte; instead of the doubling, the vowel before them is lengthened, e.g. 'from a man' is מֵאָדָם (mē'ādām) (instead of מִאָּדָם (mi''ādām)).[a]

2. On p. 10 it was shown how gutturals take Composite Shewa—ֲ ֳ ֱ instead of the simple vocal shewa; thus, while the pl. of יָשָׁר (upright) is יְשָׁרִים (y^e^šārîm), the pl. of (a word of the same class but beginning with a guttural, as) חָכָם (wise) is חֲכָמִים, ḥ^a^kāmîm (not חְכָמִים, ḥ^e^kāmîm).

3. The gutturals have a preference for the vowel Pathaḥ (ַ) under them and even before them. For example, מֶ֫לֶךְ (mélek, 'king') is a type of noun which has the vowel Seghol (ֶ) in both syllables, but a noun of the same class which has a terminal guttural is זֶ֫בַח (zébaḥ, 'sacrifice', instead of זֶ֫בֶח, zébeḥ), the guttural attracting the vowel Pathaḥ. With medial guttural it is נַ֫עַר (instead of נֶ֫עֶר).

4. The type of noun סוּס (sûs, 'horse') is a monosyllable with the vowel Šureq (וּ) between two consonants; but the same type of noun with a terminal guttural is ר֫וּחַ (read 'rúaḥ',[b] 'wind', instead of רוּח, rûḥ). The extra vowel—Pathaḥ—under the guttural arises involuntarily in pronunciation when the guttural follows a full accented vowel. This is called *Furtive Pathaḥ*. Similarly in the verb; the normal infinitive is שְׁמֹר (š^e^mōr, 'to keep') but the infinitive of a verb with a guttural third root-letter is שְׁמֹ֫עַ (š^e^mōa',[b] 'to hear').

[a] Similarly the letter ר (p. 16, Note (*b*)).

[b] The Furtive Pathaḥ is read *before* its consonant.

SUMMARY: The guttural letters אהחע:

1. Do not admit Dagheš Forte (since they cannot be doubled) but the preceding vowel is lengthened instead. (Similarly with ר.)
2. Take Composite Shewa instead of simple Vocal Shewa.
3. Prefer the vowel Pathaḥ (ַ) under them and even before them.
4. Take a Furtive Pathaḥ after a full accented vowel.

13. ACCENTS

The opening lines of Genesis, as they appear in the printed editions of the Hebrew Bible, are reproduced here, to indicate the presence of accents and their main functions. They are:

(verse 1) בְּרֵאשִׁ֖ית בָּרָ֣א אֱלֹהִ֑ים אֵ֥ת הַשָּׁמַ֖יִם וְאֵ֥ת הָאָֽרֶץ׃

(verse 2) וְהָאָ֗רֶץ הָיְתָ֥ה תֹ֙הוּ֙ וָבֹ֔הוּ וְחֹ֖שֶׁךְ עַל־פְּנֵ֣י תְה֑וֹם . . .

Each word has, apart from vowels, a small sign either below or above one of its syllables. These small signs are the *accents* and they serve:

(*a*) *To mark the tone-syllable*, i.e. to indicate the syllable to be stressed in pronunciation. In each of the first three words of verse 1 the accent is on the last syllable (Milraʿ, p. 8), showing that the stress is to be on the last syllable (bᵉrē'šîṯ bārā́' 'ᵉlōhī́m); but in הַשָּׁמַ֖יִם (haššāmáyim, v. 1) and וְהָאָ֗רֶץ (wᵉhā'áreṣ, v. 2), the accent is on the syllable last but one (Milʿel, p. 8).[a]

(*b*) *As punctuation marks*, i.e. they divide the verse into its logical constituent parts. These are of two kinds which may conveniently be called *Stops* and *Continuation marks*.[b] The two major stops being:

i. (ֽ) called *Sillûq* (סִלּוּק), which always appears under the last word of a verse, as under הָאָֽרֶץ at the end of verse 1. The

[a] In grammars all accents are indicated by a conventional arrow-head over the stressed syllable. Since most words are Milraʿ, only Milʿel words are marked.

[b] These are usually termed 'Disjunctive and Conjunctive accents' A full list of accents is given at the end of the book, Appendix, § 2.

Silluq is naturally *the greatest stop* in a verse, and regularly followed by the sign : called *Sôph*[a] *Pāsûq* (סוֹף פָּסוּק, 'end of verse').

ii. (֑) called *'Athnāḥ*[a] (אַתְנָח), as under the word אֱלֹהִ֑ים, is the second greatest stop and divides the verse into two logical parts. The values of 'Athnaḥ and Silluq are seen in the translation of verse 1. 'In the beginning God created'—first half of verse, ends with 'Athnaḥ. 'The heavens and the earth'—second half of verse, ends with Silluq, followed by the Soph Pasuq sign.

N.B. Since the sign (ֽ) is used for both the accent Silluq and the Methegh, they are to be distinguished. If this sign occurs under a word in the *middle* of a verse it must be Methegh; if it occurs under the accented syllable of a word at the *end* of a verse it is Silluq. They may both occur together, thus: מֵֽהָאָֽדָם׃ has both a Methegh and a Silluq. Silluq always occurs in the accented syllable (of the last word in a verse) but Methegh never does.

(*c*) As *musical signs* for chanting the Scriptures in the Synagogues.

SUMMARY: The accents serve (*a*) to mark the tone-syllable, (*b*) as marks of punctuation, and (*c*) as musical signs for chanting Scripture.

14. PAUSE

A word is said to be *in pause* when its accent is a major stop, i.e. a Silluq or 'Athnaḥ (pp. 20–1); in either case the word being at the end of a clause. The tendency, in speech, is to prolong the accented syllable of the last word in a sentence, i.e. when the word is in pause: thus, the word for 'water' is מַ֫יִם (máyim) in the middle of a sentence, but in pause it is מָ֑יִם—מָֽיִם׃ (mā́yim) with 'Athnaḥ or Silluq, i.e. the short vowel Pathaḥ (ַ) in the accented syllable is lengthened to Qameṣ (ָ). Similarly, 'he hath kept' is שָׁמַ֫ר (šāmár) in the middle of a sentence, but in pause it is שָׁמָ֑ר—שָׁמָֽר׃ (šāmā́r) with 'Athnaḥ or Silluq.

(The changes in pointing due to pause are dealt with more fully on pp. 137 f.)

[a] See p. 4, footnote *a*.

15. KETHIBH[a] AND QERE

An interesting feature in the printed Hebrew Bibles is that corrections of recognized errors are made in the margin or footnote, while the uncorrected words are retained in the text. The refusal to change the text, even where obvious errors are recognized, is due to the extreme reverence felt for it and acts as a safeguard against tampering with it.

(*a*) An excellent illustration of this is afforded by the impossible word אֲנְַוּ (in Jeremiah xlii 6) which obviously cannot be read. We may imagine that what happened was somewhat as follows. The Personal Pronoun 'we' is אֲנַ֫חְנוּ in Classical Hebrew, but there is a shorter form אֲנוּ which does not occur in the Bible. The scribe of the text in Jeremiah began writing the word אֲנַ֫חְנוּ but, after having written the first two letters, left it in its shorter (unclassical) form אֲנוּ. Since the manuscript was written without vowel-signs (pp. 6–7) the scribe wrote אנו instead of אנחנו. When, later, the vowel-signs were introduced, a scheme was devised for attracting the attention of the reader to the error and its correction, without altering the text. The consonants of the erroneous word (here אֲנוּ, i.e. אנו) were retained but were given the vowels of the corrected form (here אֲנַ֫חְנוּ, namely וּ ְ ַ ֲ), thereby producing an impossible form (here אֲנְַוּ). The reader is thus forced to halt at the impossible word and to refer to the margin or footnote where the correction is given.

The uncorrected word in the text is the Kᵉthîbh (כְּתִיב, 'it is written'). *The corrected reading in the margin or footnote is the Qᵉrê* (קְרֵי, 'to be read'). In the example quoted above the Kᵉthîbh is אֲנוּ and the Qᵉrê is אֲנַ֫חְנוּ.

NOTE: In the unpointed scrolls read in the Synagogues, the Kethibh (i.e. the uncorrected form) is similarly retained in the text, but no Qere (corrected form) is given in the margin or footnote. The reader is expected to be familiar with the text and to know when a word is to be corrected, i.e. to read the Qere instead of the (written) Kethibh.

(*b*) A word which has an offensive or indelicate meaning,

[a] See p. 4, footnote *a*.

though written in the text (Kethibh) is often replaced in reading (Qere, footnote) by another word—usually a euphemistic one.

(*c*) Another type of deliberate change in reading due, in this case, to reverence, is the Divine name יַהֲוֶה or יַהְוֶה (Yah^{a}weh or Yahweh). The Divine name was considered too sacred to be pronounced; so the consonants of this word were written in the text (Kethibh), but the word read (Qere) was אֲדֹנָי (meaning 'Lord'). The consonants of the (Kethibh) יהוה were given the vowels of the (Qere) אֲדֹנָי namely ֲ ֹ ָ, producing the impossible form יְהֹוָה[a] (Y^{e}hōwâ).[b] Since, however, the Divine name occurs so often in the Bible, the printed editions do not put the reading required (Qere) in the margin or footnote; the reader is expected to substitute the Qere for Kethibh, without having his attention drawn to it every time it occurs. For this reason it has been called *Qere Perpetuum*, i.e. permanent Qere.[c]

Another example of *Qere Perpetuum* is the fem. sing. Personal Pronoun הִיא (hī', 'she'), which so frequently appears in the Pentateuch in the impossible form הִוא. This is due to confusion with the masc. sing. הוּא (hu', 'he').[d] The consonants of the uncorrected form הוא (Kethibh) were given the vowel of the correction (Qere) הִיא, namely the vowel Ḥireq (ִ) and the impossible form הִוא was produced. Once again, the required reading (Qere) is not given marginally or in a footnote, because of the frequency with which this word occurs in the Bible.

16. THE ARTICLE

There is no word for the *indefinite* article in Hebrew; 'a' or 'an' is not expressed, e.g. מֶ֫לֶךְ 'king' or 'a king', עַ֫יִן 'eye' or 'an eye'. The context implies that the word is indefinite.

(*a*) The *definite* article 'the' is said to have been originally הַל

[a] The composite shewa which was under the guttural א in the word אֲדֹנָי becomes a simple shewa under the י of the Kethibh יְהֹוָה.

[b] The English Jehovah.

[c] In the Qumrân (Dead Sea) scroll of Isaiah, the Qere of the Divine name is usually written above the Kethibh, thus אדוני above יהוה. This device of substitution is early, belonging to a period before vowel-points were introduced.

[d] Before the main vowel-sounds were represented by the vowel-letters, both הוּא and הִיא were written הא.

(like the Arabic 'al'). When attached to the word it defined (e.g. הַלְמֶ֫לֶךְ 'the king'), the vowelless ל was assimilated and the following letter was consequently doubled, with Dagheš Forte (p. 15) הַמֶּ֫לֶךְ. *The article*[a], therefore, *before an ordinary* (i.e. non-guttural) *letter is* הַ *followed by Dagheš Forte.*

(*b*) When the article is prefixed to a word beginning with a guttural (אהחע) or ר then, since these letters cannot be doubled (i.e. will not admit the Dagheš Forte which should follow the article), certain adjustments in the pointing of the article have to be made, as follows:

(i) The rule (p. 16, Note (*b*), and p. 19. 1) that, if the letter to be doubled with Dagheš Forte is a guttural or ר, the preceding vowel is lengthened instead, holds good for the weaker gutturals אע and the letter ר:

א	'light' אוֹר	'*the* light' הָאוֹר	'man' אָדָם	'*the* man' הָֽאָדָם[b]
ע	'eye' עַ֫יִן	'*the* eye' הָעַ֫יִן	'city' עִיר	'*the* city' הָעִיר
ר	'head' רֹאשׁ	'*the* head' הָרֹאשׁ	'foot' רֶ֫גֶל	'*the* foot' הָרֶ֫גֶל

Before the weaker gutturals אע *and the letter* ר *the article is* הָ.

(ii) The article before the harsh gutturals הח is pointed thus:

ה	'palace' הֵיכָל	'*the* palace' הַֽהֵיכָל[b]	'glory' הוֹד	'*the* glory' הַהוֹד
ח	'darkness' חֹ֫שֶׁךְ	'*the* darkness' הַחֹ֫שֶׁךְ	'dream' חֲלוֹם	'*the* dream' הַחֲלוֹם

Before the stronger gutturals הח *the article is* הַ. No Dagheš Forte, of course, follows, nor is the vowel under the article lengthened; Dagheš Forte is said to be implicit in the harsh sounds of these gutturals.

(iii) A divergence from the above two sections occurs when the article stands before an *unaccented* הָ and עָ, and *always* before חָ, thus:

[a] By the 'article' is meant the *definite* article.

[b] Methegh two places back from accent.

'mountains' הָרִים (the הָ is *unaccented*), '*the* mountains' הֶהָרִים[a]
'dust' עָפָר („ עָ „), '*the* dust' הֶעָפָר[a]
'wise (man)' חָכָם („ חָ „), '*the* wise (man)' הֶחָכָם[a]
'valour'[b] חָ֫יִל („ חָ is *accented*), '*the* valour' הֶחָ֫יִל

Before an unaccented עָ *and* הָ *and always before* חָ *the article is* הֶ.

(iv) However, *before an accented* הָ *and* עָ *the article is* הָ, as in (i).

'a mountain' הַר (the הָ is *accented*), '*the* mountain' הָהָר
'to a mountain' הָ֫רָה („ הָ „), 'to *the* mountain' הָהָ֫רָה
'strong' עָז („ עָ „), '*the* strong' הָעָז
'iniquity' עָ֫וֶל („ עָ „), '*the* iniquity' הָעָ֫וֶל

SUMMARY: The article is pointed as follows:

(*a*) Before ordinary letters (i.e. excluding gutturals and ר) it is הַ followed by Dagheš Forte: הַמֶּ֫לֶךְ.

(*b*) (i) Before the weaker gutturals עא and ר it is הָ: הָאוֹר, הָרֹאשׁ, הָעַ֫יִן.

(ii) Before the harsh gutturals הח it is הַ: הַהֵיכָל, הַחֹ֫שֶׁךְ.

(iii) Before an *unaccented* הָ and עָ and always before חָ it is הֶ: הֶהָרִים, הֶעָפָר, הֶחָכָם.

(iv) Before an *accented* הָ and עָ it is הָ: הָהָר, הָעָז.

NOTE TO EXERCISE 1.

'The man said' is expressed in Hebrew as 'He said, (namely) the man', אָמַר הָאָדָם.

'God created' is expressed in Hebrew as 'He created, (namely) God', בָּרָא אֱלֹהִים.

The verb generally precedes its subject in Hebrew; this is the normal order.

(We shall see later that when special emphasis is laid on the subject, it comes first, e.g. הָאָדָם אָמַר means 'the *man* said'.)

[a] See note [b] on previous page.

[b] This is the pausal form of חַ֫יִל (p. 21).

EXERCISE 1

he created	בָּרָא	city (f.)	עִיר	king	מֶ֫לֶךְ
he said	אָמַר	God	אֱלֹהִים	day	יוֹם
he came	בָּא	dust	עָפָר	night	לַ֫יְלָה
to, unto	אֶל	darkness	חֹ֫שֶׁךְ	light	אוֹר
from	מִן	head	רֹאשׁ	man	אָדָם
and [a]	...וְ	temple, palace	הֵיכָל	earth, land, ground	אֲדָמָה

(1) מֶ֫לֶךְ, הַמֶּ֫לֶךְ (2) יוֹם, הַיּוֹם (3) לַ֫יְלָה, הַלַּ֫יְלָה (4) אוֹר, הָאוֹר
(5) עִיר, הָעִיר (6) רֹאשׁ, הָרֹאשׁ (7) חֹ֫שֶׁךְ, הַחֹ֫שֶׁךְ (8) הֵיכָל,
הָֽהֵיכָל[b] (9) עָפָר, הֶֽעָפָר[b] (10) הַיּוֹם וְהַלַּ֫יְלָה (11) הָאוֹר וְהַחֹ֫שֶׁךְ
(12) מֶ֫לֶךְ וְאָדָם, הַמֶּ֫לֶךְ וְהָֽאָדָם[b] (13) אֲדָמָה וְעָפָר, הָֽאֲדָמָה[b]
וְהֶֽעָפָר[b] (14) עִיר וְהֵיכָל, הָעִיר וְהָֽהֵיכָל[b] (15) בָּרָא אֱלֹהִים אָדָם
מִן־הָאֲדָמָה (16) בָּא הַמֶּ֫לֶךְ מִן הָהֵיכָל (17) אָמַר אֱלֹהִים אֶל־
הָאָדָם (18) וְאֶל־הָעִיר בָּא הַמֶּ֫לֶךְ (19) בָּרָא אֱלֹהִים אוֹר מִן־
הַחֹ֫שֶׁךְ

(1) a night, the night; (2) a day, the day; (3) a man, the man; (4) God, the God; (5) ground, the ground; (6) a palace, the palace; (7) darkness, the darkness; (8) dust, the dust. (9) God and the king. (10) The palace and the city. (11) The man and the ground. (12) The darkness and the light. (13) He created a man from the ground. (14) God said unto the king. (15) The man came unto the city. (16) The night came and the darkness. (17) And unto the man God said. (18) The king came from the city. (19) Unto the dust. (20) From the palace.

17. THE INSEPARABLE PREPOSITIONS

לְ 'to' or 'for' בְּ 'in', 'with', or 'by' כְּ 'as' or 'like'.

These prepositions have no existence as separate words but, like the article, they attach themselves, as prefixes, to the words

[a] e.g. וְאָדָם, full account given on pp. 40–1.

[b] There is a Methegh here, because this syllable is two places back from the accented syllable (pp. 7–8. 3).

they govern. They are therefore called *Inseparable Prepositions.* It seems that ל is the essential element of אֶל־[a] 'unto', בּ of the (obsolete) בֵּית 'within', כּ of כֵּן 'so'.

(A)

The pointing of the inseparable prepositions is as follows:

1. *Normally* vowelless, i.e. *with Shewa,* thus:

a king מֶ֫לֶךְ	to a king לְמֶ֫לֶךְ	in a king בְּמֶ֫לֶךְ	as a king כְּמֶ֫לֶךְ
a man אָדָם	to a man לְאָדָם	in a man בְּאָדָם	as a man כְּאָדָם

2. When the inseparable preposition is prefixed to a word whose first letter has a shewa (e.g. שְׁמוּאֵל 'Samuel') then, since two shewas cannot stand together at the beginning of a word (as לְשְׁמוּאֵל), the shewa under the prefix becomes Ḥireq (לִשְׁמוּאֵל, p. 10, Note). Hence, *before a shewa the inseparable preposition is pointed with Ḥireq,* thus:

Samuel שְׁמוּאֵל	to Samuel לִשְׁמוּאֵל	in Samuel בִּשְׁמוּאֵל
kings מְלָכִים	to kings לִמְלָכִים	in kings בִּמְלָכִים

as Samuel כִּשְׁמוּאֵל

as kings כִּמְלָכִים

3. A special case of 2 is when the inseparable preposition is prefixed to a word beginning with יְ as יְהוּדָה 'Judah'. 'To Judah' is first לִיְהוּדָה (2 above) but the י *quiesces,* i.e. it loses its consonantal character and merges into the preceding homogeneous vowel (p. 18. 2) becoming לִיהוּדָה. Hence, *before* יְ *the inseparable preposition is pointed with Ḥireq and the shewa under the* י *falls away,* thus:

Judah יְהוּדָה	to Judah לִיהוּדָה	in Judah בִּיהוּדָה
Jerusalem יְרוּשָׁלַ֫יִם[b]	to Jerusalem לִירוּשָׁלַ֫יִם	in Jerusalem בִּירוּשָׁלַ֫יִם

as Judah כִּיהוּדָה

as Jerusalem כִּירוּשָׁלַ֫יִם

4. Another special case of 2 is when the inseparable preposition is prefixed to a word whose first letter (is a guttural which) has a composite shewa, as אֲרִי 'a lion'. The combination לְאֲרִי is of course impossible (since two shewas cannot stand together at the

[a] אֶל or אֶל־.

[b] Commonly found as יְרוּשָׁלַ֫ם.

beginning of a word) so, *under the influence of the composite shewa the inseparable preposition assumes the corresponding short vowel* (p. 10, Note):

a lion אֲרִי	to a lion לַאֲרִי	in a lion בַּאֲרִי	as a lion כַּאֲרִי
Edom אֱדוֹם	to Edom לֶאֱדוֹם	in Edom בֶּאֱדוֹם	as Edom כֶּאֱדוֹם

5. An exception to 4 is the word אֱלֹהִים 'God'. The combination is first לֶאֱלֹהִים (4 above) but the א *quiesces* and loses its consonantal character (p. 18. 1), i.e. it becomes silent, thus:

God אֱלֹהִים	to God לֵאלֹהִים	in God בֵּאלֹהִים	as God כֵּאלֹהִים

6. On p. 23 it was explained that the Divine name is always written יְהוָֹה (Kethibh) but read אֲדֹנָי (Qere—'the Lord'), and that the impossible form יְהוָֹה was produced by giving the Kethibh the vowels of the Qere. The same process is carried out consistently when the inseparable preposition is prefixed to the Divine name, thus:

'Yahweh'	is written	יְהוָֹה	(Kethibh)	and read as	אֲדֹנָי 'the Lord' (Qere)
'to Yahweh'	,,	לַיהוָֹה	(,,)	,,	לַאדֹנָי [a] 'to the Lord' (Qere)
'in Yahweh'	,,	בַּיהוָֹה	(,,)	,,	בַּאדֹנָי [a] 'in the Lord' (,,)
'as Yahweh'	,,	כַּיהוָֹה	(,,)	,,	כַּאדֹנָי [a] 'as the Lord' (,,)

7. Sometimes *immediately before the tone-syllable the inseparable preposition assumes the vowel Qameṣ*, e.g. 'waters to waters' מַ֫יִם לָמָ֫יִם:[b], 'to sit' לָשֶׁ֫בֶת.

(B)

When the inseparable preposition is followed by the article, e.g. 'to *the* king' (which we should expect to be לְהַמֶּ֫לֶךְ), *the* ה *of the article* (is scarcely audible and, in fact,) *falls away*, *surrendering its vowel to the preposition*, thus: לַמֶּ֫לֶךְ. In the same way, 'to the man' (לְהָאָדָם) becomes לָאָדָם, 'to the darkness' (לְהַחֹ֫שֶׁךְ) becomes לַחֹ֫שֶׁךְ, and 'to the dust' (לְהֶעָפָר) becomes לֶעָפָר.

Just as לְהַ' becomes לַ', so בְּהַ' becomes בַּ' and כְּהַ' becomes כַּ'
,, לְהָ' ,, לָ', ,, בְּהָ' ,, בָּ' ,, כְּהָ' ,, כָּ'
,, לְהֶ' ,, לֶ', ,, בְּהֶ' ,, בֶּ' ,, כְּהֶ' ,, כֶּ'

[a] As in no. 5, the א (in לַאֲדֹנָי) quiesces, leaving לַאדֹנָי, &c.

[b] Pausal, p. 21.

(C)

The preposition מִן 'from' is usually prefixed to the word it governs, when that word has not the article. It then becomes inseparable, and is pointed as follows:

1. *Before ordinary letters* (i.e. excluding gutturals אהחע and the letter ר) e.g. שָׁאוּל 'Saul' (the combination מִנְשָׁאוּל becomes מִשָּׁאוּל—p. 15, i.e.) the vowelless נ is assimilated and the following letter is doubled by Dagheš Forte Compensative: *it* thus *becomes* מִ *followed by Dagheš Forte.*

'from a king' מִמֶּלֶךְ   'from a day' מִיּוֹם   'from a night' מִלַּיְלָה

2. *Before gutturals or* ר (e.g. אָדָם 'a man', then 'from a man' is מֵאָדָם for a hypothetical מִאָדָם, i.e.), since these letters cannot receive a Dagheš Forte, the preceding vowel, here under the preposition, is lengthened (p. 19. 1) and *the preposition is* מֵ, thus:

'from a city' מֵעִיר   'from darkness' מֵחֹשֶׁךְ   'from a head' מֵרֹאשׁ

3. *When followed by the article*, the preposition may remain separate, as מִן הַמֶּלֶךְ or become inseparable מֵהַמֶּלֶךְ; in the latter instance *the article remains intact*: 'from the man' מֵהָאָדָם, 'from the dust' מֵהֶעָפָר.

NOTE: Each of the other inseparable prepositions (ל, ב, כ) is a vowelless consonant which together with the article makes one syllable (·לְהַ, לְהָ) so that, in pronunciation, the ה is *squeezed out* and the vowelless consonant seizes its vowel (·לַ, לָ). This cannot happen when the article follows the inseparable מֵ[a], since the latter is a complete syllable in itself; therefore in this case the article remains.

SUMMARY:

(A)

The inseparable prepositions ל, ב, כ are pointed

1. Normally with shewa: לְמֶלֶךְ
2. Before a shewa they take Ḥireq: לִשְׁמוּאֵל

[a] Since the ה of the article is a guttural, the preposition is מֵ before it.

3. Before יְ they take Ḥireq, but the shewa under the י falls away: לִיהוּדָה

4. Before a composite shewa they assume the corresponding short vowel: לַאֲרִי

5. Before אֱלֹהִים they take Ṣere and the composite shewa under the א disappears: לֵאלֹהִים

6. Before יהוה they follow 5 with the vowels of the Qere: לַיהוה

7. Before the tone syllable they often take Qameṣ: לָשֶׁבֶת

(B)

When these inseparable prepositions are followed by the article, the ה of the article disappears and the prepositions assume its pointing: לָעָפָר, לָאָדָם, לַמֶּלֶךְ

(C)

When the preposition מִן becomes inseparable, then

1. Before ordinary letters (excluding the gutturals and ר) it is מִ followed by Dagheš Forte: מִמֶּלֶךְ

2. Before gutturals and ר it is מֵ: מֵרֹאשׁ, מֵאָדָם

3. Before the article it is מֵ, as in 2, and the article remains intact: מֵהָאָדָם, מֵהַמֶּלֶךְ

EXERCISE 2

he called	קָרָא	heavens (pl.)	שָׁמַיִם	Samuel	שְׁמוּאֵל
he gave	נָתַן	word, thing	דָּבָר	a people	עַם
he saw	רָאָה	woman, wife	אִשָּׁה	the ,,	הָעָם
he went, walked	הָלַךְ	no, not	[a] לֹא	Yahweh, the Lord	יהוה [b]

(1) מֶלֶךְ, לְמֶלֶךְ, מִמֶּלֶךְ; הַמֶּלֶךְ, לַמֶּלֶךְ, מִן־הַמֶּלֶךְ (2) אָדָם,
כְּאָדָם, מֵאָדָם; הָאָדָם, כָּאָדָם, מִן־הָאָדָם (3) הֵיכָל, בְּהֵיכָל,

[a] The negative precedes the word it negates, thus: 'he saw not' לֹא רָאָה.

[b] It is best to leave this word unpointed and to translate it by the conventional 'the Lord'.

מִן־הַהֵיכָל (4) הַחֹשֶׁךְ, לַחֹשֶׁךְ, כַּחֹשֶׁךְ (5) עָפָר, מֵעָפָר; הֶעָפָר,
בֶּעָפָר, מִן־הֶעָפָר (6) אֱלֹהִים, כֵּאלֹהִים, מֵאֱלֹהִים; הָאֱלֹהִים,
כָּאֱלֹהִים; מִן־הָאֱלֹהִים (7) יהוה, לַיהוה, מֵיהוה (8) אֲדָמָה,
כַּאֲדָמָה; הָאֲדָמָה, כָּאֲדָמָה (9) שְׁמוּאֵל, לִשְׁמוּאֵל, כִּשְׁמוּאֵל,
מִשְּׁמוּאֵל (10) קָרָא אֱלֹהִים לָאוֹר יוֹם וְלַחֹשֶׁךְ קָרָא לָיְלָה[a]
(11) הָלַךְ הָעָם בַּחֹשֶׁךְ וְלֹא רָאָה אוֹר (12) נָתַן שְׁמוּאֵל מֶלֶךְ לָעָם
(13) מִן־הַשָּׁמַיִם רָאָה יהוה (14) בָּרָא אֱלֹהִים אָדָם מֵעָפָר וְאִשָּׁה
מִן־הָאָדָם (15) אָמַר שְׁמוּאֵל אֶל־הָעָם: בָּא הַמֶּלֶךְ אֶל־הָעִיר
(16) קָרָא אֱלֹהִים לִשְׁמוּאֵל בַּלָּיְלָה[a] (17) נָתַן אֱלֹהִים אִשָּׁה לָאָדָם
(18) יהוה מֶלֶךְ[a] בַּשָּׁמָיִם[a] (19) הָלַךְ הַמֶּלֶךְ אֶל־הַהֵיכָל בַּלָּיְלָה
(20) נָתַן אֱלֹהִים אוֹר לָאָדָם וְלָאִשָּׁה (21) לֹא אָמַר הַמֶּלֶךְ
לִשְׁמוּאֵל דָּבָר (22) קָרָא שְׁמוּאֵל אֶל־יהוה (23) לֹא נָתַן יהוה
אוֹר לָעָם (24) הָלַךְ שְׁמוּאֵל בָּעִיר (25) רָאָה יהוה בִּשְׁמוּאֵל רֹאשׁ
לָעָם

(1) a day, in a day, from a day; the day, in the day, from the day; (2) a woman, to a woman, from a woman; the woman, to the woman, from the woman; (3) a city, like a city, from a city; the city, like the city, from the city; (4) the darkness, in the darkness, from the darkness; (5) the God, to the God, from the God; (6) the head, in the head, from the head; (7) the dust, as the dust, from the dust; (8) Samuel, in Samuel, from Samuel. (9) The Lord gave light in the heavens.[a] (10) The man came from the dust and the woman from the man. (11) God called to the king in the night.[a] (12) The king walked in the city and he saw not. (13) God gave light to the people in the city. (14) The king called to Samuel and Samuel went not. (15) The people called unto the Lord in the darkness. (16) God created a man and a woman. (17) The king came unto Samuel in the night.[a] (18) The Lord said unto Samuel. (19) The king saw a woman in the temple.

[a] Pausal—the vowel in the tone-syllable is lengthened (p. 21).

18. NOUN AND ADJECTIVE (masc. and fem. sing.)

(A)

m. sg.	horse סוּס	man אִישׁ	prophet נָבִיא	king מֶ֫לֶךְ
f. sg.	mare סוּסָה	woman אִשָּׁה	prophetess נְבִיאָה	queen מַלְכָּה

Here are four singular nouns in the masculine and feminine. There is no special termination for the masculine, but *the feminine singular noun is recognized by the accented* ָה *termination.*[a]

m. sg.	good טוֹב	evil רַע	great גָּדוֹל	high רָם
f. sg.	„ טוֹבָה	„ רָעָה	„ גְּדוֹלָה	„ רָמָה

These four examples of masc. and fem. sing. adjectives show that, while the masc. sing. has no recognized termination, *the fem. sing. adjective is formed by appending* ָה *to the masc. sing. form.*[b]

(B)

When an adjective qualifies a noun, the order of words is, e.g.:

(i)

'a good man' is expressed in Hebrew as 'a man, a good (m. one)'[c] אִישׁ טוֹב

'a good woman' „ 'a woman, a good (f. one)' אִשָּׁה טוֹבָה

The adjective *follows* the noun it qualifies and agrees with it in number and gender (as in above examples).

(ii)

'the good man' is expressed in Hebrew as 'the man, *the* good (one)' הָאִישׁ הַטּוֹב

'to the good man' „ 'to the man, *the* good (one)' לָאִישׁ הַטּוֹב

'my good man' (husband) „ 'my man, *the* good (one)' אִישִׁי[d] הַטּוֹב

'the good woman' „ 'the woman, *the* good (one)' הָאִשָּׁה הַטּוֹבָה

[a] The f. sg. ָה termination is accented; so that לַ֫יְלָה (with ָה *un*accented) is not feminine. It is a longer form of the m. sg. noun לַ֫יִל. Similarly on pp. 66 f. there is an unaccented ָה termination which has nothing to do with gender, but is an old accusative ending. Some f. sg. nouns also end in ת.

[b] Some f. sg. adjectives end in ת. For the time being, we may ignore the change in pointing, due to the additional syllable ָה appended. This is explained on pp. 35 f.

[c] The main idea is first expressed and is then qualified by what follows.

[d] The possessives are dealt with on pp. 50 f.

When the noun is *definite* [a] the adjective which qualifies it has the article.

(iii)

'the man is good' is expressed in Hebrew as 'good (is) the man' טוֹב הָאִישׁ and sometimes simply 'the man (is) good' [b] הָאִישׁ טוֹב

'the woman is good' is expressed in Hebrew as 'good (is) the woman' טוֹבָה הָאִשָּׁה and sometimes simply 'the woman (is) good' [b] הָאִשָּׁה טוֹבָה

NOTE: *The present tense of the verb 'to be'* (*'am', 'art', 'is', 'are'*) *is not expressed in Hebrew*, but is implied in the context, as above. The above examples show *that when the adjective is used predicatively it usually precedes* (though sometimes it follows)[b] *the noun.*

SUMMARY: Nouns which terminate in an accented ָה are generally fem. sing. The fem. sing. adjective is formed by appending ָה to the masc. sing.[c] The adjective follows the noun it qualifies, and agrees with it in gender and number. If the noun is definite, then the adjective has the article. When used predicatively, the adjective usually precedes (though sometimes it follows)[b] the noun.

NOTE TO EXERCISE 3.

Like the adjective, the 3rd fem. sing. of the verb in past action is formed by appending the termination ָה to the 3rd masc. sing.:

'he said'	אָמַר	'she said'	אָֽמְרָה [d]
'he called'	קָרָא	'she called'	קָֽרְאָה
'he gave'	נָתַן	'she gave'	נָֽתְנָה
'he went'	הָלַךְ	'she went'	הָֽלְכָה

[a] Even though the English may not have the article the noun may still be definite, as the third example 'my good man' implies a *definite* man. When translating, one must first put the phrase into the Hebrew order and then translate.

[b] This alternative order is used when the noun is to be emphasized: it would mean 'the *man* (or *woman*) is good'. (Cf. note to Exercise 1.)

[c] Some adjectives have a ת termination.

[d] When the accented syllable ָה is appended the vowel under the second root-letter disappears; instead of saying אָמָרָה ('āmarā́) the tendency in hurried speech is to say אָֽמְרָה ('ām^{e}rā́). Note that the methegh shows that the first syllable is open and that the vowel-sign ָ in it is 'ā' (p. 13. 2, Note).

It also follows from the Note to Exercise 1 that since

'the man said' is expressed as 'he said (namely) the man' אָמַר הָאִישׁ
'the woman said' ,, 'she said (namely) the woman' אָֽמְרָה הָאִשָּׁה

EXERCISE 3

eye (f.) עַ֫יִן	wise חָכָם	voice קוֹל	who, whom, which אֲשֶׁר
	great גָּדוֹל	man אִישׁ	that, because, when כִּי
	good טוֹב	Moses מֹשֶׁה	on, upon, over עַל
	evil (m. sg.) רַע	earth, land (f.) אֶ֫רֶץ	he הוּא
	,, (f. sg.) רָעָה	the earth הָאָ֫רֶץ[a]	he was, became הָיָה

(1) מֶ֫לֶךְ טוֹב, הַמֶּ֫לֶךְ הַטּוֹב, טוֹב הַמֶּ֫לֶךְ (2) אִשָּׁה טוֹבָה, הָאִשָּׁה
הַטּוֹבָה, טוֹבָה הָאִשָּׁה (3) דָּבָר רַע, הַדָּבָר הָרַע, רַע הַדָּבָר
(4) אֶ֫רֶץ רָעָה, הָאָ֫רֶץ הָרָעָה, רָעָה הָאָ֫רֶץ (5) אִישׁ חָכָם, הָאִישׁ
הֶחָכָם, חָכָם הָאִישׁ (6) הֵיכָל גָּדוֹל, הַהֵיכָל הַגָּדוֹל, גָּדוֹל הַהֵיכָל
(7) טוֹב הָאוֹר וְרַע הַחֹ֫שֶׁךְ (8) קָרָא הָעָם בְּקוֹל גָּדוֹל, יהוה הוּא
הָאֱלֹהִים בַּשָּׁמַ֫יִם וְעַל־הָאָ֫רֶץ (9) קָֽרְאָה הָאִשָּׁה אֶל־הַמֶּ֫לֶךְ
הֶחָכָם, טוֹב יהוה לָעָם (10) הָיָה חֹ֫שֶׁךְ גָּדוֹל עַל־הָאָ֫רֶץ
(11) רָאָה אֱלֹהִים כִּי טוֹב[b] הָאוֹר אֲשֶׁר בָּרָא (12) הָיָה מֹשֶׁה אִישׁ
גָּדוֹל בָּאָ֫רֶץ (13) רָאָה הַמֶּ֫לֶךְ כִּי חֹ֫שֶׁךְ גָּדוֹל[b] עַל־הָעִיר הָרָעָה
(14) בָּ֫אָה הָאִשָּׁה אֶל־שְׁמוּאֵל (15) אָמַר מֹשֶׁה, טוֹבָה הָאָ֫רֶץ
אֲשֶׁר נָתַן יהוה לָעָם (16) בָּרָא אֱלֹהִים אֶ֫רֶץ וְשָׁמָ֫יִם[c] (17) גָּדוֹל
הַהֵיכָל אֲשֶׁר בָּעִיר (18) הָיָה הָאָדָם כֵּאלֹהִים (19) לֹא הָיָה
כִּשְׁמוּאֵל אִישׁ חָכָם בָּאָ֫רֶץ (20) אָֽמְרָה הָאִשָּׁה, טוֹב הַדָּבָר אֲשֶׁר
אָמַר הָאִישׁ הֶחָכָם אֶל־הָעָם (21) בַּיּוֹם אוֹר, בַּלַּ֫יְלָה חֹ֫שֶׁךְ

(1) a great people, the great people, the people is great; (2) a good city, the good city, the city is good; (3) an evil day, the evil day, the day is evil; (4) a wise king, the wise king, the king is wise; (5) an evil eye, the evil eye, the eye is evil. (6) The king saw that the darkness (was)[b] great upon the land. (7) In the evil day

[a] With the article it is always הָאָ֫רֶץ.

[b] Understand 'was'. This is required by the English in a subordinate clause.

[c] Pausal, p. 21.

there was not light in the city and the people saw not. (8) The Lord is good to the people. (9) There was not a good man in the evil city. (10) The king called to the woman and she came not. (11) The people said unto Moses, 'The land which the Lord hath given is not good.'[a] (12) Samuel said unto the people, 'The Lord, He is king in the heavens and upon the earth.' (13) Moses was (for)[b] a head over the people. (14) The woman called unto the king in a loud ('great') voice. (15) The word which the Lord said unto Samuel. (16) The good woman went unto the great temple which (was)[c] in the city. (17) To the good city there was light as the day. (18) There was not in the land a man (as)[c] great as Moses.

19. GENDER AND NUMBER (of Nouns and Adjectives)

(A) Nouns

	I	II	III	IV
m. sg.	horse סוּס	prophet נָבִיא	prisoner (m.) אָסִיר	star כּוֹכָב
f. sg.	mare סוּסָה	prophetess נְבִיאָה	" (f.) אֲסִירָה	
m. pl.	horses סוּסִים	prophets נְבִיאִים	prisoners (m.) אֲסִירִים	stars כּוֹכָבִים
f. pl.	mares סוּסוֹת	prophetesses נְבִיאוֹת	" (f.) אֲסִירוֹת	

The above examples show that, while the masc. sing. has no special termination, the fem. sing. ends in ה ָ, the masc. pl. in ִים, and the fem. pl. in וֹת.

Column I represents the simplest declension of the noun. It is a monosyllable, with a full[d] vowel between two consonants; this vowel does not change by the addition of a new syllable.

[a] The Hebrew order is 'not good (is) the land which the Lord . . .'.

[b] The bracketed word is in the Hebrew expression. The student will understand from the English whether a word in brackets is to be translated or left out in the Hebrew.

[c] The bracketed word is not in the Hebrew expression, but is required by the English.

[d] Those vowels which are represented by vowel-letters are 'full' vowels; they always remain, while other vowels are often reduced.

Of the same type is קוֹץ m. (thorn), pl. קוֹצִים: חוֹמָה f. (wall), pl. חוֹמוֹת.

Column II represents a two-syllabled noun whose first syllable has a Qameṣ. When a new syllable (ים.—) is added at the end, the vowel in the first syllable disappears. This is because the accent moves forward to the new syllable (from נבִ֫יא to נבִיאִים) and, the tendency in speaking being to hurry on to the accented syllable, the Qameṣ is reduced to shewa (and instead of נָבִיאִים it becomes נְבִיאִים). In the same way the pl. of דָּבָר m. (word, thing) is דְּבָרִים (not דָּבָרִים).

Column III represents the same type of noun as Column II, except that its first letter is a guttural. Consequently, when an additional syllable appears at the end and the Qameṣ in the first syllable is reduced to shewa, it will be composite shewa under the guttural, instead of the simple shewa (p. 10).

Column IV represents a two-syllabled noun whose first syllable has a full vowel. When the additional syllable appears at the end, this vowel remains.

NOTE: (*a*) There is no neuter gender in Hebrew. Inanimate things and abstract ideas are either masculine or feminine.

(*b*) There are a number of feminine nouns whose singular does not end in ה ָ. The student will become acquainted with such nouns by practice, but some of them may be recognized in the following ways:

i. Nouns denoting the female sex are naturally feminine: e.g. אֵם 'a mother', אָתוֹן 'a she-ass'.

ii. Nouns denoting those parts of the body which occur in pairs are feminine: e.g. יָד 'a hand', עַ֫יִן 'an eye', רֶ֫גֶל 'a foot'.[a]

iii. Names of countries and towns are feminine, since they are regarded as the mothers of their inhabitants: e.g. כְּנַ֫עַן 'Canaan', יְרוּשָׁלַ֫יִם[b] 'Jerusalem'.

[a] Those parts of the body which are not duplicated are masculine, as רֹאשׁ 'head', פֶּה 'mouth'.

[b] Commonly found as יְרוּשָׁלַ֫ם.

(B) ADJECTIVES

	I	II		III	
m. sg.	good טוֹב	great גָּדוֹל	upright יָשָׁר	rich עָשִׁיר	wise חָכָם
f. sg.	טוֹבָה	גְּדוֹלָה	יְשָׁרָה	עֲשִׁירָה	חֲכָמָה
m. pl.	טוֹבִים	גְּדוֹלִים	יְשָׁרִים	עֲשִׁירִים	חֲכָמִים
f. pl.	טוֹבוֹת	גְּדוֹלוֹת	יְשָׁרוֹת	עֲשִׁירוֹת	חֲכָמוֹת

The masc. sing. adjective serves as the basis for the formation of the other genders and numbers. The fem. sing. *is formed* by appending הָ, the masc. pl. by appending ִים, and the fem. pl. by appending וֹת.

The three groups of adjectives correspond to the three groups of nouns described in (A), thus:

Column I represents the simplest form of the adjective. It is a monosyllable with a full vowel. It does not alter with the addition of a syllable.

Column II represents a two-syllabled adjective whose first vowel is Qameṣ. When an additional syllable is appended, this Qameṣ is reduced to shewa.

Column III represents the same type of adjective as Column II, except that its first letter is a guttural. In this case, the Qameṣ of the first syllable is reduced to composite shewa (under the guttural).

NOTE: The logical plurals of אִישׁ 'a man' and אִשָּׁה 'a woman' (namely, אִישִׁים and אִשּׁוֹת) are very rare and the forms usually found are אֲנָשִׁים 'men' and נָשִׁים 'women'. It must be understood that, though the fem. pl.—נָשִׁים—has the termination of a masc. pl., it is nevertheless a fem. pl. noun by nature (it means 'women'). Therefore the adjective which qualifies it, agreeing with it in number and gender, must also be fem. pl., thus: 'good women' נָשִׁים טוֹבוֹת.

20. THE DUAL NUMBER

Some Hebrew nouns have a Dual number denoting pairs of things:

singular:	יָד 'a hand'	יוֹם 'a day'	פַּעַם 'a time'
dual:	יָדַ֫יִם 'two hands'	יוֹמַ֫יִם 'two days'	פַּעֲמַ֫יִם 'twice'

The dual termination for both the masc. and the fem. is ַ֫יִם.

Note: In the case of nouns denoting objects occurring in natural pairs, the dual is often extended to have a plural meaning; e.g. יָדַ֫יִם means 'two hands' but, in certain contexts, may mean 'hands' in the plural.

Note to Exercise 4.

The 3rd person plural of the verb in past action ends in וּ for both the masculine and the feminine:

he said אָמַר	he went הָלַךְ	he called קָרָא	he gave נָתַן
she „ אָמְרָה	she „ הָלְכָה	she „ קָרְאָה	she „ נָתְנָה
they „ אָמְרוּ	they „ הָלְכוּ	they „ קָרְאוּ	they „ נָתְנוּ

EXERCISE 4

man (sg.) אִישׁ	tree עֵץ	he sat, dwelt, abode, stayed יָשַׁב
men (pl.) אֲנָשִׁים	fruit פְּרִי	he ate אָכַל
woman (sg.) אִשָּׁה	prophet נָבִיא	he took לָקַח
women (pl.) נָשִׁים	prophetess נְבִיאָה	he was הָיָה
garden גַּן	holy קָדוֹשׁ	they were (m. and f.) הָיוּ
the garden הַגָּן	also, even, indeed גַּם	all, each, every כָּל־ or כֹּל[a]
Israel יִשְׂרָאֵל	under, instead of תַּ֫חַת	

(1) סוּס טוֹב, סוּסִים טוֹבִים; סוּסָה טוֹבָה, סוּסוֹת טוֹבוֹת
(2) נָבִיא קָדוֹשׁ, נְבִיאִים קְדוֹשִׁים; נְבִיאָה קְדוֹשָׁה, נְבִיאוֹת קְדוֹשׁוֹת
(3) אִישׁ חָכָם, אֲנָשִׁים חֲכָמִים; אִשָּׁה חֲכָמָה, נָשִׁים חֲכָמוֹת
(4) עֵץ גָּדוֹל, עֵצִים גְּדוֹלִים (5) הַהֵיכָל הַגָּדוֹל, הַהֵיכָלִים

[a] See p. 13, no. 4.

הַגְּדוֹלִים (6) נָתַן יהוה לְיִשְׂרָאֵל אֶ֫רֶץ גְּדוֹלָה וְטוֹבָה (7) יָשַׁב
הַמֶּ֫לֶךְ בֶּעָפָר כָּל־הַיּוֹם וְלֹא אָכָ֑ל[a] (8) יָשְׁבָה הַנְּבִיאָה תַּ֫חַת
הָעֵץ (9) רָעִים הָיוּ הָאֲנָשִׁים אֲשֶׁר יָשְׁבוּ בָּעִיר הַגְּדוֹלָה (10) לֹא
לָקַח שְׁמוּאֵל הַנָּבִיא פְּרִי מִן־הַגָּן (11) לָקְחָה הָאִשָּׁה מִן־הַפְּרִי
אֲשֶׁר בַּגָּן וְגַם נָתְנָה לָאָדָם (12) לָקְחוּ הָאָדָם וְהָאִשָּׁה מִן־הָעֵץ
וְגַם אָכְלוּ מִן־הַפְּרִי (13) בָּ֫אוּ עַל־הָעִיר הָרָעָה כָּל־הַדְּבָרִים
אֲשֶׁר אָמְרוּ הַנְּבִיאִים הַקְּדוֹשִׁים (14) לֹא נָתְנָה הָאָ֫רֶץ פְּרִי כִּי הָיוּ
הָאֲנָשִׁים רָעִים (15) אָמַר מֹשֶׁה אֶל־כָּל־יִשְׂרָאֵל, קָדוֹשׁ הַיּוֹם
לַיהוה (16) בַּגָּן הָיוּ עֵצִים גְּדוֹלִים וְטוֹבִים (17) לֹא אָכְלוּ
הַנְּבִיאִים בַּהֵיכָל, כִּי קְדוֹשִׁים הָיוּ לַיהוה (18) רָאָה הָעָם כִּי טוֹב[b]
הַפְּרִי אֲשֶׁר לָקְחוּ הָאֲנָשִׁים מִן־הָעֵצִים אֲשֶׁר בָּאָ֫רֶץ אֲשֶׁר נָתַן
יהוה לְיִשְׂרָאֵל (19) חֲכָמִים וְטוֹבִים הָיוּ הַדְּבָרִים אֲשֶׁר אָמַר
הַנָּבִיא הֶחָכָם אֶל־הָאֲנָשִׁים אֲשֶׁר הָיוּ בַּהֵיכָל (20) קָרְאוּ הַנְּבִיאִים
בְּקוֹל גָּדוֹל, שְׁמוּאֵל הוּא נָבִיא לַיהוה (21) טוֹב יהוה לַטּוֹבִים
וְלָרָעִים

(1) a great man, great men; a great woman, great women; (2) a holy prophet, holy prophets; a holy prophetess, holy prophetesses; (3) a good word, good words; (4) a great temple, great temples. (5) The prophets went unto the holy city, for they said, 'Samuel the prophet is in the temple which is in the city, and also the king and all the people.' (6) Holy were the men who sat under the trees in the garden all the day. (7) The people dwelt (sg.) in the good land which the Lord gave to Israel. (8) The man and the woman ate from the fruit which was on the tree in the great garden. (9) Great is the Lord in the heavens and great is Israel on the earth. (10) The men went unto the land and they also[c] took from the fruit and unto the people they came and they also[c] said, 'The fruit which is in the land is good.' (11) God said unto Moses, 'The men who said that the land is not good for Israel are evil.'[d] (12) The prophets dwelt not in the evil city,

[a] Pausal. [b] Understand 'was', as is required by the English.
[c] וְגַם = and also they, &c. [d] 'Evil are the men who . . .'

for they were holy to the Lord. (13) The king saw that wise (were) the words which the holy prophet said unto the people. (14) There were not in Israel prophets (as) great as Samuel. (15) The prophetess took not from the fruit and she ate not all the day and all the night.

21. THE CONJUNCTION

The conjunction 'and'[a] is a prefixed ו, i.e. it is inseparable. It is pointed like the inseparable prepositions, with the exception of the case explained in 2 below:

1. *Ordinarily* it is vowelless, i.e. *it is pointed with shewa*—וְ:

'a man' אָדָם	'and a man' וְאָדָם
'a horse' סוּס	'and a horse' וְסוּס
'the man' הָאָדָם	'and the man' וְהָאָדָם[b]
'the horse' הַסּוּס	'and the horse' וְהַסּוּס

2. (*a*) When the conjunction is prefixed to a word whose first letter has a shewa, as שְׁמוּאֵל 'Samuel' then, since the word cannot begin with two shewas (as וְשְׁמוּאֵל) the ו takes the form וּ—וּשְׁמוּאֵל 'and Samuel'. Similarly 'words' דְּבָרִים, 'and words' וּדְבָרִים.[c]

(*b*) Before the labials במפ the conjunction also takes the form וּ:

'between' בֵּין:	'and between' וּבֵין[d] (not וְבֵין)
'Moses' מֹשֶׁה:	'and Moses' וּמֹשֶׁה (not וְמֹשֶׁה)
'here' פֹּה:	'and here' וּפֹה[d] (not וְפֹה).

[a] The conjunction may have a variety of meanings, according to the context; it may also mean 'but', 'or', &c. For the present we may take it to be 'and'.

[b] The article after the conjunction remains.

[c] The first letter in the word דְּבָרִים has Dagheš Lene, but when the conjunction וּ is prefixed, the Dagheš Lene falls away, because it is immediately preceded by a vowel (pp. 14–15).

[d] Similarly the Dagheš Lene falls away after וּ—בֵּין but וּבֵין.

It will be observed that the forms in the brackets would be difficult to articulate in ordinary speech and so the conjunction resolves into וּ. The examples in (*a*) and (*b*) show that *before shewa and the labials* במפ *the conjunction is* וּ.

3. When prefixed to a word beginning with יְ, the י (as in the case of the inseparable prepositions) quiesces into a vowel,[a] thus: 'Judah' יְהוּדָה, 'and Judah' וִיהוּדָה: 'Jerusalem' יְרוּשָׁלַיִם, 'and Jerusalem' וִירוּשָׁלַיִם.

4. Before a composite shewa it assumes the corresponding short vowel (as with the inseparable prepositions): 'I' אֲנִי, 'and I' וַאֲנִי: 'Edom' אֱדוֹם, 'and Edom' וֶאֱדוֹם.

5. An exception to 4 is אֱלֹהִים which, with the conjunction, is וֵאלֹהִים (cf. p. 30. A 5).

6. With the Kethibh יְהוָֹה (pointed with the vowels of אֲדֹנָי and read as the latter) the combination is וַיהוָֹה (and read וַאדֹנָי). (cf. p. 30. A 6).

7. When the conjunction stands *immediately before the tone-syllable* (i.e. the accented syllable), especially when it connects a pair of words, it is וָ: 'day and night' יוֹם וָלַיְלָה: 'light and darkness' אוֹר וָחֹשֶׁךְ: 'good and evil' טוֹב וָרָע.

Summary: The conjunction ו is pointed:

1. Ordinarily with shewa וְ: וְסוּס, וְהַסּוּס.
2. Before shewa and במפ it is וּ: וּשְׁמוּאֵל, וּבֵין, וּמשֶׁה, וּפֹה.
3. Before יְ the י quiesces and the conjunction has Ḥireq: וִיהוּדָה.
4. Before a composite shewa it takes the corresponding short vowel: וַאֲנִי, וֶאֱדוֹם.
5. With אֱלֹהִים it is וֵאלֹהִים.
6. With יְהוָֹה (Qere אֲדֹנָי) it is וַיהוָֹה (Qere וַאדֹנָי).
7. Immediately before the tone-syllable it is often וָ: יוֹם וָלַיְלָה.

[a] וְיְ becomes וִיְ and finally וִי (p. 18. 2).

22. THE INTERROGATIVE PRONOUNS

A. The interrogative pronoun 'who?' (subject) or 'whom?' (object)[a] is מִי. Its form is fixed and does not change: 'to whom?' לְמִי; 'from whom?' מִמִּי.

B. The interrogative pronoun 'what?' מה is pointed practically like the article:

1. Before ordinary consonants (excluding gutturals and ר) it is מַה—followed by Dagheš Forte: 'what is this?' מַה־זֶּה[b].

2. Before א and ר it is מָה: 'what (am) I?' מָה־אֲנִי.

3. Before ה and ח it is מַה: 'what (is) he?' מַה־הוּא.

4. Before a guttural with Qameṣ it is מֶה: 'what hath he done?' מֶה־עָשָׂה.

EXERCISE 5

morning בֹּקֶר	he went out יָצָא	he divided, distinguished הִבְדִּיל
evening עֶרֶב	he knew יָדַע	between בֵּין
(adj.) old זָקֵן (as noun) elder	he spoke דִּבֶּר	I אֲנִי

(1) הַשָּׁמַיִם, וְהַשָּׁמַיִם; בַּשָּׁמַיִם, וּבַשָּׁמַיִם (2) הָאָרֶץ, וְהָאָרֶץ;
בָּאָרֶץ, וּבָאָרֶץ (3) יוֹם, וְיוֹם; מִיּוֹם, וּמִיּוֹם (4) אֲנִי, וַאֲנִי; אֲדָמָה,
וַאֲדָמָה (5) מֹשֶׁה, וּמֹשֶׁה; לְמֹשֶׁה, וּלְמֹשֶׁה (6) שְׁמוּאֵל, וּשְׁמוּאֵל;
לִשְׁמוּאֵל, וְלִשְׁמוּאֵל (7) אֱלֹהִים, וֵאלֹהִים; יהוה, וַיהוה
(8) יְרוּשָׁלַיִם, וִירוּשָׁלַיִם (9) אוֹר וָחֹשֶׁךְ (10) טוֹב וָרָע (11) עֶרֶב
וָבֹקֶר (12) יוֹם וָלַיְלָה (13) פְּרִי, וּפְרִי (14) מִי אֲנִי וּמָה־אֲנִי
(15) הִבְדִּיל אֱלֹהִים בֵּין הָאוֹר וּבֵין הַחֹשֶׁךְ, בֵּין הַיּוֹם וּבֵין הַלָּיְלָה[d]
(16) לֹא הִבְדִּילוּ הָאֲנָשִׁים הָרָעִים בֵּין הַטּוֹב וּבֵין הָרָע (17) מִי
כַּיהוה[c] בַּשָּׁמַיִם וּמִי כְּיִשְׂרָאֵל[c] בָּאָרֶץ (18) בָּרָא אֱלֹהִים שָׁמַיִם
וָאָרֶץ[d] (19) טוֹבִים וַחֲכָמִים הָיוּ הַדְּבָרִים אֲשֶׁר דִּבֶּר הַנָּבִיא הַזָּקֵן

[a] Usually אֶת־מִי—as will be seen from p. 53, N.B.

[b] Observe how the ה has no value as a consonant at all. The interrogative pronoun מה is usually closely connected with the following word by a Maqqeph or, in the Bible, by a continuation accent and, by reading the two words together, the first letter of the following word is duplicated.

[c] After a vowel the Dagheš Lene falls away (pp. 14–15. (*a*), since the two words are spoken without a pause, almost as one word.

[d] Pausal.

אֶל־הַמֶּ֫לֶךְ (20) יָדַע הָאָדָם טוֹב וָרָע, כִּי אָכַל מִן־הָעֵץ אֲשֶׁר
בַּגָּן (21) אָמְרָה הָאִשָּׁה אֶל־הַזְּקֵנִים, בָּ֫אוּ אֲנָשִׁים מִיִּשְׂרָאֵל בַּלַּ֫יְלָה
וּבַבֹּ֫קֶר יָצְאוּ מִן־הָעִיר (22) לֹא הָיָה מֶ֫לֶךְ בְּיִשְׂרָאֵל, וּשְׁמוּאֵל
הַנָּבִיא הָיָה רֹאשׁ לָעָם (23) בָּעִיר הַקְּדוֹשָׁה יָשְׁבָה אִשָּׁה זְקֵנָה
וַחֲכָמָה (24) יהוה הוּא אֱלֹהִים וּמֶ֫לֶךְ בַּשָּׁמַ֫יִם וּבָאָ֫רֶץ (25) נָתַן
יהוה לְיִשְׂרָאֵל אֶ֫רֶץ טוֹבָה וּגְדוֹלָה, וְגַם נְבִיאִים גְּדוֹלִים וּקְדוֹשִׁים
(26) מַה־הַדָּבָר אֲשֶׁר דִּבֶּר אֱלֹהִים אֶל־הַנָּבִיא (27) וּבְכָל־הָעִיר
לֹא הָיָה אִישׁ טוֹב

(1) The night, and the night; in the night, and in the night; (2) the tree, and the tree; from the tree, and from the tree; (3) in the city, and in the city; (4) Jerusalem, and Jerusalem; in Jerusalem, and in Jerusalem; (5) darkness and light; (6) night and day; (7) to Israel, and to Israel; (8) an old and wise man, old and wise men. (9) Who are the men who came to the city in the evening? (10) The king was wise and good. (11) The prophets were wise and great men. (12) The Lord distinguished between the good (men)[a] and between the evil (men)[a] who were in the land. (13) In the evening and in the morning (in) every day the king called unto the Lord. (14) The prophet went out from Jerusalem, the holy city, as the word which the Lord spoke. (15) What is man whom God created? He is dust from the ground. (16) The woman said unto the people, 'The king distinguished not between (the[b]) good and (between the[b]) evil'. (17) Moses and Samuel were good and holy prophets. (18) And in all the land (there) was not a palace like the palace which was in Jerusalem. (19) The man and the woman were in the garden and from the tree they ate fruit. (20) And who is like Israel, a great nation under the heavens?

23. THE ABSOLUTE AND CONSTRUCT STATES

To illustrate what is meant by the absolute and construct states, the following two examples may be taken: (*a*) 'he is a

[a] The m. pl. adjective implies 'men'.

[b] The bracketed words are in the Hebrew thought.

man' הוּא אִישׁ, and (*b*) 'he is a man of God' הוּא אִישׁ־אֱלֹהִים. The word אִישׁ־ in (*b*) is dependent upon the next word אֱלֹהִים in such a way that the two words together אִישׁ־אֱלֹהִים make up one compound idea—'man-of God'. The dependent word אִישׁ־ is said to be in the *construct state*; whereas אִישׁ in (*a*) stands alone and is independent, and (in contradistinction) is said to be in the *absolute state*.

When two (*or more*) *words are so closely united that together they constitute one compound idea, the dependent word* (*or words*) *is* (*are*) *said to be in the Construct State.* The word (in the absolute state) upon which the construct depends, is said to be in the genitive[a] (as above אֱלֹהִים).

The construct state has, at times, a Maqqeph after it (and, in the Bible, always otherwise a continuation accent). The Maqqeph (and the continuation accent) indicate that the word (in the construct) is united with the one after it.[b]

The construct often brings about an adjustment in the form:

1.	abs. sg.	cons. sg.	abs. pl.	cons. pl.
m.	horse סוּס	horse-of סוּס־	horses סוּסִים	horses-of סוּסֵי־
f.	mare סוּסָה	mare-of סוּסַת־	mares סוּסוֹת	mares-of סוּסוֹת־

In the *simplest form* of the noun, the fem. sg. construct ends in ַת and the masc. pl. construct in ֵי. The masc. sg. and the fem. pl. do not change externally but they are recognized as constructs by the Maqqeph (and, in the Bible, also by the continuation accent) accompanying them.

NOTE: The fem. sg. noun and adjective originally terminated in ָת in the absolute. In the spoken language this ָת (āṯ) termination became thinned down to ָה (â)—the ת (ṯ) being scarcely audible and finally discarded when no word

[a] The genitive case-ending has been lost—see pp. 66–7.

[b] Since accents will rarely appear in this grammar (except for pause), the construct state will generally have a Maqqeph after it. When the student begins to read the Bible in Hebrew, he will see that the word in the construct state has either a Maqqeph or the continuation accent.

immediately followed, i.e. in the absolute. In the construct state this ָת was merely shortened to ַת in the process of hurrying on to the next word (the genitive) to complete the compound idea; the two words being spoken without a pause.[a]

The final ם of the masc. pl. was scarcely heard and finally dropped in the construct, through hurrying on to the genitive.

2. abs. sg.	cons. sg.	abs. pl.	cons. pl.
son בֵּן	son-of בֶּן־	sons בָּנִים	sons-of בְּנֵי־
hand יָד	hand-of יַד־	hands [b]יָדַ֫יִם	hands-of יְדֵי־

The vowel changes brought about in the construct state will be easily understood by bearing in mind that the compound idea (i.e. the construct and the genitive together) are spoken together practically as one word. The natural tendency, then, is to hurry on to the genitive and in doing so the word in the construct is spoken hurriedly and thus shortened as much as possible. Thus בֵּן becomes בֶּן־ in the construct and יָד becomes יַד־. In the plural, the final ם (of בָּנִים) disappears in the construct and, by hurrying on to complete the compound, the vowel (Qameṣ) in the first syllable is reduced to shewa (בְּנֵי־מֹשֶׁה —'sons-of Moses'). Similarly, the construct of the dual form יָדַ֫יִם is contracted to יְדֵי—'hands-of'.

NOTE: The reduction of the Qameṣ to shewa in the first syllable of the construct is due to the principle explained on pp. 35, 36, Column II. When the sing. noun נָבִיא is made plural by the addition of the new syllable ִים at the end and the accent moves forward on to the new syllable, the Qameṣ in the first syllable is reduced in the process of hurrying on to the accented (last) syllable (נְבִיאִים). Similarly, when נָבִיא is construct, the speaker hurries on to the genitive and the construct becomes נְבִיא־.

[a] Compare, in French, *il a* (for *at*), but *a-t-il?*

[b] Dual form.

3. abs. sg.	cons. sg.	abs. pl.	cons. pl.
word דָּבָר	word-of דְּבַר	words דְּבָרִים	words-of דִּבְרֵי
wise (man) חָכָם	wise (man)-of חֲכַם	wise (men) חֲכָמִים	wise (men)-of חַכְמֵי

When a two-syllabled word like דָּבָר is put in the construct state, two changes take place. The syllable בָר is shortened to בַר (just as יָד becomes יַד), and the Qameṣ in the first syllable דָּ is reduced to shewa, thus the absolute דָּבָר becomes דְּבַר in the construct. חָכָם is of the same type, except that its first letter is a guttural, so that, when the Qameṣ under it becomes shewa in the construct, it is a composite shewa: it becomes חֲכַם.

When the plural absolute דְּבָרִים becomes construct, then ־בָרִים becomes ־בְרֵי (just as בָּנִים becomes בְּנֵי in 2 above) resulting in דְּבְרֵי which, in turn, becomes דִּבְרֵי, (p. 10, Note). When the plural חֲכָמִים becomes construct, then ־כָמִים becomes ־כְמֵי and the resulting חֲכְמֵי becomes חַכְמֵי, i.e. the composite shewa becomes the corresponding short vowel. In the same way the absolute אֲנָשִׁים (men) becomes אַנְשֵׁי (men-of) in the construct.

Note: *The word in the construct state never takes the article.* When the compound idea is definite, it is (*not* the word in the construct but) the genitive (following it) which takes the article, thus:

Indefinite	*Definite*
a man-of God אִישׁ־אֱלֹהִים	*the* man-of-God אִישׁ־הָאֱלֹהִים[a] (not הָאִישׁ־)
a word-of truth דְּבַר־אֱמֶת	*the* word-of truth דְּבַר־הָאֱמֶת[a] (not הַדְּבַר־)

Note further the usage with proper nouns:

דְּבַר־מֹשֶׁה—*the* word-of Moses, since מֹשֶׁה[b], being a proper noun, is definite.

יַד־יהוה—*the* hand-of the Lord, „ יהוה, „ „ „

אֶרֶץ־כְּנַעַן—*the* land-of Canaan, „ כְּנַעַן, „ „ „

[a] Compare the English phrase 'the man's house', which really means '*the* house of the man'.

[b] Compare, in English, 'David's son', which means '*the* son of David'.

24. TABLE OF WORDS IN THE ABSOLUTE AND CONSTRUCT STATES

sg. abs.	sg. cons.	pl. abs.	pl. cons.	Remarks	No.
horse סוּס	סוּס	סוּסִים	סוּסֵי	Simple noun. The masc. pl. ִים changes to ֵי in the construct—general rule.	1
mare סוּסָה	סוּסַת	סוּסוֹת	סוּסוֹת	Simple noun. The fem. sg. termination ַת in the construct—general rule.	2
son בֵּן	בֶּן	בָּנִים	בְּנֵי	Pl. abs. irregular. Vowel shortened in cons. sg. Qameṣ lost in cons. pl.	3
hand יָד	יַד	יָדַ֫יִם	יְדֵי	Same as no. 3. Note how dual serves also for pl.	4
people עַם	עַם	עַמִּים	עַמֵּי	Dagheš Forte in מ of pl. Note: a vowel may be elided, but not a syllable: since pl. abs. is really עַמְמִים there is no loss of vowel.	5
prophet נָבִיא	נְבִיא	נְבִיאִים	נְבִיאֵי	The Qameṣ (under the first letter) of the sg. abs. is lost.	6
prophetess נְבִיאָה	נְבִיאַת	נְבִיאוֹת	נְבִיאוֹת	Same as no. 2.	7
word, thing דָּבָר	דְּבַר	דְּבָרִים	דִּבְרֵי	Sg. cons. loses first Qameṣ and shortens second one. Both are lost in pl. cons., the first shewa becoming Ḥireq.	8
old (man) elder זָקֵן	זְקַן	זְקֵנִים	זִקְנֵי	Second vowel of sg. abs. is Ṣere, but changes in the same way as no. 8.	9
wise (man) חָכָם	חֲכַם	חֲכָמִים	חַכְמֵי	Same as no. 8, except that the first letter is a guttural. In sg. cons. Qameṣ is replaced by composite shewa. In pl. cons. the composite shewa becomes corresponding short vowel.	10
dust עָפָר	עֲפַר			Sg. same as no. 10.	11
man אִישׁ	אִישׁ	אֲנָשִׁים[a]	אַנְשֵׁי	Pl. abs. irregular. Pl. cons. same as no. 10.	12
woman אִשָּׁה	אֵשֶׁת	נָשִׁים	נְשֵׁי	Note special form of sg. cons. The pl. has masc. termination. Pl. cons. same as no. 3.	13
eye עַ֫יִן	עֵין	עֵינַ֫יִם	עֵינֵי	Note special form of cons. sg., where the diphthong 'ai' becomes 'ê'. In the pl. the full vowel in the first syllable is not shortened, just as in no. 1.	14
star כּוֹכָב	כּוֹכַב	כּוֹכָבִים	כּוֹכְבֵי	Full vowel ô does not change. Qameṣ of sg. abs. is shortened in sg. cons. and disappears in pl. cons.	15

This Table includes most of the nouns and adjectives which have already occurred in the vocabularies.

[a] See p. 37, Note.

EXERCISE 6

Egypt מִצְרַיִם	name שֵׁם	exceedingly, very מְאֹד[a]
Jacob יַעֲקֹב	star כּוֹכָב	lo! behold! הִנֵּה
Esau עֵשָׂו	one (m.) אֶחָד[b]	
Solomon שְׁלֹמֹה	„ (f.) אַחַת	he heard, hearkened שָׁמַע

N.B. 'he hearkened to the voice-of' שָׁמַע לְקוֹל־ means 'he obeyed'.
„ in „ שָׁמַע בְּקוֹל־

(1) לֹא נָבִיא אָנִי וְלֹא בֶן־נָבִיא (2) רָאָה הַמֶּלֶךְ אִישׁ זָקֵן מְאֹד
בַּהֵיכָל וְלֹא יָדַע כִּי נְבִיא־אֱלֹהִים הוּא[c] (3) הָיָה[d] דְבַר־יהוה אֶל־
שְׁמוּאֵל בַּלָּיְלָה (4) הָלַךְ הַנָּבִיא אֶל־הֵיכַל־הַמֶּלֶךְ (5) קָרָא
מֶלֶךְ־מִצְרַיִם אֶל־מֹשֶׁה, כִּי הָיָה חֹשֶׁךְ בְּאֶרֶץ־מִצְרַיִם, וְ[e]לִבְנֵי־
יִשְׂרָאֵל הָיָה אוֹר (6) לֹא שָׁמַע הָעָם אֶל־דִּבְרֵי־הַנְּבִיאִים אֲשֶׁר
דִּבְּרוּ בְּשֵׁם־יהוה (7) וּבְגַן־הַמֶּלֶךְ הָיוּ מִכֹּל עֲצֵי־פְרִי[f] (8) הָיוּ
אַנְשֵׁי הָעִיר רָעִים מְאֹד בְּעֵינֵי־אֱלֹהִים וּבְעֵינֵי־אָדָם (9) מִכֹּל
עַמֵּי־הָאָרֶץ בָּאוּ אֶל־שְׁלֹמֹה מֶלֶךְ־יִשְׂרָאֵל, כִּי הָיָה חָכָם מְאֹד
בְּעֵינֵי־כָל־הָעַמִּים (10) יָשַׁב שְׁמוּאֵל עַל־הָאֲדָמָה בְּרֹאשׁ־בְּנֵי־
הַנְּבִיאִים (11) יָצְאוּ בְנֵי־יִשְׂרָאֵל מֵאֶרֶץ־מִצְרַיִם עַם גָּדוֹל מְאֹד,
כִּדְבַר־יהוה אֲשֶׁר דִּבֶּר אֶל־מֹשֶׁה (12) קָרָא הַמֶּלֶךְ לְכָל־חַכְמֵי־
הָאָרֶץ (13) עֵינֵי־יהוה אֶל־הַטּוֹבִים וְלֹא אֶל־הָרָעִים (14) רָאוּ
חַכְמֵי־מִצְרַיִם כִּי יַד־יהוה[c] בָּאָרֶץ (15) קָרְאוּ בְנֵי־הַנְּבִיאִים
בְּקוֹל גָּדוֹל, יהוה קְדוֹשׁ־יִשְׂרָאֵל הוּא אֶחָד וֵאלֹהֵי־כָל־הָאָרֶץ
(16) לֹא שָׁמְעוּ בְנֵי־יִשְׂרָאֵל בְּקוֹל־יהוה, וּבְעֵינֵי־מֹשֶׁה הָיָה
הַדָּבָר רַע מְאֹד (17) וְאִשָּׁה אַחַת[b] מִנְּשֵׁי־בְנֵי־הַנְּבִיאִים קָרְאָה
אֶל־שְׁמוּאֵל (18) הָיוּ בְנֵי־יִשְׂרָאֵל כַּעֲפַר־הָאֲדָמָה וּכְכוֹכְבֵי־
הַשָּׁמַיִם בָּאָרֶץ אֲשֶׁר נָתַן יהוה לְיַעֲקֹב (19) הַקּוֹל קוֹל־יַעֲקֹב

[a] Follows the adjective.

[b] This numeral is an adjective, following the noun and agreeing with it in gender.

[c] The English requires the subordinate clause to be put in the past. Understand 'was'.

[d] In English the phrase is 'the word of the Lord *came*'.

[e] The conj. here must mean 'but'. See p. 40, footnote *a*.

[f] Trees-of fruit = fruit trees (see p. 136).

וְ[a]הַיָּדַיִם יְדֵי־עֵשָׂו, כִּי לֹא הָיוּ יְדֵי־יַעֲקֹב כִּידֵי[b] עֵשָׂו (20) דִּבֶּר
מֹשֶׁה אֶל־זִקְנֵי־הָעָם כְּכֹל אֲשֶׁר אָמַר יהוה אֱלֹהֵי־יִשְׂרָאֵל
(21) הִנֵּה בָּא יוֹם־יהוה, יוֹם אֲשֶׁר הוּא חֹשֶׁךְ וְלֹא אוֹר (22) יָצָא
אֶחָד מִגְּדוֹלֵי־הָעָם וּבְקוֹל־גָּדוֹל קָרָא אֶל־אַנְשֵׁי־הָעִיר, הִנֵּה
הָעִיר בְּיַד־הַמֶּלֶךְ׃

(1) Moses was a man of God. (2) Jacob called in the name of the Lord. (3) The children of Israel were in the land of Egypt. (4) The people hearkened not to (or 'in') the voice of the old prophet who spoke in the name of the God of Israel. (5) All the elders of the city came unto Moses. (6) All the peoples of the land heard that Israel went out from the land of Egypt. (7) And I am as the dust of the ground in the eyes of the king. (8) Samuel, the prophet of God, spoke unto the great ones[c] of the people. (9) All the wise (men)[c] of the land called unto the king of Egypt with one voice, 'Behold darkness hath come upon the land.' (10) The sons of the king were evil in the eyes of the Lord. (11) The voice of the Lord is in the heavens and in the earth. (12) Solomon, the king of Israel, was very great in the eyes of all the earth. (13) The men of the evil city distinguished not between the good (ones)[c] and (between) the evil (ones). (14) The word which the prophetess spoke unto the king. (15) The Lord He is one in the heavens and the people of Israel is one upon the earth. (16) The king hearkened to the words of the prophet and he said not a(ny)thing, for he knew that he (was)[d] a man of God. (17) God gave stars in the heavens. (18) Jacob saw and behold Esau came. (19) The trees which (were) in the garden of the king were as the stars of the heavens. (20) The wives of the king were evil in the eyes of the Lord. (21) The king Solomon took a wife from the land of Egypt. (22) The elders of Israel hearkened not to the voice of Moses in the land of Egypt, for they knew not that he spoke in the name of the Lord, the God of Israel.

[a] See footnote *e*, previous page.

[b] Note the changes: יְדֵי (כְּיְדֵי becomes) כִּידֵי.

[c] Pl. m. adjective.

[d] See footnote *c*, previous page.

25. PRONOMINAL SUFFIXES (of sing. masc. noun)

I	II	III
horse (abs.) סוּס	spirit (abs.) רוּחַ	word (abs.) דָּבָר
horse-of (cons.) סוּס	spirit-of (cons.) רוּחַ	word-of (cons.) דְּבַר
my (c.) horse סוּסִי	my (c.) spirit רוּחִי	my (c.) word דְּבָרִי
thy (m.) ,, סוּסְךָ	thy (m.) ,, רוּחֲךָ	thy (m.) ,, דְּבָרְךָ
thy (f.) ,, סוּסֵךְ	thy (f.) ,, רוּחֵךְ	thy (f.) ,, דְּבָרֵךְ
his ,, סוּסוֹ	his ,, רוּחוֹ	his ,, דְּבָרוֹ
her ,, סוּסָהּ	her ,, רוּחָהּ	her ,, דְּבָרָהּ
our (c.) ,, סוּסֵנוּ	our (c.) ,, רוּחֵנוּ	our (c.) ,, דְּבָרֵנוּ
your (m.) ,, סוּסְכֶם	your (m.) ,, רוּחֲכֶם	your (m.) ,, דִּבְרְכֶם
your (f.) ,, סוּסְכֶן	your (f.) ,, רוּחֲכֶן	your (f.) ,, דִּבְרְכֶן
their (m.) ,, סוּסָם	their (m.) ,, רוּחָם	their (m.) ,, דְּבָרָם
their (f.) ,, סוּסָן	their (f.) ,, רוּחָן	their (f.) ,, דְּבָרָן

IV	V	VI
trouble (abs.) עָמָל	prophet (abs.) נָבִיא	Pronominal Suffixes for the sing. noun.
trouble-of (cons.) עֲמַל	prophet-of (cons.) נְבִיא	
my (c.) trouble עֲמָלִי	my (c.) prophet נְבִיאִי	1st sing. com. ִי
thy (m.) ,, עֲמָלְךָ	thy (m.) ,, נְבִיאֲךָ	2nd ,, masc. ְךָ
thy (f.) ,, עֲמָלֵךְ	thy (f.) ,, נְבִיאֵךְ	2nd ,, fem. ֵךְ
his ,, עֲמָלוֹ	his ,, נְבִיאוֹ	3rd ,, masc. וֹ
her ,, עֲמָלָהּ	her ,, נְבִיאָהּ	3rd ,, fem. ָהּ
our (c.) ,, עֲמָלֵנוּ	our (c.) ,, נְבִיאֵנוּ	1st pl. com. ֵנוּ
your (m.) ,, עֲמַלְכֶם	your (m.) ,, נְבִיאֲכֶם	2nd ,, masc. ְכֶם
your (f.) ,, עֲמַלְכֶן	your (f.) ,, נְבִיאֲכֶן	2nd ,, fem. ְכֶן
their (m.) ,, עֲמָלָם	their (m.) ,, נְבִיאָם	3rd ,, masc. ָם
their (f.) ,, עֲמָלָן	their (f.) ,, נְבִיאָן	3rd ,, fem. ָן

General observations. (*a*) The possessives 'my', 'thy', 'his', 'her', &c. are expressed by *suffixed* pronominal particles, as given in Column VI. From the Hebrew standpoint, 'my horse' is 'horse-of-me' סוּסִי, &c.

(*b*) Note that the 3rd fem. sing. suffix has Mappiq in the הּ (e.g. סוּסָהּ: p. 17) which is to be pronounced as a sharp 'h'; whereas the fem. sing. noun (e.g. סוּסָה) has a silent ה.

(*c*) The suffixes כֶן, כֶם (called 'heavy suffixes') attach themselves to the construct form. This is especially evident in Columns III and IV. (The addition of the heavy syllable has the same shortening effect upon the noun as a genitive has upon a preceding construct.)

(*d*) Reference may again be made to p. 32, B (ii), where it was shown that, e.g. 'my good horse' is expressed in Hebrew as 'my horse, *the* good (one)' סוּסִי הַטּוֹב.

Column I represents the simplest form of the masc. sg. noun. There is no change in pointing when pronominal suffixes are attached.

Column II represents the same type of noun as Column I but with a terminal guttural. The abs. and cons. have the Furtive Pathah (p. 19. 4). With the suffixes of the 2nd m. sg. and the 2nd m. and f. pl. the guttural has a composite shewa instead of the simple shewa.

Column III represents a two-syllabled noun with a Qameṣ in the first syllable. When this type of noun receives an additional syllable at the end—in this case the new syllable being the suffix—the accent moves on to it, and the Qameṣ in the first syllable is reduced to shewa (p. 35, A. Col. II). *Observe* that with the 2nd m. sg. suffix the Qameṣ (under the ב) has a Methegh to show that the syllable is open and that the vowel is 'ā' (p. 13. 2, Note).

Column IV represents the same type of noun as Column III but having an initial guttural. The Qameṣ in the first syllable is replaced by a composite shewa (under the guttural) when the accent moves on to the new syllable.

Column V represents a type of noun with Qameṣ in the first syllable and a 'full' vowel in the second one. As would be expected, the Qameṣ falls away in the construct and with suffixes, but the full vowel remains throughout. Note also how the א in the 2nd m. sg. and the 2nd persons pl. takes composite shewa.

26. THE INSEPARABLE PREPOSITIONS לְ, בְּ WITH SUFFIXES

The inseparable prepositions לְ and בְּ take pronominal suffixes, thus:

to me[a] (c.)	לִי	in me[b] (c.)	בִּי
,, thee (m.)	לְךָ	,, thee (m.)	בְּךָ
,, thee (f.)	לָךְ	,, thee (f.)	בָּךְ
,, him	לוֹ	,, him	בּוֹ
,, her	לָהּ	,, her	בָּהּ
,, us (c.)	לָנוּ	,, us (c.)	בָּנוּ
,, you (m.)	לָכֶם	,, you (m.)	בָּכֶם
,, you (f.)	לָכֶן	,, you (f.)	בָּכֶן
,, them (m.)	לָהֶם	,, them (m.)	בָּהֶם or בָּם
,, them (f.)	לָהֶן	,, them (f.)	בָּהֶן

The inseparable prepositions כְּ 'as, like' and מִן 'from' with pronominal suffixes are given on p. 63.

27. THE SIGN OF THE DEFINITE OBJECT

Below are given sets of examples to show how the definite object is indicated, to avoid confusing it with the subject:

(*a*) לָקַח הַבֵּן—'he took, (namely) the son'. Here הַבֵּן is the subject—'the son took', but

לָקַח אֶת־הַבֵּן—'he took the son'. Here הַבֵּן, preceded by the word אֶת־, is the object.

(*b*) לָקַח בֶּן־הַמֶּלֶךְ—'he took, (namely) the son-of the king'. Here בֶּן־הַמֶּלֶךְ is the subject—'the son-of the king took', but

לָקַח אֶת־בֶּן־הַמֶּלֶךְ—'he took the son-of the king'. Here בֶּן־הַמֶּלֶךְ, preceded by אֶת־, is the object.

[a] Or 'for me', &c.

[b] Or 'by me', &c.

(*c*) לָקַח בְּנוֹ—'he took, (namely) his son'. Here בְּנוֹ is the subject—'his son took', but

לָקַח אֶת־בְּנוֹ—'he took his son'. Here בְּנוֹ, preceded by אֶת־, is the object.

(*d*) לָקַח שְׁמוּאֵל—'he took, (namely) Samuel'. Here שְׁמוּאֵל is the subject—'Samuel took', but

לָקַח אֶת־שְׁמוּאֵל—'he took Samuel'. Here שְׁמוּאֵל, preceded by אֶת־, is the object.

The *definite object*, governed by a transitive verb, *is* usually *preceded by* the particle אֵת or אֶת־ (with Maqqeph), which draws attention to the object which is definite. In (*a*) the object is definite, since it has the article; in (*b*) the compound idea (which is the object) is definite, since the genitive has the article; in (*c*) the suffix shows that the object is a definite one; and in (*d*) the proper noun is obviously a definite (person—and here the) object.

N.B. (1) מִי לָקַח = 'who hath taken?' but אֶת־מִי לָקַח = 'whom hath he taken?'

(2) 'The man took *a* horse' is לָקַח הָאִישׁ סוּס—*in*definite object and therefore *not preceded* by the particle אֶת־.

EXERCISE 7

Abraham	אַבְרָהָם	mountain	הַר
Sarah	שָׂרָה	,, (with art.)	הָהָר
		,, (pl.)	הָרִים
covenant	בְּרִית	with[a]	עִם
dream (sg.)	חֲלוֹם *m.*	until	עַד
,, (pl.)	חֲלוֹמוֹת	he kept, watched	שָׁמַר
river	נָהָר	he cut	כָּרַת

[N.B. 'He made a covenant' is 'he cut a covenant' כָּרַת בְּרִית.]

(1) בָּרָא אֱלֹהִים אֶת־הַשָּׁמַיִם וְאֶת־הָאָרֶץ וְאֶת־כָּל־אֲשֶׁר בָּהֶם

(2) שָׁמְעוּ הָאָדָם וְהָאִשָּׁה אֶת־קוֹל־אֱלֹהִים בַּגָּן (3) וּבְיָדוֹ הַגְּדוֹלָה

[a] In the sense of 'together with', 'along with', as opposed to the insep. prep. בּ which means 'with' of instrument. It takes suffixes: עִמִּי 'with me'; עִמְּךָ 'with thee' (m).

לָקַח יהוה אֶת־עַמּוֹ יִשְׂרָאֵל מִמִּצְרַ֫יִם לוֹ לְעַם קָדוֹשׁ, וְגַם נָתַן
לָהֶם אֶת־הָאָ֫רֶץ הַטּוֹבָה מִנְּהַר־מִצְרַ֫יִם עַד־הַנָּהָר הַגָּדוֹל: וְלֹא[a]
שָׁמְרוּ אֶת־בְּרִיתוֹ אֲשֶׁר כָּרַת עִמָּם עַל־הַר־הָאֱלֹהִים וְלֹא שָׁמְעוּ
בְּקוֹלוֹ (4) שָׁמַר יהוה אֶת־יַעֲקֹב מִכָּל־רָע (5) רָאָה אֱלֹהִים
אֶת־הָאוֹר אֲשֶׁר בָּרָא וְהִנֵּה טוֹב[b] מְאֹד (6) כָּרַת שְׁמוּאֵל אֶת־
רֹאשׁ־הַמֶּ֫לֶךְ לְעֵינֵי־כָל־יִשְׂרָאֵל (7) אָמְרוּ הָעַמִּים אֲשֶׁר בָּ֫אוּ
עַל[c]־יִשְׂרָאֵל, יהוה הוּא אֱלֹהֵי־הֶהָרִים (8) וְשֵׁם־אֵשֶׁת־אַבְרָהָם[b]
שָׂרָה (9) אָמְרָה שָׂרָה אֶל־אַבְרָהָם אִישָׁהּ, הִנֵּה אִשָּׁה זְקֵנָה אֲנִי,
וְלֹא נָתַן לִי אֱלֹהִים בֵּן (10) קָרָא מֹשֶׁה בְּקוֹל גָּדוֹל, יהוה עִמָּ֫נוּ
וְגַם נָתַן בְּיָדֵ֫נוּ אֶת־הָעִיר וְאֶת־הָעָם אֲשֶׁר בָּהּ (11) הָיוּ אַנְשֵׁי־
יִשְׂרָאֵל בֶּהָרִים כָּל־הַיּוֹם עַד־הַלָּ֫יְלָה[d] (12) מֵרֹאשׁ הָהָר רָאָה
מֹשֶׁה אֶת־הָאָ֫רֶץ אֲשֶׁר נָתַן יהוה לִבְנֵי־יִשְׂרָאֵל (13) בָּ֫אוּ זִקְנֵי־
הָעָם אֶל־הֵיכַל־הַמֶּ֫לֶךְ, וְעָפָר[b] עַל־רֹאשָׁם (14) שָׁמַע אֱלֹהִים
אֶת־קוֹלִי, כִּי הוּא אוֹרִי בְּיוֹם־הַחֹשֶׁךְ (15) שָׁמַע יַעֲקֹב אֶת־
הַחֲלוֹם וְגַם שָׁמַר אֶת־הַדָּבָר, כִּי אָמַר מִן הָאֱלֹהִים הַחֲלוֹם
(16) וּבַחֲלוֹמוֹ רָאָה יַעֲקֹב וְהִנֵּה הַר גָּדוֹל מְאֹד וְרֹאשׁוֹ בַּשָּׁמָ֫יִם[d]
(17) וּבְכָל־חַכְמֵי־הָעִיר לֹא הָיָה אִישׁ אֲשֶׁר יָדַע אֶת־דְּבַר־
הַחֲלוֹם (18) הִבְדִּיל יהוה בֵּין נְבִיאֵי־מִצְרַ֫יִם וּבֵין מֹשֶׁה נְבִיאוֹ
(19) יָשְׁבוּ הַנְּבִיאִים בְּאַחַד־הָרֵי־הָאָ֫רֶץ וּבְרֹאשָׁם הָיָה שְׁמוּאֵל
(20) הִנֵּה יָדוֹ בַכֹּל, וְיַד־כָּל־אָדָם בּוֹ (21) כָּרַת אַבְרָהָם בְּרִית
עִם מֶ֫לֶךְ־הָעִיר (22) מֵהֵיכָלוֹ אֲשֶׁר בַּשָּׁמַ֫יִם רָאָה יהוה אֶת־עַמּוֹ
וְאֶת־קוֹלֵ֫נוּ שָׁמֵ֫עַ[d]

(1) God gave the woman to the man for (a) wife. (2) Samuel heard the voice of the Lord in the night. (3) Moses spoke all

[a] The conj. here means 'but'. See p. 40, footnote *a*.
[b] Supply 'was'. See p. 48, footnote *c*.
[c] 'Upon' = against.
[d] Pausal (with Silluq accent).

the words of the Lord unto the elders of Israel in the land of Egypt. (4) Sarah heard the words of the man which he spoke unto Abrâham her husband. (5) The children of Israel kept not My covenant and they distinguished not between Me[a] and (between) the gods of the land. (6) The eyes of the Lord are unto His people. (7) The woman kept the men with[b] her all the night until the light of the morning. (8) The king made a covenant with[b] the people upon the mountain of God. (9) The Lord heard our voice in the land of Egypt. (10) He distinguished Israel from all the peoples. (11) From His temple the Lord (hath) heard my voice. (12) Abraham and Sarah were very old and the Lord gave not (to) them children. (13) The woman gave the fruit unto her husband. (14) Thy people hearkened not to the words of Thy prophet and they kept not the covenant which Moses made between Thee and between us. (15) In the evening and in the morning my voice is unto the Lord and His word is with[b] me. (16) Jacob knew that the Lord was with[b] him. (17) All the wise men of Egypt said unto the king, 'Behold the God of Israel hath set ("given") his hand against (בְּ) thee and against thy people.'

28. THE PERSONAL PRONOUNS

A (Subject)	B (Object)
I (c.) אֲנִי, אָנֹכִי[c]	me (c.) אֹתִי
thou (m.) אַתָּה[d]	thee (m.) אֹתְךָ
thou (f.) אַתְּ[e]	thee (f.) אֹתָךְ
he הוּא	him אֹתוֹ
she הִיא	her אֹתָהּ
we (c.) אֲנַחְנוּ	us (c.) אֹתָנוּ

[a] בֵּין takes suffixes—בֵּינִי = 'between me', &c.

[b] See p. 53, footnote *a*.

[c] Pausal אָנֹכִי, אָנִי.

[d] Pausal אָתָּה.

[e] One of the few cases where a terminal vowelless letter has a silent shewa (p. 9, footnote *c*). The reason is that this form is an abbreviation of an original אַתִּי and the î-termination was dropped.

(Subject *contd.*)		(Object *contd.*)	
you (m.)	אַתֶּם	you (m.)	אֶתְכֶם
you (f.)	אַתֶּן	you (f.)	אֶתְכֶן
they (m.)	הֵם[a], הֵמָּה	them (m.)	אֶתְהֶם, אֹתָם
they (f.)	הֵן[a], הֵנָּה	them (f.)	אֶתְהֶן, אֹתָן

When the Personal Pronoun is the object of a verb it is *definite*, since a *particular* person is referred to; hence it is expressed by the sign of the definite object אֵת with the pronominal suffixes.

NOTE: Another form of אֵת (namely אֹת) is used with the suffixes, as אֹתִי, אֹתְךָ, except when it assumes the (so-termed) heavy suffixes כֶם, כֶן [הֶם, הֶן rarely used with this particle].

29. THE REGULAR VERB (Perfect)

he (hath) kept	שָׁמַר	he (hath) ruled	מָשַׁל
she „ „	שָֽׁמְרָה	she „ „	מָֽשְׁלָה
thou (m.) hast „	שָׁמַרְתָּ	thou (m.) hast „	מָשַׁלְתָּ
thou (f.) „ „	שָׁמַרְתְּ	thou (f.) „ „	מָשַׁלְתְּ
I (c.) (have) „	שָׁמַרְתִּי	I (c.) (have) „	מָשַׁלְתִּי
they (c.) „ „	שָֽׁמְרוּ	they (c.) „ „	מָֽשְׁלוּ
ye (m.) „ „	שְׁמַרְתֶּם	ye (m.) „ „	מְשַׁלְתֶּם
ye (f.) „ „	שְׁמַרְתֶּן	ye (f.) „ „	מְשַׁלְתֶּן
we (c.) „ „	שָׁמַרְנוּ	we (c.) „ „	מָשַׁלְנוּ

In Hebrew thinking, *an action* is regarded as being either *completed or incompleted*. Hebrew, therefore, knows of no past, present, or future tenses, but has instead a *Perfect* and an *Imperfect* (which, in a context, lend themselves to a variety of shades in meaning). For the time being, however, the Hebrew Perfect may be taken to represent action in the past ('he kept', 'he hath kept'). We shall see later that the equivalent of the English present tense is supplied by the Participle (pp. 65–6) and the

[a] Shorter form but not as frequent as the longer one.

English future tense (with other varieties) by the Imperfect (pp. 75–6).

NOTE: (*a*) The standard table of Hebrew verbs usually begins with the 3rd masc. sing. (Perfect, as מָשַׁל שָׁמַר), since this is the simplest form of the verb and conveniently serves as the basis for the others.

(*b*) The persons of the perfect are formed by taking the stem of the verb (3rd m. sg.) and *appending* pronominal particles (i.e. the essential elements of the personal pronoun to denote the person, gender, and number) thus:

שָׁמַרְתָּ	is a compound of	שָׁמַר + (אַ)תָּ(ה)	'kept	(hast)	thou	(m.)'
שָׁמַרְתְּ	,,	שָׁמַר + (אַ)תְּ	,,	,,	,,	(f.)
שְׁמַרְתֶּם	,,	שָׁמַר + (אַ)תֶּם	,,	(have)	ye	(m.)
שְׁמַרְתֶּן	,,	שָׁמַר + (אַ)תֶּן	,,	,,	,,	(f.)
שָׁמַרְנוּ	,,	שָׁמַר + (אֲ)נוּ[a]	,,	,,	we	(c.)

שָׁמַרְתִּי is due to (a false) analogy with the pronominal element of the 2nd sing.

In the 2nd pl. (masc. and fem.) the accent moves forward on to the heavy suffix (from שָׁמַר to שְׁמַרְתֶּם) and the Qameṣ in the first syllable consequently (cf. p. 35, Col. II) becomes shewa.

(*c*) If the first root-letter of the verb is a guttural (as אָמַר 'he said') there will be a composite shewa under the guttural in the 2nd pl. (אֲמַרְתֶּם 'ye have said') (instead of the simple shewa of שְׁמַרְתֶּם).

(*d*) It appears that in Hebrew thought the general or main idea is first expressed and is limited in its application by a following word or particle. Thus, 'thou (hast) kept' is 'kept (hast) thou'—שָׁמַרְתָּ—the main idea 'kept' is first given and limited in its application to 'thou' by the following pronominal particle 'thou'. Similarly:

'a good man'	is in Hebrew	'a man, a good (one)' אִישׁ טוֹב
'my man'	,,	'man-of-me' אִישִׁי
'my good man'	,,	'my man, the good (one)' אִישִׁי הַטּוֹב
'the man said'	,,	'he said, (namely) the man' אָמַר הָאִישׁ

[a] Shorter form of אֲנַחְנוּ.

30. MORE NOUNS IN THE ABSOLUTE AND CONSTRUCT STATES

The following nouns are irregular but in very frequent use:

	sg. abs.	sg. cons.	pl. abs.	pl. cons.
day	יוֹם	יוֹם	יָמִים	יְמֵי
city (f.)	עִיר	עִיר	עָרִים	עָרֵי
house	בַּ֫יִת	בֵּית	בָּתִּים[a]	בָּתֵּי
head	רֹאשׁ	רֹאשׁ	רָאשִׁים	רָאשֵׁי

EXERCISE 8

Canaan כְּנַ֫עַן

spy מְרַגֵּל

bread לֶ֫חֶם

way, path דֶּ֫רֶךְ

he did, made עָשָׂה

he remembered זָכַר

he sent, stretched out (with יָד) שָׁלַח

he ruled (over) (בְּ) מָשַׁל

he chose (בְּ) בָּחַר

(1) אַתָּה הוּא הָאֱלֹהִים וַאֲנַ֫חְנוּ עַמְּךָ בְּנֵי־בְרִיתֶ֫ךָ[b] (2) שָׁלַח מֹשֶׁה מְרַגְּלִים אֶל־אֶ֫רֶץ כְּנַ֫עַן, וְהָאֲנָשִׁים הָיוּ אַנְשֵׁי־שֵׁם, רָאשֵׁי־בְנֵי־יִשְׂרָאֵל (3) אָמַר הָאָדָם אֶל־הָאֱלֹהִים שָׁמַ֫עְתִּי אֶת־קוֹלְךָ בַּגָּן (4) אָמְרָה הָאִשָּׁה אֶל־מְרַגְּלֵי־יִשְׂרָאֵל, שָׁמַ֫עְנוּ אֶת־כָּל־אֲשֶׁר עָשָׂה יהוה לְמִצְרַ֫יִם וְגַם יָדַ֫עְנוּ[c] כִּי נָתַן לָכֶם אֶת־אֶ֫רֶץ כְּנָ֫עַן (5) לָקַ֫חְתִּי אֶתְכֶם מִמִּצְרַ֫יִם לִי לְעַם קָדוֹשׁ וְלֹא שְׁמַרְתֶּם אֶת־בְּרִיתִי וּבְקוֹלִי לֹא שְׁמַעְתֶּם, בֵּית־יַעֲקֹב (6) יָדַ֫עְתִּי[c] כִּי לֶקְחָה מִפְּרִי־עֵץ־הַגָּן וְכִי נֶתְנָה לְךָ וְאַתָּה אָכַ֫לְתָּ עִמָּהּ (7) קָרְאוּ זִקְנֵי־הָעָם אֶל־מֹשֶׁה, זָכַ֫רְנוּ[c] אֶת־הַלֶּ֫חֶם אֲשֶׁר אָכַ֫לְנוּ בְמִצְרָ֫יִם (8) אָמְרוּ הַמְרַגְּלִים[d], לָקַ֫חְנוּ מִפְּרִי־הָאָ֫רֶץ וְהִנֵּה טוֹב מְאֹד (9) יָדַ֫עְתִּי[c] כִּי

[a] See p. 13. 3, N.B.

[b] Pausal.

[c] Here the perfect is to be translated into the English present tense—the state of knowing (and remembering) being complete.

[d] See p. 18, Note to § **10**.

בְּךָ בָּחַר יהוה לְמֶלֶךְ עַל־יִשְׂרָאֵל (10) אַתָּה[a] בָּחַרְתָּ בָּנוּ מִכָּל־
הָעַמִּים וְאֹתָנוּ לָקַחְתָּ לְךָ לְעַם גָּדוֹל וְקָדוֹשׁ, וַאֲנַחְנוּ[a] לֹא שָׁמַרְנוּ
אֶת־הַבְּרִית אֲשֶׁר כָּרַתְנוּ עִמְּךָ עַל־הַר־הָאֱלֹהִים (11) אָמַר לָנוּ
הָאִישׁ, יָדַעְתִּי כִּי מְרַגְּלִים אַתֶּם מֵאֶרֶץ כְּנַעַן (12) יָשַׁב הַנָּבִיא
עַל־הָאֲדָמָה וְעָפָר עַל־רֹאשׁוֹ וּבְקוֹל גָּדוֹל קָרָא, מֶה־עָשָׂה יהוה
לָנוּ (13) זָכַרְתָּ אֹתִי אֱלֹהִים וּמֵהֵיכָלְךָ שָׁמַעְתָּ אֶת־קוֹלִי (14) מָשַׁל
שְׁמוּאֵל הַנָּבִיא בְּיִשְׂרָאֵל כִּי לֹא בָחֲרוּ[b] לָהֶם מֶלֶךְ כְּכָל־הָעַמִּים
אֲשֶׁר יָשְׁבוּ בָּאָרֶץ, וְכָל־יְמֵי־שְׁמוּאֵל הָלְכוּ בְנֵי־יִשְׂרָאֵל בְּדֶרֶךְ־
יהוה (15) הִנֵּה הֶעָרִים אֲשֶׁר בְּאֶרֶץ כְּנַעַן טוֹבוֹת וּגְדוֹלוֹת הֵנָּה
כְּעָרֵי־מִצְרָיִם (16) בְּדֶרֶךְ יהוה הָלַכְתִּי וְאֶת־דְּבָרוֹ שָׁמַרְתִּי כָּל־
הַיָּמִים (17) אַתֶּם[a] יְדַעְתֶּם כִּי הִבְדִּיל אֶתְכֶם אֱלֹהִים מִכָּל־הָעַמִּים
אֲשֶׁר תַּחַת הַשָּׁמָיִם (18) לֹא אָכַל מֹשֶׁה לֶחֶם כָּל־הַיָּמִים אֲשֶׁר
הָיָה עַל־הָהָר

(1) Abraham dwelt in the land of Egypt, for there was not bread in the land of Canaan. (2) Holy art Thou, Lord, in the heavens and in the earth. (3) Solomon the king of Israel made for him(self) a great name in the land. (4) Samuel said unto the elders of the people, 'Ye have chosen for you(rselves) a king like all the peoples and ye remembered not that the Lord He is king over all the earth.' (5) I know[c] that ye have eaten from the tree which is in the garden and that ye know[c] good and evil. (6) We know[c] that we kept not Thy covenant and that we hearkened not to the words of Thy prophet whom Thou didst send unto Thy people. (7) The spies whom the children of Israel sent unto the land of Canaan sat in the house of the woman all the night until the light of the morning. (8) The prophets said unto Samuel, 'Thou hast not taken a thing from the hand of a(ny) man all the days that thou didst rule over Israel.' (9) He saw the cities of the river and behold they (were[d]) very good. (10) The

[a] The personal pronoun is used with the verb to emphasize the person.
[b] Note that the guttural takes a composite shewa instead of the simple one.
[c] Perfect—see note *b*, p. 58.
[d] See p. 48, footnote *c*.

spies said unto Moses, 'Behold the cities which are in the land of Canaan are in the mountains'. (11) I have chosen thee for a king over my people Israel, for thou hast walked in the way of the Lord. (12) The sons of the prophets said, 'We know[a] that the Lord sent thee unto the wicked city and that He cut (off) the river for thee, for thou art His prophet'. (13) All the days that thou didst rule over my people thou didst not remember the name of the Lord. (14) The old men said unto the king, 'We dwelt in the mountains and from the fruit of the ground we ate, for we are holy men and the way of the Lord we have chosen.' (15) Behold I have taken thee, house of Israel, from a land of darkness unto a land of light and I have also kept thee from evil in the way that thou didst walk. (16) The king of Egypt said unto Moses, '[b] *Thou* hast said that the Lord, the God of Israel, hath sent thee unto His people. Who is the Lord? I know[a] not Him.'

31. FEMININE SINGULAR NOUNS WITH SUFFIXES

I	II	III
law (abs.) תּוֹרָה	lip (abs.) שָׂפָה	counsel (abs.) עֵצָה
law-of (cons.) תּוֹרַת	lip-of (cons.) שְׂפַת	counsel-of (cons.) עֲצַת
my (c.) law תּוֹרָתִי	my (c.) lip שְׂפָתִי	my (c.) counsel עֲצָתִי
thy (m.) „ תּוֹרָתְךָ	thy (m.) „ שְׂפָתְךָ	thy (m.) „ עֲצָתְךָ
thy (f.) „ תּוֹרָתֵךְ	thy (f.) „ שְׂפָתֵךְ	thy (f.) „ עֲצָתֵךְ
his „ תּוֹרָתוֹ	his „ שְׂפָתוֹ	his „ עֲצָתוֹ
her „ תּוֹרָתָהּ	her „ שְׂפָתָהּ	her „ עֲצָתָהּ
our (c.) „ תּוֹרָתֵנוּ	our (c.) „ שְׂפָתֵנוּ	our (c.) „ עֲצָתֵנוּ
your (m.) „ תּוֹרַתְכֶם	your (m.) „ שְׂפַתְכֶם	your (m.) „ עֲצַתְכֶם
your (f.) „ תּוֹרַתְכֶן	your (f.) „ שְׂפַתְכֶן	your (f.) „ עֲצַתְכֶן
their (m.) „ תּוֹרָתָם	their (m.) „ שְׂפָתָם	their (m.) „ עֲצָתָם
their (f.) „ תּוֹרָתָן	their (f.) „ שְׂפָתָן	their (f.) „ עֲצָתָן

[a] Perfect—see note *b*, p. 58.

[b] See note *a*, p. 59.

IV		V	
righteousness (abs.)	צְדָקָה	land (abs.)	אֲדָמָה
righteousness-of (cons.)	צִדְקַת	land-of (cons.)	אַדְמַת
my (c.) righteousness	צִדְקָתִי	my (c.) land	אַדְמָתִי
thy (m.) „	צִדְקָתְךָ	thy (m.) „	אַדְמָתְךָ
thy (f.) „	צִדְקָתֵךְ	thy (f.) „	אַדְמָתֵךְ
his „	צִדְקָתוֹ	his „	אַדְמָתוֹ
her „	צִדְקָתָהּ	her „	אַדְמָתָהּ
our (c.) „	צִדְקָתֵנוּ	our (c.) „	אַדְמָתֵנוּ
your (m.) „	צִדְקַתְכֶם	your (m.) „	אַדְמַתְכֶם
your (f.) „	צִדְקַתְכֶן	your (f.) „	אַדְמַתְכֶן
their (m.) „	צִדְקָתָם	their (m.) „	אַדְמָתָם
their (f.) „	צִדְקָתָן	their (f.) „	אַדְמָתָן

NOTE 1. It was pointed out on p. 44, Note, that the fem. sing. originally terminated in ַָת (āṯ), and that in the absolute state (i.e. not connected with a following word) the ת (ṯ) was (scarcely audible and therefore) discarded, so that the fem. sg. abs. termination came to be 'â' (written ָה). The original ת, however, has survived in the construct and before suffixes.[a]

2. Again (as was shown on p. 51 (*c*)), the heavy suffixes כֶם, כֶן are attached to the form of the construct. This is seen in all five columns.

Column I תּוֹרָה (corresponding to the masc. סוּס, p. 50, Col. I) represents the simplest form of the fem. sing. noun—the *full* vowel וֹ remains throughout תּוֹרָתִי, תּוֹרַת.

Column II שָׂפָה is a two-syllabled word with Qameṣ in the first syllable. This vowel is reduced to shewa in the construct and when a suffix is appended (for the reason explained on p. 51, Col. III) שְׂפָתִי, שְׂפַת.

[a] There are still some types of fem. nouns which have a ת in the abs., as נְחֹשֶׁת 'brass' or 'bronze'. See also p. 45, footnote *a*.

Column III עֵצָה is a fem. noun of a type similar to שָׂפָה in Column II, but its first letter is a guttural; consequently, the vowel (under the guttural) in the first syllable is reduced (in the construct and with suffixes) to a *composite* shewa instead of the simple shewa (cf. p. 50, Col. IV) עֲצַת, עֲצָתִי.

Column IV צְדָקָה, following Column II, becomes (hypothetically) צְדְקַת (in the construct) and צְדְקָתִי (with suffixes) which, in turn, become צִדְקַת and צִדְקָתִי (cf. p. 46. 3).

Column V אֲדָמָה is the same type of fem. noun as צְדָקָה in Column IV, but its first letter is a guttural; consequently, when the Qameṣ in the first syllable becomes shewa (in the construct and with the suffixes) producing אֲדְמַת, אֲדְמָתִי, the composite shewa under the guttural becomes the corresponding short vowel (pathaḥ)—אַדְמַת, אַדְמָתִי (cf. p. 46. 3).

32. THE DEMONSTRATIVE ADJECTIVES

this (m.)	זֶה	that (m.)	הוּא
,, (f.)	זֹאת	,, (f.)	הִיא
these (c.)	אֵלֶּה	those (m.)	הֵמָּה, הֵם
		,, (f.)	הֵנָּה, הֵן

The Demonstrative Adjectives are treated in the same way as ordinary adjectives in relation to the noun they qualify, thus:

'This man'	is expressed as	'the man, the this (one)'	הָאִישׁ הַזֶּה
'That man'	,,	'the man, the that (one)'	הָאִישׁ הַהוּא
'This woman'	,,	'the woman, the this (one)'	הָאִשָּׁה הַזֹּאת
'That woman'	,,	'the woman, the that (one)'	הָאִשָּׁה הַהִיא
'These men'	,,	'the men, the these (ones)'	הָאֲנָשִׁים הָאֵלֶּה
'Those men'	,,	'the men, the those (ones)'	הָאֲנָשִׁים [a] הָהֵם
'This is the man'	,,	'this (is) the man'	זֶה הָאִישׁ
'This is the woman'	,,	'this (is) the woman'	זֹאת הָאִשָּׁה
'These are the men'	,,	'these (are) the men'	אֵלֶּה הָאֲנָשִׁים

[a] Notice the pointing of the article with the pl. 'those' הָהֵם, &c.

33. THE PREPOSITIONS כְּ, מִן WITH SUFFIXES

The inseparable preposition כְּ (as, like) appears in poetry as a separate word in the form כְּמוֹ; and it is the latter form to which most suffixes are attached. When the preposition מִן (from) receives suffixes, a מ appears between it and most suffixes:

like me (c.)	כָּמֹ֫וֹנִי		from me (c.)	מִמֶּ֫נִּי	
,, thee (m.)	כָּמֹ֫וֹךָ		,, thee (m.)	מִמְּךָ	
,, thee (f.)	כָּמוֹךְ		,, thee (f.)	מִמֵּךְ	
,, him	כָּמֹ֫והוּ		,, him	מִמֶּ֫נּוּ	
,, her	כָּמֹ֫והָ		,, her	מִמֶּ֫נָּה	
,, us (c.)	כָּמֹ֫ונוּ		,, us (c.)	מִמֶּ֫נּוּ	
,, you (m.)	כָּכֶם		,, you (m.)	מִכֶּם	
,, you (f.)	כָּכֶן		,, you (f.)	מִכֶּן	
,, them (m.)	כָּהֶם		,, them (m.)	מֵהֶם, [מֵהֵ֫מָּה]	
,, them (f.)	כָּהֵ֫נָּה, כָּהֶן		,, them (f)	מֵהֵ֫נָּה, [מֵהֶן]	

NOTE: (a) The 1st sing. suffix is נִי.

(b) Dageš Forte (compensative) follows מ, except with the 3rd pl. suffix, on account of the guttural, when it is מֵ (p. 19. 1).

(c) מִמֶּ֫נּוּ ('from him') and מִמֶּ֫נָּה ('from her') are contractions from מִמֶּ֫נְהוּ and מִמֶּ֫נְהָ; the inserted נ implies an original reduplicated מִנְמִן which has been lost.

(d) The context determines whether מִמֶּ֫נּוּ means 'from him' or 'from us'.

(e) The 3rd sg. suffixes הוּ and הָ are earlier forms of וֹ and הָ.

(f) The medial מ is absent when the heavy suffixes כֶן, כֶם, &c, are attached.

EXERCISE 9

Sinai	סִינַי	other, another	אַחֵר
place	מָקוֹם	other (ones, pl.)	אֲחֵרִים
salvation, deliverance	יְשׁוּעָה	after, behind	אַחֲרֵי or אַחַר
fear, reverence	יִרְאָה	thus	כֹּה
blessing	בְּרָכָה	there is not / „ are „	אֵין

(1) זֶה הַיּוֹם אֲשֶׁר עָשָׂה יהוה (2) זֹאת הַתּוֹרָה אֲשֶׁר נָתַן מֹשֶׁה
לִבְנֵי־יִשְׂרָאֵל עַל־הַר־סִינָי[a] (3) אֵ֫לֶּה הַדְּבָרִים אֲשֶׁר דִּבֶּר יהוה
אֶל־מֹשֶׁה בְּאֶרֶץ־מִצְרָ֫יִם[a] (4) אָמַר יַעֲקֹב, קָדוֹשׁ הַמָּקוֹם הַזֶּה
וְאָנֹכִי לֹא יָדָ֫עְתִּי[a] (5) בַּיּוֹם הַהוּא נָתַן אֱלֹהִים יְשׁוּעָה גְדוֹלָה
לְיִשְׂרָאֵל (6) אַחַר הַדְּבָרִים הָאֵ֫לֶּה הָיָה[b] דְבַר־יהוה אֶל־אַבְרָהָם
בַּחֲלוֹם (7) כֹּה אָמַר אֱלֹהִים אֶל־הָעִיר הָרָעָה הַהִיא (8) אָמַ֫רְתִּי
אֵין יִרְאַת־אֱלֹהִים בַּמָּקוֹם הַזֶּה (9) בַּיָּמִים הָהֵם לֹא הָיָה מֶ֫לֶךְ
בְּיִשְׂרָאֵל וּשְׁמוּאֵל הָיָה הַנָּבִיא (10) הָלְכוּ בְנֵי־יִשְׂרָאֵל אַחֲרֵי
אֱלֹהִים[c] אֲחֵרִים וְלֹא זָכְרוּ אֶת־תּוֹרַת־מֹשֶׁה וְאֶת־הַבְּרִית אֲשֶׁר
כָּרַת עִמָּם יהוה עַל־הַר־סִינָי (11) אַתָּה הוּא אֱלֹהֵי־יְשׁוּעָתִי[d] וְאֵין
כָּמ֫וֹךָ (12) אָמַר מֶלֶךְ־מִצְרָ֫יִם אֵין כָּמ֫וֹךָ אִישׁ חָכָם בְּכָל־הָאָ֫רֶץ
הַגְּדוֹלָה הַזֹּאת (13) רָאָה הַמֶּ֫לֶךְ כִּי טוֹבָה[e] עֲצַת־הַנָּבִיא (14) אַתָּה
שָׁלַ֫חְתָּ בְרָכָה בִּפְרִי־אַדְמָתֵ֫נוּ (15) קָרָא עֵשָׂו בְּקוֹל גָּדוֹל, לָקַח
יַעֲקֹב אֶת־בִּרְכָתִי מִמֶּ֫נִּי (16) שָׁמַ֫רְתִּי אֶת־תּוֹרָתְךָ כָּל־הַיָּמִים
וּבְדֶרֶךְ־אֱלֹהִים[c] אֲחֵרִים לֹא הָלָ֫כְתִּי[a] (17) נָתַן אֱלֹהִים אֶת־יִרְאַת־
יַעֲקֹב עַל־כָּל־אַנְשֵׁי־הָעִיר (18) בַּלַּ֫יְלָה[f] הַהוּא הִבְדִּיל יהוה בֵּין
יִשְׂרָאֵל וּבֵין מִצְרָ֫יִם[a] (19) קְדוֹשָׁה לִי הָעִיר הַזֹּאת, כִּי בָהּ
בָּחַ֫רְתִּי לִשְׁמִי

[a] Pausal—the vowel in the tone-syllable is lengthened.

[b] See p. 48, footnote *d*. [c] 'gods', as the context shows.

[d] The idea is 'my God of salvation', i.e. 'my saving God'. See Appendix 5, p. 253. [e] See p. 48, footnote *c*. Understand 'was'.

[f] This noun is masc.; the unaccented termination is a lengthening of the word לַ֫יִל. N.B. The fem. sing. termination ָה is accented.

(1) This is the word which the Lord spoke unto His prophet. (2) This is the city which Thou hast chosen for Thy temple. (3) These are the men whom Moses sent to the Land of Canaan[a]. (4) God hath given (to) you this law upon the mountain of Sinai[a]. (5) Moses spoke all these words to the elders of Israel in the land of Egypt[a]. (6) There is none ('not') like Thee in the heavens and in the earth. (7) The blessing of the Lord is upon your ground, for ye have kept His law. (8) The king sent other men to the prophet and he came not. (9) In the city there dwelt very evil men who knew not the law of Moses. (10) We have remembered the words of the holy law and Thy covenant we have kept all the days. (11) What is this dream which I heard? (12) In Thee is our salvation, Lord, and not in other gods. (13) The elders called unto Moses, 'There is no(t) bread for the people.' (14) They have walked in the way of the gods of the land and My law they have not remembered. (15) The Lord hath given (to) you all[b] this good and great land, from these mountains unto ('until') that great river. (16) Thou (f.) hast walked after strange gods and thou didst not remember the counsel of My prophet. (17) There was not like him a prophet in all Israel who knew the Lord. (18) I sent My blessing upon thy ground, for My law is with thee all the day.

34. THE ACTIVE PARTICIPLE

The Active Participle is formed thus:

	m.sg.	f. sg.	m. pl.	f. pl.
From the root שָׁמַר (kept, watched) it is	שֹׁמֵר	שֹׁמֶ֫רֶת (or שֹׁמְרָה)	שֹׁמְרִים	שֹׁמְרוֹת
,, ,, יָשַׁב (sat, dwelt) ,,	יֹשֵׁב	יֹשֶׁ֫בֶת (or יֹשְׁבָה)	יֹשְׁבִים	יֹשְׁבוֹת
,, ,, הָלַךְ (went, walked) ,,	הֹלֵךְ	הֹלֶ֫כֶת (or הֹלְכָה)	הֹלְכִים	הֹלְכוֹת

The Active Participle is pointed with Ḥolem and Ṣere (.. ˙) for the masc. sg., to which is appended (sometimes הָ but mostly

[a] Use pausal form. See p. 21.

[b] כֹּל (with Maqqeph כָּל־) is really a noun, meaning 'whole', 'totality'. The expression 'all the land' is, in Hebrew thinking, 'the whole-of the land'. As the obj. of the vb. it is definite and is, therefore, preceded by אֶת־.

the original) ֶת ֶ for the fem. sg., ִים for the masc. pl., and וֹת for the fem. pl.

'The man keepeth'	—'The man is keeping'	הָאִישׁ שֹׁמֵר [a]
'The woman keepeth'	—'The woman is keeping'	הָאִשָּׁה שֹׁמֶרֶת
'The men keep'	—'The men are keeping'	הָאֲנָשִׁים שֹׁמְרִים
'The women keep'	—'The women are keeping'	הַנָּשִׁים שֹׁמְרוֹת
'Thou (m.) keepest'	—'Thou (m.) art keeping'	אַתָּה שֹׁמֵר
'We (m.) keep'	—'We (m.) are keeping'	אֲנַחְנוּ שֹׁמְרִים

The Participle may be regarded as a verbal adjective, agreeing in number and gender with its noun or pronoun. Though it expresses the English present tense in the above examples, it indicates rather a state of continued activity and therefore has extended uses, e.g.:

הָאִישׁ הַשֹּׁמֵר is literally 'the man, the (one) keeping' which means (*a*) 'the man who *is* keeping' when referring to present time, or (*b*) 'the man who *was* keeping' when referring to past time in the context. Another point which this example illustrates is that the Participle with the article has the force of a verb with the relative in English.

NOTE: When the last root-letter of a verb is a guttural, as שָׁמַע ('to hear'), the masc. sg. Participle שֹׁמֵעַ (for שֹׁמֵע) takes a Furtive Pathaḥ (p. 19. 4) and the fem. sg. שֹׁמַעַת (for שֹׁמֶעֶת) takes two Pathaḥs instead of two Seghols, since (p. 19. 3) the gutturals prefer the vowel Pathaḥ under them and even before them. Similarly, the masc. sg. Participle of יָדַע ('to know') is יֹדֵעַ and the fem. sing. יֹדַעַת.

35. THE OLD ACCUSATIVE ENDING ָה

Archaic Hebrew (like Classical Arabic) had three case endings: a nominative ending in *u*, a genitive ending in *i*, and an accusative ending in *a*. In Biblical Hebrew the nom. and gen.

[a] The reverse order שֹׁמֵר הָאִישׁ would emphasize the Participle.

case endings have disappeared,[a] but the accusative has persisted, not to designate the object of a transitive verb, but to denote 'direction' or 'motion towards (a place)', thus:

Egypt	מִצְרַיִם	the heavens	הַשָּׁמַיִם
towards Egypt Egyptwards	מִצְרַיְמָה	towards the heavens heavenwards	הַשָּׁמַיְמָה
the city	הָעִיר	there	שָׁם
towards the city citywards	הָעִירָה	towards there thither	שָׁמָּה

The appending of the old accusative ending ָה to denote 'direction' or 'motion towards' applies to a limited number of nouns which will become known from practice. *The accent does not move forward on to the new syllable*, but remains where it was before the ָה was appended.

NOTE: Early grammarians did not realize that this appended ָה is the old accusative ending, but they thought that it was a special device introduced and gave it the name of 'HE LOCALE'.

EXERCISE 10

righteous	צַדִּיק	wilderness	מִדְבָּר
wicked	רָשָׁע	lad, young man	נַעַר
Sheol, Hades	שְׁאֹל	he stood	עָמַד
flesh	בָּשָׂר	he went down, descended	יָרַד
messenger, angel	מַלְאָךְ	woe!	אוֹי

N.B. The pl. of הָיָה (he was) is הָיוּ (they were) (m. and f.). Similarly
,, רָאָה (he saw) is רָאוּ (they saw) ,, and
,, עָשָׂה (he did) is עָשׂוּ (they did) ,,

All these verbs are seen to belong to the same class.

(1) קוֹל קֹרֵא בַּמִּדְבָּר (2) הָאֱלֹהִים יֹשֵׁב בַּשָּׁמַיִם וּמֹשֵׁל בִּבְנֵי־אָדָם
(3) אֲנַחְנוּ קֹרְאִים אֶל־יהוה, וְהוּא שֹׁמֵעַ[b] אֶת־קוֹלֵנוּ (4) צַדִּיק

[a] The *u* in a name like שְׁמוּאֵל may be a survival of the old nominative, but survivals of the genitive in *i* are doubtful.

[b] See p. 66, Note.

אַתָּה יהוה הַנֹּתֵן לֶ֫חֶם לְכָל־בָּשָׂר (5) הַיּוֹם הַזֶּה אָנֹכִי לֹקֵחַ[a] אֹתְךָ
הַשָּׁמַ֫יְמָה (6) יָֽצְאוּ בְּנֵי־יִשְׂרָאֵל מִמִּצְרַ֫יִם הַמִּדְבָּ֫רָה (7) אַתָּה
שֹׁמֵר אֶת־דֶּ֫רֶךְ־הַצַּדִּיק, וְדֶ֫רֶךְ הָֽרָשָׁע שְׁאֹ֫לָה (8) יָרַד יַֽעֲקֹב
מִצְרַ֫יְמָה כִּי לֹא הָיָה לֶ֫חֶם בְּכָל־אֶ֫רֶץ־כְּנָֽעַן (9) הַיּוֹם הַזֶּה אַתֶּם
כֹּרְתִים בְּרִית עִם־יהוה (10) הִנֵּה אַתָּה שֹׁלֵחַ[a] מַלְאָכִים אֶל־
מֶ֫לֶךְ־מִצְרַ֫יִם וְלֹא יָדַ֫עְתָּ כִּי בֵֽאלֹהִים יְשׁוּעַת־יִשְׂרָאֵל (11) אוֹי
לָהֶם הָאֹכְלִים בָּשָׂר כָּל־הַיּוֹם וְאֶת־דְּבַר־יהוה לֹא עָשׂוּ (12) כֹּה
אָמַר יהוה, אָנֹכִי שֹׁלֵ֫חַ[a] אֹתְךָ אֶל־הָעָם הָֽרָשָׁע הַזֶּה (13) הָֽלְכוּ
בְּנֵי־הַנְּבִיאִים בַּמִּדְבָּר כָּל־הַיּוֹם וּבָעֶ֫רֶב בָּ֫אוּ הָעִ֫ירָה (14) טוֹב
לַצַּדִּיק הַשֹּׁמֵר אֶת־תּוֹרַת־יהוה, וְאוֹי לָֽרָשָׁע הָהֹלֵךְ בְּדֶ֫רֶךְ־
אֱלֹהִים אֲחֵרִים (15) וּבַֽחֲלוֹמוֹ רָאָה יַֽעֲקֹב וְהִנֵּה מַלְאֲכֵי־אֱלֹהִים
יֹרְדִים מִן־הַשָּׁמָ֫יִם (16) אָנֹכִי בֹּחֵר בְּךָ כִּי טוֹב אַתָּה בְּעֵינֵי[b]־יהוה
(17) עָשׂוּ בְנֵי־יִשְׂרָאֵל אֶת־הָרַ֫ע[c] בְּעֵינֵי־יהוה, כִּי לֹא הִבְדִּ֫ילוּ בֵּין
הַצַּדִּיק וּבֵין הָֽרָשָׁע (18) כָּל־בָּשָׂר יֹדֵ֫עַ[a] כִּי אַתָּה יהוה הַזֹּכֵר
אֶת־עַמּוֹ יִשְׂרָאֵל (19) בַּלַּ֫יְלָה הַהוּא שָׁמַע הַנַּ֫עַר וְהִנֵּה קוֹל קֹרֵא
שְׁמוּאֵל שְׁמוּאֵל (20) הַיּוֹם הַזֶּה אֲנַ֫חְנוּ עֹמְדִים עַל־הַר־הָֽאֱלֹהִים
וְשֹׁמְעִים אֶת־קוֹל־יהוה יֹצֵא מִשָּׁמָ֫יִם (21) אֵ֫לֶּה הַדְּבָרִים אֲשֶׁר
דִּבֶּר מֹשֶׁה אֶל־בְּנֵי־יִשְׂרָאֵל בְּמִדְבַּר־סִינָֽי (22) הָיָה הָֽאָדָם
כֵּֽאלֹהִים יֹדֵ֫עַ[a] טוֹב וָרָע (23) שָׁמַע הָעָם הַיֹּשֵׁב בָּהָר כִּי יָֽצָא
יִשְׂרָאֵל מִמִּצְרָֽיִם.

(1) The sons of Jacob went down to Egypt, for they heard that there was bread in Egypt. (2) Behold I am making a covenant with[d] you this day. (3) The king saw the sons of the prophets standing in the way and Samuel (was) at (בְּ) their head. (4) Woe unto you who go in the way of other gods, for there is not among ('in') you a man who knoweth the word of the Lord. (5) Thou rememberest the righteous (m. pl.) for Thou art righteous. (6) The lad cried in a loud[e] voice, 'my head, my head'. (7) And a great

[a] See p. 66, Note. [b] Constr. pl. of עַ֫יִן. [c] 'That which was evil'.
[d] See p. 53, footnote *a*. [e] In Hebrew it is 'a *great* voice'.

river (was) going forth from the garden. (8) And in his dream
the king saw a very great tree standing on the ground and its
head (was) in the heavens. (9) I am sending My angel with you
in this great wilderness. (10) God of all flesh, who heareth the
voice of Thy people, we call unto Thee for we know (Perfect)
that in Thee is our salvation. (11) The spies whom Moses sent
unto the land of Canaan stood upon the head of the mountain.
(12) Thus said the Lord unto Solomon, king of Israel, 'Thou art
wicked, for thou didst not remember the words of My law, for
thou hast taken unto thyself wives from the nations.' (13) Ye
say that ye are righteous men and that ye came down to Egypt
from Canaan for there is no bread in the land, but[a] I say that ye
are spies. (14) Jacob sent messengers unto Esau to the mountain.
(15) In that day ye said, 'We remember (Perfect) the bread which
we ate in Egypt, but[a] in this great wilderness there is no bread.'
(16) Great art Thou, Lord, who ruleth over the heavens and over
the earth. (17) The man of God came down from the mountain
to the city, as the word of the Lord.

36. PLURAL NOUNS WITH SUFFIXES

A		B	
Masc. pl.			
horses (abs.)	סוּסִים	words (abs.)	דְּבָרִים
horses-of (cons.)	סוּסֵי	words-of (cons.)	דִּבְרֵי
my (c.) horses	סוּסַי	my (c.) words	דְּבָרַי
thy (m.) „	סוּסֶ֫יךָ	thy (m.) „	דְּבָרֶ֫יךָ
thy (f.) „	סוּסַ֫יִךְ	thy (f.) „	דְּבָרַ֫יִךְ
his „	סוּסָיו	his „	דְּבָרָיו
her „	סוּסֶ֫יהָ	her „	דְּבָרֶ֫יהָ
our (c.) „	סוּסֵ֫ינוּ	our (c.) „	דְּבָרֵ֫ינוּ
your (m.) „	סוּסֵיכֶם	your (m.) „	דִּבְרֵיכֶם
your (f.) „	סוּסֵיכֶן	your (f.) „	דִּבְרֵיכֶן
their (m.) „	סוּסֵיהֶם	their (m.) „	דִּבְרֵיהֶם
their (f.) „	סוּסֵיהֶן	their (f.) „	דִּבְרֵיהֶן

[a] The conj. וֹ. See p. 40, footnote *a*.

C		D		E	
Fem. pl.				Suffixes of the pl. noun (m. and f.)	
laws (abs.)	תּוֹרוֹת	blessings (abs.)	בְּרָכוֹת		
laws-of (cons.)	תּוֹרוֹת	blessings-of (cons.)	בִּרְכוֹת		
my (c.) laws	תּוֹרוֹתַי	my (c.) blessings	בִּרְכוֹתַי	my (c.)	ַי
thy (m.) ,,	תּוֹרוֹתֶיךָ	thy (m.) ,,	בִּרְכוֹתֶיךָ	thy (m.)	ֶיךָ
thy (f.) ,,	תּוֹרוֹתַיִךְ	thy (f.) ,,	בִּרְכוֹתַיִךְ	thy (f.)	ַיִךְ
his ,,	תּוֹרוֹתָיו	his ,,	בִּרְכוֹתָיו	his	ָיו
her ,,	תּוֹרוֹתֶיהָ	her ,,	בִּרְכוֹתֶיהָ	her	ֶיהָ
our (c.) ,,	תּוֹרוֹתֵינוּ	our (c.) ,,	בִּרְכוֹתֵינוּ	our (c.)	ֵינוּ
your (m.) ,,	תּוֹרוֹתֵיכֶם	your (m.) ,,	בִּרְכוֹתֵיכֶם	your (m.)	ֵיכֶם
your (f.) ,,	תּוֹרוֹתֵיכֶן	your (f.) ,,	בִּרְכוֹתֵיכֶן	your (f.)	ֵיכֶן
their (m.) ,,	תּוֹרוֹתֵיהֶם	their (m.) ,,	בִּרְכוֹתֵיהֶם	their (m.)	ֵיהֶם
their (f.) ,,	תּוֹרוֹתֵיהֶן	their (f.) ,,	בִּרְכוֹתֵיהֶן	their (f.)	ֵיהֶן

F		G		H	
sons (abs.)	בָּנִים	fathers (abs.)	אָבוֹת	God (abs.)	אֱלֹהִים
sons-of (cons.)	בְּנֵי	fathers-of (cons.)	אֲבוֹת	God-of (cons.)	אֱלֹהֵי
my (c.) sons	בָּנַי	my (c.) fathers	אֲבוֹתַי	my (c.) God	אֱלֹהַי
thy (m.) ,,	בָּנֶיךָ	thy (m.) ,,	אֲבוֹתֶיךָ	thy (m.) ,,	אֱלֹהֶיךָ
&c.		&c.		&c.	
your (m.) ,,	בְּנֵיכֶם	your (m.) ,,	אֲבוֹתֵיכֶם	your (m.) ,,	אֱלֹהֵיכֶם
&c.		&c.		&c.	

I		J	
men (abs.)	אֲנָשִׁים	wives (women) (abs.)	נָשִׁים
men-of (cons.)	אַנְשֵׁי	wives-of (cons.)	נְשֵׁי
my (c.) men	אֲנָשַׁי	my wives	נָשַׁי
thy (m.) ,,	אֲנָשֶׁיךָ	thy ,,	נָשֶׁיךָ
&c.		&c.	
your (m.) ,,	אַנְשֵׁיכֶם	your ,,	נְשֵׁיכֶם
&c.		&c.	

NOTE: The suffixes which are attached to the pl. nouns are given in *Column E*. In the suffixes of the pl. noun there is a Yoḏ (י) which, except for the 1st sg. and the 2nd sg. fem., is silent. In early (pre-Classical) Hebrew this Yoḏ was audible in all the suffixes of the pl. noun; but, except for the two cases mentioned, it has survived only in spelling. [סוּסֶיךָ is really the constr. pl. with the suffix—'horses of thee', etc.] This Yoḏ distinguishes the pl. from the sg., especially in unpointed texts:

סוסך is to be pointed סוּסְךָ or סוּסֵךְ (thy horse), whereas

סוסיך ,, סוּסֶיךָ or סוּסַיִךְ (thy horses). Similarly

סוסו ,, סוּסוֹ (his horse), but סוסיו is סוּסָיו (his horses)

סוסנו ,, סוּסֵנוּ (our horse) ,, סוסינו ,, סוּסֵינוּ (our horses)

Columns A and C represent the simplest forms of the masc. and fem. pl. nouns.

Columns B and D represent the types of masc. and fem. pl. nouns in which the Qameṣ in the first syllable is replaced by a shewa and the shewa preceding it consequently becomes a Ḥireq (p. 46. 3).

Column G אָבוֹת is a masc. pl. noun but has the form of a fem. pl. noun, and in

Column J נָשִׁים is a fem. pl. noun but has the form of a masc. pl. noun. Both these nouns are irregular.

Column H אֱלֹהִים is singular in meaning when referring to the God of Israel (and normally takes a sing. verb) but its form is that of a pl. noun.

Column I is a variant of *Column B*—the first letter being a guttural. When the Qameṣ in the first syllable is replaced by a shewa the composite shewa under the guttural is raised to the corresponding short vowel (p. 46. 3).

NOTE: (*a*) The heavy suffixes כֶם, כֶן, הֶם, הֶן, attach themselves to the form of the construct.[a]

(*b*) The duals take the same suffixes as the pl. nouns: יָדַי, יָדֶיךָ, &c. (from יָדַיִם).

[a] See p. 51, Note (*c*).

37. SOME IRREGULAR NOUNS WITH SUFFIXES

	Singular			Plural		
	absolute	construct	with suffix	absolute	construct	with suffix
father	אָב	אֲבִי	אָבִיו, אָבִיךָ, אָבִי	אָבוֹת	אֲבוֹת	אֲבוֹתַי
son	בֵּן	בֶּן־	בְּנוֹ, בִּנְךָ, בְּנִי	בָּנִים	בְּנֵי	בָּנַי
daughter	בַּת	בַּת	בִּתּוֹ, בִּתְּךָ, בִּתִּי	בָּנוֹת	בְּנוֹת	בְּנוֹתַי
brother	אָח	אֲחִי	אָחִיו, אָחִיךָ, אָחִי	אַחִים	אֲחֵי	אַחַי
wife	אִשָּׁה	אֵשֶׁת	אִשְׁתְּךָ, אִשְׁתִּי	נָשִׁים	נְשֵׁי	נָשַׁי
house	בַּיִת	בֵּית	בֵּיתְךָ, בֵּיתִי	בָּתִּים [a]	בָּתֵּי [a]	בָּתַּי [a]
name	שֵׁם	שֶׁם־, שֵׁם	שְׁמוֹ, שִׁמְךָ. שְׁמִי	שֵׁמוֹת	שְׁמוֹת	שְׁמוֹתַי

N.B. The full list of irregular nouns is given at the end of the book.

38. POSSESSION

There is no word in Hebrew to express the English 'have', 'had', &c., and the statement of possession in point of time is made in the following ways:

'I have a son'	is in Hebrew	'there is to me a son'	יֵשׁ לִי בֵּן
'I have not a son'	,,	'there is not to me a son'	אֵין לִי בֵּן
'I have sons'	,,	'there are to me sons'	יֵשׁ לִי בָּנִים
'I have not sons'	,,	'there are not to me sons'	אֵין לִי בָּנִים
'I had a son'	,,	'there was to me a son'	הָיָה לִי בֵּן
'I had not a son'	,,	'there was not to me a son'	לֹא הָיָה לִי בֵּן
'I had sons'	,,	'there were to me sons'	הָיוּ לִי בָּנִים
'I shall have a son'	,,	'there will be to me a son'	יִהְיֶה לִי בֵּן
'I shall not have a son'	,,	'there will not be to me a son'	לֹא יִהְיֶה לִי בֵּן
'I shall have sons'	,,	'there will be (pl.) to me sons'	יִהְיוּ לִי בָּנִים
'The man has a son'	,,	'there is to the man a son'	יֵשׁ לָאִישׁ בֵּן &c.

[a] See p. 13. 3. N.B.

NOTE: (*a*) יֵשׁ and אֵין (construct of אַ֫יִן) were originally *nouns* meaning respectively 'existence' and 'non-existence' and are, on that account, used with both numbers and genders, and refer to present possession when followed by the preposition לְ.

(*b*) Possession in past or future time is expressed by the verb הָיָה, יִהְיֶה followed by the preposition לְ, and the verb must agree with its subject in number and gender. The negative used is naturally לֹא.

It will be remembered that the English possessive pronouns are expressed in Hebrew by suffixed pronominal particles and that the mere statement of possession denoted by the English genitive case (e.g. 'the man's horse') is expressed by the Hebrew construct state ('the horse-of the man'). The above chapter deals with possession in point of time.

EXERCISE 11

Rachel	רָחֵל	sheep	צֹאן	he asked	שָׁאַל
Laban	לָבָן	water (abs.)	[a] מַ֫יִם	he served	עָבַד
Joseph	יוֹסֵף	,, (cons.)	מֵי	he will be	יִהְיֶה
Pharaoh	פַּרְעֹה	why? (for what?)	לָ֫מָּה		

(1) אָמַר הַנַּ֫עַר אֶל־הַנָּבִיא אֵין לָאִשָּׁה הַזֹּאת בֵּן וְאִישָׁהּ זָקֵן מְאֹד
(2) שָׁלַ֫חְתִּי אֶת־נְבִיאַי אֶל־הָעָם הָרָשָׁע הַזֶּה וְלֹא שָׁמְעוּ אֶל־
דִּבְרֵיהֶם אֲשֶׁר דִּבְּרוּ בִשְׁמִי (3) הָיוּ בְנֵי־יִשְׂרָאֵל בְּמִדְבַּר־סִינַי
וְלֹא הָיָה מַ֫יִם לַצֹּאן אֲשֶׁר עִמָּם (4) אָמְרוּ בְנֵי־יַעֲקֹב אֶל־יוֹסֵף
יֵשׁ לָ֫נוּ אָב זָקֵן בְּאֶרֶץ־כְּנַ֫עַן, וְלֹא יָֽדְעוּ כִּי הוּא הַמֹּשֵׁל בְּכָל־
אֶרֶץ־מִצְרָ֫יִם (5) לָקַח שְׁלֹמֹה אֶת־בַּת־פַּרְעֹה לוֹ לְאִשָּׁה
(6) אָמְרוּ אַנְשֵׁי־הַמָּקוֹם יָדַ֫עְנוּ[b] אֶת־לָבָן, וְהִנֵּה רָחֵל בִּתּוֹ עִם־
הַצֹּאן אֲשֶׁר לְאָבִיהָ (7) שָׁאַל יַעֲקֹב אֶת־רָחֵל בַּת־מִי אַתְּ,
אָמְרָה רָחֵל בַּת־לָבָן אָנֹכִי (8) עָבַד יַעֲקֹב אֶת־לָבָן לְרָחֵל,

[a] The noun, like שָׁמַ֫יִם, is a plural.

[b] See p. 58, footnote *c*.

וְהוּא נָתַן לוֹ אֶת־בִּתּוֹ הַגְּדוֹלָה לְאִשָּׁה תַּ֫חַת[a] רָחֵל (9) אַתָּה
אֱלֹהֵינוּ וַאֲנַ֫חְנוּ עַמֶּ֫ךָ[b] אַתָּה אָבִ֫ינוּ וַאֲנַ֫חְנוּ בָנֶ֫יךָ (10) קָרָא פַרְעֹה
לְכָל־זְקֵנָיו וּלְכָל־חֲכָמָיו, וּלְעֵינֵיהֶם עָשָׂה מֹשֶׁה כְּכֹל[c] אֲשֶׁר אָמַר
יהוה (11) אֵ֫לֶּה שְׁמוֹת־בְּנֵי־יִשְׂרָאֵל אֲשֶׁר יָֽרְדוּ מִצְרַ֫יְמָה אֶל־
יוֹסֵף (12) לֹא לָקַח יַעֲקֹב אִשָּׁה מִבְּנוֹת־כְּנַ֫עַן, כִּי רָעוֹת[d] הֵ֫נָּה
בְּעֵינֵי־אָבִיו מְאֹד (13) לָ֫מָּה לֹא אָמַ֫רְתָּ לִּי כִּי אִשְׁתְּךָ הִיא, וַאֲנִי
לֹא יָדַ֫עְתִּי (14) אָמַר לָבָן אֶל־יַעֲקֹב, נָשֶׁ֫יךָ בְּנוֹתַי הֵ֫נָּה וּבָנֶ֫יךָ בָּנַי
וְצֹאנְךָ צֹאנִי וְכֹל אֲשֶׁר לְךָ לִי הוּא (15) אָמַר יהוה אֶל־יַעֲקֹב,
שִׁמְךָ יִהְיֶה יִשְׂרָאֵל (16) קָֽרְאָה רָחֵל אֶת־שֶׁם־בְּנָהּ יוֹסֵף, כִּי
אָֽמְרָה יִהְיֶה לִּי בֵּן אַחֵר (17) אָמַר יוֹסֵף אֶל־פַּרְעֹה, הִנֵּה אָבִי
וְאַחַי וּנְשֵׁיהֶם וּבְנֵיהֶם וּבְנוֹתֵיהֶם וְצֹאנָם וְכָל־אֲשֶׁר לָהֶם בָּ֫אוּ
מִצְרַ֫יְמָה (18) רָאוּ אֲבוֹתֵ֫ינוּ אֶת־כָּל־אֲשֶׁר עָשָׂה יהוה לְפַרְעֹה
וּלְמִצְרָ֫יִם (19) אָנֹכִי יהוה אֱלֹהֶ֫יךָ וְאָנֹכִי יָרַדְתִּי עַל־הַר־סִינַי
בַּיּוֹם הַגָּדוֹל הַהוּא (20) לָ֫מָּה יָשַׁ֫בְתְּ בֶּעָפָר, בַּת־יִשְׂרָאֵל, כִּי
הָֽלְכוּ בָנַ֫יִךְ אַחֲרֵי עֵינֵיהֶם וְגַם עָֽבְדוּ אֱלֹהִים אֲחֵרִים (21) וּמַה־
שֹׁאֵל[e] יהוה מִמְּךָ, בֵּית־יַעֲקֹב

(1) The children of Israel served the king of Canaan, for they did (the) evil in the eyes of the Lord and they hearkened not to the words of His law. (2) I have served thee for Rachel thy daughter, and why hast thou not kept thy covenant with me? (3) Thou art the God of our fathers, who keepest me from all evil. (4) I knew not that she is his wife and that he is a prophet of God. (5) Laban said unto Jacob, 'Why hast thou taken my gods from my house?' (6) Jacob came down to Egypt, he and his sons and his wives and his sheep and all that (belonged) to him, unto Joseph his son, who (was) ruling over the land. (7) Thou hast said, 'Behold thy son will be a great man in the land, and behold I have not a son and my wife is very old.' (8) Their gods are of wood (עֵץ) which the hands of man (have)

[a] 'Instead of'.
[b] Pausal form with Athnaḥ (p. 21).
[c] Translate 'according to all'.
[d] Understand 'were'. See p. 48, footnote *c*.
[e] Emphasizing participle.

made. (9) Jacob kept the sheep which (belonged) to Laban, the father of Rachel. (10) In that day My house will be on the head of the holy mountain which I have chosen for My name. (11) Thou, Lord, dwellest in the heavens and Thou knowest what the wicked (m. pl.) have done to me, and I am righteous in the eyes of the sons of man. (12) The king called the name of his son Solomon. (13) Your eyes have seen that the Lord hath cut (off) the waters of the river for you, for he said, 'Israel will be My people.' (14) Ye shall have ('there shall be to you') a place in My temple for My holy ones (m. pl.). (15) The sons of Jacob said, 'We know that thou art he who ruleth over this great land and that we are in thy hand[a].' (16) Thus I have said unto My prophets who spoke in My name, and why have ye not hearkened to their words? (17) The woman said unto the prophet, 'I asked not a son from the Lord, for He hath taken him from me.' (18) All the blessings of the Lord came upon your land, as[b] the man of God spoke.

39. THE IMPERFECT OF THE REGULAR VERB

The Imperfect generally denotes an incompleted action. For the time being it may be regarded loosely as representing the English future tense.

he will keep	יִשְׁמֹר	he will judge	יִשְׁפֹּט [c]
she „ „	תִּשְׁמֹר	she „ „	תִּשְׁפֹּט
thou (m.) wilt „	תִּשְׁמֹר	thou (m.) wilt „	תִּשְׁפֹּט
thou (f.) „ „	תִּשְׁמְרִי	thou (f.) „ „	תִּשְׁפְּטִי
I (c.) will „	אֶשְׁמֹר	I (c.) will „	אֶשְׁפֹּט
they (m.) „ „	יִשְׁמְרוּ	they (m.) „ „	יִשְׁפְּטוּ
they (f.) „ „	תִּשְׁמֹרְנָה	they (f.) „ „	תִּשְׁפֹּטְנָה
ye (m.) „ „	תִּשְׁמְרוּ	ye (m.) „ „	תִּשְׁפְּטוּ
ye (f.) „ „	תִּשְׁמֹרְנָה	ye (f.) „ „	תִּשְׁפֹּטְנָה
we (c.) „ „	נִשְׁמֹר	we (c.) „ „	נִשְׁפֹּט

[a] The sing. 'hand' means 'power'.

[b] A prep. cannot govern a verb. We must, therefore, rephrase 'as (that) which . . .' . . . כַּאֲשֶׁר.

[c] Note Dagheš lene in פּ.

It will be observed that whereas the *Perfect suffixes* pronominal particles, the *Imperfect prefixes* them. The explanation for this may be: In the Perfect, the (completed) act is regarded as the main or general idea (and therefore stated first), while its application is determined by the pronominal particle (i.e. the doer) which follows. In the Imperfect, however, since the act is incompleted, the doer seems to be the main idea (to be expressed first) and the (incompleted) act (following the pronominal particle) limits the scope of the doer.

The prefixes for the Imperfect are איתנ (which have been made into the mnemonic אֵיתָן). The א is the 1st sg. prefix, the י the 3rd masc., the ת the 3rd fem. and 2nd masc., and the נ is the 1st pl. prefix.

The masc. pl. ends in וּ and the fem. pl. in נָה, thus:

3rd masc. sg.	יִשְׁמֹר	3rd masc. pl.	יִשְׁמְרוּ
2nd ,, ,,	תִּשְׁמֹר	2nd ,, ,,	תִּשְׁמְרוּ
3rd fem. ,,	תִּשְׁמֹר	3rd fem. ,,	תִּשְׁמֹ֫רְנָה
2nd ,, ,,	תִּשְׁמְרִי	2nd ,, ,,	תִּשְׁמֹ֫רְנָה

The context determines whether תִּשְׁמֹר means 'thou (m.) wilt keep' or 'she will keep' and whether תִּשְׁמֹ֫רְנָה means 'they (f.) will keep' or 'you (f.) will keep'.

40. THE IMPERATIVE

The Imperative is the shortest form of the verb inflected on the analogy of the Imperfect, so that its form appears to be that of the Imperfect without a prefix, thus:

keep thou (m.)	שְׁמֹר	judge thou (m.)	שְׁפֹט
,, thou (f.)	שִׁמְרִי [a]	,, thou (f.)	שִׁפְטִי [b]
,, ye (m.)	שִׁמְרוּ [a]	,, ye (m.)	שִׁפְטוּ [b]
,, ye (f.)	שְׁמֹ֫רְנָה	,, ye (f.)	שְׁפֹ֫טְנָה

[a] From שְׁמְרִי and שְׁמְרוּ

[b] From שְׁפְטִי and שְׁפְטוּ

41. NEGATIVE COMMANDS OR PROHIBITIONS

A negative command or prohibition is expressed by the familiar 'Thou shalt not . . .', 'Ye shall not . . .', i.e. *by the negative with the Imperfect*; the *negative* is *never used with* the *Imperative.*

Thou (m.) shalt not keep is (i) לֹא תִשְׁמֹר for permanent prohibition, and (ii) אַל תִּשְׁמֹר for immediate prohibition. (In colloquial English (i) means 'Never keep', and (ii) 'Do not keep —now'.)

NOTE: It will be pointed out later (pp. 114. (*b*) and (*c*)) that, in one instance in the regular verb and frequently in weak verbs, the Imperfect has a shortened form. When an immediate prohibition is expressed, אַל is used with the shortened form of the Imperfect—where there is one.

EXERCISE 12

judgement, justice	מִשְׁפָּט	he judged	שָׁפַט
righteousness	צֶדֶק		
truth	אֱמֶת	he pursued	רָדַף
Sabbath	שַׁבָּת	he persecuted (with acc.)	רָדַף
face (pl.)	פָּנִים	he pursued (after)	רָדַף אַחֲרֵי
before, i.e. to the face-of	לִפְנֵי־		
before me, i.e. to my face	לְפָנַי		

N.B. The pl. of הָיָה (he was) is הָיוּ (they [m. & f.] were).
,, (m.) of יִהְיֶה (he will be) is יִהְיוּ (they [m.] will be). Similarly
,, of רָאָה (he saw) is רָאוּ (they [m. & f.] saw), and
,, (m.) of יִרְאֶה (he will see) is יִרְאוּ (they [m.] will see).

(1) דִּבֶּר אֱלֹהִים אֶל־מֹשֶׁה נְבִיאוֹ פָּנִים אֶל־פָּנִים (2) מִי אֲנִי
וּמַה־בֵּית־אָבִי כִּי אֶמְשֹׁל בָּעָם הַגָּדוֹל הַזֶּה, וְאָנֹכִי נָעַר[a] (3) בְּךָ
בָּחַרְתִּי לְמֶלֶךְ עַל־יִשְׂרָאֵל, וְאַתָּה תִשְׁפֹּט אֶת־עַמִּי בְּצֶדֶק
וּבְמִשְׁפָּט, כִּי צַדִּיק אָנֹכִי, יהוה אֱלֹהֶיךָ (4) מִשְׁפַּט־צֶדֶק יִהְיֶה

[a] Pausal form.

לָכֶם בָּאָרֶץ אֲשֶׁר אָנֹכִי נֹתֵן לָכֶם (5) הִנְנִי[a] שֹׁלֵחַ אֹתְךָ אֶל־אַנְשֵׁי־
הָעִיר הַזֹּאת, וַאֲנִי יָדַעְתִּי כִּי לֹא יִשְׁמְעוּ אֶל־דְּבָרֶיךָ (6) שְׁמֹר
אֶת־יוֹם־הַשַּׁבָּת, כִּי קָדוֹשׁ הַיּוֹם לַיהוה אֱלֹהֶיךָ (7) זִכְרוּ אֶת־
תּוֹרַת־יהוה אֲשֶׁר נָתַן לָכֶם עַל־הַר־סִינַי בְּיַד־מֹשֶׁה (8) צֶדֶק
צֶדֶק תִּרְדֹּף, כִּי צַדִּיק אָנִי[b] (9) לֹא תִכְרֹת בְּרִית עִם־הָעַמִּים
הָאֵלֶּה, כִּי אֶת־הָרַע בְּעֵינַי עָשׂוּ (10) רִדְפוּ אַחֲרֵי־הָאֲנָשִׁים כִּי
יָצְאוּ מִן־הָעִיר הַמִּדְבָּרָה (11) אַל־תִּשְׁלְחוּ מַלְאָכִים אֶל־פַּרְעֹה,
כִּי לֹא בְמִצְרַיִם יְשׁוּעַת־יִשְׂרָאֵל (12) אוֹי לָכֶם הָרֹדְפִים אֶת־
הַצַּדִּיק, וְיִרְאַת־יהוה אֵין בָּכֶם (13) מַה־בֶּן־אָדָם כִּי תִזְכֹּר
אֹתוֹ (14) עִמְדוּ לִפְנֵי־יהוה בְּיִרְאָה וְעִבְדוּ אֹתוֹ בֶּאֱמֶת (15) לֹא
יִהְיוּ לְךָ אֱלֹהִים אֲחֵרִים לְפָנָי[b c] (16) כָּרַת אֱלֹהִים לִפְנֵיכֶם[c] אֶת־
מֵי־הַנָּהָר (17) אָנֹכִי שֹׁלֵחַ אֶת־מַלְאָכִי לִפְנֵיכֶם וְהוּא יִשְׁמֹר
אֶתְכֶם בַּדֶּרֶךְ אֲשֶׁר אַתֶּם הֹלְכִים (18) שִׁפְטוּ, הַשָּׁמַיִם[d], בֵּינִי וּבֵין
עַמִּי, כִּי אֵין צַדִּיק בָּאָרֶץ (19) בַּיּוֹם הַהוּא אֶשְׁפֹּט אֶת־הָעִיר
הָרְשָׁעָה הַזֹּאת, כִּי אֵין בָּהּ מִשְׁפָּט (20) מִשְׁפְּטֵי צֶדֶק וֶאֱמֶת
(21) אוֹי לָהֶם הָאֹמְרִים לָמָּה תִקְרְאוּ בְּשֵׁם־יהוה

(1) *Thou*,[e] Lord, wilt keep me from all evil, for I (have) walked before Thee[c] in righteousness and in truth. (2) These are the judgements which Moses gave to the children of Israel in the wilderness of Sinai. (3) Judge thou me with righteousness, for I am righteous. (4) Remember ye the words of My law and keep ye My covenant all the days that ye are in the land which I give to you. (5) *Thou*[e] wilt rule over this people with righteousness, as thy father before thee. (6) Who am I that I should judge thy people? (7) Why, Lord, wilt Thou pursue me in the day and in the night? (8) Say ye, 'There is none ("not") holy as the Lord

[a] הִנֵּה takes suffixes: הִנְנִי (also הִנֵּנִי) 'behold I', הִנְּךָ 'behold thou'.

[b] Pausal form.

[c] See vocab., p. 77.

[d] The vocative is expressed by the article, here 'O heavens'.

[e] Use pronoun for emphasis.

our God who dwelleth in the heavens and ruleth over the sons of man with judgement.' (9) Thy law is truth and Thy word is truth. (10) The men of the city said unto Jacob, 'Make thou a covenant between thee and between us, between thy children and between our children.' (11) Remember thou the day that thou didst stand upon the mountain of Sinai before the Lord thy God. (12) The children of Israel kept the day of the Sabbath all the days of the prophet. (13) Hear thou (f.) the word of the Lord which He hath spoken, O Daughter of Israel. (14) Thou wilt pursue the wicked (m. pl.) to Sheol, and the (ones) who remember[a] Thee Thou wilt keep. (15) One judgement shalt thou have ('there shall be to thee') for the good (m. pl.) and for the wicked (m. pl.). (16) Thus said the Lord, 'Thou wilt not rule over Israel, for thou art wicked in the eyes of the Lord.' (17) Pursue ye not (after) these men, for they are in the mountains.

42. THE INFINITIVES

There are two Infinitives in Hebrew, known as:

(*a*) the Infinitive Absolute: שָׁמוֹר, שָׁפוֹט and

(*b*) the Infinitive Construct: שְׁמֹר, שְׁפֹט.

The Infinitive is a verbal noun, ending in '-ing', as in the phrase 'seeing is believing'.

(*a*) The Infinitive Absolute functions in syntax, thus:

שָׁמַר—'he hath kept': שָׁמוֹר שָׁמַר 'he hath indeed (or surely) kept'
שָׁמַר שָׁמוֹר 'he hath kept—continually'.

יִשְׁמֹר—'he will keep'. שָׁמוֹר יִשְׁמֹר 'he will indeed (or surely) keep'
יִשְׁמֹר שָׁמוֹר 'he will keep—continually'.

The Infinitive Absolute expresses emphasis when it immediately precedes the finite verb, and duration when it immediately follows it.[b]

(*b*) The Infinitive Construct with the preposition לְ expresses

[a] M. pl. part. with art.—'the (ones) remembering'.

[b] The Infinitive Absolute is sometimes used to represent the Imperative.

the English Infinitive:[a] לִשְׁמֹר ‘to keep’, לִמְשֹׁל ‘to rule’, לִשְׁפֹּט ‘to judge’.[b]

Note: When the third root-letter is a guttural (as שָׁמַע ‘to hear’) both Infinitives (שָׁמוֹעַ and שְׁמֹעַ) have Furtive Pathaḥ under the guttural (p. 19. 4).

43. ‘HE’ INTERROGATIVE

The simple question is introduced by the prefixed particle הֲ:

‘Thou (m.) hast kept’ שָׁמַרְתָּ; ‘hast thou (m.) kept?’ הֲשָׁמַרְתָּ

‘Thou (m.) hast not kept’ לֹא שָׁמַרְתָּ; ‘hast thou (m.) not kept?’ הֲלֹא שָׁמַרְתָּ[c]

‘There is’ יֵשׁ; ‘is there?’ הֲיֵשׁ

Before a simple shewa it is הַ: ‘do ye know?’ הַיְדַעְתֶּם: likewise before gutturals it is הַ: ‘is there not?’ הַאֵין, ‘art thou?’ הַאַתָּה, except when the guttural has Qameṣ when it is הֶ, as הֶעָצוּם הוּא = is he mighty?

EXERCISE 13

commandment	מִצְוָה	small (m. sg.)	קָטֹן, קָטָן
,, (pl.)	מִצְוֹת[d]	(f. sg.)	קְטַנָּה
		(pl.)	קְטַנִּים, קְטַנּוֹת
peace	שָׁלוֹם		
(it is) well (with) (לְ)	שָׁלוֹם	he dreamt	חָלַם
sun	שֶׁמֶשׁ	if	אִם

(1) בָּא שְׁמוּאֵל הָעִ֫ירָה לִשְׁפֹּט אֶת־הָעָם, וְכָל־אִישׁ אֲשֶׁר הָיָה לוֹ דְּבַר־מִשְׁפָּט הָלַךְ אֶל־הַנָּבִיא (2) אָמְרוּ אַנְשֵׁי־הָעִיר הָרְשָׁעָה,

[a] The uses of the Infinitive Construct are given on pp. 131 ff.

[b] The Inf. Const. שְׁפֹט with prefixed לְ becomes לִשְׁפֹּט; the פּ now has Dagheš lene (p. 14. (*a*)). This happens only with prefixed לְ, since the combination is regarded as a single word. With prefixed בְּ, however, it is בִּשְׁפֹט.

[c] הֲלֹא is often translated as ‘surely’. הֲלֹא שָׁמַרְתָּ may, in certain contexts, mean ‘surely thou hast kept’, anticipating a positive answer.

[d] This pl. is usually written defectively מִצְוֹת (miṣwōṯ—the ו is a consonant) instead of מִצְווֹת as might be expected.

בָּא הָאִישׁ הַזֶּה אֶל־עִירֵ֫נוּ וְהִנֵּה שָׁפוֹט יִשְׁפֹּט אֹתָ֫נוּ (3) אָמַר יַעֲקֹב
אֶל־יוֹסֵף בְּנוֹ הַקָּטָן, מַה־הַחֲלוֹם הַזֶּה אֲשֶׁר חָלָ֫מְתָּ הֲמָשׁוֹל
תִּמְשֹׁל בָּ֫נוּ (4) בָּ֫אוּ מַלְאָכִים מֵעָרֵי־כְנַ֫עַן לִכְרוֹת בְּרִית־שָׁלוֹם
עִם־יִשְׂרָאֵל (5) שָׁאַל אֹתָהּ הַנָּבִיא, הֲשָׁלוֹם לָךְ, הֲשָׁלוֹם לְאִישֵׁךְ,
הֲשָׁלוֹם לַנָּ֫עַר (6) נָתַן אֱלֹהִים אֶת־הַשֶּׁ֫מֶשׁ בַּשָּׁמַ֫יִם לִמְשֹׁל בַּיּוֹם
וְאֶת־הַכּוֹכָבִים לִמְשֹׁל בַּלָּ֫יְלָה (7) אָמַר יַעֲקֹב אֶל־רָחֵל אִשְׁתּוֹ,
הֲתַ֫חַת אֱלֹהִים אָנֹכִי אֲשֶׁר לֹא נָתַן לָךְ בֵּן (8) זָכוֹר תִּזְכֹּר אֶת־
יוֹם־הַשַּׁבָּת לִשְׁמֹר אֹתוֹ (9) אָמְרוּ בְנֵי־יַעֲקֹב אֶל־אֲבִיהֶם, שָׁאוֹל
שָׁאַל אֹתָ֫נוּ הָאִישׁ הַמֹּשֵׁל בְּאֶ֫רֶץ־מִצְרַ֫יִם, הֲיֵשׁ לָכֶם אָב
(10) לָ֫מָּה שְׁלַחְתֶּם לִשְׁאֹל בֵּאלֹהֵי[a]־כְנַ֫עַן, הַאֵין אֱלֹהִים בְּיִשְׂרָאֵל
(11) יָדֹ֫עַ[b] יָדַ֫עְתִּי כִּי קָדוֹשׁ הַמָּקוֹם הַזֶּה לַיהוה (12) עָמַד כָּל־
הָעָם עַל־הַר־סִינַי מִגָּדוֹל וְעַד־קָטֹן לִשְׁמֹ֫עַ[b] אֶת־דִּבְרֵי־אֱלֹהִים
(13) אִם שָׁמ֫וֹעַ[b] תִּשְׁמְעוּ בְּקוֹלִי וְאֶת־מִצְוֹתַי תִּשְׁמְרוּ בֶּאֱמֶת, לֹא
יִהְיֶה בָכֶם רָ֫ע (14) אָמַר שְׁמוּאֵל אֶל־הַמֶּ֫לֶךְ, אִם קָטֹן אַתָּה
בְּעֵינֶ֫יךָ זְכֹר כִּי רֹאשׁ־יִשְׂרָאֵל אָ֫תָּה (15) רָאוּ עֵינֵיכֶם אֶת־כָּל־
אֲשֶׁר עָשָׂה לָכֶם יהוה בְּמִצְרַ֫יִם וּבַמִּדְבָּר הַגָּדוֹל הַזֶּה (16) אָמַר
יַעֲקֹב אֶל־לָבָן, הֲלֹא לְרָחֵל בִּתְּךָ הַקְּטַנָּה עָבַ֫דְתִּי עִמָּךְ[c]
(17) הֲלֹא כָל־הָאָ֫רֶץ לְפָנֶ֫יךָ וְשָׁם נָהָר גָּדוֹל וּמַ֫יִם לַצֹּאן אֲשֶׁר
עִמְּךָ, וְלָ֫מָּה לֹא יִהְיֶה שָׁלוֹם בֵּינִי וּבֵינֶ֫ךָ

(1) The king went unto the prophet to enquire of[a] (שָׁאַל בְּ) the word of God. (2) The woman said to him, 'Did I ask a son from the Lord? for He hath taken him from me.' (3) Ye shall indeed remember all[d] that Pharaoh, the king of Egypt, hath done unto you. (4) I have indeed heard that there is none ('not') like thee in all the land, who knoweth the word of the Lord. (5) Hast thou not a son who will rule over my people? (6) Jacob

[a] 'To enquire of' means to consult the oracle.

[b] Note the Furtive Pathaḥ under the terminal guttural.

[c] Pausal for עִמְּךָ.

[d] See p. 65, footnote *b*—'the whole of (that) which'.

asked the men of the place who were there, 'Do ye know (perf.) Laban?' (7) All the children of Israel came to the holy city to choose for them(selves) a king like all the peoples of the land. (8) I indeed know that the Lord is with thee and that He hath gone from me. (9) Have we not served Thee in truth and why wilt Thou pursue us to Sheol? (10) The spies of Israel were small in the eyes of the peoples of Canaan, for they were very great men. (11) The Lord hath come to judge His people this day. (12) The men said unto Joseph, 'A dream we dreamt in one night, I and he.' (13) If thou shalt indeed keep My commandments and the words of My law thou shalt remember, behold thou shalt rule over Israel in peace. (14) It shall be well for all who are with thee in the house, for thou hast kept our word. (15) The sun giveth light to the sons of man. (16) All the wise (men) came to hear his words, for his name had gone forth in all the land. (17) Will ye keep my commandments in truth? (18) Thy son shall not rule over my people, for thou art small in the eyes of the Lord.

44. SEGHOLATE NOUNS

	(king)	(book)	(holiness)	
Nouns of the type	מֶ֫לֶךְ	סֵ֫פֶר	קֹ֫דֶשׁ	are evolved from the originals
	[מַלְךְ	סִפְר	קֻדְשׁ][a]	which, in the first stage, received
the vowel Seghol	[מַ֫לֶךְ	סִ֫פֶר	קֻ֫דֶשׁ][b]	and by a further step, these forms
became	מֶ֫לֶךְ	סֵ֫פֶר	קֹ֫דֶשׁ	—the classical forms.

Because these types of nouns received the *helping vowel Seghol* they are classed as Segholates. It will be observed from the tables below that the original forms have survived with the suffixes of the sg.,[c] thus:

[a] The forms with the archaic case-endings (see p. 66. **35**) were $malk^{u}$, $malk^{i}$, &c., $sifr^{u}$, $sifr^{i}$, &c. When the case-endings were dropped, the forms *malk*, *sifr*, &c., remained.

[b] It can easily be understood how מַלְךְ became מַ֫לֶךְ and סִפְר became סֵ֫פֶר, &c.

[c] The original מַלְךְ, סִפְר with suffixes remained מַלְכִּי, סִפְרִי, as we should have expected.

Singular					
king (abs.)	מֶ֫לֶךְ	book (abs.)	סֵ֫פֶר	holiness (abs.)	קֹ֫דֶשׁ
king-of (cons.)	מֶ֫לֶךְ	book-of (cons.)	סֵ֫פֶר	holiness-of (cons.)	קֹ֫דֶשׁ
my (c.) king	מַלְכִּי	my (c.) book	סִפְרִי	my (c.) holiness	קָדְשִׁי[a]
thy (m.) ,,	מַלְכְּךָ	thy (m.) ,,	סִפְרְךָ	thy (m.) ,,	קָדְשְׁךָ
&c.		&c.		&c.	
Plural					
kings (abs.)	מְלָכִים	books (abs.)	סְפָרִים	holinesses (abs.)	קֳדָשִׁים[b]
kings-of (cons.)	מַלְכֵי	books-of (cons.)	סִפְרֵי	holinesses-of (cons.)	קָדְשֵׁי
my (c.) kings	מְלָכַי	my (c.) books	סְפָרַי	my (c.) holinesses	קֳדָשַׁי
thy (m.) ,,	מְלָכֶ֫יךָ	thy (m.) ,,	סְפָרֶ֫יךָ	thy (m.) ,,	קֳדָשֶׁ֫יךָ
your (m.) ,,	מַלְכֵיכֶם[c]	your (m.) ,,	סִפְרֵיכֶם[c]	your (m.) ,,	קָדְשֵׁיכֶם[c]
&c.		&c.		&c.	

NOTE: (*a*) When the terminal letter of a Segholate noun is a guttural then, since the guttural prefers the vowel Pathaḥ before it (p. 19. 3), the form will be as זֶ֫רַע ('seed') instead of זֶ֫רֶע. Coming from the original זַרְע its form with the suffixes of the sing. will be זַרְעִי, זַרְעֲךָ (the latter with composite shewa under the guttural).

With a medial guttural the form of this type is נַ֫עַר ('lad') instead of נֶ֫עֶר, the guttural preferring Pathaḥ under it and even before it.[d] 'His lad' is נַעֲרוֹ, 'thy lad'—נַעַרְךָ, etc.

(*b*) Since the guttural nouns in the above examples (as well as in some other types, see tables at the end of the book) do not receive the helping vowel Seghol, there is some objection to the use of the term Segholate to embrace such types of

[a] Read 'Qodšî'—the vowel in the first syllable is a Qameṣ-Ḥaṭuph.

[b] For קֳדָשִׁים—the shewa has been promoted to the short vowel, Qameṣ-Ḥaṭuph, and so read 'Qodāšîm'.

[c] Observe how, once again, the heavy suffixes כֶם, הֶם attach themselves to the form of the construct.

[d] Since the vowel was not modified, the basic original form was preserved.

nouns. However, merely as a convenient term, if its deficiencies are remembered, it may be employed

(*c*) There are some variants from the above standard table of Segholate nouns; these will be indicated when they occur. Three frequently occurring variants are בֶּ֫גֶד (garment), צֶ֫דֶק (righteousness), and קֶ֫בֶר (grave) which seem to have come from the originals בִּגְד, צִדְק, and קִבְר, since with the suffixes of the sg. they are בִּגְדִי, בִּגְדְךָ, צִדְקִי, קִבְרִי, etc., and the construct pls. are בִּגְדֵי, קִבְרֵי, etc.

45. אֵת—'WITH'

There are two kinds of אֵת which are derived from different origins. The one אֵת which introduces the definite object appears in the form אֹת׳ with the suffixes—אֹתִי 'me', אֹתְךָ 'thee', etc. (pp. 55–6). The other אֵת meaning 'with', 'along with'[a] appears in the form אִתּ׳, with the suffixes, as below:

with me (c.)	אִתִּי	with us (c.)	אִתָּ֫נוּ
„ thee (m.)	אִתְּךָ	„ you (m.)	אִתְּכֶם
„ thee (f.)	אִתָּךְ	„ you (f.)	אִתְּכֶן
„ him	אִתּוֹ	„ them (m.)	אִתָּם
„ her	אִתָּהּ	„ them (f.)	אִתָּן

N.B. Be careful to distinguish between אֹתִי, אֹתְךָ 'me', 'thee', &c.
and אִתִּי, אִתְּךָ 'with me', 'with thee'.

46. THE PASSIVE PARTICIPLE

The Passive Participle follows the same principles as the active: from the root שָׁמַר ('to keep') the form is:

	masc.	fem.
'is kept' (sg.)	שָׁמוּר	שְׁמוּרָה
'are kept' (pl.)	שְׁמוּרִים	שְׁמוּרוֹת

[a] In Genesis xvii. 21 we find both types of אֵת in the same half-verse: וְאֶת־בְּרִיתִי אָקִים אֶת־יִצְחָק—'and My covenant I shall establish with Isaac'. The first אֶת־ is the sign of the def. obj., while the second one means 'with'.

Like the Active Participle, the Passive is a verbal adjective: 'The matter is kept' is הַדָּבָר שָׁמוּר. 'The matter which is kept' is 'the matter, the (one) kept' הַדָּבָר הַשָּׁמוּר. (See pp. 65 f.).

NOTE: When the third letter of a verb is a guttural, as יָדַע ('to know'), the Passive Participle m. sg. יָדוּעַ ('known') has a Furtive Pathaḥ (p. 19. 4).

EXERCISE 14

stone (f.)	אֶבֶן	wisdom (ḥoḵmâ)	חָכְמָה
,, (pl.)	אֲבָנִים	he placed, set	שָׂם
ear (f.)	אֹזֶן	he wrote	כָּתַב
,, (dual)	אָזְנַיִם		
servant, slave	עֶבֶד	he called (to)[a]	קָרָא לְ
,, ,, (pl.)	עֲבָדִים	he read (in)	קָרָא בְּ
Jordan	יַרְדֵּן	dead	מֵת

(1) אַתָּה הוּא מַלְכִּי וֵאלֹהֵי־יְשׁוּעָתִי[b] וְאֵין כָּמוֹךָ (2) יָצָא אַבְרָהָם
מִבֵּית־אָבִיו וּמֵאַרְצוֹ כִּדְבַר־יהוה (3) קָרָא הַמֶּלֶךְ לְעַבְדּוֹ
הַמֹּשֵׁל בְּכָל־אֲשֶׁר לוֹ (4) עָשׂוּ בְנֵי־יִשְׂרָאֵל כְּכָל[c]־הַכָּתוּב בְּסֵפֶר־
הַתּוֹרָה אֲשֶׁר קָרְאוּ הַנְּבִיאִים בְּאָזְנֵי־הָעָם (5) מֹשֶׁה עַבְדִּי מֵת,
וְאַתָּה תִּהְיֶה[d] לְרֹאשׁ עַל־יִשְׂרָאֵל תַּחַת מֹשֶׁה (6) אָמַר יהוה אֶל־
שְׁלֹמֹה בַּחֲלוֹם, כִּי שָׁאַלְתָּ חָכְמָה מִמֶּנִּי לִשְׁפֹּט אֶת־עַמִּי בְּצֶדֶק,
גַּם זֹאת[e] נְתוּנָה לְךָ כִּי טוֹב הַדָּבָר אֲשֶׁר שָׁאַלְתָּ מִמֶּנִּי בְּעֵינַי עַד־
מְאֹד (7) לָקַח אִתּוֹ אַבְרָהָם אֲנָשִׁים מֵעַבְדֵי־בֵיתוֹ וּמִן־הֶעָרִים
אֲשֶׁר כָּרְתוּ בְרִית אִתּוֹ, וּבַלַּיְלָה הַהוּא רָדַף אַחֲרֵי הַמְּלָכִים

[a] It means 'summoned' or 'named', according to the context. קָרָא אֶל implies prayer.

[b] 'My God of salvation', i.e. 'my saving God'. See Appendix 5, p. 253.

[c] 'According to all'.

[d] From the account of the Imperfect on pp. 75–6 it will be seen that, since the Imperfect 3rd m. sg. (of הָיָה) is יִהְיֶה, then the 2nd m. sg. will be תִּהְיֶה.

[e] 'This (thing)'.

(8) אֱלֹהֵי־הָעַמִּים הֵמָּה עֵץ[a] וָאֶבֶן, אָזְנַיִם לָהֶם וְלֹא יִשְׁמְעוּ[b], עֵינַיִם
לָהֶם וְלֹא יִרְאוּ[b] (9) דְּרָכַי דַּרְכֵי־צֶדֶק וְתוֹרָתִי אֱמֶת (10) וְאִשָּׁה
אַחַת מִנְּשֵׁי־בְנֵי־הַנְּבִיאִים קָרְאָה אֶל־הַנָּבִיא, הִנֵּה עַבְדְּךָ אִישִׁי
מֵת, וּבַבַּיִת אֵין אִתִּי דָּבָר לִי וּלְבָנַי (11) כִּתְבוּ אֶת־הַדְּבָרִים
הָאֵלֶּה עַל־אֲבָנִים גְּדוֹלוֹת וְיִקְרְאוּ בָם בְּנֵיכֶם וּבְנֵי־בְנֵיכֶם כִּי
כָּרַת יהוה לִפְנֵיכֶם אֶת־מֵי־הַיַּרְדֵּן (12) וְהַיָּמִים הָאֵלֶּה יְמֵי־
קֹדֶשׁ[c] הֵמָּה (13) וְכֹל אֲשֶׁר עָשָׂה שְׁלֹמֹה וְדִבְרֵי־חָכְמָתוֹ הֲלֹא הֵם
כְּתוּבִים בְּסֵפֶר־מַלְכֵי־יִשְׂרָאֵל (14) זָכַרְנוּ[d] אֶת־לַחְמֵנוּ אֲשֶׁר
אָכַלְנוּ בְמִצְרָיִם (15) וְהַסְּפָרִים הָאֵלֶּה שְׁמוּרִים הֵמָּה בְּהֵיכַל־
הַמֶּלֶךְ (16) שִׁמְעוּ אֶת־הַדָּבָר אֲשֶׁר אָנֹכִי קֹרֵא בְּאָזְנֵיכֶם
(17) קָרָא הַמֶּלֶךְ בַּסֵּפֶר אֶת־כָּל־הַמִּצְוֹת וְאֶת־כָּל־הַמִּשְׁפָּטִים

(1) Remember me, Lord my God, for I am Thy servant and Thy word is with me all the day. (2) The prophet wrote all these things in his book, for he said, 'Our sons and the sons of our sons will read in it all that our eyes have seen.' (3) The people cried in a loud voice, 'The Lord hath given in(to) our hands[e] this city and her king.' (4) The servants of Pharaoh said, 'This is the hand of God.' (5) The ways of the wicked (m. pl.) are to Sheol, but[f] the righteous (m. pl.) shall see the light of the day. (6) The children of Israel took from the stones of that place and in the Jordan they placed them. (7) Thou, Lord, givest (to) all flesh its ('his') bread. (8) With our ears we have heard the words of God coming forth from the heavens. (9) The fear of the Lord is the way of wisdom and the words of His law are righteousness and truth. (10) Knowest thou not that the men who (were) pursuing thee in Egypt are dead? (11) The prophet read before the people the words which (were) written in the book of the law which (was) in the temple. (12) In His wisdom He created the heavens and the earth and all which is in them. (13) The

[a] 'Wood'.

[b] The Imperfect denotes continuance, so that it could be translated here as a (permanent) English present tense.

[c] 'Days of holiness', i.e. 'holy days', see p. 136. **63.**

[d] See footnote *c*, p. 58.

[e] Use the sg. 'hand' meaning 'power'.

[f] Conjunction ו.

kings of the nations said, 'Their gods are the gods of the mountains.' (14) Your fathers were slaves to Pharaoh in Egypt. (15) All my ways are written in Thy book before Thee and all[a] is known to Thee.

47. PREPOSITIONS WITH SUFFIXES OF THE PLURAL (NOUN)

In the vocabulary of Exercise 9 two forms of the preposition 'after', 'behind' were given, namely אַחַר and אַחֲרֵי. The longer form אַחֲרֵי is treated as a dual construct (just as רַגְלֵי is a dual construct from רֶגֶל 'foot'), so that the suffixes which it receives are those which go with the plural nouns (as with Duals, note (*b*), p. 71).

Again, in the poetical books of the Bible, the prepositions אֶל־ 'to' and עַל 'upon' are often found in the longer forms אֱלֵי and עֲלֵי[b] and are similarly treated; that is, the suffixes which are attached to these prepositions are those of the plural nouns also, as below:

unto—אֶל[c] (in poetry אֱלֵי)		upon—עַל (in poetry עֲלֵי)		after, behind—אַחַר or אַחֲרֵי	
unto me (c.)	אֵלַי	upon me (c.)	עָלַי	after me (c.)	אַחֲרַי
,, thee (m.)	אֵלֶיךָ	,, thee (m.)	עָלֶיךָ	,, thee (m.)	אַחֲרֶיךָ
,, thee (f.)	אֵלַיִךְ	,, thee (f.)	עָלַיִךְ	,, thee (f.)	אַחֲרַיִךְ
,, him	אֵלָיו	,, him	עָלָיו	,, him	אַחֲרָיו
,, her	אֵלֶיהָ	,, her	עָלֶיהָ	,, her	אַחֲרֶיהָ
,, us (c.)	אֵלֵינוּ	,, us (c.)	עָלֵינוּ	,, us (c.)	אַחֲרֵינוּ
,, you (m.)	אֲלֵיכֶם	,, you (m.)	עֲלֵיכֶם	,, you (m.)	אַחֲרֵיכֶם
,, you (f.)	אֲלֵיכֶן	,, you (f.)	עֲלֵיכֶן	,, you (f.)	אַחֲרֵיכֶן
,, them (m.)	אֲלֵיהֶם	,, them (m.)	עֲלֵיהֶם	,, them (m.)	אַחֲרֵיהֶם
,, them (f.)	אֲלֵיהֶן	,, them (f.)	עֲלֵיהֶן	,, them (f.)	אַחֲרֵיהֶן

NOTE: (i) How the heavy suffixes attach themselves to the form of the construct.

[a] הַכֹּל—'the whole'. See p. 65, footnote *b*.

[b] Cf. the prepositional idea in לִפְנֵי ('to the face of') and לְעֵינֵי ('to the eyes of'), meaning 'before'.

[c] אֶל is generally used after verbs of motion and speech.

(ii) Another preposition which is similarly treated is תַּ֫חַת 'below', 'beneath', 'instead of': תַּחְתַּי 'below me', תַּחְתֶּ֫יךָ 'below thee', תַּחְתָּיו 'below him', etc.

48. COHORTATIVE AND JUSSIVE

There is an extension of the Imperfect to express emphasis or effort.

(*a*) In the 1st pers. it is called *Cohortative*, which *is denoted by appending the syllable* ָה *to the 1st pers. Imperfect*, thus:

Ordinary Imperfect— אֶשְׁמֹר 'I shall keep' נִשְׁמֹר 'we shall keep'

Cohortative ,, —אֶשְׁמְרָה 'I *will* keep' 'let me keep' נִשְׁמְרָה 'we *will* keep' 'let us keep'

(*b*) Corresponding to the Cohortative is the *Emphatic Imperative* which also has an ָה appended to the Imperative sg. masc.

Ordinary Imperative: שְׁמֹר 'keep thou (m.)'
Emphatic ,, : שָׁמְרָה 'keep thou (m.) indeed'

(*c*) The Imperfect is often used with a *Jussive* force—'let him ...' but wherever the final vowel can possibly be shortened this is done.[a] יִשְׁפֹּט הַמֶּ֫לֶךְ means 'the king will judge', but in certain contexts may mean 'let the king judge'.

EXERCISE 15

sea	יָם	in order that, for the sake of	לְמַ֫עַן
,, (pl.)	יַמִּים	for my sake, &c.	לְמַעֲנִי, לְמַעַנְךָ
nation	גּוֹי	where?	אַיֵּה
distress, trouble	צָרָה	he reigned	מָלַךְ
alone	לְבַד		
I alone, &c. (with suff.)	לְבַדִּי, לְבַדְּךָ		

(1) לָ֫מָּה שָׁלַ֫חְתָּ אֵלַי לִשְׁאֹל אֶת־דְּבַר־יהוה, אַיֵּה אֱלֹהֵי־כְנַ֫עַן אֲשֶׁר עָבַ֫דְתָּ כָּל־יָמֶ֫יךָ וְאַיֵּה נְבִיאֵיהֶם (2) דִּבֶּר אֵלֵ֫ינוּ הָאִישׁ

[a] One part only of the regular verb has a shortening for the Jussive (p. 114. (*b*)), while several of the weak verbs have shortened forms.

כַּדְּבָרִים[a] הָאֵלֶּה וְלֹא שָׁמַע אֶל־דִּבְרֵי־עֲבָדָיו (3) לָמָּה רָדַפְתָּ
אַחֲרַי כָּאִישׁ הָרֹדֵף אַחֲרֵי־עַבְדּוֹ, יִשְׁפֹּט[b] יהוה בֵּינִי וּבֵינֶךָ כִּי
צַדִּיק אָנֹכִי בְּעֵינָיו (4) אֶשְׁמְרָה אֶת־תּוֹרָתְךָ יהוה אֱלֹהַי, כִּי אַתָּה
לְבַדְּךָ יְשׁוּעָתִי בְּיוֹם־צָרָה (5) נִכְרְתָה בְרִית אֲנִי וְאַתָּה לְמַעַן
יִהְיֶה שָׁלוֹם בֵּין עַמִּי וּבֵין עַמְּךָ כָּל־הַיָּמִים (6) שָׁפְטָה אֹתִי
בְּמִשְׁפָּט כִּי עַבְדְּךָ אָנֹכִי, זָכְרָה אֹתִי אֱלֹהַי כִּי אֵלֶיךָ עֵינָי
(7) רָאוּ בְנֵי־יִשְׂרָאֵל וְהִנֵּה מִצְרַיִם[c] רֹדְפִים אַחֲרֵיהֶם וְהַיָּם
לִפְנֵיהֶם (8) קִרְאוּ אֶל־יהוה אֱלֹהֵי־אֲבוֹתֵינוּ, כִּי הוּא אָבִינוּ
הַשֹּׁמֵעַ אֶת־קוֹל־בָּנָיו הַקֹּרְאִים אֵלָיו בַּצָּרָה (9) כֹּה אָמַר יהוה,
לֹא אִתְּכֶם לְבַדְּכֶם אָנֹכִי כֹּרֵת אֶת־הַבְּרִית הַזֹּאת כִּי גַּם עִם־
בְּנֵיכֶם אֲשֶׁר יִהְיוּ אַחֲרֵיכֶם (10) אָמְרוּ בְנֵי־יַעֲקֹב, בָּאָה עָלֵינוּ
הַצָּרָה הַזֹּאת עַל־דְּבַר־אָחִינוּ הַקָּטָן (11) אֶזְכְּרָה אֶת־מִשְׁפָּטֶיךָ
יהוה, כִּי מִשְׁפְּטֵי־צֶדֶק[d] הֵמָּה (12) אָמְרוּ זִקְנֵי־הָעָם אֶל־שְׁמוּאֵל,
נִבְחֲרָה[e] לָנוּ מֶלֶךְ כְּכָל־הַגּוֹיִם, וְהוּא יִמְלֹךְ עָלֵינוּ בְּצֶדֶק
(13) תִּמְלֹךְ אַתָּה לְבַדְּךָ בָּעִיר אֲשֶׁר בָּחַרְתָּ (14) לָמָּה אָמְרוּ
הַגּוֹיִם אַיֵּה אֱלֹהֵיהֶם, וְאַתָּה יהוה תִּשְׁמֹר אֹתָנוּ לְמַעַנְךָ כַּאֲשֶׁר
אָמַרְתָּ (15) אָמַר אֱלֹהִים נִבְרְאָה אָדָם אֲשֶׁר יִמְשֹׁל בָּאָרֶץ
וּבַיַּמִּים וּבְכָל־אֲשֶׁר בָּהֶם (16) אָמְרוּ אֵלָיו רָאשֵׁי־יִשְׂרָאֵל,
מָלְכָה אַתָּה עָלֵינוּ כִּי טוֹב אַתָּה בְּעֵינֵי־כָל־הָעָם (17) הֲשָׁפוֹט
תִּשְׁפֹּט אֶת־הָעָם הַגָּדוֹל הַזֶּה לְבַדֶּךָ (18) וְאֶתְכֶם לְבַדְּכֶם הִבְדִּיל
לוֹ[f] יהוה מִכָּל־הַגּוֹיִם לְגוֹי קָדוֹשׁ

(1) Abraham pursued (after) them all the night to the wilderness, for they took the son of his brother with them. (2) Let us write all these things in a book in order that our children who

[a] The insep. prep. כ should be translated here 'according to'.

[b] Jussive force.

[c] Translate 'Egyptians'. Often the name of the country represents its people collectively, and may therefore have a pl. verb.

[d] 'Judgements of righteousness', i.e. 'righteous (or right) judgements', see p. 136. 63.

[e] Note that the guttural takes a composite shewa under it instead of the simple shewa vocal.

[f] 'Unto himself'.

shall be after us shall read in it that the Lord cut (off) the waters of the sea before us. (3) Remember Thy covenant with us, Lord, for Thy sake and for the sake of Thy great name. (4) The heads of the people said unto the king, 'Let us send messengers unto the land of Egypt for we are in distress' (use art.). (5) The nations have come upon us and in the day and in the night they have pursued us. (6) Have I not indeed said that thy (f.) son shall reign over Israel after me? (7) The nations say, 'Is this the people which the Lord hath chosen for Him(self)?' (8) I will call (Cohort.) unto[a] the Lord my God, for in Him is my salvation and not in another god. (9) Jacob said unto Joseph his son, 'Shalt thou indeed reign over me and over thy father's house?' (10) In my dream I heard a voice calling unto me, 'Where are the gods which ye have served? Call ye unto[a] them and not unto Me.' (11) The nations of the earth serve the sun and the stars of the heavens, and they know (perf.) not that the Lord hath created them for the sake of His great name. (12) The servant of the king said unto the wicked men who (were) with him, '*I* (pronoun) will reign over this people instead of the king whom they have chosen.' (13) From the head of the mountain the prophet saw the river which goeth to the sea (by) the way of the wilderness. (14) In that day God spoke unto me face to face. (15) Judge me not, Lord, for I am in distress (use art.).

49. WAW CONSECUTIVE

Special care is to be taken in this chapter, since the usage described here is characteristic and regular in Biblical Hebrew. Taking two separate sentences: (i) 'The king kept the word of the Lord' שָׁמַר הַמֶּ֫לֶךְ אֶת־דְּבַר־יהוה and (ii) 'He judged the people in truth' שָׁפַט אֶת־הָעָם בְּצֶ֫דֶק the verb in each sentence is naturally in the Perfect. *If*, however, these *two sentences referring to the past are* not separate but *in the one continuous narration*, thus: 'The king kept the word of the Lord and he judged the people in truth', then *only the first verb* ('kept') *is in the*

[a] See p. 85, footnote *a*.

Perfect while the following verb ('and he judged') *is in the Imperfect with a prefixed Waw*:

שָׁמַר הַמֶּ֫לֶךְ אֶת־דְּבַר־יהוה וַיִּשְׁפֹּט אֶת־הָעָם בְּצֶ֫דֶק

Conversely, *in a continuous narration referring to the future*, as 'The king will keep the word of the Lord and he will judge the people in truth', *only the first verb* ('will keep') *is in the Imperfect, while the following verb* ('and he will judge') *is in the Perfect with a prefixed Waw*:

יִשְׁמֹר הַמֶּ֫לֶךְ אֶת־דְּבַר־יהוה וְשָׁפַט אֶת־הָעָם בְּצֶ֫דֶק

Early grammarians thought that the connecting Waw (ו) had the strange effect of *converting* the tense of a verb into its opposite and they therefore called it 'Waw Conversive'. Though this seems, at first glance, to be the effect of this prefixed Waw, it does not seem reasonable to suppose that a conjunction could *convert* a completed action into an continuous one or vice versa. Later grammarians noted that this usage was confined to consecutive narratives and they therefore termed it 'Waw Consecutive'. Though the latter observation is correct, it nevertheless does not account for this phenomenon, but modern scholarship traces it back to the earliest known Semitic languages and concludes that this type of prefixed Waw has *preserved* forms and uses of a Perfect and a Preterite which go far back into Semitic usage, whence it has been called *Waw Conservative*. (See Appendix 4, p. 252, for special note).

N.B. Because the term 'Waw Consecutive' is so familiar it seems advisable to retain it, but it must be remembered that this is done purely for convenience' sake.

NOTE: (*a*) The Waw Consecutive which is attached to the Perfect is pointed like the Waw Conjunction:

He will judge and he will keep—יִשְׁפֹּט וְשָׁמַר

He will judge and he will rule—יִשְׁפֹּט וּמָשַׁל

You will judge and you will keep—תִּשְׁפְּטוּ וּשְׁמַרְתֶּם

You will judge and you will say—תִּשְׁפְּטוּ וַאֲמַרְתֶּם

You will judge and you will know—תִּשְׁפְּטוּ וִידַעְתֶּם

(*b*) The Waw Consecutive which is attached to the Imperfect is ו pointed with Pathaḥ and followed by Dagheš Forte:[a]

He judged and he kept—שָׁפַט וַיִּשְׁמֹר

They judged and they kept—שָׁפְטוּ וַיִּשְׁמְרוּ

But before the 1st sing. prefix א it is וָ (since א will not admit Dagheš Forte the vowel is lengthened):

I judged and I kept—שָׁפַטְתִּי וָאֶשְׁמֹר.

(*c*) Waw Consecutive with the Perfect moves the accent to the last syllable wherever possible, as 'Thou hast kept'—שָׁמַרְתָּ but 'and thou wilt keep'—וְשָׁמַרְתָּ; while Waw Consecutive with the Imperfect tends to push the accent back wherever possible—this is apparent in the weak verbs, e.g. 'he will sit' יֵשֵׁב but 'and he sat' וַיֵּשֶׁב.[b]

(*d*) There must be nothing between the Waw Consecutive and the verb, so that 'he judged and he kept not' is simply שָׁפַט וְלֹא שָׁמַר.

(*e*) Where the Imperfect has a shortened form (i.e. in one case in the regular verb—p. 114. (*b*)—and frequently in the weak verbs) the Waw Consecutive is attached to this instead of to the long form; e.g. the Imperfect of הָיָה ('he was, it was') is יִהְיֶה ('he will be, it will be') which has a shortened form[c] יְהִי (p. 217), so that the Imperfect of this verb with Waw Consecutive is וַיְהִי[d] (instead of וַיִּהְיֶה, and means 'and he was, and it was', the latter often being translated 'and it came to pass').

(*f*) Often a verse or even a chapter opens with a verb which has the Waw Consecutive, as וַיְהִי 'and it came to pass'; this, rather than implying a continuation with what has preceded, has little more force than 'now it happened'. In the same way וְהָיָה = 'and it shall come to pass'.

[a] The conjunction in the cognate language Arabic is also 'wa'. The Dagheš Forte represents the natural tendency [in speech] to duplicate the consonant following an unaccented short vowel [here Pathaḥ].

[b] When the accent is thrown back the last syllable is now closed and unaccented; its vowel is therefore shortened.

[c] The shortened form is also that used for the Jussive (p. 88. (*c*)).

[d] Incidentally note that the Dagheš Forte is omitted from the י for euphony—p. 18, Note.

EXERCISE 16

inhabitant, dweller (part.)	יֹשֵׁב	he slew, killed	הָרַג
blood	דָּם	(to say) saying	לֵאמֹר[a]
blood(shed)	דָּמִים (pl.)	as, when (with Perf.)	כַּאֲשֶׁר
life	חַיִּים (pl.)	that, when (with Imperf.)	כִּי
judge	שֹׁפֵט (part.)	he spilt, shed	שָׁפַךְ
there	שָׁם	he cried	צָעַק
thither	שָׁמָּה		

(1) יָשַׁב אַבְרָהָם בְּאֶרֶץ־כְּנַעַן וַיִּכְרֹת בְּרִית־שָׁלוֹם עִם יֹשְׁבֵי־
הָאָרֶץ (2) שָׁמוֹר תִּשְׁמֹר אֶת־מִצְוֹתַי וְזָכַרְתָּ כִּי אָנֹכִי יהוה אֱלֹהֶיךָ
(3) שֹׁפְטִים יִהְיוּ לָכֶם בְּכָל־עָרֵיכֶם וְשָׁפְטוּ אֶת־הָעָם בְּצֶדֶק
(4) רָאוּ בְּנֵי־יַעֲקֹב כִּי יוֹסֵף הוּא הַמֹּשֵׁל בְּכָל־אֶרֶץ־מִצְרָיִם
וַיִּזְכְּרוּ אֶת־הַחֲלוֹמוֹת אֲשֶׁר חָלָם (5) אָמַר אַבְרָהָם אֶל־שָׂרָה,
הִנֵּה אֲנַחְנוּ בָּאִים מִצְרַיְמָה וְהָיָה כִּי יִרְאוּ אֹתָךְ עַבְדֵי־פַרְעֹה
וְאָמְרוּ אִשְׁתּוֹ זֹאת, וְהָרְגוּ אֹתִי וְלָקְחוּ אֹתָךְ בֵּיתָה־פַּרְעֹה: אִמְרִי
כִּי אָחִיךְ אָנֹכִי (6) אִם יִרְדֹּף עֵשָׂו אַחֲרֵי יַעֲקֹב וְהָרַג אֹתוֹ לָמָּה
לִי חַיִּים (7) בַּיּוֹם הַהוּא, אָמַר יהוה, יִהְיֶה בֵּיתִי בְּרֹאשׁ־הָהָר
הַזֶּה, וּבָאוּ שָׁמָּה כֹּל גּוֹיֵי־הָאָרֶץ, וְיָדְעוּ כִּי אֲנִי הוּא הָאֱלֹהִים
וְאֵין אַחֵר לְפָנָי (8) בָּאוּ אֵלָיו זִקְנֵי־יִשְׂרָאֵל וַיִּבְחֲרוּ[b] בוֹ לְמֶלֶךְ
עֲלֵיהֶם, כַּאֲשֶׁר דִּבֶּר יהוה אֶל־שְׁמוּאֵל (9) לָקַח הַנַּעַר סֵפֶר
וַיִּכְתֹּב בּוֹ אֶת־דִּבְרֵי־הַנָּבִיא (10) שָׁמַעְתִּי אֶת־קוֹל־עַמִּי בַּצָּרָה
וָאֶזְכֹּר אֶת־בְּרִיתִי אִתָּם (11) וְהָיָה אִם לֹא יִשְׁמְעוּ אֶל־דְּבָרֶיךָ
וְלָקַחְתָּ מִמֵּי־הַנָּהָר וְשָׁפַכְתָּ עַל־הָאֲדָמָה, וְהָיוּ הַמַּיִם לְדָם
לְעֵינֵיהֶם: לָקַח מֹשֶׁה מַיִם מֵהַנָּהָר וַיִּשְׁפֹּךְ עַל־הָאֲדָמָה, וַיִּהְיוּ
לְדָם לְעֵינֵי־זִקְנֵי־יִשְׂרָאֵל (12) אָמַר יַעֲקֹב אֶל־בָּנָיו, יִשְׁמְעוּ

[a] From the verb אָמַר—weak verb (pp. 161 ff.).

[b] Composite shewa under guttural.

מַלְכֵי־הָאָרֶץ אֶת־הַדָּבָר הַזֶּה וּבָאוּ עָלֵינוּ וְהָרְגוּ אֹתָנוּ (13) וַיְהִי
שְׁמוּאֵל נָבִיא לְיִשְׂרָאֵל וַיִּשְׁפֹּט אֶת־הָעָם בְּצֶדֶק כָּל־יְמֵי־חַיָּיו
(14) יָרְדוּ בְנֵי־יַעֲקֹב מִצְרַיְמָה וַיִּשְׁלְחוּ מַלְאָכִים לִפְנֵיהֶם אֶל־
יוֹסֵף לֵאמֹר הִנֵּה בֵית־אָבִיךָ וְכָל־אֲשֶׁר לָהֶם בָּאוּ אֵלֶיךָ מִצְרָיְמָה
(15) וַיְהִי[a] דְבַר־יהוה אֵלַי לֵאמֹר בֶּן־אָדָם מָה־אַתָּה שֹׁמֵעַ
(16) עֲבָדִים הָיוּ אֲבוֹתֵינוּ לְפַרְעֹה בְּמִצְרַיִם וַיִּצְעֲקוּ[b] אֶל־יהוה
אֱלֹהֵינוּ (17) אָמַר אַבְרָהָם אֶל־עַבְדּוֹ הַמֹּשֵׁל בְּכָל־אֲשֶׁר לוֹ,
הִנְנִי שֹׁלֵחַ אֹתְךָ אֶל־בֵּית־אָבִי, וְהָלַכְתָּ שָׁמָּה וְלָקַחְתָּ אִשָּׁה לִבְנִי
מִשָּׁם (18) יהוה הָלַכְתִּי לְפָנֶיךָ בְּצֶדֶק וְאֶשְׁמֹר אֶת־תּוֹרָתְךָ בֶּאֱמֶת
(19) זָכַרְתָּ אֶת־בְּרִיתְךָ אִתָּנוּ וַתִּכְרֹת לְפָנֵינוּ אֶת־מֵי־הַנָּהָר
כַּאֲשֶׁר אָמַרְתָּ, וּמֵהַנָּהָר לָקַחְנוּ אֲבָנִים גְּדוֹלוֹת וַנִּכְתֹּב עֲלֵיהֶן
אֶת־הַדְּבָרִים אֲשֶׁר רָאוּ עֵינֵינוּ, לְמַעַן יִקְרְאוּ בָהֶן בָּנֵינוּ הַבָּאִים
אַחֲרֵינוּ אֵת כָּל־אֲשֶׁר עָשָׂה יהוה לָנוּ (20) הִנֵּה דְּמֵי־אָחִיךָ
צֹעֲקִים[b] אֵלַי מִן־הָאֲדָמָה (21) כִּי יִהְיֶה לְךָ דְּבַר־מִשְׁפָּט אֲשֶׁר
אֵינֶנּוּ[c] בַּתּוֹרָה הַזֹּאת, וְהָלַכְתָּ אֶל־הַמָּקוֹם אֲשֶׁר בָּחַרְתִּי לִשְׁמִי
וְשָׁאַלְתָּ אֶת־הַשֹּׁפֵט אֲשֶׁר יִהְיֶה שָׁם בַּיָּמִים הָהֵם

(1) I have remembered Thy law, my God, and I have kept Thy commandments all the days of my life. (2) The Lord saw our distress and He remembered that we are His people, the children of His covenant. (3) The man and his wife were in the garden and they heard the voice of God calling unto[d] them. (4) Thou shalt not shed blood and thou shalt know that I am the Lord who judgeth all flesh with judgement and there is not a righteous man before Me. (5) Pharaoh took all his people with him and he pursued (after) the children of Israel in the wilderness unto the sea.[e] (6) And it shall come to pass in that day that (waw consec.) Thy servants will cry unto[d] Thee from this place which Thou hast chosen for Thy house and Thou wilt remember them and wilt hear their voice. (7) This day thine

[a] See p. 48, footnote *d*.
[b] Composite shewa under guttural.
[c] אֵין takes suffixes; here 'he (or it) is not'.
[d] See p. 85, footnote *a*.
[e] Old acc. case-ending.

eyes have seen that the Lord hath given thee in my hand and I slew thee not. (8) The king stood before the people and he made a covenant with them to keep the way of the Lord all the days. (9) Jacob dwelt in the house of Laban and he kept his sheep. (10) In that day the Lord our God will judge Egypt and all thy servants will come down unto me and they shall say, 'The Lord is righteous.' (11) The children of Israel stood upon the holy mountain and they heard the voice of God coming forth from the heavens. (12) And it came to pass after these things that (waw consec.) Solomon reigned over Israel and he judged the people with his wisdom which the Lord had given (to) him and his name was great in all the land. (13) The kings of Canaan saw that the children of Israel were[a] in the land and they sent messengers unto the inhabitants of the mountains saying, 'Behold the people of Israel hath gone forth from Egypt and behold he is in our land and he will take our cities from us and he will dwell in them and all our people will be servants to him.' (14) Behold I am going unto the elders of Israel and I shall say unto them, 'The God of your fathers hath seen all that Pharaoh hath done to you and He will keep His word which He spoke unto Abraham, and the children of Israel shall go forth from Egypt a very great nation.' And it shall come to pass if they shall not hearken unto my words and they shall ask, 'Who art thou and who hath sent thee to us?', then (waw consec.) I will take water from the sea and I will pour upon the ground before them and the water shall be(come for) blood. (15) Keep my way from evil, Lord, and the nations of the earth shall know that Thou art my God and that I am Thy servant.

50. STATIVE VERBS

There are three types of verb, represented respectively by שָׁמַר ('he kept'), כָּבֵד ('he was heavy') and קָטֹן ('he was small'). The distinguishing feature is the vowel in the second syllable of the perfect stem: in שָׁמַר it is *a*, in כָּבֵד it is *e*, and in קָטֹן it is *o*. These verbs, therefore, fall into three classes, designated as *a*, *e*, and *o*.

[a] See p. 48, footnote *c*. 'Were' is required by the English, but not by the Hebrew.

The meanings of the above two verbs of the *e* and *o* classes show that they indicate *states*-of-being, as opposed to verbs of action or motion. *They are therefore known as Stative Verbs.* Below is a table giving their conjugation:

		PERFECT	IMPERFECT	PERFECT	IMPERFECT
Sing.	3. m.	כָּבֵד	יִכְבַּד	קָטֹן	יִקְטֹן
	3. f.	כָּבְדָה	תִּכְבַּד	קָטְנָה	תִּקְטֹן
	2. m.	כָּבַ֫דְתָּ	תִּכְבַּד	קָטֹ֫נְתָּ	&c.
	2. f.	כָּבַדְתְּ	תִּכְבְּדִי	קָטֹנְתְּ	
	1. c.	כָּבַ֫דְתִּי	אֶכְבַּד	קָטֹ֫נְתִּי	
Plur.	3. m.	כָּבְדוּ	יִכְבְּדוּ	קָטְנוּ	
	3. f.		תִּכְבַּ֫דְנָה		
	2. m.	כְּבַדְתֶּם	תִּכְבְּדוּ	קְטָנְתֶּם	(Qᵉtontem)
	2. f.	כְּבַדְתֶּן	תִּכְבַּ֫דְנָה	קְטָנְתֶּן	
	1. c.	כָּבַ֫דְנוּ	נִכְבַּד	קָטֹ֫נּוּ	(for קָטֹנְנוּ)
Sing.	1. c. COHORTATIVE	אֶכְבְּדָה			

		IMPERATIVE	PARTICIPLE	IMPERATIVE	PARTICIPLE
Sing.	m.	כְּבַד	כָּבֵד		קָטֹן
	f.	כִּבְדִי	כְּבֵדָה		
Plur.	m.	כִּבְדוּ	כְּבֵדִים		
	f.	כְּבַ֫דְנָה	כְּבֵדוֹת		

INFINITIVE: abs. כָּבוֹד, constr. כְּבַד

The Statives diverge, in pointing, from the *a* type:

(i) Both the *e* and *o* verbs (כָּבֵד and קָטֹן) have the Imperfect in *a* (יִכְבַּד and יִקְטֹן) instead of *o* (יִשְׁמֹר). The Imperative is also in *a* (כְּבַד) instead of *o* (שְׁמֹר).

(ii) The m. sg. Participle has the same form as the 3rd m. sg. Perfect, but the context determines which it is. There can be no confusion between the f. sg. Part. (כְּבֵדָה) and the 3rd f. sg. Perf. (כָּבְדָה).

(iii) The Perfect of the *e* type is regular in pointing: כָּבַדְתִּי, כָּבַדְתָּ but in the Perfect of the *o* type the *o* vowel predominates: קָטֹנְתִּי, קָטֹנְתָּ, קְטָנְתֶּם (Qᵉṭontem), except in the 3rd f. sg. (קָֽטְנָה) and the 3rd pl. (קָֽטְנוּ).

NOTE: There are several verbs which are Stative in meaning though the Perfect has not the *e* or *o* vowel in the second syllable. In such cases the Imperfect and the Imperative are in *a*, e.g.:

	('he lay, slept')	('he was bereaved')
Perf.	שָׁכַב	שָׁכַל
Impf.	יִשְׁכַּב	יִשְׁכַּל
Imperat.	שְׁכַב	

(Such verbs will be indicated in the vocabularies and the Imperfect will be given.)

EXERCISE 17

Isaac	יִצְחָק	he was great	גָּדַל (impf. יִגְדַּל)
work, service	עֲבוֹדָה	he lay, slept	שָׁכַב („ יִשְׁכַּב)
grave	קֶבֶר	he buried	קָבַר
death (abs.)	מָוֶת	he commanded	צִוָּה
„ (cons.)	מוֹת[a]	he was able	יָכֹל
„ (with suff.)	מוֹתִי	now, I pray (thee or you)	נָא
he was old	זָקֵן (impf. יִזְקַן)		
he was hungry	רָעֵב („ יִרְעַב)		

(1) לֹא יָדַע יִצְחָק כִּי יַעֲקֹב בְּנוֹ הַקָּטָן הוּא[b] הָעֹמֵד לְפָנָיו, כִּי
כָבְדוּ עֵינָיו וְלֹא רָאָה׃ וִידֵי[c]־יַעֲקֹב הָיוּ כִּידֵי[c]־עֵשָׂו אָחִיו (2) צִוָּה
פַרְעֹה אֶת־עֲבָדָיו לֵאמֹר תִּכְבַּד[d] הָעֲבוֹדָה עַל־בְּנֵי־יִשְׂרָאֵל, כִּי
הֵמָּה צֹעֲקִים אֶל־אֱלֹהֵיהֶם מֵעֲבוֹדָתָם (3) קָטֹנְתָּ[e] בְּעֵינֵי־יהוה, כִּי

[a] In articulation it is seen how 'máweṯ' (מָוֶת) becomes 'mauṯ' and then 'môṯ' (מוֹת־).

[b] See p. 48, footnote *c*.

[c] Note the changes from יָדֵי (וְיָדֵי—וִידֵי) to וִידֵי, כִּידֵי.

[d] Jussive force—'let be heavy'.

[e] Translate into the English present tense, since the state is a complete one.

לֹא שָׁמַרְתָּ אֶת־דְּבָרוֹ (4) כִּי שָׁפַכְתָּ דָמִים וַיִּקְטַן הַדָּבָר בְּעֵינֶיךָ,
לֹא יִמְלֹךְ בִּנְךָ אַחֲרֶיךָ (5) צַדִּיק אַתָּה יהוה הַנֹּתֵן לָרָעֵב[a] אֶת־
לַחְמוֹ (6) הָיוּ בְנֵי־יִשְׂרָאֵל בְּמִדְבַּר־סִינַי וַיִּרְעַב הָעָם וַיִּצְעֲקוּ
אֶל־מֹשֶׁה לֵאמֹר לָמָּה יָצְאוּ עֲבָדֶיךָ מִמִּצְרַיִם, כִּי מָוֶת בַּמִּדְבָּר
הַגָּדוֹל הַזֶּה, כִּי אֵין לֶחֶם לָנוּ וּלְנָשֵׁינוּ וּלְבָנֵינוּ, וְאֵין מַיִם לַצֹּאן
אֲשֶׁר אִתָּנוּ (7) לֹא תִשְׁכַּב בְּהֵיכַל־יהוה כִּי קָדוֹשׁ הַמָּקוֹם
לֵאלֹהֶיךָ, וְהָאִישׁ אֲשֶׁר לֹא יִשְׁמֹר אֶת־הַמִּצְוָה הַזֹּאת מִשְׁפַּט־מָוֶת
לוֹ (8) דִּבְּרוּ הַמְרַגְּלִים[b] אֶל־מֹשֶׁה לֵאמֹר בָּעֶרֶב יָרַדְנוּ מֵהָהָר
הָעִירָה וַנִּשְׁכַּב שָׁם בַּלַּיְלָה הַהוּא (9) יִגְדַּל שִׁמְךָ בְּכָל־הָאָרֶץ
וְרָאוּ הַגּוֹיִם כִּי אֲנַחְנוּ עִמָּךְ[c] (10) לֹא יָכֹלְתִּי[d] לִשְׁפֹּט אֶת־כָּל־הָעָם
לְבַדִּי (11) הִנֵּה אַתֶּם בָּאִים אֶל־הָאָרֶץ אֲשֶׁר נָתַן לָכֶם יהוה
וּשְׁמַרְתֶּם אֶת־עֲבוֹדָתוֹ, כַּאֲשֶׁר צִוָּה אֶתְכֶם מֹשֶׁה עַבְדּוֹ (12) הִנֵּה
זֶה בֵּית־אֱלֹהִים וְלֹא יָדַעְתִּי וָאֶשְׁכַּב שָׁם (13) וַיְהִי הַנַּעַר
בְּהֵיכַל־יהוה וַיִּגְדַּל וַיְהִי לְאִישׁ, וַיִּשְׁמֹר אֶת־עֲבוֹדַת־יהוה וַיִּרְדֹּף
אֶת־הַצֶּדֶק וְאֶת־הָאֱמֶת (14) וַיְהִי אַחֲרֵי מוֹת־יַעֲקֹב וַיִּזְכֹּר יוֹסֵף
אֶת־מִצְוַת־אָבִיו אֲשֶׁר צִוָּה אֹתוֹ לִפְנֵי־מוֹתוֹ לֵאמֹר אַל־נָא
תִקְבֹּר אֹתִי בְּמִצְרַיִם, קָבְרָה[e]־נָּא אֹתִי בְּאֶרֶץ־כְּנַעַן וְשָׁכַבְתִּי עִם־
אֲבוֹתַי שָׁם (15) וַיְהִי דְבַר־יהוה אֵלָיו בַּחֲלוֹם־הַלַּיְלָה לֵאמֹר
אָנֹכִי אֱלֹהֵי־אַבְרָהָם וֵאלֹהֵי־אָבִיךָ יִצְחָק וְשָׁמַרְתִּי אֹתְךָ מִכָּל־רָע

(1) The children of Israel served Pharaoh the king of Egypt and the work was heavy upon them exceedingly and they cried unto the Lord the God of their fathers from their work. (2) Jacob placed a stone under his head and he slept there that night and it came to pass in the morning that (waw consec.) he remembered the dream which he (had) dreamt. (3) The spies said unto the woman, 'If the elders of the city shall ask thee saying, "Where are the men who came unto thee in the night?" then (waw consec.) thou shalt say unto them, "Pursue ye (after) them, for they went

[a] Participle. [b] See p. 18, Note. [c] Pausal.
[d] Translate into the English present tense, since the state is a complete one.
[e] Emphatic Imperative.

forth from the city (by) the way of the river."' (4) If thou shalt indeed keep the commandments of the Lord thy God and thou shalt serve Him in truth, thou shalt not be hungry for[a] bread all thy days. (5) The heads of the people said unto Samuel, 'Behold thou art old (perf.) and thy sons have not walked in the way of the Lord, and who will be a prophet and a judge over us after thy death?' (6) This grave is thine; bury thy dead there. (7) And the children of Israel were in the wilderness and they kept the day of the Sabbath as[b] the Lord commanded Moses. (8) And it came to pass after the death of Solomon that they remembered (waw consec.) all that he had done unto them and they placed not his son over them and they chose another man for a king. (9) Jacob spoke unto Laban saying, 'Behold I am going forth to the house of my father in the land of Canaan, for thou hast not remembered my work which I have worked with thee all these days.' (10) These men have done that which is evil (use art.) in the eyes of the Lord and they will go down to Sheol[c] before your eyes[d] and ye shall know that the Lord judgeth the wicked. (11) Behold I am giving (to) you (the) life and (the) death, and ye shall choose the way of life and ye shall pursue it all your days. (12) Joseph said unto them, 'Behold our father commanded us before his death to bury him with his fathers in the grave which is in the land of Canaan.' (13) The Lord hath given (to) thee wisdom and thy name hath become great in the land and from all the cities (they) come to ask of thee matters of judgement. (14) Isaac spoke unto Jacob his younger (small) son saying, 'Behold Esau thy brother cometh to the house and he will hear that thou hast taken his blessing and he will pursue (after) thee to shed thy blood.' (15) Art thou able (perf.) to rule over this great people (thou) alone?

51. GENERAL DESCRIPTION OF THE REGULAR VERB

The Hebrew verb is normally *triliteral*, i.e., its root consists of three letters. The triliteral root, without vowels or affixes, gives the root idea of the verb—שׁמר of 'keep'-ing, משׁל of

[a] Use the art. [b] See p. 75, footnote *b*. [c] Old acc. case-ending.

[d] In Hebrew it is '*to* your eyes', meaning 'in your sight'.

'rule'-ing, without any reference to person, gender, number, tense, or mood. These modifications are supplied by the vowels, as שָׁמַר ('he hath kept') 3rd m. sg. Perfect, שְׁמֹר ('keep thou') m. sg. Imperative, and by the pronominal particles, suffixed, as שָׁמַרְתָּ ('thou hast kept') 2nd m. sg. Perfect, and prefixed, as תִּשְׁמֹר ('thou wilt keep') 2nd m. sg. Imperfect.

The Hebrew verb-root is conjugated under seven heads. They are:

1. Simple Active	שָׁבַר	'he hath broken'	called QAL (קַל)
2. Simple Passive[b]	נִשְׁבַּר	'he was broken'	,, NIPH'AL[a] (נִפְעַל)
3. Intensive Active	שִׁבֵּר	'he hath utterly broken, smashed, shattered'	,, PI'EL (פִּעֵל)
4. Intensive Passive	שֻׁבַּר	'he was utterly broken, smashed, shattered'	,, PU'AL (פֻּעַל)

To clarify the meaning of the next three forms we may take the Qal גָּדַל 'he was great', from which is derived:

5. Causative Active	הִגְדִּיל	'he hath made great,[c] ,, magnified'	called HIPH'IL (הִפְעִיל)
6. Causative Passive	הָגְדַּל[d]	'he was made great, ,, magnified'	,, HOPH'AL (הָפְעַל)
7. Reflexive	הִתְגַּדֵּל	'he hath made himself great, ,, magnified himself'	,, HITHPA'EL (הִתְפַּעֵל)

NOTE: (*a*) The first of these has been called קַל—QAL—which means 'light' by contrast with the other six which are *derived* from the same root.[e] The verb פָּעַל (pā'al) 'did, performed' has been taken to serve as the prototype of the derived forms; thus, the Simple Passive is the נִפְעַל NIPH'AL, the Intensive Active is the פִּעֵל PI'EL, &c.

(*b*) Note carefully that the Pi'el, Pu'al, and Hithpa'el have Dagheš Forte Characteristic in the second root-letter (see p. 15 (*b*) (ii)), thus giving greater weight to the stem and intensifying the meaning.

(*c*) The table of the regular verb given before was in Qal. The other six derived forms are given separately in the chapters which follow.

[a] See p. 4, footnote *a*. [b] Also reflexive: see p. 102, first Note.

[c] Compare the English causatives 'to raise' (from 'rise'), 'to seat' (from 'sit'), and 'to fell' (from 'fall').

[d] Read 'Hogdal'. [e] And sometimes referred to as כְּבֵדִים 'heavy'.

52. NIPHAL

Perfect

he hath been broken he was ,,	נִשְׁבַּר	he hath been burned he was ,,	נִשְׂרַף
she ,, ,,	נִשְׁבְּרָה	she ,, ,,	נִשְׂרְפָה
thou (m.) wast ,,	נִשְׁבַּרְתָּ	thou (m.) wast ,,	נִשְׂרַפְתָּ
thou (f.) ,, ,,	נִשְׁבַּרְתְּ	thou (f.) ,, ,,	נִשְׂרַפְתְּ
I (c.) was ,,	נִשְׁבַּרְתִּי	I (c.) was ,,	נִשְׂרַפְתִּי
they (c.) were ,,	נִשְׁבְּרוּ	they (c.) were ,,	נִשְׂרְפוּ
ye (m.) ,, ,,	נִשְׁבַּרְתֶּם	ye (m.) ,, ,,	נִשְׂרַפְתֶּם
ye (f.) ,, ,,	נִשְׁבַּרְתֶּן	ye (f.) ,, ,,	נִשְׂרַפְתֶּן
we (c.) ,, ,,	נִשְׁבַּרְנוּ	we (c.) ,, ,,	נִשְׂרַפְנוּ

Imperfect

he will be broken	יִשָּׁבֵר	he will be burned	יִשָּׂרֵף
she ,,	תִּשָּׁבֵר	she ,,	תִּשָּׂרֵף
thou (m.) wilt ,,	תִּשָּׁבֵר	thou (m.) wilt ,,	תִּשָּׂרֵף
thou (f.) ,,	תִּשָּׁבְרִי	thou (f.) ,,	תִּשָּׂרְפִי
I (c.) shall ,,	אֶשָּׁבֵר (אִשָּׁבֵר)	I (c.) shall ,,	אֶשָּׂרֵף (אִשָּׂרֵף)
they (m.) will ,,	יִשָּׁבְרוּ	they (m.) will ,,	יִשָּׂרְפוּ
they (f.) ,,	תִּשָּׁבַרְנָה	they (f.) ,,	תִּשָּׂרַפְנָה
ye (m.) ,,	תִּשָּׁבְרוּ	ye (m.) ,,	תִּשָּׂרְפוּ
ye (f.) ,,	תִּשָּׁבַרְנָה	ye (f.) ,,	תִּשָּׂרַפְנָה
we (c.) shall ,,	נִשָּׁבֵר	we (c.) shall ,,	נִשָּׂרֵף

Cohortative

let me (c.) ,,	אֶשָּׁבְרָה	let me (c.) ,,	אִשָּׂרְפָה

Imperative

be thou (m.) broken	הִשָּׁבֵר	be thou (m.) burned	הִשָּׂרֵף
,, thou (f.) ,,	הִשָּׁבְרִי	,, thou (f.) ,,	הִשָּׂרְפִי
,, ye (m.) ,,	הִשָּׁבְרוּ	,, ye (m.) ,,	הִשָּׂרְפוּ
,, ye (f.) ,,	הִשָּׁבַרְנָה	,, ye (f.) ,,	הִשָּׂרַפְנָה

PARTICIPLE

being broken (m. sg.)	נִשְׁבָּר	being burned (m. sg.)	נִשְׂרָף
" (f. sg.)	נִשְׁבָּרָה	" (f. sg.)	נִשְׂרָפָה
" (m. pl.)	נִשְׁבָּרִים	" (m. pl.)	נִשְׂרָפִים
" (f. pl.)	נִשְׁבָּרוֹת	" (f. pl.)	נִשְׂרָפוֹת

INFINITIVE

absolute	נִשְׁבֹּר and הִשָּׁבֹר	נִשְׂרֹף and הִשָּׂרֹף
construct	הִשָּׁבֵר	הִשָּׂרֵף

NOTE: The Niphal, in some verbs, preserves a 'middle' or reflexive meaning.[a] The Niphal Perfect נִשְׁמַר may also mean 'he kept himself', the Imperfect יִשָּׁמֵר 'he will keep himself', and the Imperative הִשָּׁמֵר 'keep thyself', &c. The verbs which are of this kind will have the reflexive meaning given.

The Perfect of the Niphal is formed by prefixing the syllable נִ to the root. The pronominal suffixes are the same as those of the Qal, the 3rd masc. sg. serving as the basis for suffixing them.

NOTE: The context determines whether נִשְׁבְּרָה is 3rd fem. sg. Niphal Perf. ('she was broken') or 1st pl. Cohortative Qal ('let us break').

The Imperfect יִשָּׁבֵר is a contraction of יִנְשָׁבֵר, the נ of the Niphal having been assimilated, so that *throughout the Imperfect Niphal there is a Dagheš Forte* (Compensative) *in the first root-letter of the verb.* (If the first root-letter is a guttural, then, in the Niphal Imperfect, since the guttural cannot receive the Dagheš, the preceding vowel, Ḥireq (under the prefix), is lengthened to Ṣere; 'he will be left' is יֵעָזֵב (pp. 156 ff.).

As with the Imperfect Qal, so with the Imperfect Niphal, the consonants איתנ (mnemonically written אֵיתָן) are *prefixed* to denote the persons. The pl. masc. ends in וּ and the pl. fem. in נָה. There is no shortened form for the Jussive; it is the same as the 3rd m. sg. Imperf. and the context indicates when it is Jussive.

NOTE: The form אִשָּׂרֵף is frequently found, as well as אֶשָּׂרֵף, but the Cohortative is always אִשָּׂרְפָה.

[a] The significance of the Niphal thus oscillates between reflexive and passive.

The Imperative has the letter ה before the root—הִשָּׁבֵר.

Distinguish carefully between:

The Participle m. sg.	נִשְׁבָּר (he is being broken)	and the	3rd m. sg. Perf.	נִשְׁבַּר
,, f. sg.	נִשְׁבָּרָה (she ,,)	,,	3rd f. sg. ,,	נִשְׁבְּרָה

Note: There are some verbs which are found in Niphal only and not in Qal at all, as נִמְלַט 'he escaped',[a] נִלְחַם 'he fought',[b] and, in the English translation, may not have either a passive or reflexive meaning. It is possible that some of these verbs come from an obsolete Qal which has disappeared from the language or which does not happen to occur in the Old Testament.

EXERCISE 18

N.B. In the vocabularies which follow (and in the general vocabulary at the end of the book) the 3rd masc. sg. Perf. (in Qal, unless otherwise stated) will be given as the root of the verb, and the English translation of it will be the Infinitive, thus: לָקַח 'to take', אָמַר 'to say'. The student is now sufficiently advanced to know that this conventional rendering is the most convenient manner of giving the roots of verbs in vocabularies, as is done in the dictionaries of other languages.

David	דָּוִד	to hide oneself, to be hidden	סתר	in Niphal	נִסְתַּר
chair, throne	כִּסֵּא	to fight	לחם	,,	נִלְחַם
		,, against	,,	,,	,, בְּ
congregation	עֵדָה	to capture			לָכַד
scribe	סֹפֵר	to burn			שָׂרַף
fire (f.)	אֵשׁ	midst (abs.)			תָּוֶךְ[c]
yet, more, again	עוֹד	,, (const.)			תּוֹךְ

(1) נִכְרְתוּ מֵי־הַיַּרְדֵּן לִפְנֵי בְנֵי־יִשְׂרָאֵל (2) אִם שָׁמוֹר תִּשְׁמֹר אֶת־מִצְוֹתַי וְהָלַכְתָּ בְּדֶרֶךְ־דָּוִד אָבִיךָ לֹא יִכָּרֵת לְךָ אִישׁ יֹשֵׁב

[a] 'Got himself off'.

[b] √לחם = joined; נִלְחַם 'joined himself to' = 'struggled, fought with'.

[c] Cf. p. 97, footnote *a* on מָוֶת.

עַל כִּסֵּא־יִשְׂרָאֵל (3) בִּדְבַר־יהוה נִבְרְאוּ הַשָּׁמַ֫יִם וּבְחָכְמָתוֹ
הָאָ֫רֶץ (4) נִקְרְאוּ סֹפְרֵי־הַמֶּ֫לֶךְ לְפָנָיו וַיִּכְתְּבוּ בַּסֵּ֫פֶר כְּכֹל אֲשֶׁר
צִוָּה אֹתָם (5) לֹא יִקָּרֵא עוֹד שִׁמְךָ יַעֲקֹב כִּי יִשְׂרָאֵל יִהְיֶה שְׁמֶ֫ךָ[a]
כִּי נִלְחַ֫מְתָּ עִם מַלְאַךְ־אֱלֹהִים וְגַם יָכֹ֫לְתָּ לוֹ (6) יֵצְאוּ דָּוִד וַאֲנָשָׁיו
וַיִּלָּחֲמוּ בְּיֹשְׁבֵי־הָהָר וַיִּלְכְּדוּ אֶת־עִירָם וַיִּשְׂרְפוּ אֹתָהּ בָּאֵשׁ
(7) נִלְכְּדָה הָעִיר וַתִּנָּתֵן בְּיָדָם וַתִּשָּׂרֵף בָּאֵשׁ, הִיא וְכָל־אֲשֶׁר בָּהּ
(8) אַתֶּם יְדַעְתֶּם כִּי יהוה הוּא הַנִּלְחָם לָנוּ (9) נִסְתְּרָה דַרְכִּי
מֵאֱלֹהַי וְאֶת־קוֹלִי בַּצָּרָה לֹא שָׁמֵעַ (10) עֵינַי אֶל־כָּל־דַּרְכֵיכֶם,
אָמַר יהוה, כִּי לֹא נִסְתְּרוּ מִלְּפָנָי (11) דִּבְּרָה הָאִשָּׁה אֶל־מְרַגְּלֵי־
יִשְׂרָאֵל לֵאמֹר הִסָּתְרוּ בֶּהָרִים יוֹמַ֫יִם וַהֲלַכְתֶּם לְדַרְכְּכֶם, וְהָיָה
כִּי תִלָּחֲמוּ[b] בָּעִיר הַזֹּאת וְהִיא תִנָּתֵן בְּיַד־יִשְׂרָאֵל וּזְכַרְתֶּם אֹתִי
וְאֶת־בֵּית־אָבִי (12) שָׁמַע הָאָדָם אֶת־קוֹל־אֱלֹהִים בַּגָּן וַיִּסָּתֵר
בְּתוֹךְ הָעֵצִים (13) רָאוּ בְנֵי־הַנְּבִיאִים כִּי נִלְקַח הַנָּבִיא מֵעֵינֵיהֶם
הַשָּׁמַ֫יְמָה וַיִּצְעֲקוּ בְקוֹל גָּדוֹל אָבִ֫ינוּ אָבִינוּ (14) מֵת[c] שְׁמוּאֵל הַנָּבִיא
וַיִּקָּבֵר בְּבֵיתוֹ אֲשֶׁר בָּהָר (15) נִבְחַר דָּוִד לְמֶ֫לֶךְ עַל כָּל־יִשְׂרָאֵל
כִּדְבַר־שְׁמוּאֵל אֲשֶׁר דִּבֶּר אֵלָיו לִפְנֵי־מוֹתוֹ (16) אֶקָּבְרָה־נָּא
בְּקֶ֫בֶר־אֲבוֹתַי בְּאֶ֫רֶץ־כְּנָ֫עַן (17) אִשָּׁפְטָה־נָּא בְּמִשְׁפָּט יהוה כִּי
שֹׁפֵט־צֶ֫דֶק אָ֫תָּה (18) הִבָּ֫דְלוּ[d] מִתּוֹךְ הָעֵדָה הָרָעָה הַזֹּאת, כִּי כֹה
אָמַר יהוה, אָנֹכִי אֶשְׁפֹּט אֹתָם לְעֵינֵי־עֲדַת־יִשְׂרָאֵל וְיָצְאָה מִמֶּ֫נִּי
אֵשׁ וְאָכְלָה אֹתָם וְאֶת־כָּל־אֲשֶׁר לָהֶם (19) לֹא תִלָּחֵם בִּבְנֵי־
עֵשָׂו כִּי אָחִ֫יךָ הוּא

(1) The children of Israel went into the midst of the sea and the waters were cut off before them, as the Lord spoke unto Moses. (2) The men of the wicked city said, 'Let us burn his house and all that is in it.' (3) I heard the voice of the Lord in the mountains and I hid (myself). (4) Jacob died in the land of Egypt and he was buried with his fathers in the land of Canaan.

[a] Pausal form of שִׁמְךָ. [b] Composite shewa under guttural.

[c] This form is also a Perfect and has this meaning here: 'he died'.

[d] Niphal in the reflexive sense, 'separate yourselves'.

(5) David sent messengers unto the people saying, 'The city hath been captured, as the king hath commanded.' (6) The Lord spoke unto Moses saying, 'When the children of Israel shall be in the land which I am giving (to) them and they shall see great cities and they shall say, "Who is able to fight against the inhabitants of cities as these?"' (7) Thou sittest upon a throne of righteousness and judgest the sons of man. (8) In my dream I heard a voice calling, 'Woe to them who are hungry for evil,[a] for the day of judgement hath come.' (9) The wise men of the land were in the palace, and they were called before the king. (10) The scribe was taken and he was burnt before all the congregation of Israel, and the matter was written in the book of the days. (11) The Lord spoke and the heavens were created and the waters were poured out upon the face of the earth. (12) In that day there shall be no more death in the land and every man shall sit under his tree in peace. (13) Why hast thou hidden thyself from (before) me? hast thou eaten from the fruit of the tree which is in the midst of the garden?

53. PIEL

From the Qal שָׁבַר 'he hath broken' is derived the Piel שִׁבֵּר 'he hath utterly broken, he hath shattered'. The *Piel has the Daghes̆ Forte Characteristic in the second root-letter throughout the conjugation.* Some verbs are found in Piel without a primary Qal, as בִּקֵּשׁ 'he hath sought'.

PERFECT

he (hath) shattered		שִׁבֵּר	he (hath) sought		בִּקֵּשׁ
she	,,	שִׁבְּרָה	she	,,	בִּקְשָׁה
thou (m.) hast	,,	שִׁבַּרְתָּ	thou (m.) hast	,,	בִּקַּשְׁתָּ
thou (f.)	,,	שִׁבַּרְתְּ	thou (f.)	,,	בִּקַּשְׁתְּ
I (c.) have	,,	שִׁבַּרְתִּי	I (c.) have	,,	בִּקַּשְׁתִּי
they (c.)	,,	שִׁבְּרוּ	they (c.)	,,	בִּקְשׁוּ
ye (m.)	,,	שִׁבַּרְתֶּם	ye (m.)	,,	בִּקַּשְׁתֶּם
ye (f.)	,,	שִׁבַּרְתֶּן	ye (f.)	,,	בִּקַּשְׁתֶּן
we (c.)	,,	שִׁבַּרְנוּ	we (c.)	,,	בִּקַּשְׁנוּ

[a] Use the art.

Imperfect

he will shatter	יְשַׁבֵּר	he will seek	יְבַקֵּשׁ
she ,,	תְּשַׁבֵּר	she ,,	תְּבַקֵּשׁ
thou (m.) wilt ,,	תְּשַׁבֵּר	thou (m.) wilt ,,	תְּבַקֵּשׁ
thou (f.) ,,	תְּשַׁבְּרִי	thou (f.) ,,	תְּבַקְשִׁי
I (c.) will ,,	אֲשַׁבֵּר	I (c.) will ,,	אֲבַקֵּשׁ
they (m.) ,,	יְשַׁבְּרוּ	they (m.) ,,	יְבַקְשׁוּ
they (f.) ,,	תְּשַׁבֵּ֫רְנָה	they (f.) ,,	תְּבַקֵּ֫שְׁנָה
ye (m.) ,,	תְּשַׁבְּרוּ	ye (m.) ,,	תְּבַקְשׁוּ
ye (f.) ,,	תְּשַׁבֵּ֫רְנָה	ye (f.) ,,	תְּבַקֵּ֫שְׁנָה
we (c.) ,,	נְשַׁבֵּר	we (c.) ,,	נְבַקֵּשׁ

Cohortative

let me ,, I *will* ,,	אֲשַׁבְּרָה	let me ,, I *will* ,,	אֲבַקְשָׁה

Imperative

shatter thou (m.)	שַׁבֵּר	seek thou (m.)	בַּקֵּשׁ
,, ,, (f.)	שַׁבְּרִי	,, ,, (f.)	בַּקְשִׁי
,, ye (m.)	שַׁבְּרוּ	,, ye (m.)	בַּקְשׁוּ
,, ,, (f.)	שַׁבֵּ֫רְנָה	,, ,, (f.)	בַּקֵּ֫שְׁנָה

Participle

shattering (m. sg.)	מְשַׁבֵּר	seeking (m. sg.)	מְבַקֵּשׁ
,, (f. sg.)	מְשַׁבֶּ֫רֶת (מְשַׁבְּרָה)	,, (f. sg.)	מְבַקֶּ֫שֶׁת (מְבַקְשָׁה)
,, (m. pl.)	מְשַׁבְּרִים	,, (m. pl.)	מְבַקְשִׁים
,, (f. pl.)	מְשַׁבְּרוֹת	,, (f. pl.)	מְבַקְשׁוֹת

Infinitive

absolute	שַׁבֹּר, שַׁבֵּר	בַּקֹּשׁ, בַּקֵּשׁ
construct	שַׁבֵּר	בַּקֵּשׁ

Once again, the 3rd m. sg. serves as the basis for the other persons and gender, in the Perfect and Imperfect, and the pronominal suffixes (for the Perfect) and prefixes (for the Imperfect) are constant. *The Participle has a prefixed* מ.

N.B. (1) The Dagheš Forte which is characteristic in the 2nd root-letter is sometimes absent in certain forms. The second example בִּקֵּשׁ happens to be one of these verbs, when the medial root-letter ק is vowelless, i.e. when it has a shewa: the 3rd pl. Perf. בִּקְּשׁוּ is found as בִּקְשׁוּ, the doubling of the medial root-letter having been omitted for euphony (pp. 17 f.). Similarly, the Cohortative sg. is found as אֲבַקְשָׁה.

(2) There are a few Piel verbs of the type גִּדַּל with *a* in the second syllable. This is the original form and it has remained in most parts of the Perfect—בִּקַּשְׁתָּ, בִּקַּשְׁנוּ, &c.

EXERCISE 19

heart	לֵבָב, לֵב	to gather	קָבַץ in Qal
,, (with suff.)	לְבָבִי, לִבִּי	and also in Piel	קִבֵּץ.
,, (pl.)	לְבָבוֹת, לִבּוֹת	to be gathered; to gather together, assemble (reflexive)[c] קבץ in Niphal	נִקְבַּץ
seed	זֶרַע[a]		
,, (with suff.)	זַרְעִי	to speak דבר in Piel	דִּבֶּר[d]
tablet	לוּחַ[b]	to count	סָפַר
,, (pl.)	לוּחוֹת	to relate, to recount ספר in Piel	סִפֵּר
Joshua	יְהוֹשֻׁעַ	to escape מלט in Niphal	נִמְלַט
gold	זָהָב	to find	מָצָא

(1) סִפֵּר לָהֶם יוֹסֵף אֶת־הַחֲלוֹמוֹת אֲשֶׁר חָלַם וְלֹא יָכְלוּ לְדַבֵּר
אִתּוֹ בְּשָׁלוֹם (2) שָׁמַע אַבְרָהָם וְהִנֵּה קוֹל מְדַבֵּר אֵלָיו לֵאמֹר
הֲיָכֹל אָדָם לְסַפֵּר אֶת־כֹּכְבֵי־הַשָּׁמַיִם, כִּי כֹה יִהְיֶה זַרְעֲךָ בָּאָרֶץ
הַזֹּאת (3) וַיְדַבֵּר[e] יהוה אֶל־מֹשֶׁה לֵאמֹר קַבֵּץ אֵלֶיךָ אֶת־זִקְנֵי־
יִשְׂרָאֵל וְדִבַּרְתָּ אֲלֵיהֶם כַּדְּבָרִים הָאֵלֶּה (4) אֱלֹהִים בְּאָזְנֵינוּ
שָׁמַעְנוּ, אֲבוֹתֵינוּ סִפְּרוּ לָנוּ (5) שְׁמֹר אֶת־הַדְּבָרִים הָאֵלֶּה, כְּתֹב
אֹתָם עַל לוּחַ־לִבֶּךָ[f] אֲנִי יהוה דִּבַּרְתִּי (6) וַיְהִי בַּיּוֹם הַהוּא, וּמֹשֶׁה
שֹׁמֵר אֶת־צֹאנוֹ בַּמִּדְבָּר וְהִנֵּה אִשׁ לְפָנָיו וּמַלְאַךְ־יהוה מְדַבֵּר

[a] Segholate noun with terminal guttural; see p. 83, Note (*a*).
[b] Furtive Pathaḥ; see p. 19. 4.
[c] Niphal has often a reflexive force, p. 102, first Note.
[d] When followed by a noun it is דִּבֶּר and in pause it is דִּבֵּר.
[e] For the absence of the Dagheš Forte in the Yoḍ, see p. 18, Note.
[f] Pausal, see p. 137 (*c*).

אֵלָיו מִתּוֹךְ־הָאֵשׁ (7) בַּקְּשׁוּ אֶת־יהוה בְּלֵב נִשְׁבָּר וְעִבְדוּ אֹתוֹ
בְּיִרְאָה, וְנִמְלַטְתֶּם מֵהָרָעָה אֲשֶׁר דִּבֶּר עֲלֵיכֶם[a] (8) שָׁמַע דָּוִד כִּי
הַמֶּלֶךְ מְבַקֵּשׁ אֶת־מוֹתוֹ וַיִּמָּלֵט מִיָּדוֹ וַיִּסָּתֵר בֶּהָרִים, וַיִּקָּבְצוּ
אֵלָיו אֲנָשִׁים מִיִּשְׂרָאֵל וַיְהִי דָוִד לְרֹאשׁ עֲלֵיהֶם (9) אִמָּלְטָה־נָּא
מִיַּד־הָרְשָׁעִים אֲשֶׁר בִּקְשׁוּ אֶת־מוֹתִי (10) אָמַר הָרָשָׁע בְּלִבּוֹ
אֵין אֱלֹהִים בַּשָּׁמַיִם וְאֵין מִשְׁפָּט בָּאָרֶץ (11) שָׁאַל הָאִישׁ אֶת־
יוֹסֵף לֵאמֹר אֶת־מִי אַתָּה מְבַקֵּשׁ (12) נִקְבְּצוּ כָּל רָאשֵׁי־הָעָם
אֶל־דָּוִד וַיְדַבְּרוּ אֵלָיו לֵאמֹר הִנֵּה־נָא זָקַנְתָּ וְלֹא יָדַעְתָּ אֶת־יוֹם־
מוֹתְךָ, וְאַתָּה הוּא הַיֹּצֵא וְהַבָּא לְפָנֵינוּ, וּמִי יִהְיֶה לְרֹאשׁ עָלֵינוּ
אַחֲרֶיךָ (13) בָּאוּ כָּל מַלְכֵי־הָאָרֶץ וַיְבַקְשׁוּ אֶת־פְּנֵי־הַמֶּלֶךְ
שְׁלֹמֹה לִשְׁמֹעַ אֶת־חָכְמָתוֹ אֲשֶׁר נָתַן אֱלֹהִים בְּלִבּוֹ (14) שָׁמַע
פַּרְעֹה אֶת־דִּבְרֵי יוֹסֵף וַיְדַבֵּר אֶל־עֲבָדָיו לֵאמֹר הֲנִמְצָא בְכָל־
אַרְצִי אִישׁ חָכָם כָּמֹהוּ הַיֹּדֵעַ אֶת־דְּבַר־הָאֱלֹהִים, כִּי אֵין דָּבָר
נִסְתָּר מִמֶּנּוּ (15) יָרַד מֹשֶׁה מֵהַר־סִינַי וּבְיָדוֹ לוּחוֹת־הַבְּרִית,
וַיְדַבֵּר אֶל־יְהוֹשֻׁעַ לֵאמֹר מַה־הַקּוֹל הַזֶּה בְּאָזְנָי: וַיְסַפֵּר לוֹ
יְהוֹשֻׁעַ כִּי עָשׂוּ לָהֶם בְּנֵי־יִשְׂרָאֵל אֱלֹהֵי־זָהָב וַיִּקְרְאוּ לִפְנֵיהֶם
אֵלֶּה אֱלֹהֶיךָ יִשְׂרָאֵל: וַיְהִי כַּאֲשֶׁר שָׁמַע מֹשֶׁה אֶת־דִּבְרֵי־יְהוֹשֻׁעַ
וַיְשַׁבֵּר אֶת־הַלּוּחוֹת עַל־הָאֲדָמָה (16) דַּבֵּר אֶל־בְּנֵי־יִשְׂרָאֵל
וְאָמַרְתָּ אֲלֵיהֶם, לֹא תִרְדֹּף אַחֲרֵי עֶבֶד־אָחִיךָ כִּי יִמָּלֵט מִיָּדוֹ,
וְזָכַרְתָּ כִּי עֲבָדִים הָיוּ אֲבוֹתֵיכֶם בְּאֶרֶץ־מִצְרָיִם (17) צָעֲקוּ
אֵלֶיךָ וְלֹא שָׁמַעְתָּ בִּקְשׁוּ אֹתְךָ וַתִּסָּתֵר מִפְּנֵיהֶם (18) בַּיּוֹם הַהוּא,
אָמַר יהוה, אֲקַבֵּץ אֶתְכֶם אֵלַי מִבֵּין הַגּוֹיִם וְשָׁפַטְתִּי אֹתָם וּבִקַּשְׁתִּי
מִיָּדָם אֶת־דְּמֵי־בָנַי (19) עָשָׂה לוֹ הַמֶּלֶךְ כִּסֵּא־זָהָב

(1) Thus said the Lord, 'Seek ye peace with all your heart and pursue it (in) every day.' (2) Joshua gathered together all the heads of Israel and he spoke in their ears all the words which the Lord commanded. (3) Thy fear[b] is in my heart, Lord, and the light of Thy countenance I seek (Imperf.). (4) The Lord gave (to) Moses the tablets of the covenant and upon the stones were written the

[a] 'Against you'. [b] Meaning 'the fear of Thee'.

judgements and the commandments which the Lord commanded Israel. (5) Gather Thy sheep unto Thee from among the peoples and they shall know that Thou art the God of their fathers. (6) Esau pursued (after) Jacob his brother and he sought to shed his blood and Jacob escaped from his hand. (7) Behold a day cometh and (there) shall go forth a man who is not from the seed of David and he will sit upon the throne of Israel. (8) A messenger came unto David and he spoke unto him saying 'Escape thou to the wilderness, for the king knoweth that thou wast hidden in this place and he will come to shed thy blood.' (9) Remember thou (m.) these words which I speak unto thee and thou shalt serve the Lord thy God with all thy heart. (10) All the inhabitants of the wicked city gathered together and they sought the men who had come unto his house and they found them not. (11) Moses did as the Lord commanded him and he spoke to the elders of the people.

54. PUAL

Perfect

he was shattered	שֻׁבַּר		he was sought	בֻּקַּשׁ
she "	שֻׁבְּרָה		she "	בֻּקְּשָׁה
thou (m.) wast "	שֻׁבַּרְתָּ		thou (m.) wast "	בֻּקַּשְׁתָּ
thou (f.) "	שֻׁבַּרְתְּ		thou (f.) "	בֻּקַּשְׁתְּ
I (c.) was "	שֻׁבַּרְתִּי		I (c.) was "	בֻּקַּשְׁתִּי
they (c.) were "	שֻׁבְּרוּ		they (c.) were "	בֻּקְּשׁוּ
&c.			&c.	

Imperfect

he will be shattered	יְשֻׁבַּר		he will be sought	יְבֻקַּשׁ
she "	תְּשֻׁבַּר		she "	תְּבֻקַּשׁ
thou (m.) wilt be "	תְּשֻׁבַּר		thou (m.) wilt "	תְּבֻקַּשׁ
thou (f.) "	תְּשֻׁבְּרִי		thou (f.) "	תְּבֻקְּשִׁי
I (c.) will be "	אֲשֻׁבַּר		I (c.) will "	אֲבֻקַּשׁ
&c.			&c.	

COHORTATIVE

let me be shattered I *will* ,,	אֲשֻׁבְּרָה	let me be sought I *will* ,,	אֲבֻקְּשָׁה

IMPERATIVE

———	———

PARTICIPLE

being shattered (m. sg.)	מְשֻׁבָּר	being sought (m. sg.)	מְבֻקָּשׁ
,, ,, (f. sg.)	מְשֻׁבֶּרֶת (מְשֻׁבָּרָה)	,, ,, (f. sg.)	מְבֻקֶּשֶׁת (מְבֻקָּשָׁה)
&c.		&c.	

INFINITIVE

שֻׁבֹּר (abs.) . . . (cons.)	בֻּקֹּשׁ (abs.) . . . (cons.)

No examples of Pual Imperative are found.

Except for the vowel under the first root-letter the pointing of the Pual follows that of the Piel. The Participle, likewise, has a prefixed מ. *Dagheš Forte is Characteristic in the second root-letter of the Pual.*

EXERCISE 20

mother	אֵם	to scatter פזר in Piel	פִּזֵּר (or פִּזַּר)
,, (with suff.)	אִמִּי		
,, (pl.)	אִמּוֹת	to sanctify קדשׁ in Piel	קִדֵּשׁ
Aaron	אַהֲרֹן	to honour / to harden כבד in Piel	כִּבֵּד
priest	כֹּהֵן		
shepherd	רֹעֶה	to praise הלל in Piel	הִלֵּל
glory	כָּבוֹד	to praise שׁבח in Piel	שִׁבַּח
world, eternity	עוֹלָם	for ever	עַד־עוֹלָם or לְעוֹלָם

(1) כִּסְאֲךָ אֱלֹהִים לְעוֹלָם וְיֻשַּׁבְתָּ עָלָיו בְּצֶדֶק (2) הֻלְלוּ[a] אֶת־יהוה כָּל־גּוֹיִם שֻׁבְּחוּ אֹתוֹ כָּל־יֹשְׁבֵי־הָאָרֶץ, כִּי גָּדוֹל עַד־הַשָּׁמַיִם כְּבוֹדוֹ (3) בֻּקַּשׁ הַדָּבָר וַיִּמָּצֵא וְהִנֵּה אֱמֶת דִּבֵּר הָאִישׁ,

[a] The Dagheš Forte Characteristic is often omitted (see p. 107, N.B. (1)).

וַיְסֻפַּר לַמֶּלֶךְ לֵאמֹר הִנֵּה נִמְצָאִים בָּעִיר אֲנָשִׁים רְשָׁעֵי־לֵב
הַמְבֻקְּשִׁים אֶת־דְּמֵי־מַלְכֵּנוּ (4) דַּבֵּר אֶל־הָאֶבֶן הַזֹּאת בְּשְׁמִי
וְיֻצְאוּ מִמֶּנָּה מַיִם וְקֻדַּשְׁתָּ אֹתִי לְעֵינֵי־בְנֵי־יִשְׂרָאֵל: וַיְדַבֵּר מֹשֶׁה
אֶל־הָאֶבֶן וַיִּשָּׁפְכוּ מִמֶּנָּה מַיִם כִּדְבַר־יהוה (5) עָמְדוּ בְנֵי־אַהֲרֹן
הַכֹּהֲנִים בְּבֵית־יהוה וַיְהַלְלוּ אֶת־שְׁמוֹ לֵאמֹר גָּדוֹל יהוה וּמְהֻלָּל
מְאֹד בְּעִיר־אֱלֹהֵינוּ (6) קַדֵּשׁ אֶת־אַהֲרֹן אָחִיךָ וְאֶת־בָּנָיו וְהָיוּ
כֹּהֲנִים לִי הֵמָּה וְזַרְעָם אַחֲרֵיהֶם עַד־עוֹלָם, וְשָׁמְרוּ אֶת־עֲבוֹדָתִי
בְּהֵיכָלִי (7) כַּבֵּד אֶת־אָבִיךָ וְאֶת־אִמֶּךָ לְמַעַן תִּהְיֶה בִרְכָתִי
עָלֶיךָ בָּאָרֶץ אֲשֶׁר אָנֹכִי נֹתֵן לָךְ (8) עָשָׂה לוֹ יוֹסֵף שֵׁם גָּדוֹל
בָּאָרֶץ, וַיְהִי מְכֻבָּד מְאֹד בְּעֵינֵי־חַכְמֵי־מִצְרָיִם (9) זִכְרוּ אֶת־
יוֹם־הַשַּׁבָּת לְקַדֵּשׁ אֹתוֹ (10) הַשָּׁמַיִם מְסַפְּרִים כְּבוֹד־יהוה
וְהָאָרֶץ מְהַלֶּלֶת אֶת־שְׁמוֹ (11) לָמָּה תְכַבְּדוּ אֶת־לְבַבְכֶם כַּאֲשֶׁר
כִּבְּדוּ אֲבוֹתֵיכֶם אֶת־לְבָבָם לְפָנַי (12) וַיְהִי אַחֲרֵי הַדְּבָרִים
הָאֵלֶּה וַיְכַבֵּד פַּרְעֹה אֶת־לִבּוֹ וְלֹא שָׁמַע אֶל־מֹשֶׁה (13) כֹּה
אָמַר יהוה אֶל־הָעִיר יְרוּשָׁלַיִם, הִנְנִי מְפַזֵּר אֶת־בָּנַיִךְ בְּתוֹךְ
הַגּוֹיִם, וְהָיוּ מְפֻזָּרִים כַּצֹּאן אֲשֶׁר אֵין לָהֶם רֹעֶה, וּבִקְשׁוּ וְלֹא
יִמָּצְאוּ, וְשָׁאֲלוּ הַגּוֹיִם אַיֵּה הָעָם אֲשֶׁר יָצָא מִמִּצְרָיִם: וְהָיָה כִּי
יִקְרְאוּ אֵלַי בְּלֵב נִשְׁבָּר וְשָׁמַעְתִּי אֶת־קוֹלָם וְקִבַּצְתִּי אֹתָם אֵלַי
כְּרֹעֶה אֲשֶׁר יְקַבֵּץ אֶת־צֹאנוֹ (14) בְּתוֹךְ קְדוֹשֶׁיךָ תְּהֻלַּל וְשִׁמְךָ
יְכֻבַּד לְעוֹלָם

(1) Moses stood upon the mountain of God at[b] the head of the children of Israel and he sanctified them before the Lord and he spoke unto them saying, 'This day the Lord is coming down upon this mountain and He will speak unto you.' (2) Thy children shall praise Thy name for ever, for Thou art our father who is

[a] The Dagheš Forte Characteristic is often omitted (see p. 107, N.B. (1)).
[b] Use the insep. prep. ב.

in the heavens and hearkeneth to the voice of the (ones) who call[a] unto[b] Thee in truth. (3) Thou hast scattered us among the nations who know (Perf.) Thee not, for we hardened our heart and kept not the ways of Thy holy law. (4) Aaron the priest made gods of gold for the people from the gold which they gave (to) him, for they (had) cried unto him, 'Where is thy brother Moses? For he hath not come down from the mountain and we know (Perf.) not what hath become of (say 'to') him' [הָיָה לוֹ]. (5) Let us praise the name of the Lord among the nations and let us recount His glory in all the world. (6) We have been scattered like sheep (use art.) which have no shepherd, but Thou [וְאַתָּה], for the sake of Thy name, wilt gather us together unto Thee from among the nations. (7) Honour ye an old man, for in him is wisdom. (8) God hath chosen the day of the Sabbath and He hath sanctified it for the glory of His great name. (9) The spies whom Moses sent to the land of Canaan were men of wisdom, exceedingly honoured[c] in the congregation of Israel. (10) The Lord spoke unto Moses saying, 'Behold thou hast become small [√קָטֹן] in Mine eyes, for thou didst not honour Me before Israel and thou didst not speak unto the stone as I said.' (11) It is good to praise the Lord and to sanctify His great name. (12) I shall be found if I shall be sought in truth, said the Lord, for I hearken to the voice of the righteous. (13) In that day the Lord gave salvation to Israel and the inhabitants of the city were scattered before them. (14) All that thou seekest is given to thee. (15) I am old (Perf. verb) and I know not a righteous man seeking bread.

55. HIPHIL

From the Qal גָּדַל 'he was great' is derived the Hiphil (Causative) הִגְדִּיל[d] 'he caused to be great', 'he magnified'; from the Qal מָלַךְ 'he reigned' is derived the Hiphil הִמְלִיךְ 'he caused to reign', 'he made king'.

[a] Use the act. part. m. pl. with the art.—'the (ones) calling'.

[b] See p. 85, footnote *a*.

[c] Pual part. m. pl., since the part. is a verbal adj.

[d] Note that the Dagheš in the דּ is lene in the consonant beginning the syllable (p. 14. (*a*)) with no vowel immediately preceding.

Perfect

he (hath) made great	הִגְדִּיל	he (hath) made to reign	הִמְלִיךְ
she ,,	הִגְדִּ֫ילָה	she ,,	הִמְלִ֫יכָה
thou (m.) hast ,,	הִגְדַּ֫לְתָּ	thou (m.) hast ,,	הִמְלַ֫כְתָּ
thou (f.) ,,	הִגְדַּלְתְּ	thou (f.) ,,	הִמְלַכְתְּ
I (c.) have ,,	הִגְדַּ֫לְתִּי	I (c.) have ,,	הִמְלַ֫כְתִּי
they (c.) ,,	הִגְדִּ֫ילוּ	they (c.) ,,	הִמְלִ֫יכוּ
ye (m.) ,,	הִגְדַּלְתֶּם	ye (m.) ,,	הִמְלַכְתֶּם
ye (f.) ,,	הִגְדַּלְתֶּן	ye (f.) ,,	הִמְלַכְתֶּן
we (c.) ,,	הִגְדַּ֫לְנוּ	we (c.) ,,	הִמְלַ֫כְנוּ

Imperfect

he will make great	יַגְדִּיל	he will make to reign	יַמְלִיךְ
she ,,	תַּגְדִּיל	she ,,	תַּמְלִיךְ
thou (m.) wilt ,,	תַּגְדִּיל	thou (m.) wilt ,,	תַּמְלִיךְ
thou (f.) ,,	תַּגְדִּ֫ילִי	thou (f.) ,,	תַּמְלִ֫יכִי
I (c.) shall ,,	אַגְדִּיל	I (c.) shall ,,	אַמְלִיךְ
they (m.) will ,,	יַגְדִּ֫ילוּ	they (m.) will ,,	יַמְלִ֫יכוּ
they (f.) ,,	תַּגְדֵּ֫לְנָה	they (f.) ,,	תַּמְלֵ֫כְנָה
ye (m.) ,,	תַּגְדִּ֫ילוּ	ye (m.) ,,	תַּמְלִ֫יכוּ
ye (f.) ,,	תַּגְדֵּ֫לְנָה	ye (f.) ,,	תַּמְלֵ֫כְנָה
we (c.) shall ,,	נַגְדִּיל	we (c.) shall ,,	נַמְלִיךְ

Cohortative

let me make great I *will* ,,	אַגְדִּ֫ילָה	let me make to reign I *will* ,,	אַמְלִ֫יכָה
let us ,, we *will* ,,	נַגְדִּ֫ילָה	let us ,, we *will* ,,	נַמְלִ֫יכָה

Jussive

let him ,,	יַגְדֵּל	let him ,,	יַמְלֵךְ

Imperfect
(with Waw Consecutive)

and he made great	וַיַּגְדֵּל	and he made to reign	וַיַּמְלֵךְ

IMPERATIVE

make thou (m.) great	הַגְדֵּל	make thou (m.) to reign	הַמְלֵךְ
,, (f.) ,,	הַגְדִּילִי	,, (f.) ,,	הַמְלִיכִי
,, ye (m.) ,,	הַגְדִּילוּ	,, ye (m.) ,,	הַמְלִיכוּ
,, (f.) ,,	הַגְדֵּלְנָה	,, (f.) ,,	הַמְלֵכְנָה

PARTICIPLE

making great (m. sg.)	מַגְדִּיל	making to reign (m. sg.)	מַמְלִיךְ
,, (f. sg.)	מַגְדִּילָה	,, (f. sg.)	מַמְלִיכָה
,, (m. pl.)	מַגְדִּילִים	,, (m. pl.)	מַמְלִיכִים
,, (f. pl.)	מַגְדִּילוֹת	,, (f. pl.)	מַמְלִיכוֹת

INFINITIVE

absolute	הַגְדֵּל	absolute	הַמְלֵךְ
construct	הַגְדִּיל	construct	הַמְלִיךְ

(*a*) The Perfect of the Hiphil is formed by prefixing ה to the root of the verb—הִמְלִיךְ. The Imperfect יַמְלִיךְ is for יְהַמְלִיךְ; the ה of the Hiphil is assimilated and the vowelless י assumes its pointing (cf. as under similar conditions the inseparable preposition with the article, p. 28. (B)). The Imperative has the prefixed ה.

(*b*) It is to be noted very carefully that *the Hiphil is the only part of the regular verb which has a shortened form of the Imperfect*, thus: יַמְלִיךְ (Imperf.) is shortened to יַמְלֵךְ (Jussive); יַגְדִּיל to יַגְדֵּל, and *that the Waw Consecutive takes the shortened form of the Imperfect* when there is one (p. 92, Note (*e*)), so that, e.g., 'and he made great' is וַיַּגְדֵּל (and not וַיַּגְדִּיל): 'and he made to reign' is וַיַּמְלֵךְ (and not וַיַּמְלִיךְ).

N.B.: There is usually no shortening for the 1st sing.: it is simply וָאַמְלִיךְ—this is important.

(*c*) It was pointed out on p. 77 that *negative commands of immediate application are expressed by* אַל *with the shortened form of the Imperfect*, where one exists, so that 'make not to reign —*now*—' is אַל תַּמְלֵךְ (while the permanent prohibition 'make not to reign—*never*—' is לֹא תַמְלִיךְ).

(*d*) As in the case of other derived forms there are some verbs which are found in Hiphil but not in Qal &c.: the verb 'to destroy' is הִשְׁמִיד.

56. HOPHAL

Perfect

he was made great	הָגְדַּל (hogdal)	he was made to reign	הָמְלַךְ (homlak)
she ,,	הָגְדְּלָה	she ,,	הָמְלְכָה
thou (m.) wast ,,	הָגְדַּלְתָּ	thou (m.) wast ,,	הָמְלַכְתָּ
&c.		&c.	
they (c.) were ,,	הָגְדְּלוּ	they (c.) were ,,	הָמְלְכוּ
&c.		&c.	

Imperfect

he will be made great	יָגְדַּל (yogdal)	he will be made to reign	יָמְלַךְ (yomlak)
she ,,	תָּגְדַּל	she ,,	תָּמְלַךְ
&c.		&c.	
they (m.) ,,	יָגְדְּלוּ	they (m.) ,,	יָמְלְכוּ
they (f.) ,,	תָּגְדַּלְנָה	they (f.) ,,	תָּמְלַכְנָה
&c.		&c.	

Imperative

———

Participle

being made great (m. sg.)	מָגְדָּל[a]	being made to reign (m. sg.)	מָמְלָךְ[a]
&c.		&c.	

Infinitive

הָגְדֵּל (abs.)	הָמְלֵךְ (abs.)

[a] Often with 'u' under the מ—מֻגְדָּל, מֻמְלָךְ

EXERCISE 21

הִקְהִיל	to gather together (transitive) קהל in Hiphil	שְׁכֶם	Shechem
נִקְהַל	,, (intransitive[a]) ,, in Niphal	קָהָל	assembly, gathering
הִסְתִּיר	to hide (transitive) סתר in Hiphil	בְּכוֹר	firstborn
נִסְתַּר	,, oneself ,, in Niphal	אֹיֵב	enemy
הִשְׁחִית	to destroy שחת in Hiphil	שָׁלֵם	perfect
הִשְׁמִיד	to destroy שמד in Hiphil	שָׁאוּל	Saul

(1) בַּיּוֹם הַהוּא הִמְלִיךְ דָּוִד אֶת־שְׁלֹמֹה בְנוֹ עַל־יִשְׂרָאֵל (2) בָּאוּ
כֹּל אַנְשֵׁי־יִשְׂרָאֵל שְׁכֶמָה לְהַמְלִיךְ אֶת־שָׁאוּל עֲלֵיהֶם, כִּי בוֹ
בָּחַר יהוה לְמֶלֶךְ, וַיַּמְלֵךְ אֹתוֹ שָׁם שְׁמוּאֵל הַנָּבִיא: וַיְדַבֵּר
שְׁמוּאֵל בְּאָזְנֵי־הָעָם לֵאמֹר הִנֵּה שָׁמַעְתִּי בְקוֹלְכֶם כְּכֹל אֲשֶׁר
אֲמַרְתֶּם וָאַמְלִיךְ עֲלֵיכֶם מֶלֶךְ, וְהִנֵּה מַלְכְּכֶם לִפְנֵיכֶם: וְהָיָה אִם
שָׁמוֹר יִשְׁמֹר אֶת־מִצְוֹת־יהוה וְעָשָׂה כְּכֹל[b] הַכָּתוּב בְּסֵפֶר־תּוֹרַת־
מֹשֶׁה וְהָיָה לְבָבוֹ שָׁלֵם עִם יהוה אֱלֹהָיו, הִנֵּה יהוה אֱלֹהֵיכֶם יִהְיֶה
אִתְּכֶם וְהוּא יִלָּחֵם לָכֶם וְנָתַן לָכֶם יְשׁוּעָה מִכָּל־אֹיְבֵיכֶם, וְנָתַן
אֶת־יִרְאַתְכֶם[c] עַל־כָּל־גּוֹיֵי הָאָרֶץ (3) דַּבֵּר אֶל־פַּרְעֹה וְאָמַרְתָּ
אֵלָיו, כֹּה אָמַר יהוה אֱלֹהֵי־יִשְׂרָאֵל, הִנְנִי שֹׁלֵחַ אֶת־מַלְאָכִי
בְּתוֹכְכֶם וְהָרַג אֶת־כָּל־בְּכוֹרֵי מִצְרַיִם, מִבְּכוֹר־פַּרְעֹה הַיֹּשֵׁב
עַל־כִּסְאוֹ וְעַד בְּכוֹר־הָעֶבֶד, וְהִבְדַּלְתִּי בַּיּוֹם הַהוּא בֵּין יִשְׂרָאֵל
וּבֵין מִצְרַיִם וְיָדַעְתָּ כִּי אֲנִי יהוה (4) וַיְדַבֵּר יהוה אֶל־מֹשֶׁה
לֵאמֹר הַקְהֵל אֶת־רָאשֵׁי־הָעָם וְאֶת־שֹׁפְטָיו וְדִבַּרְתָּ אֲלֵיהֶם
לֵאמֹר הִבָּדְלוּ מִתּוֹךְ הַקָּהָל הָרָשָׁע הַזֶּה, כִּי יהוה מַשְׁחִית אֶת־
הַמָּקוֹם הַזֶּה וְיָרְדוּ שְׁאֹלָה, הֵמָּה וּנְשֵׁיהֶם וּבְנֵיהֶם וּבְנוֹתֵיהֶם וְצֹאנָם
וְכָל־אֲשֶׁר לָהֶם (5) הִסְתִּירָה הָאִשָּׁה אֶת־מְרַגְּלֵי־יִשְׂרָאֵל אִתָּהּ
בַּבַּיִת, וַיְבַקְשׁוּ אֹתָם זִקְנֵי־הָעִיר וְלֹא מָצְאוּ אֹתָם (6) בַּיּוֹם הַהוּא

[a] Or 'to be gathered together'; 'to gather together' (intransitive, used as a plural or collective only. [b] 'According to all . . .'. [c] 'Fear of you'.

אַסְתִּיר אֶת־פָּנַי מֵהֶם, וּבָאוּ עֲלֵיהֶם אֹיְבֵיהֶם וְהִשְׁחִיתוּ אֶת־
עָרֵיהֶם וְלָקְחוּ אֶת־כָּל־הַזָּהָב הַנִּמְצָא בְּבֵית־יהוה וְשָׂרְפוּ אֶת־
הַבַּיִת הַקָּדוֹשׁ (7) רָאָה אֱלֹהִים כִּי הִשְׁחִית כָּל־בָּשָׂר אֶת־דַּרְכּוֹ
עַל־הָאָרֶץ (8) אָמְרוּ אֲלֵיהֶם הַמַּלְאָכִים, הִמָּלְטוּ־נָא הָהָרָה כִּי
אֲנַחְנוּ מַשְׁחִיתִים אֶת־הָעִיר (9) לָמָּה הִסְתַּרְתָּ אֶת־פָּנֶיךָ מִמֶּנִּי,
הֲלֹא אֲנִי עַבְדֶּךָ (10) מִן הַשָּׁמַיִם הִשְׁמַעְתָּ אֶת־קוֹלְךָ וַתְּדַבֵּר
אֵלֵינוּ מִתּוֹךְ הָאֵשׁ (11) רָאָה אֱלֹהִים אֶת־הָאוֹר אֲשֶׁר עָשָׂה וְהִנֵּה
טוֹב[a] מְאֹד, וַיַּבְדֵּל בֵּין הָאוֹר וּבֵין הַחֹשֶׁךְ (12) בְּנֵי בְכוֹרִי אַתָּה
יִשְׂרָאֵל אֲשֶׁר בָּחַרְתִּי מִכָּל־הַגּוֹיִם לְהַבְדִּיל אֶתְכֶם לִי לְגוֹי קָדוֹשׁ׃

(1) Mine enemies have come upon me and they have sought my death; destroy them, Lord, for they have done evil to me. (2) Moses stood upon the mountain and he hid his face (from) before the glory of the Lord. (3) In that day Solomon was made to reign over Israel and all the people called before him, 'May the name of the king Solomon be great (Imperf.)[b] in all the world as the name of his father David.' (4) Hide not Thy face from me, my God, and destroy me not. (5) All the children of Israel gathered together against (עַל) Moses and against Aaron and they spoke unto them saying, 'Is not all the congregation holy unto the Lord and in the midst of them[c] is His glory?' (6) Behold I have made thy name great and I destroyed thine enemies from (upon) the face of the earth and thou hast not distinguished between Me and between the gods of the nations. (7) The prophet went forth from the city and he gathered unto him all the priests who (were) keeping[d] the service of the Lord and he spoke unto them according to ('as') all that the Lord (had) commanded him. (8) Ye shall not destroy the trees which give fruit when you (will) fight against the inhabitants of Canaan. (9) Because thy heart was perfect with Me as the heart of David My servant, this thing shall not be in thy days. (10) Thus shalt

[a] The English subordinate clause requires the addition 'was'.

[b] With Jussive effect. See p. 88 (*c*).

[c] i.e. 'in their midst'. תָּוֶךְ, with suffix, becomes תּוֹכִי, &c.

[d] 'The (ones) keeping'—see p. 66.

thou speak unto Pharaoh the king of Egypt, 'Behold I am going forth in thy land and I shall slay all the firstborn, from the firstborn of man until the firstborn of the sheep.' (11) I indeed know that thou art mine enemy and that thou hast spoken evil against me before the king. (12) If I shall hide (myself) in the mountains behold there Thou art and (if) I go down (waw consec. with Perf.) to Sheol[a] even there thou wilt pursue me. (13) Ye shall not distinguish between a man and between his servant in (the) judgement and ye shall not honour the face of an old man. (14) Rachel took the gods of her father and she hid them with her, and Laban sought them and he found them not.

57. HITHPAEL

From the Qal (e.g. גָּדַל 'to be great') is derived the reflexive Hithpael (הִתְגַּדֵּל[b] 'to make oneself great') *with a Dagheš Forte Characteristic in the second root-letter*, as below:

PERFECT

he (hath) made himself great he (hath) magnified himself	הִתְגַּדֵּל	he (hath) made himself holy he (hath) sanctified himself	הִתְקַדֵּשׁ
she ,, ,, herself	הִתְגַּדְּלָה	she ,, ,, herself	הִתְקַדְּשָׁה
thou (m.) hast magnified thyself	הִתְגַּדַּלְתָּ	thou (m.) hast sanctified thyself	הִתְקַדַּשְׁתָּ
thou (f.) ,, thyself	הִתְגַּדַּלְתְּ	thou (f.) ,, thyself	הִתְקַדַּשְׁתְּ
I (c.) have magnified myself	הִתְגַּדַּלְתִּי	I (c.) have sanctified myself	הִתְקַדַּשְׁתִּי
they (c.) have magnified themselves	הִתְגַּדְּלוּ	they (c.) have sanctified themselves	הִתְקַדְּשׁוּ
ye (m.) have magnified yourselves	הִתְגַּדַּלְתֶּם	ye (m.) have sanctified yourselves	הִתְקַדַּשְׁתֶּם
ye (f.) have magnified yourselves	הִתְגַּדַּלְתֶּן	ye (f.) have sanctified yourselves	הִתְקַדַּשְׁתֶּן
we (c.) have magnified ourselves	הִתְגַּדַּלְנוּ	we (c.) have sanctified ourselves	הִתְקַדַּשְׁנוּ

[a] Old acc. case-ending. [b] The Dagheš in the ג is, of course, lene.

Imperfect

he will magnify himself	יִתְגַּדֵּל	he will sanctify himself	יִתְקַדֵּשׁ
she ,, herself	תִּתְגַּדֵּל	she ,, herself	תִּתְקַדֵּשׁ
thou (m.) wilt magnify thyself	תִּתְגַּדֵּל	thou (m.) wilt sanctify thyself	תִּתְקַדֵּשׁ
thou (f.) wilt magnify thyself	תִּתְגַּדְּלִי	thou (f.) wilt sanctify thyself	תִּתְקַדְּשִׁי
I (c.) shall magnify myself	אֶתְגַּדֵּל	I (c.) shall sanctify myself	אֶתְקַדֵּשׁ
they (m.) will magnify themselves	יִתְגַּדְּלוּ	they (m.) will sanctify themselves	יִתְקַדְּשׁוּ
they (f.) will magnify themselves	תִּתְגַּדֵּלְנָה	they (f.) will sanctify themselves	תִּתְקַדֵּשְׁנָה
ye (m.) will magnify yourselves	תִּתְגַּדְּלוּ	ye (m.) will sanctify yourselves	תִּתְקַדְּשׁוּ
ye (f.) will magnify yourselves	תִּתְגַּדֵּלְנָה	ye (f.) will sanctify yourselves	תִּתְקַדֵּשְׁנָה
we (c.) shall magnify ourselves	נִתְגַּדֵּל	we (c.) shall sanctify ourselves	נִתְקַדֵּשׁ

Cohortative

let me magnify myself	אֶתְגַּדְּלָה	let me sanctify myself	אֶתְקַדְּשָׁה
let us ,, ourselves	נִתְגַּדְּלָה	let us ,, ourselves	נִתְקַדְּשָׁה

Imperative

magnify thyself (m.)	הִתְגַּדֵּל	sanctify thyself (m.)	הִתְקַדֵּשׁ
,, ,, (f.)	הִתְגַּדְּלִי	,, ,, (f.)	הִתְקַדְּשִׁי
,, yourselves (m.)	הִתְגַּדְּלוּ	,, yourselves (m.)	הִתְקַדְּשׁוּ
,, ,, (f.)	הִתְגַּדֵּלְנָה	,, ,, (f.)	הִתְקַדֵּשְׁנָה

Participle

magnifying himself	מִתְגַּדֵּל	sanctifying himself	מִתְקַדֵּשׁ
,, herself	מִתְגַּדְּלָה, מִתְגַּדֶּלֶת	,, herself	מִתְקַדְּשָׁה, מִתְקַדֶּשֶׁת
,, themselves (m.)	מִתְגַּדְּלִים	,, themselves (m.)	מִתְקַדְּשִׁים
,, ,, (f.)	מִתְגַּדְּלוֹת	,, ,, (f.)	מִתְקַדְּשׁוֹת

Infinitives

הִתְגַּדֵּל	הִתְקַדֵּשׁ

(*a*) The Hithpael is formed by prefixing הִתְ to the root of the verb.

(*b*) The Imperfect יִתְקַדֵּשׁ is a contraction of יְהִתְקַדֵּשׁ (as in the Hiphil, p. 114. (*a*)) but in the Imperative the ה remains.

(*c*) The Participle has מִתְ prefixed to the root.

(*d*) The context determines whether

הִתְקַדֵּשׁ is 3rd m. sg. Perf., Imperat., or Infin.
הִתְקַדְּשׁוּ is 3rd m. pl. Perf. or Imperat.
תִּתְקַדֵּשׁ is the 3rd f. sg. or 2nd m. sg. Imperf.

NOTE: When a verb beginning with an *s*-sound is put in the Hithpael, e.g. שָׁמַר, the resulting form (הִתְשַׁמֵּר) becomes הִשְׁתַּמֵּר, i.e. the first root-letter שׁ and the ת of the prefixed syllable הִתְ are transposed. Similarly, the Hithpael of סָתַר is הִסְתַּתֵּר. The rule is: *When the first root-letter of a verb is a sibilant* שס, *in Hithpael it is transposed with the* ת *of the Prefix.*

This process is carried still further when the first root-letter is צ as in צָדֵק ('to be just'), the Hithpael being הִצְטַדֵּק, i.e. not only does transposition take place, but the (sharp) ת becomes a dull ט. When the first root-letter of a verb is a dental (ד, ט, ת) the ת of the prefixed syllable הִתְ is often assimilated to it, as הִטַּהֵר for הִתְטַהֵר ('to purify oneself'). The assimilation of the ת sometimes takes place even with other letters, as הִנַּבֵּא for הִתְנַבֵּא; הִזַּכּוּ for הִתְזַכּוּ.

NOTE TO EXERCISE 22. In order to make the succeeding exercises fuller we may here anticipate chap. 70 and introduce the familiar וַיֹּאמֶר ('and he said') and the other persons which follow from it. The verb אָמַר is said to be weak, since its first root-letter א is both a guttural and a quiescent letter, bringing about certain modifications in pointing. The Imperfect is יֹאמַר ('he will say') but with waw consecutive it is וַיֹּאמֶר ('and he said'). Following from this:

'and they (m.) said' is וַיֹּאמְרוּ
'and thou (m.) hast said'
'and she said' } is וַתֹּאמֶר
'and ye (m.) have said' is וַתֹּאמְרוּ
'and we (c.) said' is וַנֹּאמֶר &c.

EXERCISE 22

prayer	תְּפִלָּה	to hide oneself חבא in Hithpael	הִתְחַבֵּא
spirit, wind (f.)	רוּחַ[a]	to walk (to and fro) הלך in Hithpael	הִתְהַלֵּךְ
,, (with suff.)	רוּחִי		
,, (pl.)	רוּחוֹת	to prophesy נבא in Hithpael (also found in Niphal)	הִתְנַבֵּא
opposite, against, before	נֶגֶד	to pray פלל in Hithpael	הִתְפַּלֵּל
war	מִלְחָמָה	to lift up, bear, carry	נָשָׂא

(1) נָשָׂא יַעֲקֹב אֶת־עֵינָיו וְהִנֵּה עֵשָׂו בָּא וַאֲנָשִׁים אִתּוֹ, וַיִּתְפַּלֵּל
יַעֲקֹב אֶל־יהוה לֵאמֹר יהוה אֱלֹהֵי־אַבְרָהָם וֵאלֹהֵי־יִצְחָק אָבִי,
אַתָּה אָמַרְתָּ אֵלַי אָנֹכִי אֶשְׁמֹר אֹתְךָ מִכָּל־רָע: שָׁמְרָה־נָּא אֹתִי
מִיַּד־אָחִי מִיַּד־עֵשָׂו כִּי בָא עָלַי לְהִלָּחֵם בִּי (2) בָּאוּ אֲנָשִׁים
מֵאֹיְבֵי־דָוִד וַיְסַפְּרוּ לְשָׁאוּל לֵאמֹר הֲלֹא דָוִד מִסְתַּתֵּר בְּעִיר־
הַנְּבִיאִים: וַיֹּאמֶר שָׁאוּל אֶל־עֲבָדָיו, רִדְפוּ אַחֲרָיו וְלֹא יִמָּלֵט מִיָּדִי:
וַיִּהְיוּ מַלְאֲכֵי־שָׁאוּל בַּדֶּרֶךְ וְהִנֵּה קְהַל־נְבִיאִים עֹמְדִים וּמִתְנַבְּאִים
נֶגְדָּם, וּשְׁמוּאֵל הַנָּבִיא בְּרֹאשָׁם, וַתְּהִי עַל־מַלְאֲכֵי־שָׁאוּל רוּחַ־
אֱלֹהִים וַיִּתְנַבְּאוּ גַּם הֵמָּה (3) וַיְהִי הַיּוֹם וַיִּתְנַשֵּׂא אֶחָד מֵעַבְדֵי־
הַמֶּלֶךְ וַיֹּאמֶר בְּלִבּוֹ אָנֹכִי אֶמְלֹךְ עַל־יִשְׂרָאֵל: וַיִּתְקַבְּצוּ אֵלָיו
אֲנָשִׁים מֵרָאשֵׁי־הָעָם וַיַּמְלִיכוּ אֹתוֹ עֲלֵיהֶם וַיִּשְׁלְחוּ מַלְאָכִים
לְכָל־עָרֵי־יִשְׂרָאֵל לֵאמֹר מִי דָוִד וּמַה־בֵּיתוֹ כִּי יִמְלֹךְ בְּיִשְׂרָאֵל,
הִנֵּה בָּחַרְנוּ בְאִישׁ מִזֶּרַע־שָׁאוּל לִמְלֹךְ עָלֵינוּ (4) הִנֵּה יָמִים בָּאִים
וְהָיוּ בָנֶיךָ בַּצָּרָה וּבָאוּ אֶל־הַבַּיִת הַגָּדוֹל וְהַקָּדוֹשׁ הַזֶּה וְהִתְפַּלְלוּ
אֵלֶיךָ בְּרוּחַ נִשְׁבָּרָה וּבְלֵבָב שָׁלֵם וּבָאָה תְפִלָּתָם בְּאָזְנֶיךָ וְזָכַרְתָּ
אֹתָם וְלֹא תַסְתִּיר עוֹד אֶת־פָּנֶיךָ מֵהֶם (5) בַּיּוֹם הַהוּא, אָמַר
יהוה, אֶשְׁפֹּךְ אֶת־רוּחִי עַל־כָּל־בָּשָׂר וְלֹא תִהְיֶה עוֹד מִלְחָמָה
וְהָיָה שָׁלוֹם בְּכָל־הָעוֹלָם וְצֶדֶק יִמְשֹׁל בְּלֵב־הָאָדָם (6) לָמָּה
יִתְהַלֵּל הָרָשָׁע לְנֶגֶד עֵינֶיךָ, בְּיוֹם־הַמִּשְׁפָּט לֹא יִמָּלֵט: וַאֲנִי

[a] See p. 19. 4.

אֶתְפַּלֵּל אֶל־יהוה הֲשֹׁמֵעַ אֶל־תְּפִלַּת־עַבְדּוֹ (7) וַיִּשְׁמְעוּ הָאָדָם
וְאִשְׁתּוֹ אֶת־קוֹל־הָאֱלֹהִים מִתְהַלֵּךְ בַּגָּן לְרוּחַ־הַיּוֹם וַיִּתְחַבְּאוּ
בְּתוֹךְ הָעֵצִים (8) אָמוֹר אָמַרְתִּי בְּלִבִּי, לֹא אֲדַבֵּר עוֹד אֶל־הָעָם
הַזֶּה כִּי אֵין בָּהֶם יִרְאַת־אֱלֹהִים וַיֹּאמֶר יהוה אֵלַי הִתְנַבֵּא עוֹד
בִּשְׁמִי לִפְנֵי הֵיכַל־הַמֶּלֶךְ, הֲלֹא אָנֹכִי שָׁלַחְתִּי אֹתְךָ (9) וַיֹּאמֶר
מֹשֶׁה אֶל־בְּנֵי־יִשְׂרָאֵל הִתְקַדְּשׁוּ אַתֶּם וּנְשֵׁיכֶם וּבְנֵיכֶם, כִּי יהוה
אֱלֹהֵינוּ יֵרֵד עַל־הָהָר הַזֶּה וְנָתַן לָנוּ אֶת־תּוֹרָתוֹ (10) יֵצְאוּ בְּנֵי־
יִשְׂרָאֵל לְהִלָּחֵם בְּאֹיְבֵיהֶם וַתִּכְבַּד עֲלֵיהֶם הַמִּלְחָמָה וַיִּצְעֲקוּ
אֶל־יהוה אֱלֹהֵיהֶם

(1) In that day My spirit shall rule over the heart of man, said the Lord, and they shall walk (Hithp.) before Me in righteousness and in truth. (2) The Lord said unto me, 'Let me destroy this people and a great nation shall come forth from thee', and I prayed unto Him saying, 'Destroy them not, Lord, for they are Thy children.' (3) The spirit of God is in all the world and the glory of His name is in every place. (4) The children of Israel lifted up their eyes and behold a great sea (was) before them and they gathered together and they said, 'Behold the Egyptians (say 'Egypt') are pursuing (after) us and we shall not escape from their hand.' (5) This is the prayer which Solomon prayed unto the Lord, 'If it is good in the eyes of the Lord, then ('and') He shall give wisdom in the heart of His servant, in order that I may judge Thy people with a perfect heart.' (6) And God spoke unto Abraham and he said unto him, 'Go thou (to and fro[a]) in the land, for it is thine and thy seed's for ever.' (7) Saul saw the sons of the prophets prophesying in the city and the spirit of God was upon him and he prophesied, also he, with them. And the men who saw him said, 'Is Saul also among the prophets?' (8) I have walked before Thee with a perfect heart, for Thy law (was) before me in the day and in the night. (9) David saw that Saul (was) pursuing (after) him and that he (was) seeking his

[a] Hithpael.

death and he hid himself in the wilderness and no man knew his
place. (10) Moses commanded Aaron his brother saying, 'Sanctify
thyself, thou and thy sons with thee, before the Lord.' (11) And
the heart of the king raised itself against the Lord and he said
unto his servants, 'Go ye through (Hithp.) in the land and seek
ye the prophets of the Lord and say ye unto them, 'Ye shall
prophesy no more in the land, for thus hath the king commanded.'
(12) Let me walk (Hithp.) in the light of Thy face, O Lord;
pour out upon me the spirit of Thy wisdom.

58. VERBAL SUFFIXES (of the Perfect)

The verb may receive pronominal suffixes. Often, instead of
the verb followed by the Personal Pronoun (object), as שָׁמַר אֹתוֹ
'he hath kept him', we find שְׁמָרוֹ—the verb with pronominal
suffix. Below is given a table of the Qal Perfect with verbal
suffixes attached:

he (hath) kept שָׁמַר		*she (hath) kept* שָׁמְרָה	
he (hath) kept me (c.)	שְׁמָרַ֫נִי	she (hath) kept me (c.)	שְׁמָרַ֫תְנִי
,, thee (m.)	שְׁמָרְךָ	,, thee (m.)	שְׁמָרַתְךָ
,, thee (f.)	שְׁמָרֵךְ	,, thee (f.)	שְׁמָרָ֫תֶךְ
,, him	שְׁמָרוֹ / שְׁמָרָ֫הוּ	,, him	שְׁמָרַ֫תְהוּ / שְׁמָרַ֫תּוּ
,, her	שְׁמָרָהּ	,, her	שְׁמָרַ֫תָּה
,, us (c.)	שְׁמָרָ֫נוּ	,, us (c.)	שְׁמָרַ֫תְנוּ
,, you (m.)	——	,, you (m.)	——
,, you (f.)	——	,, you (f.)	——
,, them (m.)	שְׁמָרָם	,, them (m.)	שְׁמָרָ֫תַם
,, them (f.)	שְׁמָרָן	,, them (f.)	שְׁמָרָ֫תַן

thou (m.) hast kept שָׁמַ֫רְתָּ

thou (m.) hast kept me (c.)		שְׁמַרְתַּ֫נִי
,,	him	שְׁמַרְתּוֹ שְׁמַרְתָּ֫הוּ
,,	her	שְׁמַרְתָּ֫הּ
,,	us (c.)	שְׁמַרְתָּ֫נוּ
,,	them (m.)	שְׁמַרְתָּם
,,	them (f.)	שְׁמַרְתָּן

thou (f.) hast kept שָׁמַרְתְּ

thou (f.) hast kept me (c.)		שְׁמַרְתִּ֫ינִי
,,	him	שְׁמַרְתִּ֫יהוּ
,,	her	שְׁמַרְתִּ֫יהָ
,,	us (c.)	שְׁמַרְתִּ֫ינוּ
,,	them (m.)	שְׁמַרְתִּים
,,	them (f.)	שְׁמַרְתִּין

I (c.) (have) kept שָׁמַ֫רְתִּי

———		
I (c.) (have) kept thee (m.)		שְׁמַרְתִּ֫יךָ
,,	thee (f.)	שְׁמַרְתִּיךְ
,,	him	שְׁמַרְתִּ֫יהוּ שְׁמַרְתִּיו
,,	her	שְׁמַרְתִּ֫יהָ
———		
,,	you (m.)	שְׁמַרְתִּיכֶם
,,	you (f.)	שְׁמַרְתִּיכֶן
,,	them (m.)	שְׁמַרְתִּים
,,	them (f.)	שְׁמַרְתִּין

they (c.) (have) kept שָֽׁמְרוּ

they (c.) (have) kept me (c.)		שְׁמָר֫וּנִי
,,	thee (m.)	שְׁמָר֫וּךָ
,,	thee (f.)	שְׁמָרוּךְ
,,	him	שְׁמָר֫וּהוּ
,,	her	שְׁמָר֫וּהָ
,,	us (c.)	שְׁמָר֫וּנוּ
,,	you (m.)	———
,,	you (f.)	———
,,	them (m.)	שְׁמָרוּם
,,	them (f.)	שְׁמָרוּן

---

ye (m. and f.) (have) kept

שְׁמַרְתֶּם, שְׁמַרְתֶּן

ye (m. and f.) (have) kept me (c.)
שְׁמַרְתּ֫וּנִי

&c. as the 3rd pl.

we (c.) (have) kept

שָׁמַ֫רְנוּ

we (c.) (have) kept thee (m.)
שְׁמַרְנ֫וּךָ

&c. as the 3rd pl.

GENERAL NOTE:

(*a*) The suffixes attached to the verb are practically the same
as those which are attached to the noun and preposition.
The 1st sg. suffix נִי has already been met with the prepositions כְּ and מִן (מִמֶּֽנִּי, כָּמֹֽונִי).

(*b*) When the verb receives a suffix the accent moves forward
on to the new syllable and the Qameṣ in the first syllable
is consequently reduced to shewa (p. 36), e.g. שָׁמַר but
שְׁמָרַ֫נִי, שְׁמָרֹו; שָׁמַ֫רְתִּי but שְׁמַרְתִּ֫יךָ, שְׁמַרְתִּ֫יו.

3rd m. sg. When the accent moves forward to the suffix,
changes in pointing take place. In שָׁמַר the vowel under
the מ is in a closed syllable and is short, but when the
suffix is attached the ר no longer closes that syllable but
opens the next one רֹו, רַ֫נִי, so that the short vowel Pathaḥ
under the מ is now in an open unaccented syllable; it is
therefore lengthened to Qameṣ (see p. 7. 2).

When the 1st sg. suffix נִי is attached, the 3rd radical takes
a linking vowel (due to the natural mode of speech).

3rd f. sg. The 3rd f. sg. Perfect Qal שָׁמְרָה was originally
שָׁמְרַת (just as the f. sg. noun termination הָ was originally
תָ—p. 61, Note 1). It was shown (pp. 60 ff., 82 ff.) that
original forms often survive with the suffixes, so that when
the 3rd f. sg. Perf. takes suffixes, the original ת remains:
שְׁמָרַ֫תְנִי.

שְׁמָרַ֫תּוּ is a contraction from the alternative form שְׁמָרַ֫תְהוּ,
the latter having the older suffix, and similarly שְׁמָרַ֫תָּה is
contracted from שְׁמָרַ֫תְהָ.

The 3rd pl. (m. and f.) suffixes have the short vowel (Pathaḥ)
since they are in closed unaccented syllables.

2nd m. sg. שָׁמַרְתָּ with suffix of the 1st sg. becomes שְׁמַרְתַּנִי—on the analogy of שְׁמָרַנִי.

2nd f. sg. שָׁמַרְתְּ was originally שָׁמַרְתִּי[a] from which the terminal י disappeared. With suffixes the original form, with Yodh, remains: שְׁמַרְתִּינִי.

2nd m. and f. pl. שְׁמַרְתֶּם was originally שְׁמַרְתּוּם and
שְׁמַרְתֶּן ,, שְׁמַרְתּוּן, so that

'you (m.) (have) kept me (c.)' would be שְׁמַרְתּוּמְנִי and
'you (f.) ,, ' ,, שְׁמַרְתּוּנְנִי, but
in the masc. verb the medial מ disappeared (like the ם in the pl. constr.) and the נ likewise disappeared in the fem. verb, both producing שְׁמַרְתּוּנִי, so that it is left to the context to determine whether the verb is masc. or fem.

NOTE: (*c*) The context determines whether שְׁמַרְתִּיהוּ is 'I (have) kept him' or 'thou (f.) hast kept him'. Similarly with the 3rd f. sg. and the 3rd pl. suffixes.

(*d*) שְׁמַרְתִּינִי cannot be 'I have kept me' but must be 'thou (f.) hast kept me'. שְׁמַרְתִּיךְ cannot be 'thou (f.) hast kept thee' but is 'I (have) kept thee' (since the first members of these pairs are reflexives and are expressed by Niphal or Hithpael).

It will be understood that normally *only the active verbs can take suffixes*; Niphal, Pual, Hophal, and Hithpael, being reflexives and passives, cannot govern an object and therefore do not take suffixes[b]; so now examples of Piel and Hiphil with suffixes will be given to complete the scheme:

[a] Occasionally preserved in the O.T. but in the impossible form שָׁמַרְתִּי (Kethibh altered to Qere).

[b] Except with Inf. Cons. which is considered a verbal noun ending in '-ing'—הִשָּׂרְפוֹ = 'his being burnt' (p. 133, Note).

PIEL: he (hath) sought בִּקֵּשׁ	HIPHIL: he (hath) made king הִמְלִיךְ
he (hath) sought me (c.) בִּקְשַׁנִי	he (hath) made me (c.) king הִמְלִיכַנִי
,, thee (m.) בִּקֶּשְׁךָ	,, thee (m.) king הִמְלִיכְךָ
,, him בִּקְשׁוֹ &c.	,, him king הִמְלִיכוֹ &c.
she ,, me בִּקְשַׁתְנִי	she ,, me king הִמְלִיכַתְנִי
thou (m.) hast ,, me בִּקַּשְׁתַּנִי	thou (m.) hast ,, me king הִמְלַכְתַּנִי
I (c.) (have) ,, thee (m.) בִּקַּשְׁתִּיךָ	I (c.) (have) ,, thee (m.) king הִמְלַכְתִּיךָ
they (c.) ,, me בִּקְשׁוּנִי	they (c.) ,, me king הִמְלִיכוּנִי
ye (m. and f.) ,, me בִּקַּשְׁתּוּנִי	ye (m. and f.) ,, me king הִמְלַכְתּוּנִי
we (c.) ,, thee (m.) בִּקַּשְׁנוּךָ	we (c.) ,, thee (m.) king הִמְלַכְנוּךָ

EXERCISE 23

soul, life (f.)	נֶפֶשׁ[a]	to pass over, transgress	עָבַר
to sell	מָכַר	to fear, be afraid	יָרֵא (stative)
to steal	גָּנַב	to be afraid of	יָרֵא מִן or מִפְּנֵי
to leave, forsake	עָזַב	to fear (reverence)	יָרֵא אֶת

(1) מֵרֹאשׁ־הָהָר רָאָה מֹשֶׁה אֶת־אֶרֶץ־כְּנַעַן וְשָׁמָּה לֹא בָא, כִּי עָבַר אֶת־מִצְוַת־יהוה וְלֹא קִדְּשׁוֹ לְעֵינֵי־עֲדַת בְּנֵי־יִשְׂרָאֵל

[a] Segholate: with suff. נַפְשִׁי.

(2) מְכַרְתָּ֫נוּ בְּיַד־אֹֽיְבֵ֫ינוּ וְכָל־הַיּוֹם שְׁאָל֫וּנוּ אַיֵּה אֱלֹהֵיכֶם
(3) שִׁמְעוּ־נָא אֶת־דְּבָרַי, רִשְׁעֵי[a]־יִשְׂרָאֵל, יהוה לְקָחַ֫נִי מֵאַחֲרֵי־
הַצֹּאן וַיֹּ֫אמֶר אֵלַי, בֶּן־אָדָם הִנָּבֵא[b] עַל־עַמִּי רָעָה, כִּי עָזְבוּ אֶת־
תּוֹרָתִי וְאֶת־הָרַע בְּעֵינַי עָשׂוּ: וְהָיָה בְּיוֹם־הַמִּשְׁפָּט וְצָעֲקוּ אֵלַי
לֵאמֹר עֲזַבְתָּ֫נוּ יהוה וְלַעֲבָדִים נִמְכַּ֫רְנוּ, כִּי עָבַ֫רְנוּ[c] אֶת־בְּרִיתֶ֫ךָ[d]
(4) וַיְהִי בַּלַּ֫יְלָה הַהוּא, וְעַבְדֵי שָׁאוּל שֹׁכְבִים עַל־הָאֲדָמָה, וַיִּהְיוּ
שָׁאוּל וְדָוִד לְבַדָּם, וַיֹּ֫אמֶר אֵלָיו דָּוִד, אַתָּה יָדַ֫עְתָּ כִּי נְתָנְךָ יהוה
בְּיָדִי וְלֹא הֲרַגְתִּ֫יךָ, כִּי אֶת־יהוה אָנֹכִי יָרֵא, יִשְׁפֹּט יהוה בֵּינִי
וּבֵינֶ֫ךָ[d] (5) אַתָּה בְּחַרְתָּ֫נוּ מִכָּל־הָעַמִּים וּבְמִצְוֹתֶ֫יךָ קִדַּשְׁתָּ֫נוּ
(6) שִׁבְּח֫וּךָ כָּל־הַגּוֹיִם וּלְשִׁמְךָ נָתְנוּ כָבוֹד (7) רְדָפ֫וּנִי רְשָׁעִים
מְבַקְשֵׁי־נַפְשִׁי, וְאַתָּה הִסְתַּרְתַּ֫נִי מֵהֶם (8) שָׁמַע יוֹסֵף אֶת־הַחֲלוֹם
אֲשֶׁר חָלַם עֶ֫בֶד־פַּרְעֹה וַיְסַפֵּר לוֹ אֶת־דְּבַר־הַחֲלוֹם וַיֹּ֫אמֶר
אֵלָיו בְּעוֹד יוֹמַ֫יִם וְעָמַדְתָּ עַל־מְקוֹמְךָ לִפְנֵי־פַרְעֹה, וּזְכַרְתַּ֫נִי
לְפָנָיו, כִּי גָנוֹב גְּנָב֫וּנִי מִבֵּית־אָבִי וּלְעֶ֫בֶד מְכָר֫וּנִי מִצְרַ֫יְמָה
(9) וַיְדַבֵּר מֹשֶׁה אֶל־אַהֲרֹן לֵאמֹר הַקְהֵל אֶת־הָעָם נֶ֫גֶד הָהָר
וְקִדַּשְׁתָּם שָׁם לִפְנֵי יהוה (10) הַגֹּנֵב אִישׁ וּמְכָרוֹ מִשְׁפַּט־מָ֫וֶת לוֹ
(11) פִּזַּרְתָּ֫נוּ בַּגּוֹיִם וְגַם שָׁם לֹא עֲזַבְתָּ֫נוּ[c] (12) וְהָיָה בַּיּוֹם הַהוּא
וְהִכְרַתִּי אֶת־עַמִּי בְּאֶרֶץ־אֹיְבֵיהֶם וְקִבַּצְתִּים אֵלַי מִשָּׁם (13) וַיֹּ֫אמֶר
יַעֲקֹב אֶל־לָבָן, יָד֫וֹעַ יָדַ֫עְתָּ אֶת־עֲבוֹדָתִי אֲשֶׁר עֲבַדְתִּ֫יךָ[c] וָאֶשְׁמֹר
אֶת־צֹאנְךָ כָּל־הַיָּמִים הָאֵ֫לֶּה, וְלָ֫מָּה רָדַ֫פְתָּ אַחֲרָי לֹא גָנַ֫בְתִּי
אֶת־אֱלֹהֶ֫יךָ וְאֵין אִתִּי מִכֹּל אֲשֶׁר לָךְ[e]: וְלֹא יָדַע יַעֲקֹב כִּי גְנָבָ֫תַם
רָחֵל אִשְׁתּוֹ (14) יְדַעְתִּיךָ בְּמִצְרַ֫יִם בַּת־יִשְׂרָאֵל וּבַמִּדְבָּר לֹא
עֲזַבְתִּיךָ[c] (15) אַתָּה הִבְדַּלְתָּם מִכֹּל גּוֹיֵי־הָאָ֫רֶץ וְהֵ֫מָּה לֹא כִבְּדוּךָ

[a] Const. pl. of רָשָׁע.
[b] This verb is used both in Niphal and Hithpael. See previous vocabulary.
[c] Composite shewa under guttural instead of simple shewa vocal.
[d] Pausal.
[e] Pausal for לְךָ.

(16) הִנֵּה הִמְלַכְתִּיךָ עַל־יִשְׂרָאֵל וַאֲשְׁמִיד אֶת־אֹיְבֶיךָ מִפָּנֶיךָ
(17) הִנֵּה אָנֹכִי אִתְּךָ וּשְׁמַרְתִּיךָ בַּדֶּרֶךְ וְעָבַרְתָּ בְשָׁלוֹם בָּאָרֶץ
וְיֵֽרְאוּ מִמְּךָ יֹשְׁבֶיהָ

Use verbal suffixes wherever possible.

(1) Thou hast remembered me, Lord, in the day of my distress and Thou hast not forsaken me in the hands[a] of mine enemies. (2) Those who seek (say 'the seekers of'—const. pl. of participle) my life have pursued me and *Thou* (pronoun) hast scattered them before me like (the) sheep in the wilderness which have no shepherd. (3) This day I have sanctified thee for a priest to the Lord and thou shalt serve in the temple of the Lord, thou and thy sons after thee all the days. (4) Our enemies have destroyed us and they have burned Thy holy city. (5) And Moses prayed unto the Lord, saying, 'Why hast thou sent me unto Pharaoh? For behold the children of Israel are crying unto me, saying, "The Lord will judge thee, for Pharaoh hath hardened his heart against us and our service hath become heavy upon us unto death" (say 'until the death').' (6) The man who ruleth over the land asked us and he said unto us, 'Where is the lad? Why hath he not come down with you to Egypt?' (7) And the Lord said, 'Shall I hide from My servant Abraham the judgement of this wicked city? For I know him and his heart is perfect with Me.' (8) I have sold them in(to) the hand of the king of Canaan, for they have transgressed My covenant and they honoured Me not in the eyes of the nations. (9) Praise thou, my soul, thy God; recount His glory in all the world. (10) Behold I am taking all the prophets who are found in this city and I shall hide them in the mountains, for I know that the king seeketh their life, and I fear the Lord. (11) Why hast thou said, house of Israel, the Lord hath forsaken thee? Hast not *thou* (pronoun) forsaken Him? (12) The messenger spoke unto the prophet and he said unto him, 'The king hath sent me unto thee saying, "Pray thou for us unto the Lord"'; and the prophet said 'I will pray'.

[a] The sg. 'hand' means 'power'.

59. VERBAL SUFFIXES (of the Imperfect)

	QAL: *he will keep* יִשְׁמֹר		*they (m.) will keep* יִשְׁמְרוּ
he will keep me (c.)	יִשְׁמְרֵ֫נִי יִשְׁמְרֵ֫נִּי	they (m.) will keep me (c.)	יִשְׁמְר֫וּנִי
,, thee (m.)	ᵃיִשְׁמָרְךָ יִשְׁמְרֶ֫ךָ	,, thee (m.)	יִשְׁמְרוּךָ
,, thee (f.)	יִשְׁמְרֵךְ	,, thee (f.)	יִשְׁמְרוּךְ
,, him	יִשְׁמְרֵ֫הוּ יִשְׁמְרֶ֫נּוּ	,, him	יִשְׁמְר֫וּהוּ
,, her	יִשְׁמְרֶ֫הָ יִשְׁמְרֶ֫נָּה	,, her	יִשְׁמְר֫וּהָ
,, us (c.)	יִשְׁמְרֵ֫נוּ	,, us (c.)	יִשְׁמְר֫וּנוּ
,, you (m.)	ᵃיִשְׁמָרְכֶם	,, you (m.)	יִשְׁמְרוּכֶם
,, you (f.)	ᵃיִשְׁמָרְכֶן	,, you (f.)	יִשְׁמְרוּכֶן
,, them (m.)	יִשְׁמְרֵם	,, them (m.)	יִשְׁמְרוּם
,, them (f.)	יִשְׁמְרֵן	,, them (f.)	יִשְׁמְרוּן

Similarly תִּשְׁמֹר with suffixes is
תִּשְׁמְרֵ֫נִי, תִּשְׁמָרְךָ ᵃ (תִּשְׁמְרֶ֫ךָ) &c.

אֶשְׁמֹר with suffixes is
אֶשְׁמָרְךָ ᵃ, אֶשְׁמְרֵ֫הוּ &c.

נִשְׁמֹר becomes נִשְׁמָרְךָ ᵃ &c.

Likewise תִּשְׁמְרוּ with suffixes is
תִּשְׁמְרֵ֫נִי, תִּשְׁמְר֫וּהוּ &c.

תִּשְׁמֹ֫רְנָה with suffixes is
the same as 2 m. pl. above.

NOTE: (a) The suffix with the sg. Imperf. has the *e* vowel: יִשְׁמְרֵם, יִשְׁמְרֵ֫נִי (whereas the suffix with the sg. Perf. has *a*: שְׁמָרַ֫נִי, שְׁמָרָם).

(b) The 2nd and the 3rd fem. pl. follow the תִּשְׁמְרוּ type when the suffixes are attached.

(c) Since the change of persons in the Imperfect occurs at the beginning of the word, the suffixed forms remain constant at the end.

ᵃ The vowel under the מ is *o*—Qameṣ-Ḥaṭuph.

(*d*) The alternative forms of the sg. Imperf. with suffixes have (what is called) a NUN Demonstrative or Energic assimilated before the suffix which has, therefore, Dagheš Forte; i.e. יִשְׁמְרֶךָּ for יִשְׁמְרֶנְךָ. This alternative form is more frequent in Pause.

(Note: The unassimilated form is sometimes found in poetry.)

PIEL: *he will seek* יְבַקֵּשׁ	HIPHIL: *he will make king* יַמְלִיךְ
he will seek me (c.) יְבַקְשֵׁנִי [a]	he will make me (c.) king יַמְלִיכֵנִי
„ thee (m.) יְבַקֶּשְׁךָ	„ thee (m.) king יַמְלִיכְךָ
„ him יְבַקְשֵׁהוּ	„ him „ יַמְלִיכֵהוּ
they (m.) will seek me (c.) יְבַקְשׁוּנִי	they (m.) will make me (c.) king יַמְלִיכוּנִי

The rest of the table can be worked out from the preceding page.

THE IMPERATIVE WITH SUFFIXES

	QAL: *keep thou* (*m.*) שְׁמֹר	PIEL: *seek thou* (*m.*) בַּקֵּשׁ	HIPHIL: *make thou* (*m.*) *king* הַמְלֵךְ
Sing.:			
	keep me (c.) שָׁמְרֵנִי	seek me (c.) בַּקְשֵׁנִי [a]	make me (c.) king הַמְלִיכֵנִי
	„ him שָׁמְרֵהוּ	„ him בַּקְשֵׁהוּ	„ him „ הַמְלִיכֵהוּ
Plur.:			
	„ me (c.) שִׁמְרוּנִי	„ me (c.) בַּקְשׁוּנִי	„ me (c.) „ הַמְלִיכוּנִי
	„ him שִׁמְרוּהוּ	„ him בַּקְשׁוּהוּ	„ him „ הַמְלִיכוּהוּ

60. THE INFINITIVE CONSTRUCT (with Suffixes)

my (c.) keeping שָׁמְרִי keeping me (c.) שָׁמְרֵנִי

thy (m.) keeping שָׁמְרְךָ

keeping thee (m.) שָׁמְרְךָ

thy (f.) keeping, keeping thee (f.) שָׁמְרֵךְ

his „ „ him שָׁמְרוֹ

her „ „ her שָׁמְרָהּ

our (c.) „ „ us (c.) שָׁמְרֵנוּ

[a] Often without Dagheš in the vowelless ק. See pp. 17–18.

your (m.) keeping,	keeping	you (m.)	שָׁמָרְכֶם
your (f.)	,,	,,	you (f.)	שָׁמָרְכֶן
their (m.)	,,	,,	them (m.)	שָׁמְרָם
their (f.)	,,	,,	them (f.)	שָׁמְרָן

N.B. The pointing of the Infinitives Construct of the derived forms when attaching suffixes is the same as that of their respective sg masc. Imperatives when *they* attach suffixes.

This table shows that the Infinitive Construct is a kind of verbal noun ending in '-ing'.[a] The suffixes of the Infinitive Construct may denote either the subject or the object, except in the case of the 1st sg. and the 2nd masc. sg. which have special suffixes for the subject and the object (שָׁמְרִי and שָׁמְרֵנִי, &c.).

The following construction is characteristic of Biblical style:

a. 'and it came to pass when he remembered' is rendered as

'and it came to pass as his remembering' וַיְהִי כְּזָכְרוֹ or

,, in ,, וַיְהִי בְּזָכְרוֹ

'and it came to pass when the king remembered' is rendered

,, as the-remembering-of the king[b] וַיְהִי כִּזְכֹּר הַמֶּלֶךְ

b. 'and it shall come to pass when he shall remember' is rendered

,, as his remembering וְהָיָה כְּזָכְרוֹ or

,, in ,, וְהָיָה בְּזָכְרוֹ

'and it shall come to pass when the king shall remember' is

,, as the-remembering-of the king[b]

וְהָיָה כִּזְכֹּר הַמֶּלֶךְ

The Infinitive Construct, with preposition and suffix, may occur together with the Perfect or the Imperfect, as a verbal noun. Before translating an English sentence with a subordinate clause, always convert the sentence into idiomatic Hebrew thought, as above.

[a] e.g. as in the phrase 'seeing is believing'.
[b] i.e. 'the king's remembering'.

NOTE: The Infinitives Construct of the passives and the reflexives may also assume prefixed prepositions and pronominal suffixes, thus:
'and it came to pass when she was burned' is rendered as 'and it came to pass in her being-burned' וַיְהִי בְּהִשָּׂרְפָהּ; 'and it came to pass when the city was burned' is rendered as 'and it came to pass in the being-burned of the city' וַיְהִי בְּהִשָּׂרֵף הָעִיר.

EXERCISE 24

Hebrew עִבְרִי	strong חָזָק	to trust בָּטַח
Egyptian מִצְרִי		to forget שָׁכַח

(1) וַיֹּאמֶר מֹשֶׁה אֶל־הָעִבְרִי לָמָּה תִרְדֹּף[a] אֶת־אָחִיךָ, וַיֹּאמֶר
אֵלָיו הָעִבְרִי מִי שָׂמְךָ לְרֹאשׁ וּלְשֹׁפֵט עָלֵינוּ, הַ[b]אֹמֵר אַתָּה לְהָרְגֵנִי
כַּאֲשֶׁר הָרַגְתָּ אֶת־הַמִּצְרִי: וַיְסַפֵּר הַדָּבָר בְּאָזְנֵי־פַרְעֹה וַיְבַקֵּשׁ
לְהָרְגוֹ: וַיְהִי כִּשְׁמֹעַ מֹשֶׁה אֶת־הַדָּבָר הַזֶּה וַיִּמָּלֵט לְנַפְשׁוֹ
הַמִּדְבָּרָה (2) וַיְהִי יַעֲקֹב זָקֵן מְאֹד וַיְדַבֵּר אֶל־יוֹסֵף בְּנוֹ וַיֹּאמֶר
אֵלָיו, הִנְנִי הֹלֵךְ בְּדֶרֶךְ כָּל־בָּשָׂר: אַל־נָא תִקְבְּרֵנִי בְּמִצְרָיִם
(3) וְהָיָה כִּי יִשְׁאָלְךָ בִנְךָ לֵאמֹר מָה־הָעֲבוֹדָה הַזֹּאת, וְאָמַרְתָּ
אֵלָיו, בַּיּוֹם הַזֶּה יָצְאוּ אֲבוֹתֵינוּ מִמִּצְרַיִם מִבֵּית־עֲבָדִים (4) וַיְהִי
בְּעָזְבָם אֶת־הָעִיר וַתִּגְנֹב רָחֵל אֶת־אֱלֹהֵי־אָבִיהָ וַיִּרְדֹּף לָבָן
אַחֲרֵיהֶם וַיְבַקֵּשׁ אֶת־אֱלֹהָיו וְלֹא מְצָאָם (5) וַיֹּאמֶר שָׁאוּל אֶל־
שְׁמוּאֵל, כַּבְּדֵנִי־נָא נֶגֶד זִקְנֵי־עַמִּי, וַיֹּאמֶר שְׁמוּאֵל אָנֹכִי אֲכַבֶּדְךָ
כִּי רֹאשׁ־יִשְׂרָאֵל אָתָּה (6) זָכְרֵנִי אֱלֹהַי כִּי בְךָ בָטַחְתִּי, אַל־נָא
תִשְׁכָּחֵנִי כִּי יְשׁוּעָתִי אָתָּה (7) לֹא שָׁמְעוּ בְנֵי־יִשְׂרָאֵל אֶל־מֹשֶׁה
בְּדַבְּרוֹ אֲלֵיהֶם, כִּי הִכְבִּיד עֲלֵיהֶם פַּרְעֹה אֶת־הָעֲבוֹדָה (8) דַּבֵּר
אֲלֵיהֶם בִּשְׁמִי וְאָמַרְתָּ, כֹּה אָמַר יהוה, לֹא שְׁכַחְתִּים וְלֹא
עֲזַבְתִּים: וּבְהִתְפַּלְלָם אֵלַי בְּרוּחַ נִשְׁבָּרָה אָנֹכִי אֶזְכְּרֵם וּמֵאֶרֶץ

[a] The Imperf., in this context, has a frequentative effect—'why dost thou pursue?' i.e. 'why dost thou keep on pursuing?'
[b] Hē interrogative.

אֹיְבֵיהֶם אֲקַבְּצֵם אֵלָי (9) שָׁמַע הַמֶּלֶךְ אֶת־דִּבְרֵי־הַנָּבִיא וַיִּכְתְּבֵם
בַּסֵּפֶר לְמַעַן לֹא יִשְׁכְּחוּ דְּבָרָיו (10) הַלְלוּ אֶת־יהוה כָּל־גּוֹיִם,
שַׁבְּחוּהוּ כָּל־יֹשְׁבֵי־הָאָרֶץ (11) וַיִּצְעֲקוּ בְנֵי־יִשְׂרָאֵל וַיֹּאמְרוּ טוֹב
הָיָה לָנוּ בְּאֶרֶץ מִצְרַיִם בְּאָכְלֵנוּ לֶחֶם וּבָשָׂר (12) וַיִּלְכְּדוּ אֶת־
הָעִיר וַיִּשְׂרְפוּהָ בָּאֵשׁ וַיִּמְכְּרוּ אֶת־יֹשְׁבֶיהָ לַעֲבָדִים (13) הֲלֹא
שָׁמַעְתָּ אֶת־דִּבְרֵי־הָרָשָׁע בְּאָמְרוֹ כָּל־הַיּוֹם אֵין אֱלֹהִים
(14) וַיִּלָּחֶם דָּוִד בְּאֹיְבָיו וַיְפַזְּרֵם וַיִּרְדְּפֵם הַמִּדְבָּרָה וְלֹא נִמְלַט
אֶחָד מֵהֶם (15) אֶת־הַצֶּדֶק וְאֶת־הָאֱמֶת תִּרְדֹּף, בַּקְּשֵׁם בְּכָל־
לְבָבֶךָ (16) יְבַקְשׁוּנִי וְלֹא יִמְצָאוּנִי כִּי אֵין בְּלִבָּם יִרְאַת־יהוה

Wherever possible attach the verbal suffixes.

(1) Trust ye in the Lord with all your heart and serve ye Him in truth. (2) And it came to pass as he heard (inf. cons. and suff.) the words of the messenger that he cried (waw consec.) in a loud voice, 'Woe to us for we have been sold into the hand of our enemies'; and he prayed unto the Lord and he said, 'Lord, God of our fathers, remember us in the day of our distress.' (3) And it came to pass when they crossed (inf. constr.) the Jordan that they fought (waw consec.) against the city and they captured it. (4) And Solomon was a lad when his father David caused him to reign over Israel. (5) We have not forgotten Thee, Lord, and the words of Thy law are written upon the tablets of our heart. (6) Saul took his men with him and he pursued (after) them all the night and he found them not; and it came to pass in the morning and behold they (were) lying upon the ground in the midst of the trees. (7) This is the prayer which David prayed when he escaped (inf. const. and suff.) from the hand of Saul, 'Thou art righteous, Lord, for Thou hast kept me from the hand of those who seek ('seekers-of' const. pl. part.) my life and from the hand of the wicked king who sayeth all the day, "Let us pursue him until (the) death".' (8) Speak thou unto the king and thou shalt say unto him, 'Why hath thy heart lifted thee up and thou hast spoken these words against the Lord? Hast thou

indeed forgotten the commandment which thy father commanded thee before his death, saying: "Honour the Lord all the days of thy life"?' (9) The priest took the small son of the king and he hid him in the temple of the Lord, for they told (to) him saying: 'Behold the king is dead and they are seeking all the sons of his house to slay them.' (10) The sons of Jacob saw Joseph and they knew him not, for he was a lad when they sold him to Egypt. (11) I asked her saying: 'The daughter of whom art thou?' and it came to pass when I heard that she (was) thy daughter then (waw consec.) I spoke unto her these words.

61. THE RELATIVE PRONOUN

The Relative Pronoun is the indeclinable אֲשֶׁר ('who, which', &c.). Note in the following examples how the English relatives 'where', 'whither', &c. are expressed in Hebrew:

WHERE: 'The place where he dwelt' is expressed as
'The place *which* he dwelt *there*' הַמָּקוֹם אֲשֶׁר יָשַׁב שָׁם

WHENCE: 'The place whence he came' is expressed as
'The place *which* he came *thence*' הַמָּקוֹם אֲשֶׁר בָּא מִשָּׁם

WHITHER: 'The place whither he went' is expressed as
'The place *which* he went *thither*' הַמָּקוֹם אֲשֶׁר הָלַךְ שָׁמָּה

WHOSE: 'The man whose book I took' is expressed as
'The man *who* I took *his book*' הָאִישׁ אֲשֶׁר לָקַחְתִּי אֶת־סִפְרוֹ

TO WHOM: 'The man to whom I gave a book' is expressed as
'The man *who* I gave *to him* a book' הָאִישׁ אֲשֶׁר נָתַתִּי[a] לוֹ סֵפֶר

FROM WHOM: 'The man from whom I took a book' is expressed as
'The man *who* I took *from him* a book' הָאִישׁ אֲשֶׁר לָקַחְתִּי מִמֶּנּוּ סֵפֶר

LIKE WHOM: 'The man like whom he was' is expressed as
'The man *who* he was *like him*' הָאִישׁ אֲשֶׁר הָיָה כָּמוֹהוּ

The above English relatives should be resolved into their component elements before translating into Hebrew and, conversely, the Hebrew relative pronoun with the following element should be compounded into the corresponding English relative.

[a] Contracted from נָתַנְתִּי: pp. 148 ff.

62. DEGREES OF COMPARISON

Hebrew has no special forms for the Degrees of Comparison, but they are expressed thus:

'David is greater than Saul' דָּוִד גָּדוֹל מִשָּׁאוּל i.e. David is great from (in comparison with) Saul.

'David is the greatest of his brothers' is (*a*) דָּוִד הַגָּדוֹל מֵאֶחָיו or בְּאֶחָיו

or (*b*) דָּוִד גְּדוֹל־אֶחָיו

i.e. David is (*a*) *the* great (one) *from* or *among* his brothers, or

(*b*) *the* great-one-of his brothers.

The Comparative Degree is expressed by a מִן *of Comparison* following the adjective; i.e. attached to the word with which the noun is compared.[a]

The Superlative Degree is expressed in two ways:

(*a*) the adjective has the article and is followed by מִן or בְּ attached to the word with which the noun is compared, or

(*b*) the adjective is put in the construct state and is dependent upon the word with which the noun is compared.

63. SHORTAGE OF ADJECTIVES

Hebrew has a very limited number of adjectives, but the effect of limiting the application of a noun may be obtained by putting it in the construct state, when the following genitive limits the application of the noun in the same way as would a following adjective; e.g.

'a godly man' is אִישׁ־אֱלֹהִים i.e. a man-of God.

'a holy mountain' ,, הַר־קֹדֶשׁ i.e. a mountain-of holiness.

'golden vessels' ,, כְּלֵי־זָהָב i.e. vessels-of gold.

'the holy mountain'[a] ,, הַר־הַקֹּדֶשׁ
'my holy mountain'[b] ,, הַר־קָדְשִׁי
} since the construct cannot take the article or suffix; it is the genitive which is made definite by the article or suffix.

'an eloquent man' אִישׁ־דְּבָרִים is expressed by circumlocution: man-of words.

[a] מִן implies 'separation', 'distinction', and so seems to have suggested 'comparison'.

[a] .e. '*the* mountain of holiness'.

[b] i.e. '*my* mountain of holiness'. See Appendix 5, p. 253.

64. CHANGES IN POINTING DUE TO PAUSE

(*a*) It was shown on p. 21 that when a word is *in pause* the vowel in the tone-syllable is lengthened, as שָׁמַר becomes שָׁמָֽר׃, שָׁמָ֑ר in pause.

Other changes in pointing due to pause are:

(*b*) In a Milraʿ word the accent is often pushed back to the penultimate syllable whose vowel, if short, is lengthened; e.g. אַתָּה ('thou') becomes אָֽתָּה׃, אָ֑תָּה in pause.

(*c*) A vocal shewa becomes the nearest short vowel, i.e. Seghol, and the accent is thrown back on to it; e.g. פְּרִי ('fruit') becomes פֶּֽרִי׃, פֶּ֑רִי; יָדְךָ ('thy hand') becomes יָדֶֽךָ׃, יָדֶ֑ךָ; שִׁמְךָ ('thy name') comes from (a hypothetical) שְׁמְךָ which in pause is שְׁמֶֽךָ׃, שְׁמֶ֑ךָ.

(*d*) A composite shewa becomes the corresponding short vowel, is then lengthened and the accent is pushed back on to it: e.g. אֲנִי ('I') becomes אָֽנִי׃, אָ֑נִי in pause.

(*e*) Some Segholate nouns of the מֶ֫לֶךְ type revert to the original form in pause, as חֶ֫רֶב ('sword') originally חַרְבּ and then חַ֫רֶב becomes חָֽרֶב׃, חָ֑רֶב in pause.

(*f*) With regard to the verb, the vowel of the second syllable (e.g. in שָׁמַר; יִשְׁמֹר, תִּשְׁמֹר) which is lost when the accent moves forward on to an additional syllable (שָֽׁמְרָה, שָֽׁמְרוּ; יִשְׁמְרוּ, תִּשְׁמְרוּ) reappears in pause, is lengthened if short, and the accent moves back on to it, as:

שָֽׁמְרָה but שָׁמָֽרָה׃, שָׁמָ֑רָה; שָֽׁמְרוּ but שָׁמָֽרוּ׃, שָׁמָ֑רוּ;
יִשְׁמְרוּ but יִשְׁמֹֽרוּ׃, יִשְׁמֹ֑רוּ; תִּשְׁמְרוּ but תִּשְׁמֹֽרוּ׃, תִּשְׁמֹ֑רוּ.[a]

EXERCISE 25

silver כֶּ֫סֶף	to sin חָטָא
cattle, herd בָּקָר	to fall נָפַל
now עַתָּה	only רַק

(1) וַיֹּ֫אמֶר מֹשֶׁה אֶל־יְהוֹשֻׁעַ, כִּי יִהְיוּ בְנֵי־יִשְׂרָאֵל בָּאָ֫רֶץ אֲשֶׁר

[a] The sign ׀ here is Silluq.

הֵ֫מָּה בָאִים שָׁ֫מָּה וְרָאוּ אֶת־הֶעָרִים הַגְּדוֹלוֹת וְהַחֲזָקוֹת בְּרָאשֵׁי
הֶהָרִים וְיֵֽרְאוּ מִפְּנֵי־יֹשְׁבֵיהֶן, וְדִבַּרְתָּ אֲלֵיהֶם לֵאמֹר בִּטְחוּ בַיהוה
אֱלֹהֵיכֶם, כִּי מַלְאָכוֹ יִלָּחֵם לָנוּ (2) אַתָּה הוּא אֱלֹהֵי־צִדְקִי[a]
הַשְׁמִ֫עַ אֶל־תְּפִלָּתִי בְּקָרְאִי אֵלֶיךָ (3) שֹׁפְטֵי־צֶ֫דֶק[b] יִהְיוּ לָכֶם
בָּאָ֫רֶץ אֲשֶׁר אַתֶּם בָּאִים שָׁ֫מָּה, כִּי צַדִּיק אָנִי (4) שָׁפְטֵם אֱלֹהַי כִּי
אַנְשֵׁי־דָמִים הֵמָּה וַיְבַקְשׁוּ אֶת־נַפְשִׁי (5) וַיְהִי אַחֲרֵי הַדְּבָרִים
הָאֵ֫לֶּה וַיֹּ֫אמֶר פַּרְעֹה אֶל־יוֹסֵף, עַתָּה יָדַ֫עְתִּי כִּי אִישׁ חָכָם אַתָּה
אֲשֶׁר אֵין כָּמֹ֫וךָ בְּכָל־הָאָ֫רֶץ: וְהִנֵּה כָּל־אַרְצִי בְּיָדֶךָ הִיא וְרַק
בְּדְבַר־הַכִּסֵּא אֶגְדַּל מִמֶּ֫ךָּ (6) שָׁלַח יַעֲקֹב מַלְאָכִים לְפָנָיו אֶל־
עֵשָׂו אָחִיו לֵאמֹר עִם־לָבָן אֲחִי־אִמֹּ֫נוּ יָשַׁבְתִּי עַד־עָ֫תָּה: וַיְהִי־לִי
צֹאן וּבָקָר וְכֶ֫סֶף וְזָהָב וַעֲבָדִים, וְהִנְנִי הֹלֵךְ אַ֫רְצָה כְּנָ֫עַן
(7) מְבַקְשֵׁי־יהוה אָכְלוּ לֶ֫חֶם וְעֹזְבֵי־דְרָכָיו לְעוֹלָם יִרְעָ֫בוּ:
(8) דִּבְרֵי־חָכְמָה טוֹבִים מִכָּ֫סֶף, וְיִרְאַת־אֱלֹהִים מִזָּהָב (9) וַיֹּ֫אמֶר
דָּוִד אֶל־שְׁמוּאֵל, הֲטוֹב אָנֹכִי מֵאַחַי כִּי בָחַ֫רְתָּ בִּי, וּבֵית־אָבִי
הוּא הַקָּטֹן בְּיִשְׂרָאֵל (10) נָפַל יְהוֹשֻׁ֫עַ עַל־פָּנָיו אַ֫רְצָה וַיִּתְפַּלֵּל
אֶל־יהוה לֵאמֹר לָ֫מָּה עֲזַבְתָּ֫נוּ יהוה כִּי נָפְלוּ בָנֶ֫יךָ לִפְנֵי אֹיְבֵיהֶם,
וְאַתָּה אָמַ֫רְתָּ אֵלַי הִנְנִי בְתוֹכְכֶם וְאָנֹכִי אֶלָּחֵם לָכֶם: וַיֹּ֫אמֶר אֵלָיו
יהוה לָ֫מָּה אַתָּה נֹפֵל עַל־פָּנֶ֫יךָ, חָטָא יִשְׂרָאֵל כִּי לָקְחוּ מִן־הַזָּהָב
וּמִן־הַכֶּ֫סֶף וַיַּסְתִּ֫ירוּ לָהֶם: וְעַתָּה יִמָּ֫צְאוּ[c] הָאֲנָשִׁים אֲשֶׁר עָבְרוּ
אֶת־מִצְוֺתִי וְשָׁפַטְתָּ֫ אֹתָם לְעֵינֵי כָל־עֲדַת־יִשְׂרָאֵל (11) יָרַד
אֱלֹהִים עַל הַר־קָדְשׁוֹ[a] וַיְדַבֵּר אֶל־עַמּוֹ כְּדַבֵּר אָב אֶל־בָּנָיו
(12) אֱלֹהִים יֹשֵׁב עַל כִּסֵּא־קָדְשׁוֹ[a] וּמַלְאֲכֵי־אֵשׁ עֹמְדִים לְפָנָיו
בְּיִרְאָה (13) בָּ֫אוּ יַעֲקֹב וּבֵיתוֹ אֶל־הַמָּקוֹם אֲשֶׁר נִלְחַם אִתּוֹ
מַלְאַךְ־אֱלֹהִים שָׁם וַיִּשְׁכְּבוּ שָׁם בַּלַּ֫יְלָה הַהוּא (14) שָׁלַח אֱלֹהִים
חֹ֫שֶׁךְ גָּדוֹל בְּאֶ֫רֶץ מִצְרַ֫יִם אֲשֶׁר לְפָנָיו לֹא הָיָה כָּמֹ֫הוּ, וּבַמָּקוֹם

[a] See pp. 84 (*c*) and 136. **63**, footnote *b*.
[b] i.e. 'righteous judges'.
[c] Jussive force, 'let them be found'.

אֲשֶׁר יָֽשְׁבוּ בוֹ בְּנֵי־יִשְׂרָאֵל הָיָה אוֹר (15) טוֹב מוֹתִי מֵחַיַּי כִּי
עֲזַבְתָּ֫נִי בְּיוֹם־צָרָה (16) בָּרָא אֱלֹהִים עֵץ־פְּרִי אֲשֶׁר זַרְעוֹ בוֹ

(1) The children came to the place whence ('which—from there') they crossed the sea when Pharaoh pursued (after) them. (2) In the heavens and in the earth there is none greater than Thee. (3) And Joshua spoke unto the people and he said unto them, 'This is the city against which ("which—against her") we shall fight and the Lord will give it into our hand; and now, let the men who are afraid of the battle separate themselves from the midst of the people until we have captured (inf. const. and suff.) the city.' (4) The spies saw the house where they had slept (in) that night and they remembered the woman who sold them not into the hand of the elders of her city. (5) Thy children have sinned to Thee and Thy holy words ('thy words of holiness') they have forgotten. (6) And now, hearken ye to my voice, according to ('as') all which I speak unto you; forget ye not. (7) The Lord will remember us, for the sake of His holy name,[a] if not for our sake. (8) Why wilt thou pursue me? Am I better than a dead man in thine eyes? (9) Thou art my God of salvation in whom I trust ('who, I trust in Thee') and unto Thee I call. (10) It is good for the people whose God is the Lord and woe to the nations who know Him not. (11) It is better to trust in the Lord than to trust in the sons of man. (12) Abraham went forth from the land of Egypt and he had sheep and cattle and servants.

65. THE WEAK VERB

A verb is said to be weak when it deviates from the regular or normal type, due to (*a*) a guttural letter, (*b*) a quiescent letter, or (*c*) a letter, such as נ, which is liable to assimilate, being among the root-letters; for in each case adjustments have to be made. For example:

(*a*) The verb עָזַב ('to leave') is weak, since the first root-letter is a guttural. In the normal verb (שָׁמַר) the Niphal Imperfect (יִשָּׁמֵר) has Dagheš Forte compensative in the first root-letter

[a] 'His name of holiness'.

(since the נ of the Niphal (יִנְשָׁמֵר) is assimilated); but the Niphal of the verb עָזַב cannot be יִעָּזֵב since the guttural cannot receive a Dagheš, and so the preceding vowel is lengthened in compensation, producing יֵעָזֵב.

(*b*) The verb יָטַב ('to be good') is weak, since its first root-letter is a quiescent. In the normal verb שָׁכַב (Stative in meaning: 'to lie') the Imperfect Qal is יִשְׁכַּב, but the Imperfect Qal of יָטַב is first יִיְטַב and the vowelless י quiesces producing יִיטַב (see p. 18. 2).

(*c*) The verb נָפַל ('to fall') is weak, since the first root-letter is נ which, when vowelless between two consonants, is usually assimilated. The Imperfect Qal of the normal שָׁמַר is יִשְׁמֹר, but of נָפַל the Imperfect Qal is first יִנְפֹּל and then the medial נ is assimilated producing יִפֹּל.

In each of the above examples, the peculiarity of one of the root-letters forces the verb to deviate from the normal type. By simply applying the rules which govern these peculiar letters, the variant forms can be worked out, as indicated above.

66. CLASSIFICATION OF WEAK VERBS

In order to classify conveniently the different types of weak verbs, the letters of the word פָּעַל ('to do, perform'[a]) are employed, thus: the first root-letter of *any* verb is known as its פ Pē, the second root-letter as its ע 'Ayin, and the third root-letter as its ל Lāmeḏ. The weak verbs are therefore described thus:

The verb עָזַב ('to leave') is a Pe Guttural verb.
,, ,, בָּחַר ('to choose') is an 'Ayin Guttural verb.
,, ,, שָׁמַע ('to hear') is a Lameḏ Guttural verb.
,, ,, נָפַל ('to fall') ,, Pe Nun verb.
,, ,, נָגַע ('to touch') ,, Pe Nun and Lameḏ Guttural verb; it is doubly weak.

[a] See p. 100, Note (*a*), for analogy.

67. PE NUN VERBS

QAL

Perf.:	he hath fallen	נָפַל	Not used in Perf. Qal but is displaced by Niphal	(נִגַּשׁ)
	she ,,	נָֽפְלָה		
	thou (m.) hast ,,	נָפַ֫לְתָּ &c.		
Imperf.:	he will fall	יִפֹּל	he will draw near	יִגַּשׁ
	she ,,	תִּפֹּל	she ,,	תִּגַּשׁ
	thou (m.) wilt ,,	תִּפֹּל	thou (m.) wilt ,,	תִּגַּשׁ
	thou (f.) ,,	תִּפְּלִי	thou (f.) ,,	תִּגְּשִׁי
	I (c.) shall ,,	אֶפֹּל	I (c.) shall ,,	אֶגַּשׁ
	they (m.) will ,,	יִפְּלוּ	they (m.) will ,,	יִגְּשׁוּ
	they (f.) ,,	תִּפֹּ֫לְנָה	they (f.) ,,	תִּגַּ֫שְׁנָה
	ye (m.) ,,	תִּפְּלוּ	ye (m.) ,,	תִּגְּשׁוּ
	ye (f.) ,,	תִּפֹּ֫לְנָה	ye (f.) ,,	תִּגַּ֫שְׁנָה
	we (c.) shall ,,	נִפֹּל	we (c.) shall ,,	נִגַּשׁ
Cohort.:	let me (c.) fall	אֶפְּלָה	let me (c.) draw near	אֶגְּשָׁה
	,, us (c.) ,,	נִפְּלָה	,, us (c.) ,,	נִגְּשָׁה
Imper.:	fall thou (m.)	נְפֹל	draw thou (m.) near	גַּשׁ [a] (emph. גְּשָׁה [a])
	,, (f.)	נִפְלִי	,, (f.) ,,	גְּשִׁי
	,, ye (m.)	נִפְלוּ	,, ye (m.) ,,	גְּשׁוּ
	,, (f.)	נְפֹ֫לְנָה	,, (f.) ,,	גַּ֫שְׁנָה
Part.:	falling (m. sg.)	נֹפֵל	[drawing near (m. sg.)	נֹגֵשׁ]
	,, (f. sg.)	נֹפֶ֫לֶת &c.	*not used*	
Inf. Abs.		נָפוֹל		נָגוֹשׁ
Const.		נְפֹל		גֶּ֫שֶׁת [a]
,,	with ל	לִנְפֹּל		לָגֶ֫שֶׁת
,,	with suffix	נָפְלִי		גִּשְׁתִּי

[a] The Dagheš in the גּ is Lene.

In the נָפַל type only the Imperfect is weak, since the vowelless נ between the two consonants is assimilated and the following letter has a Dagheš Forte (יִפֹּל for יִנְפֹּל).

The other type נָגַשׁ has several additional peculiarities:

In the *Imperfect* the vowel in the second syllable is *a* (cf. p. 97, Note).

In the *Imperative* the נ, though initial, has disappeared.

In the *Infinitive Construct* the נ has also disappeared but the feminine termination ת is assumed, making it a Segholate noun (pp. 82 f.). When the preposition ל is prefixed it is pointed with Qameṣ, since it comes immediately before the tone-syllable (p. 30. 7). *Note carefully* the form of the Infinitive Construct with the suffixes—גִּשְׁתִּי, &c. (p. 84. (*c*)).

Niphal (of the Pe Nun Verb)

The Perfect and Participle Qal of נָגַשׁ are not used, but are replaced by these parts in the Niphal (most likely in a kind of reflexive meaning), while the other parts of the Niphal are not used. Therefore to give a complete table of the Niphal we may introduce the verb נצל which is used in the Niphal to mean 'to be delivered', 'to escape'.

Perf.:	he hath drawn near	נִגַּשׁ	he was delivered	נִצַּל
	she ,,	נִגְּשָׁה	she ,,	נִצְּלָה
	thou (m.) hast ,,	נִגַּשְׁתָּ	thou (m.) wast ,,	נִצַּלְתָּ
		&c.		&c.
Imperf.:	not used	[יִנָּגֵשׁ]	he will be delivered	יִנָּצֵל
			she ,,	תִּנָּצֵל
				&c.
Imper.:	not used	[הִנָּגֵשׁ]	be thou (m.) delivered, escape	הִנָּצֵל
			,, (f.) ,,	הִנָּצְלִי
				&c.
Part.:	drawing near (m. sg.)	נִגָּשׁ	being delivered (m. sg.)	נִצָּל
	,, (f. sg.)	נִגָּשָׁה	,, (f. sg.)	נִצָּלָה
		&c.		&c.
Inf.:	not used	[הִנָּגֵשׁ]		הִנָּצֵל

In the Perfect נִגַּשׁ (for נִנְגַּשׁ) and the Participle נִגָּשׁ (for נִנְגָּשׁ) the Pe Nun shows assimilation. The rest of the Niphal is regular, since it is only the prefixed נ of Niphal which is assimilated (יִנָּצֵל for יִנְנָצֵל, &c.).

Hiphil (of the Pe Nun Verb)

The Hiphil of נָגַשׁ 'to cause to draw near', 'to bring near' is הִגִּישׁ for הִנְגִּישׁ, and the Imperfect is יַגִּישׁ for יַנְגִּישׁ, as below. The Hiphil of נָפַל 'to cause to fall', 'to cast' is הִפִּיל for הִנְפִּיל and the Imperfect is יַפִּיל for יַנְפִּיל, as below.

Perf.:	he (hath) brought near	הִגִּישׁ	he (hath) cast	הִפִּיל
	she ,,	הִגִּ֫ישָׁה	she ,,	הִפִּ֫ילָה
	thou (m.) hast ,,	הִגַּ֫שְׁתָּ	thou (m.) hast ,,	הִפַּ֫לְתָּ
	they (c.) have ,,	הִגִּ֫ישׁוּ	they (c.) have ,,	הִפִּ֫ילוּ
		&c.		&c.
Imperf.:	he will bring near	יַגִּישׁ	he will cast	יַפִּיל
	she ,,	תַּגִּישׁ	she ,,	תַּפִּיל
	thou (m.) wilt ,,	תַּגִּישׁ	thou (m.) wilt ,,	תַּפִּיל
	thou (f.) ,,	תַּגִּ֫ישִׁי	thou (f.) ,,	תַּפִּ֫ילִי
	I (c.) shall ,,	אַגִּישׁ	I (c.) shall ,,	אַפִּיל
		&c.		&c.
Cohort.:	let me (c.) ,,	אַגִּ֫ישָׁה	let me (c.) ,,	אַפִּ֫ילָה
Shortened Imperf. Jussive	let him bring near	יַגֵּשׁ	let him ,,	יַפֵּל
Imperf. with Waw Consecutive	and he brought near	וַיַּגֵּשׁ	and he ,,	וַיַּפֵּל
Imper.:	bring thou (m.) near	הַגֵּשׁ (emph. הַגִּ֫ישָׁה)	cast thou (m.)	הַפֵּל (emph. הַפִּ֫ילָה)
	,, (f.) ,,	הַגִּ֫ישִׁי	,, (f.)	הַפִּ֫ילִי
		&c.		&c.
Part.:	bringing near (m. sg.)	מַגִּישׁ	casting (m. sg.)	מַפִּיל
	,, (f. sg.)	מַגִּישָׁה	,, (f. sg.)	מַפִּילָה
		&c.		&c.
Inf. absolute:		הַגֵּשׁ		הַפֵּל
construct:		הַגִּישׁ		הַפִּיל

In every part of the Pe Nun Hiphil the נ is assimilated.

Hophal (of the Pe Nun Verb)

The Hophal Perfect of נָגַשׁ is הֻגַּשׁ (instead of הָגַּשׁ reduced from הָנְגַּשׁ); the Qibbuṣ (*u*) and Qameṣ-Ḥaṭuph (*o*) belong to the same class of vowels and often alternate, as for example the Segholate noun גֹּדֶל ('greatness') is with suffixes גָּדְלְךָ and גֻּדְלוֹ, &c. A usual feature of inflection is that *o* becomes *u* when followed by a doubled letter, e.g. כֹּל 'all', but כֻּלּוֹ 'all of him'; חֹק 'statute', but חֻקּוֹ 'his statute'. Similarly here. The Imperfect Hophal is יֻגַּשׁ (*and not* יָגַּשׁ):

Perf.:	he was brought near	הֻגַּשׁ	he was cast	הֻפַּל
	she ,,	הֻגְּשָׁה	she ,,	הֻפְּלָה
	thou (m.) wast ,,	הֻגַּשְׁתָּ	thou (m.) wast ,,	הֻפַּלְתָּ
		&c.		&c.
Imperf.:	he will be brought near	יֻגַּשׁ	he will be cast	יֻפַּל
	she ,,	תֻּגַּשׁ	she ,,	תֻּפַּל
		&c.		&c.

There is no Imperative (p. 115).

Part.:	being brought near (m. sg.)	מֻגָּשׁ	being cast (m. sg.)	מֻפָּל
	,, (f. sg.)	מֻגָּשָׁה	,, (f. sg.)	מֻפָּלָה
		&c.		&c.
Inf. absolute:		הֻגַּשׁ		הֻפַּל
construct:		הֻגַּשׁ		הֻפַּל

Note: (*a*) There are some verbs whose initial נ is not assimilated. This is generally the case when the second root-letter is a guttural אהחע; e.g. the Imperfect Qal of נָחַל ('to inherit') is יִנְחַל,[a] the Hiphil Perfect is הִנְחִיל ('to cause to inherit') and the Imperfect Hiphil is יַנְחִיל. Similarly the Imperfect Qal of נָהַג ('to lead') is יִנְהַג[a] and the Hiphil form Perfect is הִנְהִיג. The נ before the guttural is not assimilated, so that this type of verb is in this respect really regular, and does not come under the category of Pe Nun.

[a] The Pathaḥ is due to the guttural (see p. 166).

(*b*) From some Pe Nun roots nouns are derived; e.g. מַשָּׂא ('burden') from נָשָׂא ('to lift up, bear'), מַטָּע ('plant') from נָטַע ('to plant'), מַתָּנָה ('gift') from נָתַן ('to give'), מַסָּע ('journey') from נָסַע ('to journey').

EXERCISE 26

sword (f.)	חֶ֫רֶב	to smite, plague	נָגַף, imperf. יִגֹּף
plague	מַגֵּפָה	to tell, declare נגד in Hiphil	הִגִּיד
lord, master	אָדוֹן	to save, deliver נצל in Hiphil	הִצִּיל
warrior, hero, mighty man	גִּבּוֹר	to be delivered נצל in Niphal	נִצַּל
		much, great	רַב
		many (pl.)	רַבִּים

(1) לָקַח שָׁאוּל אֶת־חַרְבּוֹ וַיִּפֹּל עָלֶ֫יהָ וַיֹּ֫אמֶר אֶל־נַעֲרוֹ אַל־
אֶפְּלָה בְּיַד־אֹיְבָי (2) הִפִּיל יהוה עַל־יֹשְׁבֵי־הָעִיר אַבְנֵי־אֵשׁ
מִשָּׁמַ֫יִם וַיַּשְׁמֵד אֹתָם מֵעַל פְּנֵי־הָאֲדָמָה (3) שָׁלַח יהוה מַגֵּפָה
בְּיִשְׂרָאֵל וַיִּגֹּף בָּעָם כָּל־הַיּוֹם הַהוּא וַיִּפְּלוּ מֵהֶם רַבִּים, כִּי לֹא
בָטְחוּ בוֹ וַיֹּאמְרוּ טוֹב הָיָה לָ֫נוּ בְּמִצְרַ֫יִם וְעַתָּה נִפֹּל בַּחֶ֫רֶב
לִפְנֵי־מַלְכֵי־כְנָ֫עַן (4) לֹא הִגִּידָה הַמַּלְכָּה כִּי עִבְרִיָּה הִיא[a] וְכִי
יָצָא דְבַר־הַמֶּ֫לֶךְ לְהַשְׁמִיד אֹתָהּ וְאֶת־בֵּית־אָבִ֫יהָ וְאֶת־עַמָּהּ
(5) וַיֹּ֫אמֶר הַמֶּ֫לֶךְ אֶל־יִצְחָק, לֹא יָדַ֫עְתִּי מִי עָשָׂה אֶת־הַדָּבָר
הָרָע הַזֶּה וְאַתָּה לֹא הִגַּ֫דְתָּ לִי וְאָנֹכִי לֹא שָׁמַ֫עְתִּי (6) קָרָא פַרְעֹה
אֶל־יוֹסֵף וַיֹּ֫אמֶר אֵלָיו, הַגֵּד הֻגַּד לִי כִּי אִישׁ חָכָם אַתָּה יֹדֵעַ
חֲלוֹמוֹת, וְעַתָּה הַגֶּד[b]־לִי אֶת־הַחֲלוֹם אֲשֶׁר חָלַ֫מְתִּי (7) וַתִּכְבַּ֫דְנָה
עֵינֵי־יִצְחָק וַיֹּ֫אמֶר אֶל־יַעֲקֹב הָעֹמֵד לְפָנָיו, גֹּשָׁה[c] אֵלַי וְיָדַ֫עְתִּי
הַאַתָּה בְּנִי עֵשָׂו אִם־לֹא (8) וַיִּגַּשׁ יְהוּדָה אֶל־יוֹסֵף וַיֹּ֫אמֶר אֵלָיו,
יְדַבֶּר[b]־נָא עַבְדְּךָ דָבָר בְּאָזְנֵי־אֲדֹנִי: הִנֵּה אָבִ֫ינוּ זָקֵן מְאֹד, וְהָיָה

[a] Understand 'was', as required by the English.

[b] With the Maqqeph following, the word is deprived of its accent and, being a closed syllable, its vowel is shortened.

[c] Emphatic imperative.

אִם לֹא יִהְיֶה הַנַּעַר אִתָּנוּ וָמֵת[a]׃ וְעַתָּה אִם טוֹב בְּעֵינֶיךָ אָנֹכִי
אֶהְיֶה עֶבֶד לַאֲדֹנִי תַּחַת אָחִי וְהָלַךְ הוּא הַבַּיְתָה אֶל־אָבִיו׃ וַיְהִי
כִּשְׁמֹעַ יוֹסֵף אֶת־דְּבָרָיו וַיֹּאמֶר אֲלֵיהֶם גְּשׁוּ־נָא אֵלַי וַיִּגְּשׁוּ אֵלָיו׃
וַיְדַבֵּר אֲלֵיהֶם לֵאמֹר אֲנִי יוֹסֵף אֲשֶׁר מְכַרְתֶּם אֹתִי מִצְרָיְמָה
(9) צָעַק מֹשֶׁה אֶל־יהוה לֵאמֹר לָמָּה שְׁלַחְתַּנִי אֶל־פַּרְעֹה כִּי
הִכְבִּיד עֲלֵיהֶם אֶת־הָעֲבוֹדָה וְהַצֵּל לֹא הִצַּלְתָּ אֶת־עַמֶּךָ (10) כֹּה
אָמַר יהוה, אַל־תְּבַקֵּשׁ אֶת־יְשׁוּעַת־מִצְרַיִם כִּי נָפוֹל תִּפֹּל
מִצְרַיִם בֶּחָרֶב[b] (11) וַיֻּגַּד לְדָוִד לֵאמֹר הִנֵּה גִּבּוֹרֵי שָׁאוּל בָּאִים
לְהָרְגֶךָ וַיִּמָּלֵט דָּוִד בַּלַּיְלָה הַהוּא וַיִּנָּצֵל מִיָּדָם׃ וַיְהַלֵּל אֶת־שֵׁם־
יהוה וַיֹּאמַר אֵלֶיךָ יהוה הִתְפַּלַּלְתִּי וּמִכָּל־צָרוֹתַי הִצַּלְתָּנִי
(12) יָרְאוּ בְּנֵי־יִשְׂרָאֵל מִגֶּשֶׁת אֶל־הַגִּבּוֹר, וַיְהִי הַדָּבָר רַע מְאֹד
בְּעֵינֵי־דָוִד וַיֹּאמֶר בְּלִבּוֹ אֶכְרְתָה אֶת־רֹאשׁוֹ מֵעָלָיו וְיֵדְעוּ אֹיְבֵינוּ
כִּי יֵשׁ אֱלֹהִים בְּיִשְׂרָאֵל וַאֲנַחְנוּ בֹּטְחִים בּוֹ (13) הַצִּילֵנִי יהוה כִּי
בָּאוּ הַמַּיִם עַד־הַנָּפֶשׁ (14) אַתָּה הוּא אֲדוֹן־הָעוֹלָם, הַמַּצִּיל אֶת־
הַצַּדִּיק בְּקָרְאוֹ אֵלֶיךָ (15) הִנְנִי שֹׁלֵחַ עָלֶיךָ אֶת־גּוֹיֵי־הָאָרֶץ
וְנִלְחֲמוּ בְךָ וְנָפְלוּ כָּל־גִּבּוֹרֶיךָ בַּחֶרֶב בְּיוֹם־הַמִּלְחָמָה (16) לָמָּה
נִקְהַלְתֶּם עָלַי, בְּנֵי־יִשְׂרָאֵל, הֲלֹא אָמַרְתִּי אֲלֵיכֶם לֹא תִלָּחֲמוּ
בְּמַלְכֵי־כְנַעַן וְלֹא תִנָּגְפוּ לִפְנֵיהֶם, כִּי אֵין בָּכֶם יהוה

(1) Abraham took his men with him and he pursued (after) the kings and he fell upon them in the night and they (were) sleeping on the ground and they were smitten by sword before him. (2) Why didst thou not tell (to) me that she is thy wife, for I knew not and the Lord hath plagued me and all my house. (3) And Abraham drew near unto the Lord and he said: ‘If there are righteous men in this city, wilt thou destroy them with the

[a] ‘Then he will die.’

[b] Pausal form (p. 137. (*e*)) causes change in pointing of preposition.

wicked?' And the Lord said unto him: 'If righteous men shall be found there I will not destroy the city.' (4) And the children of Israel praised the Lord and they said: 'Great is the Lord our God, for He heard our voice in (the) distress and He delivered us from the hand of Egypt.' (5) David took a great stone and he wrote upon it the name of the Lord and he said unto the warrior of the enemy, 'Thou comest upon me with the sword and I come upon thee with the name of the God of Israel, and thou shalt fall into my hand and I shall take thy sword from (upon) thee to cut off thy head.' (6) Thus said the great and mighty king unto Israel, 'Where are the gods of Egypt? Did they indeed deliver them from my hand? And where is the Lord your God in whom ye trust ("who—ye trust in Him")? Even ye shall not be delivered from my hand and why shall ye fall by my sword?' And the warriors of the people told the prophet the words of the mighty king which his messenger spoke unto the people. And the prophet said unto them: Thus said the Lord unto the great king, 'Because thou hast said in thy heart, "I am the lord of the world and there is none stronger than I", behold I will cause thee to fall (down) from (upon) thy throne and another shall reign instead of thee.' (7) The elders of the people found the man who stole the gold and the silver and they brought him near unto Joshua for (the) judgement. (8) Esau said unto Jacob, 'Why hast thou sent the sheep and the cattle to me? There is much with me, my brother.' (9) Deliver me from the hands of those who seek ('the seekers of') my life, for they say, 'There is no salvation for him in the Lord.' (10) The sons of Jacob saw Joseph and they said: 'Behold the man of dreams cometh' and they sought to slay him. And Judah said unto them, 'Let us sell him for a slave', and he delivered him from their hand. (11) Joshua went forth to fight against the city and it fell into his hand and all its inhabitants were smitten before him by the sword. (12) Behold I am sending all my plagues in Pharaoh and in his people and they shall know that there is none like Me.

68. THE VERBS נָתַן AND לָקַח

Perf.:	he hath given	נָתַן	
she	,,	נָֽתְנָה	
thou (m.) hast	,,	נָתַ֫תָּ	(for נָתַ֫נְתָּ)
thou (f.)	,,	נָתַתְּ	(for נָתַנְתְּ)
I (c.) have	,,	נָתַ֫תִּי	(for נָתַ֫נְתִּי)
they (c.)	,,	נָֽתְנוּ	
ye (m.)	,,	נְתַתֶּם	(for נְתַנְתֶּם)
ye (f.)	,,	נְתַתֶּן	(for נְתַנְתֶּן)
we (c.)	,,	נָתַ֫נּוּ	(for נָתַ֫נְנוּ)

Imperf.:	he will give	יִתֵּן	(for יִנְתֵּן)
she	,,	תִּתֵּן	
thou (m.) wilt	,,	תִּתֵּן	
thou (f.)	,,	תִּתְּנִי	
I (c.) shall	,,	אֶתֵּן	
they (m.) will	,,	יִתְּנוּ	
they (f.)	,,	תִּתֵּ֫נָּה	(for תִּתְנֶ֫נָה)
ye (m.)	,,	תִּתְּנוּ	
ye (f.)	,,	תִּתֵּ֫נָּה	(for תִּתְנֶ֫נָה)
we (c.) shall	,,	נִתֵּן	

Cohort.: let me (c.) give אֶתְּנָה

Part. active: giving (m. sg.) נֹתֵן
,, (f. sg.) נֹתֶ֫נֶת
&c.

passive: given (m. sg.) נָתוּן
,, (f. sg.) נְתוּנָה
&c.

Imper.: give thou (m.) תֵּן
,, (f.) תְּנִי
,, ye (m.) תְּנוּ
,, (f.) תֵּ֫נָּה (for תְּנֶ֫נָה)

Inf. absolute: נָתוֹן

Inf. construct: תֵּת (for תֶּ֫נֶת)
,, with ל לָתֵת
,, ,, suffix תִּתִּי
&c.

נָתַן has a further peculiarity in that its *third* root-letter נ when vowelless in the middle of a word is also assimilated: נָתַתָּ for נָתַנְתָּ, &c. The Imperfect and the Imperative (following it) have Ṣere in the second syllable (יִתֵּן and תֵּן) instead of Ḥolem. The (hypothetical) form of the Infinitive Construct—תֶּנֶת—is a Segholate, originally תִּנְתְּ in which the medial נ is assimilated leaving תִּתְּ which has remained with the suffixes—תִּתִּי—but without the suffix the terminal ת cannot have Dagheš, so the preceding vowel (Ḥireq) is lengthened (to Ṣere)—תֵּת. With prefixed ל (pointed Qameṣ immediately before the tone-syllable) the Dagheš Lene falls away, since a vowel immediately precedes it.

The verb לָקַח behaves exactly as if it were a Pe Nun verb; i.e. when the ל is vowelless in the middle of a word it is assimilated; thus the Imperf. is יִקַּח for יִלְקַח (just as the ל of the article is assimilated—pp. 23 f. (*a*)):

Perf.:	he hath taken	לָקַח
	she ,,	לָקְחָה
	thou (m.) hast ,,	לָקַחְתָּ
	&c. (regular)	
Imper.:	take thou (m.)	קַח
	,, (f.)	קְחִי
	,, ye (m.)	קְחוּ
	,, (f.)	קַחְנָה
Imperf.:	he will take	יִקַּח
	she ,,	תִּקַּח
	thou (m.) wilt ,,	תִּקַּח
	thou (f.) ,,	תִּקְחִי
	I (c.) shall ,,	אֶקַּח
		&c.
Part. active:	taking (m. sg.)	לֹקֵחַ
	,, (f. sg.)	לֹקַחַת
		&c.
passive:	taken (m. sg.)	לָקוּחַ
	,, (f. sg.)	לְקוּחָה
		&c.
Inf. absolute:		לָקוֹחַ
construct:	קַחַת; with ל,	לָקַחַת
	with suffix	קַחְתִּי
		&c.
Cohort.:		
	let me (c.) ,,	אֶקְחָה
	,, us (c.) ,,	נִקְחָה

The verb לָקַח behaves like נָגַשׁ, except where the rules of the guttural (the third root-letter) operate: namely, the masc. sg.

participles (active לֹקֵחַ and passive לָקוּחַ) and the Infinitive Absolute (לָקוֹחַ) take a furtive Pathaḥ (pp. 19. 4 and 173), and the fem. sing. active Participle (לֹקַחַת for לֹקֶחֶת) and the Infinitive Construct (קַחַת for קֶחֶת) have Pathaḥs instead of Seghols, since the guttural attracts Pathah under it and before it (pp 19. 3 and 173). The Pathaḥ in the second syllable of the Imperfect is also due to the guttural.

Note: It was pointed out on pp. 17 f. that Dagheš Forte is often omitted in a letter with a shewa and that often the omission is not indicated by Raphe (p. 18, Note), so that the

3rd m. pl. Imperf. Qal is found as	יִקְחוּ	(for יִקְּחוּ)
2nd m. pl. ,, ,,	תִקְחוּ	(,, תִּקְּחוּ)
and the 1st c. Cohort. ,,	אֶקְחָה	(,, אֶקְּחָה).

NIPHAL

Perf.:	he hath been given	נִתַּן (for נִנְתַּן)	he hath been taken	נִלְקַח
	she ,,	נִתְּנָה (for נִנְתְּנָה)	she ,,	נִלְקְחָה
	thou (m.) hast ,,	נִתַּתָּ (for נִנְתַּנְתָּ)	thou (m.) hast ,,	נִלְקַחְתָּ
Imperf.:	he will be given	יִנָּתֵן &c. (regular)	he will be taken	יִלָּקַח (pathah before guttural—p. 172)
Imper.:	be thou (m.) given	הִנָּתֵן &c. (regular)	be thou (m.) taken	הִלָּקַח (pathaḥ before guttural—p. 173)
Part.:	being given (m. sg.)	נִתָּן (for נִנְתָּן)	being taken (m. sg.)	נִלְקָח &c.
Inf. absolute:		הִנָּתֹן (regular)		הִלָּקֹחַ (furtive pathaḥ)
construct:		הִנָּתֵן (regular)		הִלָּקַח (pathaḥ before guttural)

Note: These two verbs are found in Passives other than the Niphal; לָקַח in the Perfect and Imperfect and נָתַן in the Imperfect only, viz.:

Perf.:	he hath been taken	לֻקַּח	*Imperf.*:	he will be taken	יֻקַּח
	she ,,	לֻקְּחָה		she ,,	תֻּקַּח
	thou (m.) hast ,,	לֻקַּ֫חְתָּ		&c.	
	[No Perf. Pass. of נָתַן found.]			he will be given	יֻתַּן

The form of the Perfect is that of a regular Pual and that of the Imperfect is a Pe Nun Hophal; but since these verbs are not found in Piel or Hiphil the above forms are less likely to be survivals of the passives Pual and Hophal. Some grammarians have therefore been led to regard the above forms as examples of a passive Qal.

EXERCISE 27

child (m.) boy	יֶ֫לֶד	two (m.) שְׁנַ֫יִם const.	שְׁנֵי־
,, (f.) girl	יַלְדָּה	,, (f.) שְׁתַּ֫יִם ,,	שְׁתֵּי־
		to bear (child)	יָלַד
grace	חֵן		
,, (with suff.)	חִנִּי	to return, come back	שָׁב[a]

(1) רָאוּ בְנֵי־הָֽאֱלֹהִים אֶת־בְּנוֹת־הָֽאָדָם כִּי טוֹבוֹת הֵ֫נָּה[b] וַיִּקְחוּ לָהֶם נָשִׁים מִכֹּל אֲשֶׁר בָּחָ֫רוּ[c] (2) רָאָה אַבְרָהָם וְהִנֵּה אֲנָשִׁים עֹבְרִים בַּדֶּ֫רֶךְ וַיִּקַּח לֶ֫חֶם וַיִּתֵּן לִפְנֵיהֶם וַיֹּ֫אמֶר אֲלֵיהֶם, אִכְלוּ־נָא אִתִּי לֶ֫חֶם וַהֲלַכְתֶּם לְדַרְכְּכֶם: וְלֹא יָדַע אַבְרָהָם כִּי מַלְאֲכֵי־אֱלֹהִים הֵ֫מָּה[b] אֲשֶׁר שָׁלַח יהוה לְהַשְׁחִית אֶת־הָעִיר הָֽרְשָׁעָה וּלְהַצִּיל אֶת־בֶּן־אָחִיו מִשָּׁם (3) לֹא הִגִּ֫ידָה לָהֶם שָׂרָה כִּי אֵ֫שֶׁת־אַבְרָהָם הִיא וַיִּקְחוּ אֹתָהּ אֶל־פַּרְעֹה: וַיִּגֹּף יהוה אֶת־פַּרְעֹה וְאֶת־עֲבָדָיו עַל־דְּבַר שָׂרָה: וַיְהִי כִּשְׁמֹ֫עַ פַּרְעֹה כִּי אֵ֫שֶׁת אַבְרָהָם הִיא וַיֹּ֫אמֶר אֵלָיו לָ֫מָּה לֹא הִגַּ֫דְתָּ לִּי כִּי אִשְׁתְּךָ הִיא וָאֶקַּח אֹתָהּ לִי, וְעַתָּה הִנֵּה אִשְׁתְּךָ לְפָנֶ֫יךָ, קַח אֹתָהּ וַהֲלַ֫כְתָּ בְּשָׁלוֹם מֵאַרְצִי: וַיִּתֵּן לוֹ צֹאן וּבָקָר וְכֶ֫סֶף וְזָהָב וַעֲבָדִים רַבִּים (4) צִוָּה יִצְחָק אֶת־יַעֲקֹב בְּנוֹ לֵאמֹר לֹא תִקַּח אִשָּׁה מִבְּנוֹת־כְּנָ֫עַן,

[a] The root is שׁוּב, but the ו is absorbed in Perf., see p. 196.

[b] The English requires 'were' to be supplied.

[c] Pausal—p. 137.

כִּי רָעוֹת הֵנָּה בְּעֵינֵי מְאֹד וְהָלַכְתָּ אֶל־בֵּית־אִמְּךָ וְלָקַחְתָּ אִשָּׁה
מִשָּׁם (5) וַיֹּאמֶר לָבָן אֶל־יַעֲקֹב, הַגִּידָה לִּי מָה־אֶתֵּן לָךְ וַיֹּאמֶר
יַעֲקֹב תְּנָה לִּי אֶת־רָחֵל בִּתְּךָ הַקְּטַנָּה לְאִשָּׁה: וַיֹּאמֶר לָבָן, טוֹב
תִּתִּי אֹתָהּ לְךָ מִתִּתִּי[a] אֹתָהּ לְאִישׁ אַחֵר, כִּי אָחִי וּבְשָׂרִי אָתָּה[b]
(6) בָּא שְׁכֶם לִפְנֵי־אָבִיו וַיֹּאמֶר אֵלָיו, קְחָה לִּי אֶת־בַּת־יַעֲקֹב
לְאִשָּׁה, כִּי מָצְאָה חֵן בְּעֵינַי[c] מְאֹד: וַיְדַבֵּר אֲבִי־שְׁכֶם אֶל־יַעֲקֹב
וְאֶל־בָּנָיו לֵאמֹר הִנֵּה מָצְאָה הַיַּלְדָּה חֵן בְּעֵינֵי־שְׁכֶם בְּנִי, תְּנוּ
אֹתָהּ לוֹ לְאִשָּׁה, וּלְקַחְתֶּם אֶת־בְּנֹתֵינוּ לָכֶם לְנָשִׁים וְאֶת־בְּנוֹתֵיכֶם
תִּתְּנוּ לָנוּ, וִישַׁבְתֶּם בְּשָׁלוֹם אִתָּנוּ, הֲלֹא כָל־הָאָרֶץ לִפְנֵיכֶם:
וַיֹּאמְרוּ אֵלָיו בְּנֵי־יַעֲקֹב, אִם־תִּשְׁמְעוּ בְּקוֹלֵנוּ כְּכֹל אֲשֶׁר נְדַבֵּר
אֲלֵיכֶם, נָתוֹן נִתֵּן אֶת־בְּנֹתֵינוּ לָכֶם לְנָשִׁים וְאֶת־בְּנוֹתֵיכֶם נִקַּח
לָנוּ וְיָשַׁבְנוּ אִתְּכֶם בָּאָרֶץ: וְאִם לֹא תִשְׁמְעוּ בְקוֹלֵנוּ וְלָקַחְנוּ אֶת־
הַיַּלְדָּה וְהָלָכְנוּ[b] (7) וַיְהִי כִּשְׁמֹעַ יַעֲקֹב אֶת־דִּבְרֵי־בָנָיו וַיֹּאמֶר
אֲלֵיהֶם, אַתֶּם יְדַעְתֶּם כִּי שְׁנַיִם יָלְדָה לִּי רָחֵל אִשְׁתִּי וְהָאֶחָד יָצָא
וְלֹא שָׁב, וְהָיָה כִּי תִקְחוּ אֶת־אָחִיו הַקָּטָן אִתְּכֶם מִצְרַיְמָה, וּמֵת
גַּם הוּא בַדָּרֶךְ[b] (8) צִוָּה שְׁלֹמֹה וַיִּתְּנוּ לוֹ חֶרֶב, וַיֹּאמֶר אֶל־עֲבָדָיו,
נִכְרְתָה אֶת־הַיֶּלֶד לִשְׁנַיִם, כִּי זֹאת אֹמֶרֶת בְּנִי הוּא וְזֹאת[d] אֹמֶרֶת
לֹא כִּי בְנִי הוּא: וַיְהִי כִּשְׁמֹעַ אֵם־הַיֶּלֶד אֶת־מִשְׁפַּט־הַמֶּלֶךְ
וַתִּפֹּל לְפָנָיו אַרְצָה וַתֹּאמֶר, תְּנוּ לָהּ אֶת־הַיֶּלֶד וְכָרוֹת אַל־
תִּכְרְתוּ אֹתוֹ: וַיֹּאמֶר הַמֶּלֶךְ אֶל־כָּל־הָעֹמְדִים לְפָנָיו זֹאת אֵם־
הַיָּלֶד[b] (9) צִוָּה יְהוֹשֻׁעַ אֶת־הָעָם לֵאמֹר בְּתֵת יהוה אֶת־הָעִיר
בְּיֶדְכֶם, שָׂרוֹף תִּשְׂרְפוּ אֹתָהּ בָּאֵשׁ, וְאֶת־צֹאנָהּ וְאֶת־זְהָבָהּ תִּקְחוּ

[a] The מִן of comparison: 'better than my giving her', i.e. 'better than that I should give her' (pp. 132 ff., 136).

[b] Pausal—p. 137.

[c] 'To find grace in the eyes of' means 'to please'.

[d] 'This (one) . . . and this (one)' is idiomatic for 'the one . . . and the other'.

לָכֶם (10) יָשַׁב הַנָּבִיא לְבַדּוֹ עַל־רֹאשׁ־הָהָר וַיִּתְפַּלֵּל אֶל־יְהוָה
לֵאמֹר, קַח אֶת־נַפְשִׁי מִמֶּנִּי כִּי טוֹב מוֹתִי מֵחַיָּי[a] (11) אִם אֶסָּתֵר
בֶּהָרִים שָׁם תִּמְצָאֵנִי וְיָרַדְתִּי[b] שְׁאֹלָה גַּם מִשָּׁם יָדְךָ תִּקָּחֵנִי

(1) David saw that the Lord had given (to) him salvation and that his enemy had fallen to the ground dead before him and he took his sword and he cut off his head with it. And the Lord gave (to) him grace in the eyes of the people and they called in one voice and they said, 'Behold David is the greatest (say "the great one") among [בְּ] the warriors of Israel.' And the thing was very bad in the eyes of Saul. (2) Isaac saw that his son Esau (was) standing before him and he said unto him, 'Behold thy brother Jacob came and he took thy blessings instead of thee, and I knew not that he (was) thy brother.' (3) Thou hast given Thy fear in my heart, Lord, and mine enemies shall see that in Thee I have trusted. (4) The Lord spoke unto Joshua and he said unto him, 'This is the land which I have given to Abraham and to his seed unto ("until") eternity.' (5) The sons of Jacob stood before Pharaoh and they said unto him: 'Behold we are men of cattle and now, if thy servants have found grace in thine eyes, give (to) us, we pray thee [נָא], a place in the land and we will dwell there in peace.' (6) The man came forth from the midst of the trees where ('which . . . there') he was hidden and he said unto the Lord: 'The woman which thou hast given to me, *she* (use pronoun) took from the fruit of the tree and she gave to me.' (7) Rachel bare a son and they called his name Joseph, for they said: 'The Lord will give (to) thee another son.' (8) David sent his men unto the woman to take her unto him for a wife, for they told (to) him that her husband (was) dead; and they took her unto him to the wilderness where he had hidden himself from (before) Saul. (9) The priest said unto the woman, 'The Lord hath heard thy prayer and thou shalt bear a son and they will call his name Samuel.' (10) Joshua commanded the priests of the people saying: 'Take ye great stones and write ye upon them all these blessings, as Moses commanded

[a] The מִן of comparison.

[b] Understand '(and) if . . .'.

us before his death.' (11) The wicked man saw the gold and the silver in the palace of the king and he took from it and he hid (it) in the ground. (12) Hide not Thy face from me and Thy holy spirit ('Thy spirit of holiness'[a]) take not from me, for Thy servant am I.

69. PE GUTTURAL VERBS

The peculiarities of the gutturals are that they cannot receive Dagheš Forte, they take a composite shewa instead of simple shewa, and they require the vowel Pathaḥ under them and even before them, so that corresponding adjustments must be made when the verb has a guttural among its root-letters. Below is a Table of a verb whose first root-letter is a guttural, i.e. a Pe Guttural verb:

Qal

Perf.:	he hath forsaken	עָזַב	*Imperf.*:	he will forsake		יַעֲזֹב
	she	" עָֽזְבָה		she	"	תַּעֲזֹב
	thou (m.) hast	" עָזַבְתָּ		thou (m.) wilt	"	תַּעֲזֹב
	thou (f.)	" עָזַבְתְּ		thou (f.)	"	תַּעַזְבִי
	I (c.) have	" עָזַבְתִּי		I (c.) shall	"	אֶעֱזֹב
	they (c.)	" עָֽזְבוּ		they (m.) will	"	יַעַזְבוּ
				they (f.)	"	תַּעֲזֹבְנָה
	ye (m.)	" עֲזַבְתֶּם		ye (m.)	"	תַּעַזְבוּ
	ye (f.)	" עֲזַבְתֶּן		ye (f.)	"	תַּעֲזֹבְנָה
	we (c.)	" עָזַבְנוּ		we (c.) shall	"	נַעֲזֹב
Part. active:	forsaking (m. sg.)	עֹזֵב				
		&c.	*Cohort.*:	let me (c.)	"	אֶעֶזְבָה
passive:	forsaken (m. sg.)	עָזוּב		" us (c.)	"	נַעַזְבָה
	" (f. sg.)	עֲזוּבָה				
Inf. absolute:		עָזוֹב	*Imper.*:	forsake thou (m.)		עֲזֹב
construct:		עֲזֹב		"	(f.)	עִזְבִי
	with ל	לַעֲזֹב		"	ye (m.)	עִזְבוּ
	with suffix	עָזְבִי		"	(f.)	עֲזֹבְנָה

[a] See Appendix 5, p. 253.

In the Perfect the 2nd pl. m. and f. (עֲזַבְתֶּם and עֲזַבְתֶּן) have Ḥaṭeph-Pathaḥ under the guttural (instead of the simple shewa of the regular verb שְׁמַרְתֶּם).

In the Imperfect the composite shewa replaces the simple shewa under the guttural, corresponding with the vowel under the prefix (יַעֲזֹב, אֶעֱזֹב) and when another shewa follows the Ḥaṭeph-vowel, the latter becomes the corresponding short vowel (יַעַזְבוּ, אֶעֶזְבָה, נַעַזְבָה).

The *Imperative* f. sg. being a hypothetical עְזְבִי becomes עִזְבִי; similarly the m. pl. עִזְבוּ.

The *Active Participle* and the *Infinitive Absolute* are regular.

The *Infinitive Construct* has a composite shewa ·under the guttural (עֲזֹב) instead of the simple shewa of the regular verb— שְׁמֹר) and with a prefixed preposition the latter has the corresponding short vowel (לַעֲזֹב—p. 30. 4).

NOTE ON THE IMPERFECT QAL: Originally the form of the Imperfect Qal was (יַשְׁמֻר) 'yašmur' which became 'yešmur', 'yešmor' and finally 'yišmor'. The original *a* vowel of the first syllable is preserved in the Pe Guttural verb by the Guttural. In the case of the Pe Guttural Stative verb, there is an arrested development; e.g. the verb חָזַק 'to be strong' has the Imperfect יֶחֱזַק (the *a* vowel in the second syllable 'yeḥ[a]zaq' being due to the Stative—pp. 95 ff.), i.e. the original 'yaḥ[a]zaq' became 'yeḥ[e]zaq' and did not develop any further because of the guttural.

QAL

Imperf.:	he will be strong	יֶחֱזַק		he will be pleasant		יֶעֱרַב
	she	,,	תֶּחֱזַק	she	,,	תֶּעֱרַב
	thou (m.) wilt	,,	תֶּחֱזַק	thou (m.) wilt	,,	תֶּעֱרַב
	thou (f.)	,,	תֶּחֶזְקִי	thou (f.)	,,	תֶּעֶרְבִי
	I (c.) shall	,,	אֶחֱזַק	I (c.) shall	,,	אֶעֱרַב
	they (m.) will	,,	יֶחֶזְקוּ	they (m.) will	,,	יֶעֶרְבוּ
	they (f.)	,,	תֶּחֱזַקְנָה	they (f.)	,,	תֶּעֱרַבְנָה
	ye (m.)	,,	תֶּחֶזְקוּ	ye (m.)	,,	תֶּעֶרְבוּ
	ye (f.)	,,	תֶּחֱזַקְנָה	ye (f.)	,,	תֶּעֱרַבְנָה
	we (c.) shall	,,	נֶחֱזַק	we (c.) shall	,,	נֶעֱרַב

Imper.: be thou (m.) strong			חֲזַק
,,	(f.)	,,	חִזְקִי
,, ye	(m.)	,,	חִזְקוּ
,,	(f.)	,,	חֲזַקְנָה

SPECIAL NOTE: There are some Pe Guttural verbs with the (harsh) guttural ח, as חָמַד 'to desire', which take a simple shewa in the Imperfect—יַחְמֹד: similarly the Imperf. of חָשַׁךְ 'to be dark' is יֶחְשַׁךְ. As a point of analogy showing how the harsh guttural often differs from the weaker ones, it will be remembered that (e.g. p. 24. (*b*) (ii)) it sometimes does not cause the preceding vowel to be lengthened when it rejects a Dagheš Forte.

NIPHAL

The Niphal Perfect נִשְׁמַר 'nišmar' was originally נַשְׁמַר 'našmar' and so the Niphal Perfect of the Pe Guttural verb was originally נַעֲזַב which (just as יַחֲזַק became יֶחֱזַק) became נֶעֱזַב.

The Imperfect Niphal of the regular verb (יִשָּׁמֵר for יִנְשָׁמֵר) has Dagheš Forte in the first root-letter, but when this letter is a guttural the preceding vowel (Ḥireq) is lengthened (to Ṣere) instead: (יֵעָזֵב for יִעָּזֵב).

Perf.:			*Imperf.*:		
he hath been forsaken		נֶעֱזַב	he will be forsaken		יֵעָזֵב
she	,,	נֶעֶזְבָה	she	,,	תֵּעָזֵב
thou (m.) hast	,,	נֶעֱזַבְתָּ	thou (m.) wilt	,,	תֵּעָזֵב
thou (f.)	,,	נֶעֱזַבְתְּ	thou (f.)	,,	תֵּעָזְבִי
I (c.) have	,,	נֶעֱזַבְתִּי	I (c.) shall	,,	אֵעָזֵב
			they (m.) will	,,	יֵעָזְבוּ
they (c.)	,,	נֶעֶזְבוּ	they (f.)	,,	תֵּעָזַבְנָה
ye (m.)	,,	נֶעֱזַבְתֶּם	ye (m.)	,,	תֵּעָזְבוּ
ye (f.)	,,	נֶעֱזַבְתֶּן	ye (f.)	,,	תֵּעָזַבְנָה
we (c.)	,,	נֶעֱזַבְנוּ	we (c.) shall	,,	נֵעָזֵב

Imper.: be thou (m.) forsaken הֵעָזֵב
„ (f.) „ הֵעָזְבִי
„ ye (m.) „ הֵעָזְבוּ
„ (f.) „ הֵעָזַבְנָה

Part.:
being forsaken (m. sg.) נֶעֱזָב
&c.

Inf. absolute: נַעֲזוֹב
construct: הֵעָזֵב
„ with suffix הֵעָזְבִי
&c.

N.B. The Niphal Perf. of חָמַד is נֶחְמַד
„ Participle „ is נֶחְמָד

Hiphil

The earlier form of the Hiphil הִגְדִּיל 'higdîl' was הַגְדִּיל 'hagdîl' so that the Hiphil Perfect of עָבַר ('to pass over') had the form הַעֲבִיר which became הֶעֱבִיר ('to cause to pass over, to bring over'). Cf. Niph. Perf. above.

Perf.:
he (hath) brought over הֶעֱבִיר
she „ הֶעֱבִירָה
thou (m.) hast „ הֶעֱבַרְתָּ
thou (f.) „ הֶעֱבַרְתְּ
I (c.) (have) „ הֶעֱבַרְתִּי

they (c.) „ הֶעֱבִירוּ
ye (m.) „ הֶעֱבַרְתֶּם
ye (f.) „ הֶעֱבַרְתֶּן
we (c.) „ הֶעֱבַרְנוּ

Cohort.:
let me (c.) bring over אַעֲבִירָה

Perf. with Waw Consec.:
and thou (m.) wilt bring over וְהֶעֱבַרְתָּ
&c.

Part.: bringing over (m. sg.) מַעֲבִיר
&c.

Inf. absolute: הַעֲבֵר
construct: הַעֲבִיר

Imperf.:
he will bring over יַעֲבִיר
she „ תַּעֲבִיר
thou (m.) wilt „ תַּעֲבִיר
thou (f.) „ תַּעֲבִירִי
I (c.) shall „ אַעֲבִיר
they (m.) will „ יַעֲבִירוּ
they (f.) „ תַּעֲבֵרְנָה
ye (m.) „ תַּעֲבִירוּ
ye (f.) „ תַּעֲבֵרְנָה
we (c.) shall „ נַעֲבִיר

Shortened Imperf. Jussive:
let him bring over יַעֲבֵר

Imperf. with Waw Consec.:
and he brought over וַיַּעֲבֵר

Imper.:
bring thou (m.) over הַעֲבֵר
„ (f.) „ הַעֲבִירִי
„ ye (m.) „ הַעֲבִירוּ
„ (f.) „ הַעֲבֵרְנָה

Note carefully that the Hiphil has a shortened form of the Imperfect for the Jussive, that the waw consecutive attaches itself to the shortened form of the Imperfect (but see also p. 114 (*b*) N.B.), and that the negative command of immediate application is אַל with the shortened form of the Imperfect.

HOPHAL: *Perf.*: he was brought over הָעֳבַר (ho'ŏbar) &c.[a]
she ,, הָעָבְרָה (ho'oberâ) &c.
thou (m.) wast ,, הָעֳבַרְתָּ &c.

Imperf.: he will be brought over יָעֳבַר &c. (yo'ŏbar)

No Imperative.

Part.: being brought over (m. sg.) מָעֳבָר &c.

Infinitive: הָעֳבֵר

Since the characteristic of the Piel, Pual, and Hithpael is the doubling of the *second* root-letter with Dagheš Forte, the initial guttural of the Pe Guttural verb is unaffected, so that in these conjugations it is regular:

'he renewed' is חִדֵּשׁ 'he will renew' is יְחַדֵּשׁ Piel
'he renewed himself' is הִתְחַדֵּשׁ 'he will renew himself' is יִתְחַדֵּשׁ Hithpael.

EXERCISE 28

ark, box, coffin	אָרוֹן	sign	אֹת
		,, (pl.)	אֹתוֹת
pit, dungeon	בּוֹר	to be angry	קָצַף
		,, with	קָצַף עַל
camp	מַחֲנֶה	so, thus	כֵּן
friend, neighbour	רֵעַ[b]	to be dark	חָשַׁךְ[c]

(1) וַיְדַבֵּר יְהוֹשֻׁעַ אֶל־הַכֹּהֲנִים הַנֹּשְׂאִים אֶת־אֲרוֹן בְּרִית־יהוה לֵאמֹר עִבְרוּ בְּמַחֲנֶה לִפְנֵי אֲחֵיכֶם הַיַּרְדֵּנָה וַעֲמַדְתֶּם בְּמֵי־הַנָּהָר,

[a] The vowel in the first syllable of the Hophal is *o*; here, because of the guttural having a composite shewa the syllable has been opened, but the vowel in it is still *o*.

[b] 'One . . . another' is expressed in Hebrew as 'a man . . . his friend'.

[c] Imperf. יֶחְשַׁךְ; see p. 97, Note.

וְהָיָה בְּעָמְדְכֶם בַּנָּהָר וְנִכְרְתוּ מֵימָיו לִפְנֵיכֶם עַד עֲבֹר כָּל־
עֲדַת בְּנֵי־יִשְׂרָאֵל, וְהָיָה כְּעָבְרָם אֶת־הַיַּרְדֵּן וְשָׁבוּ הַמַּיִם
לִמְקוֹמָם (2) עָשָׂה אֱלֹהִים כְּכֹל אֲשֶׁר דִּבֶּר מֹשֶׁה וַיַּעֲבֵר רוּחַ
גְּדוֹלָה וַחֲזָקָה עַל אֶרֶץ מִצְרַיִם וַתֶּחְשַׁךְ כָּל־הָאָרֶץ וְלֹא רָאָה
אִישׁ אֶת־[a]רֵעֵהוּ (3) רָאָה הַמִּצְרִי כִּי יהוה[b] עִם־יוֹסֵף וַיַּעֲזֹב בְּיָדוֹ
אֶת־בֵּיתוֹ וְאֶת־כָּל־אֲשֶׁר לוֹ (4) וַיִּגַּשׁ אֵלָיו אֶחָד מֵעַבְדֵי־פַרְעֹה
וַיֹּאמֶר אֵלָיו, חֲטָאוּ עֲבָדֶיךָ לְפַרְעֹה וַיִּקְצֹף עָלֵינוּ פַּרְעֹה וַיִּתֵּן
אֹתָנוּ בַּבּוֹר, וְשָׁם אִתָּנוּ נַעַר עִבְרִי, וַנַּחֲלוֹם חֲלוֹם בְּלַיְלָה אֶחָד,
וַיְהִי בַבֹּקֶר וַנְּסַפֵּר לוֹ אֶת־הַחֲלוֹם אֲשֶׁר חָלַמְנוּ וַיַּגֶּד לָנוּ אֶת־
דְּבַר־הַחֲלוֹם, וְכַאֲשֶׁר הִגִּיד לָנוּ כֵּן הָיָה (5) נָשָׂא יְהוֹשֻׁעַ אֶת־
עֵינָיו וְהִנֵּה אִישׁ עֹמֵד לְפָנָיו וְחֶרֶב בְּיָדוֹ, וַיֹּאמֶר אֵלָיו יְהוֹשֻׁעַ הֲלָנוּ
אַתָּה אִם[c] לְאֹיְבֵינוּ: וַיֹּאמֶר הָאִישׁ אָנֹכִי מַלְאַךְ־אֱלֹהִים אֲשֶׁר
שְׁלָחַנִי יהוה לְהִלָּחֵם לָכֶם, וְעַתָּה חֲזַק כִּי אַתָּה תַּעֲבִיר אֶת־הָעָם
הַזֶּה אֶל־הָאָרֶץ אֲשֶׁר נָתַן לָהֶם יהוה: וַיֹּאמֶר יְהוֹשֻׁעַ, אִם מָצָא
עַבְדְּךָ חֵן בְּעֵינֵי־אֲדוֹנִי, תְּנָה לִי אֹת כִּי מַלְאַךְ־אֱלֹהִים אַתָּה
(6) וְכָל־דִּבְרֵי־הַמֶּלֶךְ אֲשֶׁר חָטָא וַאֲשֶׁר הֶחֱטִיא אֶת־יִשְׂרָאֵל
וְכֹל אֲשֶׁר עָשָׂה הִנָּם כְּתוּבִים בְּסֵפֶר דִּבְרֵי־הַיָּמִים[d] לְמַלְכֵי־
יִשְׂרָאֵל (7) הִנֵּה נָתַתִּי לָכֶם אֶת־יוֹם־הַשַּׁבָּת לִבְרִית־עוֹלָם
וּשְׁמַרְתֶּם אֹתוֹ בְּכָל־לְבַבְכֶם כִּי אֹת הִיא בֵּינִי וּבֵינֵיכֶם (8) כִּי
יַהֲרֹג אִישׁ אֶת־רֵעֵהוּ וְהוּא לֹא בִקֵּשׁ אֶת מוֹתוֹ, וּבָא אֶל אַחַת־
הֶעָרִים אֲשֶׁר הִבְדִּיל מֹשֶׁה וְהִגִּיד אֶת־הַדָּבָר אֶל־הַשֹּׁפְטִים וְיָשַׁב
שָׁם עַד מוֹת־הַכֹּהֵן הַגָּדוֹל: וְהָיָה אִם יִרְדֹּף אַחֲרָיו אֲחִי־הַמֵּת
וּמְצָאוֹ בַּדֶּרֶךְ וְהָרַג אֹתוֹ, הִנֵּה דָּמוֹ בְרֹאשׁוֹ, כִּי לֹא עָשָׂה כַּכָּתוּב
בַּסֵּפֶר הַזֶּה וְלֹא הִצִּיל אֶת־נַפְשׁוֹ (9) וַיֹּאמֶר יהוה אֶל־אַבְרָהָם,

[a] 'One . . . another' is expressed in Hebrew as 'a man . . . his friend'.
[b] Supply 'was' in the English.
[c] Here has the meaning 'or'.
[d] i.e. the chronicles.

עֲבֹר בָּאָ֫רֶץ הַזֹּאת כִּי לְךָ נְתַתִּ֫יהָ וּלְזַרְעֲךָ עַד־עוֹלָם׃ וַיֹּ֫אמֶר
אַבְרָהָם, יהוה אֱלֹהִים מַה־תִּתֶּן לִי וְאֵין לִי בֵן וְשָׂרָה אִשְׁתִּי זְקֵנָה
מְאֹד (10) רָאָה פַּרְעֹה כִּי יָצְאוּ בְנֵי־יִשְׂרָאֵל מֵאַרְצוֹ וְלֹא שָׁבוּ
מִצְרַ֫יְמָה וַיְחַזֵּק אֶת־לִבּוֹ וַיִּקַּח אֶת־עַמּוֹ אִתּוֹ וַיִּרְדֹּף אַחֲרֵיהֶם
(11) הִנֵּה זָקַ֫נְתִּי וְלֹא רָאוּ עֵינַי צַדִּיק נֶעֱזָב וְזַרְעוֹ מְבַקֵּשׁ לָחֶם
(12) וּבַאֲרוֹן־הַקֹּ֫דֶשׁ הָיוּ שְׁנֵי[a]־לוּחוֹת הַבְּרִית אֲשֶׁר נָתַן יהוה
לְמֹשֶׁה עַל הַר־סִינָי (13) מִי יַעֲמֹד לְפָנֶיךָ יהוה בְּשָׁפְטְךָ אֶת־
הָעוֹלָם (14) לָ֫מָּה שְׁכַחְתַּ֫נִי יהוה וַתַּעַזְבֵ֫נִי בְּיַד אֹיְבָי (15) עֲבֹר
לִפְנֵי־הָעָם, אַתָּה וְהַכֹּהֲנִים אִתְּךָ וְדִבַּרְתָּ אֲלֵיהֶם לֵאמֹר הִתְחַזְּקוּ
וּבִטְחוּ בַּיהוה (16) בַּיּוֹם הַהוּא, אָמַר יהוה, הֶעָרִים תֵּעָזַ֫בְנָה
כַּמִּדְבָּר וְאָמְרוּ הָעֹבְרִים אַיֵּה הָעָם הַיֹּשֵׁב בָּהֵ֫נָּה

(1) And Joseph dreamed another dream and he told (it) to his father, and he said unto him,.'Behold in my dream the sun and the stars (were) falling before me to the earth.'[b] And his father was angry with him exceedingly and he said, 'Shall we indeed fall before thee to the earth[b] as before a king?' And he kept the matter in his heart. (2) Moses returned to Egypt, for all the men who (were) seeking his life were dead; and he stood before Pharaoh, he and Aaron his brother, and he spoke all the words which the Lord had commanded him. (3) Ye shall not cause your children to pass through (the) fire, as the way of the nations among whom ye dwell ('which ye dwell among them'). (4) And it came to pass as the people heard (inf. constr.) the words of Joshua that (waw consec.) they said unto him: 'The Lord the God of our fathers we will serve and His law we will keep all the days, and we will hearken in thy voice as we hearkened to Moses.' (5) If a man shall have a Hebrew servant and the servant shall take unto himself a wife and he shall have children and if he shall say, 'I will not forsake my wife and my children in the house

[a] Construct of שְׁנַיִם, lit. 'a pair of' (see p. 243 (*b*)).

[b] 'Earthwards'—אַ֫רְצָה, with old acc. case-ending.

of my master', then (waw consec.) they shall bring him near unto the judges of his city and the master shall tell (to) them the words of his servant and the servant shall serve him for ever. (6) Because (כִּי) thou hast pursued him and thou hast said in thy heart, 'I will slay him', behold thy blood is on ('in') thy head. (7) The prophet sat in the dust and he called in a great voice, 'Behold Thy city is forsaken and Thy holy temple ("Thy temple of holiness"[a]) is burned to the ground, for the king hath sinned before Thee and he caused Thy people to sin.' (8) And the Lord spoke unto Joshua saying: 'Be strong, for I will not forsake thee and My angel shall be with thee as he was with Moses My servant.' (9) If the sheep of thy neighbour shall be in the way and there is no shepherd with them, thou shalt not leave them in the way but (כִּי) thou shalt indeed gather them unto thee and thou shalt send to tell (to) thy neighbour, and thou shalt remember that I am the Lord thy God. (10) All the wise men of Pharaoh came and they stood before him and they heard the dream which he related to them and they knew not what to tell (to) him for they were exceedingly afraid. (11) Forget ye not the signs which I have given to you in Egypt and on the sea and ye shall tell (to) your children and (to) your children's children.

70. PE 'ALEP̱ VERBS

The letter א, besides being a guttural, is also a quiescent letter (pp. 18 f.) and, in the case of five verbs, it quiesces and loses its consonantal value; these verbs therefore form a class in themselves and are called Pe 'Alep̱ verbs. They are: אָכַל 'to eat' ('devour, consume'); אָבַד 'to perish', 'to be lost'; אָמַר 'to say'; אָבָה 'to be willing'; and אָפָה 'to bake' (the latter two being Lameḏ He verbs as well as Pe 'Alep̱s—doubly weak).

[a] See Appendix 5, p. 253.

Qal

Perf.:	he hath eaten	אָכַל
	she „	אָכְלָה
		&c.
	ye (m.) have „	אֲכַלְתֶּם
	ye (f.) „	אֲכַלְתֶּן
		&c.
Imper.:	eat thou (m.)	אֱכֹל
	„ (f.)	אִכְלִי
	„ ye (m.)	אִכְלוּ
	„ (f.)	אֱכֹ֫לְנָה
Part.:	eating (m. sg.)	אֹכֵל
Inf. absolute:		אָכוֹל
construct:		אֱכֹל
	with ל	לֶאֱכֹל

Imperf.:	he will eat	יֹאכַל[a]
	she „	תֹּאכַל
	thou (m.) wilt „	תֹּאכַל
	thou (f.) „	תֹּאכְלִי
	I (c.) shall „	אֹכַל (for אֹאכַל)
	they (m.) will „	יֹאכְלוּ
	they (f.) „	תֹּאכַ֫לְנָה
	ye (m.) „	תֹּאכְלוּ
	ye (f.) „	תֹּאכַ֫לְנָה
	we (c.) shall „	נֹאכַל
Cohort.:	let me eat	אֹכְלָה (for אֹאכְלָה)

The Qal Perfect is the same as that of the Pe Guttural verb. The Imperfect is יֹאכַל (instead of an expected יֶאֱכֹל). The א attracts Ḥaṭeph-Seghol in preference to the Ḥaṭeph-Pathaḥ, as seen from the Imperative and the Infinitive Construct (אֱכֹל).

Note: The verb אָמַר 'to say' behaves in a special way in the Infinitive Construct with the prefixed preposition, being לֵאמֹר instead of לֶאֱמֹר, and the א is silent. The 3rd sg. m. Imperfect יֹאמַר with waw consecutive is:

(*a*) וַיֹּאמַ֑ר in pause, followed *immediately* by the words spoken, without any intervening word or words, thus: 'He called unto his servants and he said: "Hear ye my words"'

קָרָא אֶל־עֲבָדָיו וַיֹּאמַ֑ר שִׁמְעוּ אֶת־דְּבָרָֽי׃

(*b*) Generally וַיֹּ֫אמֶר; i.e. יֹאמֶר with the accent put back one place, so that the last syllable being closed and now

[a] In pause: יֹאכֵ֑ל &c.

unaccented is shortened. 'He called unto his servants and he said unto them: 'Hear ye my words''

קָרָא אֶל־עֲבָדָיו וַיֹּאמֶר אֲלֵיהֶם שִׁמְעוּ אֶת־דְּבָרָי׃

With the	3rd f. sg. 2nd m. sg.	it is similarly	וַתֹּאמֶר
,, ,,	1st pl.	,, ,, ,,	וַנֹּאמֶר
but ,, ,,	1st sg.	it is	וָאֹמַר [a]

The other conjugations follow the Pe Guttural. The real divergence of the Pe 'Aleп̱ is in the Imperfect Qal.

EXERCISE 29

serpent	נָחָשׁ	then	אָז	to perish, be lost	אָבַד
naked	עֵירֹם	lest	פֶּן־	to open (the eyes)	פָּקַח [b]
(pl.)	עֵירֻמִּים				

(1) וַיֹּאמֶר הַנָּחָשׁ אֶל־הָאִשָּׁה, הֲצִוָּה אֶתְכֶם אֱלֹהִים לֵאמֹר, לֹא תֹאכְלוּ מִכֹּל עֲצֵי־הַגָּן׃ וַתֹּאמֶר אֵלָיו הָאִשָּׁה, מִפְּרִי־עֲצֵי־הַגָּן אָכוֹל נֹאכֵל, וּ[c]מִפְּרִי־הָעֵץ אֲשֶׁר בְּתוֹךְ־הַגָּן אָמַר אֱלֹהִים לֹא תֹאכְלוּ מִמֶּנּוּ׃ וַיֹּאמֶר הַנָּחָשׁ, יֹדֵעַ אֱלֹהִים כִּי בְּיוֹם אֲכָלְכֶם מִמֶּנּוּ תִּפָּקַחְנָה עֵינֵיכֶם וִידַעְתֶּם אֶת־הַטּוֹב וְאֶת־הָרָע׃ וַתִּקַּח הָאִשָּׁה מִפְּרִי־הָעֵץ וַתֹּאכַל וַתִּתֵּן גַּם לְאִישָׁהּ וַיֹּאכַל עִמָּהּ׃ וַיִּשְׁמְעוּ אֶת־קוֹל־יהוה אֱלֹהִים מִתְהַלֵּךְ בַּגָּן לְרוּחַ הַיּוֹם וַיִּתְחַבְּאוּ בְּתוֹךְ הָעֵצִים כִּי עֵירֻמִּים הֵמָּה[d]׃ וַיֹּאמֶר אֱלֹהִים אֶל־הָאָדָם, מִי הִגִּיד לְךָ כִּי עֵירֹם אָתָּה הֲמִן־הָעֵץ אֲשֶׁר אָמַרְתִּי לְךָ לֹא־תֹאכַל מִמֶּנּוּ אָכָלְתָּ׃ וַיֹּאמֶר הָאָדָם, הָאִשָּׁה אֲשֶׁר נָתַתָּ לִי הִיא נָתְנָה לִי וָאֶקַּח מִיָּדָהּ וָאֹכֵל (2) הִשָּׁמְרוּ[e] לָכֶם מְאֹד פֶּן־תֹּאמְרוּ בִּלְבַבְכֶם נַעַבְדָה אֶת־אֱלֹהֵי־הַגּוֹיִם אֲשֶׁר אֲנַחְנוּ יֹשְׁבִים בְּתוֹכָם וַהֲלַכְתֶּם אַחֲרֵיהֶם, כִּי

[a] It was pointed out on p. 114 (*b*), N.B., that the 1st sg. has no shortened form of the Imperfect.

[b] Used only for opening *the eyes*.

[c] The context determines the function of the conjunction; here it means 'but' (see p. 40, footnote *a*).

[d] Supply 'were'.

[e] 'Watch yourselves', i.e. 'take heed'.

שָׁפוֹט אֶשְׁפֹּט אֶתְכֶם, וְיָֽצְאָה מִמֶּ֫נִּי אֵשׁ וְאָֽכְלָה אֶתְכֶם וַאֲבַדְתֶּם
מֵעַל פְּנֵי־הָאֲדָמָה (3) וַיֹּ֫אמֶר מֹשֶׁה, הִנֵּה אָנֹכִי בָּא[a] אֶל־בְּנֵי־
יִשְׂרָאֵל וְאָמַרְתִּ֫י אֲלֵיהֶם אֱלֹהֵי־אֲבוֹתֵיכֶם שְׁלָחַ֫נִי אֲלֵיכֶם לְהַצִּיל
אֶתְכֶם מִיַּד־מִצְרַ֫יִם, וְאָמְרוּ אֵלַי מַה־שְּׁמוֹ, מָה־אֹמַר אֲלֵיהֶם
(4) נָשָׂא הַנָּבִיא אֶת־קוֹלוֹ וַיֹּאמַר עֵירֹם יָצָא הָאָדָם אֶל־הָעוֹלָם
וְעֵירֹם שָׁב אֶל־הָאֲדָמָה, יהוה נָתַן וַיהוה לָקָח: מְהֻלָּל שֵׁם־יהוה
עַד־עוֹלָם (5) לָ֫מָּה תֹאמַר, יַעֲקֹב, עֲזָבַ֫נִי יהוה וַיַּסְתֵּר אֶת־פָּנָיו
מִמֶּ֫נִּי, הֲלֹא[b] אַתָּה עֲזַבְתּוֹ וַתַּעֲבֹד אֶת־אֱלֹהֵי־כְנָעַן (6) אֱמֹר אֶל־
אַהֲרֹן אָחִ֫יךָ וְאֶל־בָּנָיו הַכֹּהֲנִים, קְדוֹשִׁים אַתֶּם לֵאלֹהֵיכֶם (7) יָרַד
כְּבוֹד־יהוה בַּמַּחֲנֶה וַיְדַבֵּר יהוה אֶל־מֹשֶׁה לֵאמֹר שָׁמַ֫עְתִּי אֶת־
קוֹל בְּנֵי־יִשְׂרָאֵל הָאֹמְרִים מִי יַאֲכִילֵ֫נוּ בָּשָׂר כִּי טוֹב הָיָה לָ֫נוּ
בְּאֶרֶץ־מִצְרַ֫יִם בְּאָכְלֵנוּ בָּשָׂר, וְעַתָּה הִנְנִי מַאֲבִיד אֹתָם מֵעַל פְּנֵי־
הָאֲדָמָה וְלֹא יִזָּכֵר שְׁמָם עַד־עוֹלָם: וַיְהִי כִּשְׁמֹ֫עַ מֹשֶׁה אֶת־
דִּבְרֵי־יהוה וַיִּפֹּל עַל־פָּנָיו אַ֫רְצָה וַיֹּאמַר יהוה אֱלֹהֵי אֲשֶׁר
עָמַ֫דְתִּי לְפָנֶ֫יךָ בֶּאֱמֶת, אַל־נָא תַשְׁחֵת אֶת־הָעָם הַזֶּה, פֶּן־יֹאמְרוּ
הַגּוֹיִם כִּי לֹא יָ֫כֹלְתָּ לְהִלָּחֵם בֵּאלֹהֵי־כְנַ֫עַן וַתֵּהָרֵג בַּמִּדְבָּר
(8) וַיְהִי כַּאֲשֶׁר שָׂ֫מוּ לְפָנָיו לֶ֫חֶם לֶאֱכֹל וַיֹּ֫אמֶר אֲלֵיהֶם, אִם טוֹב
בְּעֵינֵיכֶם לֹא אֹכַל עַד־אֲשֶׁר דִּבַּ֫רְתִּי אֶת־דְּבָרָי: וַיֹּ֫אמְרוּ אֵלָיו
דַּבֶּר־נָא כִּי שֹׁמְעִים אֲנָֽחְנוּ: וַיֹּאמַר, עֶ֫בֶד אַבְרָהָם אָנֹכִי: וַיֹּ֫אמֶר
אֵלַי אֲדוֹנִי לֹא תִקַּח אִשָּׁה לִבְנִי לְיִצְחָק מִבְּנוֹת־הַכְּנַעֲנִי אֲשֶׁר
אָנֹכִי יֹשֵׁב בְּאַרְצוֹ, וְעַתָּה קַח לְךָ אֲנָשִׁים מֵעַבְדֵי־בֵיתִי וְהָלַכְתָּ֫
אֶל־בֵּית־אָבִי וְלָֽקַחְתָּ֫ אִשָּׁה לִבְנִי מִשָּׁם: וַיְהִי בָּ֫עֶרֶב וְהִנְנִי עֹמֵד[c]
בַּדֶּ֫רֶךְ וְהִנֵּה הַיַּלְדָּה לְפָנָי וַתַּגֵּד לִי אֶת־שְׁמָהּ וְאֶת־שֵׁם בֵּית־
אָבִיהָ: וַיְהִי כְּשָׁמְעִי אֶת־דְּבָרֶ֫יהָ וָאֶפֹּל עַל־פָּנַי וָאֲהַלֵּל אֶת־
שֵׁם־יהוה אֲשֶׁר לֹא עָזַב אֶת־אֲדוֹנִי (9) בָּא הַנָּבִיא אֶל בֵּית־
הָאִשָּׁה אֲשֶׁר הָיָה שָׁם הַיֶּ֫לֶד הַמֵּת וַיִּתְפַּלֵּל אֶל־יהוה כָּל־

[a] Participle.

[b] 'Surely'. See p. 80, footnote *c*.

[c] Understand 'was' (standing).

הַלָּֽיְלָה׃ וַיְהִי בַבֹּקֶר וַתִּפָּקַחְנָה עֵינֵי־הַיֶּלֶד, וַתִּקַּח הָאִשָּׁה אֶת־
בְּנָהּ וַתֹּאמַר עַתָּה יָדַעְתִּי כִּי אִישׁ־אֱלֹהִים אָתָּה

(1) Thus shalt thou say unto the house of Jacob: 'Behold a great camp cometh against you and the enemy shall capture your cities and he will take your sons and daughters with him to his land and there will be only old men in the cities.' (2) What shall we say unto Thee, Lord? Are we not Thy children and Thou our father, and why shall we perish before[a] Thine eyes? (3) The king lifted up his voice and he said: 'Great is the Lord who delivereth those who trust (participle with article[b]) in Him, but (conjunction) those who forsake[c] His law will surely perish from (upon) the face of the ground.' (4) Destroy me not, Lord, lest the wicked (pl.) shall say in their heart, 'The righteous (man) hath perished and there is no salvation for him in God'. (5) Samuel and the king sat (down) to eat bread before the Lord, and the elders of Israel with them. (6) And God said unto the man: 'Because thou hast transgressed My commandment and thou hast taken from the fruit of the tree which is in the midst of the garden, behold thou shalt indeed work the ground and in (the) distress thou shalt eat bread.' (7) The daughters of the dead man came unto Moses and they said unto him: 'Behold our father is dead and he was not in the congregation of the wicked (pl.) whom the Lord destroyed, and why shall his name perish from the midst of Israel, for he hath not a son'. And Moses brought near their judgement before the Lord. (8) 'Behold I have sent upon them the serpents and they ate the fruit of their land until [עַד־אֲשֶׁר] they had not bread to eat, and they have not returned yet unto Me', said the Lord. (9) A fire came down from heaven and consumed them and they perished, they and all that they had. (10) Thou hast watched over us in the wilderness and from the heavens Thou hast sent (to) us bread to eat and Thou hast not forsaken us. (11) The spies opened their eyes and behold before them (was) a great city. (12) The woman gave (to) me from the fruit and I ate; and I hid myself for I knew that I am naked.

[a] '*To* Thine eyes'.

[b] i.e. 'the (ones) trusting'.

[c] Cons. pl. part.—'the forsakers of . . .'.

71. ʽAYIN GUTTURAL VERBS

When the second root-letter of a verb is a guttural—i.e. when it is an ʽAyin Guttural verb—its pointing is modified because of the guttural, thus:

Qal

Perf.:	he hath chosen		בָּחַר	*Imperf.*:	he will choose		יִבְחַר
	she	,,	בָּֽחֲרָה		she	,,	תִּבְחַר
	thou (m.) hast	,,	בָּחַרְתָּ		thou (m.) wilt	,,	תִּבְחַר
	thou (f.)	,,	בָּחַרְתְּ		thou (f.)	,,	תִּבְחֲרִי
	I (c.) have	,,	בָּחַרְתִּי		I (c.) shall	,,	אֶבְחַר
					they (m.) will	,,	יִבְחֲרוּ
	they (c.)	,,	בָּֽחֲרוּ		they (f.)	,,	תִּבְחַרְנָה
	ye (m.)	,,	בְּחַרְתֶּם		ye (m.)	,,	תִּבְחֲרוּ
	ye (f.)	,,	בְּחַרְתֶּן		ye (f.)	,,	תִּבְחַרְנָה
	we (c.)	,,	בָּחַרְנוּ		we (c.) shall	,,	נִבְחַר

Part.						
active:	choosing (m. sg.)	בֹּחֵר &c.	*Cohort.*:	let me (c.)	,,	אֶבְחֲרָה
				let us (c.)	,,	נִבְחֲרָה
passive:	chosen (m. sg.)	בָּחוּר &c.				

Inf. absolute:		בָּחוֹר	*Imper.*:	choose thou	(m.)	בְּחַר
construct:		בְּחֹר	,,		(f.)	בַּחֲרִי
,,	with ל	לִבְחֹר	,,	ye	(m.)	בַּחֲרוּ
,,	with suffix	בָּחֳרוֹ	,,		(f.)	בְּחַרְנָה

The Perfect is normal except that the 3rd f. sg. and the 3rd pl. have a composite shewa under the guttural. Similarly in *the Imperfect* 2nd f. sg., 3rd m. pl., and 2nd m. pl., and Cohortative; while in the other persons the vowel under the guttural is

Pathaḥ. Note how in the Imperative f. sg. and m. pl. the first radical (which, in the Imperfect, has a shewa) assumes the short vowel corresponding to the following composite shewa.

Niphal

Perf.:	he was chosen		נִבְחַר	*Imperf.*:	he will be chosen		יִבָּחֵר
	she	,,	נִבְחֲרָה		she	,,	תִּבָּחֵר
	thou (m.) wast	,,	נִבְחַרְתָּ		thou (m.) wilt	,,	תִּבָּחֵר
	thou (f.)	,,	נִבְחַרְתְּ &c.		thou (f.)	,,	תִּבָּחֲרִי &c.
	they (c.) were	,,	נִבְחֲרוּ &c.		they (m.)	,,	יִבָּחֲרוּ &c.
Part.:	being chosen (m. sg.)		נִבְחָר &c.	*Imper.*:	be thou (m.) chosen		הִבָּחֵר &c.
Inf. absolute:			נִבְחֹר	*Inf. construct*:			הִבָּחֵר

The Niphal of the 'Ayin Guttural is practically normal, except that the composite shewa replaces the simple shewa under the guttural.

Piel

In Piel, Pual, and Hithpael the second root-letter is doubled and has Dagheš Forte, but when the second root-letter is a guttural or ר the preceding vowel is lengthened instead. This regularly occurs when the second root-letter is א (as מֵאֵן for מִאֵן 'to refuse') or ר (as בֵּרֵךְ for בִּרֵךְ 'to bless'). When the second root-letter is the harsh הח or even ע the preceding vowel is usually not lengthened (as שִׁחֵת 'to destroy', מִהֵר 'to hurry', בִּעֵר 'to burn'); the doubling is said to be implicit. Though strictly not an 'Ayin Guttural verb ברך may here be classed as one, since in Piel the medial ר behaves as a guttural in not receiving Dagheš Forte:

Perf.: he (hath) blessed	בֵּרֵךְ (for בִּרֵּךְ)	*Imperf.*: he will bless	יְבָרֵךְ (for יְבַרֵּךְ)
she ,,	בֵּרְכָה	she ,,	תְּבָרֵךְ
thou (m.) hast ,,	בֵּרַכְתָּ	thou (m.) wilt ,,	תְּבָרֵךְ
thou (f.) ,,	בֵּרַכְתְּ	thou (f.) ,,	תְּבָרְכִי
I (c.) have ,,	בֵּרַכְתִּי	I (c.) shall ,,	אֲבָרֵךְ
they (c.) ,,	בֵּרְכוּ	they (m.) will ,,	יְבָרְכוּ
		they (f.) ,,	תְּבָרֵכְנָה
ye (m.) ,,	בֵּרַכְתֶּם	ye (m.) ,,	תְּבָרְכוּ
ye (f.) ,,	בֵּרַכְתֶּן	ye (f.) ,,	תְּבָרֵכְנָה
we (c.) ,,	בֵּרַכְנוּ	we (c.) shall ,,	נְבָרֵךְ
Imper.: bless thou (m.)	בָּרֵךְ	*Cohort.*: let me (c.) ,,	אֲבָרְכָה
,, (f.)	בָּרְכִי	let us (c.) ,,	נְבָרְכָה
,, ye (m.)	בָּרְכוּ	*Imperf. with Waw Consecutive*:	
,, (f.)	בָּרֵכְנָה	and he blessed	וַיְבָרֶךְ
Part.: blessing (m. sg.)	מְבָרֵךְ &c.	*Infinitives*:	בָּרֵךְ

NOTE: When the Imperfect יְבָרֵךְ receives the waw consecutive the accent is retarded one place, so that the *closed syllable* רֵךְ being now *unaccented* shortens its vowel, becoming רֶךְ (just as אֵת becomes אֶת־)—וַיְבָרֶךְ.

PUAL

Perf.: he was blessed	בֹּרַךְ (for בֻּרַּךְ)	*Imperf.*: he will be blessed	יְבֹרַךְ (for יְבֻרַּךְ)
she ,,	בֹּרְכָה	she ,,	תְּבֹרַךְ
thou (m.) wast ,,	בֹּרַכְתָּ	thou (m.) wilt ,,	תְּבֹרַךְ
thou (f.) ,,	בֹּרַכְתְּ	thou (f.) ,,	תְּבֹרְכִי
I (c.) was ,,	בֹּרַכְתִּי	I (c.) shall ,,	אֲבֹרַךְ
they (c.) were ,,	בֹּרְכוּ	they (m.) will ,,	יְבֹרְכוּ
		they (f.) ,,	תְּבֹרַכְנָה

Perf.:		*Imperf.*:	
ye (m.) were blessed	בֹּרַכְתֶּם	ye (m.) will be blessed	תְּבֹרְכוּ
ye (f.) ,,	בֹּרַכְתֶּן	ye (f.) ,,	תְּבֹרַכְנָה
we (c.) ,,	בֹּרַכְנוּ	we (c.) shall ,,	נְבֹרַךְ

Part.:		*Infinitives*:	בֹּרַךְ
(being) blessed (m. sg.)	מְבֹרָךְ &c.		

NOTE: The alternate *o* vowel for the *u* of Pual is analogous to the process explained on page 144 on the Hophal of the Pe Nun verb (which is הֻגַּשׁ *u* for הָגַּשׁ *o*).

Hithpael

Perf.:		*Imperf.*:	
he (hath) blessed himself	הִתְבָּרֵךְ	he will bless himself	יִתְבָּרֵךְ
she herself	הִתְבָּרְכָה &c.	she herself	תִּתְבָּרֵךְ &c.
Imper.: bless thyself (m.)	הִתְבָּרֵךְ &c.	*Part.*: blessing himself	מִתְבָּרֵךְ &c.
Infinitives:	הִתְבָּרֵךְ		

The following illustrates the pointing of an 'Ayin Guttural verb in Piel, Pual, and Hithpael where, though Dagheš Forte is absent in the guttural, there is no lengthening of the preceding vowel:

Piel		Pual	
Perf.: he (hath) comforted	נִחַם	he was comforted	נֻחַם
Imperf.: he will comfort	יְנַחֵם	he will be comforted	יְנֻחַם
Imper.: comfort thou (m.)	נַחֵם		
Part.: comforting (m. sg.)	מְנַחֵם	being comforted (m. sg.)	מְנֻחָם
Infinitives:	נַחֵם		נֻחַם

Hithpael

Perf.: he (hath) comforted himself	הִתְנַחֵם
Imperf.: he will comfort himself	יִתְנַחֵם
Imper.: comfort thyself (m.)	הִתְנַחֵם
Part.: comforting himself	מִתְנַחֵם
Infinitives:	הִתְנַחֵם

EXERCISE 30

gift, offering	מִנְחָה	time, season	עֵת
famine, hunger	רָעָב	with suffix	עִתּוֹ
kindness (segholate)	חֶ֫סֶד	pl.	עִתִּים

(1) וַיְהִי אַחֲרֵי הַדְּבָרִים הָאֵ֫לֶּה וַיֶּחֱזַק הָרָעָב בְּמִצְרַ֫יִם וַתִּרְעַב
כָּל־הָאָ֫רֶץ וַיִּצְעַק כָּל־הָעָם אֶל־פַּרְעֹה לֵאמֹר תְּנָה לָ֫נוּ לֶ֫חֶם
לֶאֱכֹל׃ וַיֹּ֫אמֶר אֲלֵיהֶם פַּרְעֹה לָ֫מָּה תִצְעֲקוּ אֵלַי, בַּקְּשׁוּ לֶ֫חֶם
מִיּוֹסֵף וְהוּא יִתֵּן לָכֶם׃ וַיִּשְׁלְחוּ אֶל־יוֹסֵף לֵאמֹר לָ֫מָּה יֹאבְדוּ
עֲבָדֶ֫יךָ בָּרָעָב׃ וַיֹּ֫אמֶר אֲלֵיהֶם יוֹסֵף, מִכְרוּ לִי אַדְמַתְכֶם וְנָתַתִּ֫י
לָכֶם לֶחֶם׃ וַיִּמְכְּרוּ לוֹ אֶת־אַדְמָתָם וַיִּתֵּן לָהֶם לֶחֶם׃ רַק
הַכֹּהֲנִים לְבַדָּם לֹא מָכְרוּ לוֹ אֶת־אַדְמָתָם, כִּי קֹ֫דֶשׁ הִיא
לֵאלֹהֵי־מִצְרָ֫יִם (2) וְאַבְרָהָם זָקֵן מְאֹד וַיְבָ֫רֶךְ אֹתוֹ אֱלֹהִים וַיְהִי־
לוֹ צֹאן וּבָקָר וְכֶ֫סֶף וְזָהָב וַעֲבָדִים רַבִּים׃ וַיִּתְפַּלֵּל אַבְרָהָם
אֶל־יהוה וַיֹּאמַר לָ֫מָּה לִי כָּל־הַכָּבוֹד הַזֶּה וְלִי לֹא נָתַ֫תָּ זָ֫רַע׃
וְאַתָּה אָמַ֫רְתָּ אֵלַי הִנֵּה זַרְעֲךָ יִהְיֶה כְּכוֹכְבֵי־הַשָּׁמַ֫יִם וְכַעֲפַר־
הָאָ֫רֶץ אֲשֶׁר אִם יָכֹל אִישׁ לִסְפֹּר אֹתָם כֹּה יִסָּפֵר זַרְעֶ֫ךָ
(3) וַיְהִי כִּשְׁמֹ֫עַ עֵשָׂו אֶת־דִּבְרֵי־אָבִיו וַיִּצְעַק בְּקוֹל גָּדוֹל, בָּרֲכֵנִי
גַּם אֹתִי אָבִי׃ וַיֹּ֫אמֶר יִצְחָק, בָּא אֵלַי אָחִ֫יךָ וַאֲבָרְכֵ֫הוּ וָאֶתֵּן
אֹתְךָ לוֹ לְעֶ֫בֶד וְהוּא יִמְשֹׁל בְּךָ׃ וַיֹּ֫אמֶר עֵשָׂו הַ[a]בְרָכָה אַחַת אֵין

[a] The Hē Interrogative. Before a shewa the composite shewa under the ה becomes the corresponding short vowel (p. 80). This הַ cannot be confused with the article, since there is no following Dagheš Forte.

לְךָ אָבִי׃ וַיֹּאמֶר יִצְחָק הִנֵּה בֵּרַכְתִּי אֹתוֹ, גַּם בָּרוּךְ יִהְיֶה׃
וַיֹּאמֶר עֵשָׂו בְּלִבּוֹ, אַחֲרֵי מוֹת־אָבִי אֲהַרְגָה אֶת־אָחִי (4) צִוָּה
יַעֲקֹב אֶת־עֲבָדָיו לֵאמֹר כִּי יִשְׁאַל אֶתְכֶם עֵשָׂו אָחִי לְמִי אַתֶּם
וּלְמִי אֵלֶּה לִפְנֵיכֶם, וַאֲמַרְתֶּם, לְיַעֲקֹב עַבְדְּךָ מִנְחָה הִיא שְׁלוּחָה
לַאֲדוֹנִי לְעֵשָׂו לִמְצֹא חֵן בְּעֵינָיו וְהִנֵּה הוּא אַחֲרֵינוּ (5) בָּעֵת
הַהִיא, אָמַר יהוה, יִהְיֶה רָעָב בְּכָל־הָאָרֶץ, רָעָב לֹא לַלֶּחֶם
כִּי לִשְׁמֹעַ אֶת־דְּבַר־יהוה׃ וּבְךָ יִתְבָּרְכוּ כֹּל גּוֹיֵי־הָאָרֶץ, כִּי
שֵׁם־יהוה נִקְרָא עָלֶיךָ (6) אֲבָרְכָה אֶת־יהוה בְּכָל־עֵת, בִּקְהַל־
עַמִּים אֲהַלְלֶנּוּ׃ כִּי גָדוֹל עַד־שָׁמַיִם חַסְדּוֹ, וּבְכָל־הָאָרֶץ כְּבוֹדוֹ
(7) בָּרוּךְ אַתָּה יהוה הַנֹּתֵן לְכָל־בָּשָׂר אֶת־לַחְמוֹ בְּעִתּוֹ (8) בָּרְכוּ
אֶת־יהוה כָּל־קְדוֹשָׁיו, סַפְּרוּ אֶת־חֲסָדָיו בְּכָל־עֵת (9) וַיְדַבֵּר
יהוה אֶל־מֹשֶׁה לֵאמֹר בְּחַר לְךָ אֲנָשִׁים מֵרָאשֵׁי־יִשְׂרָאֵל וְשָׁלַחְתָּ
אֹתָם אַרְצָה כְנָעַן׃ וּרְאוּ אֶת־הָאָרֶץ הֲטוֹבָה[a] הִיא אִם[b] רָעָה
וְאֶת־הֶעָרִים הַגְּדוֹלוֹת[a] הֵנָּה אִם[b] קְטַנּוֹת, וְלָקְחוּ מִפְּרִי־הָאָרֶץ
וְשָׁבוּ אֶל־הַמַּחֲנֶה וְהִגִּידוּ לָעָם אֵת אֲשֶׁר רָאוּ׃ וַיִּבְחַר מֹשֶׁה
אַנְשֵׁי־אֱמֶת וַיִּשְׁלָחֵם אַרְצָה כְנַעַן כַּאֲשֶׁר צִוָּה אֹתוֹ יהוה כֵּן עָשָׂה׃

(1) Joseph saw his brothers among the (ones) coming to Egypt and he drew near unto them and he asked them, saying: 'Is it well with (ל) your old father?' and they said, 'It is well, and behold our small brother hath come down with us'. (2) The servant of Abraham said unto them, 'Behold I stood in the way and I asked the girl, saying, "Is there a place in thy house for me and for the men who are with me?"; and she said: "There is place for my lord and for his men." And I gave (to) her the silver. And now, my master is old and the Lord hath blessed him, and he hath given all that he hath to his son Isaac whom Sarah his wife hath borne to him. And now, if it is good in your eyes, let us ask (Cohort.) the girl if she will be a wife to the son of my master, and she shall go after me to the house of my master.' (3) The priest of the city came forth and he blessed Abraham

[a] See footnote on previous page. [b] 'or'.

and he said: 'Blessed art thou to the Lord who hath given thine enemies in thy hand; and now give (to) us the people, and the gold and the silver take thou for thyself'. (4) The prophet called unto the people who had gathered together upon the mountain and he said: 'Choose ye this day between the Lord and (between) the gods of Canaan'. (5) And the Lord spoke unto Moses saying, 'Why dost[a] thou cry unto Me? Speak unto them and they shall go into the midst of the sea and they shall see that I shall not forsake them.' (6) David brought the priest near unto him and he inquired of [בּ] the Lord saying, 'Wilt Thou give this city in my hand when I shall fight against it?' (7) Jacob saw Rachel and he drew near unto her and he said, 'The daughter of whom art thou?'; and she said unto him, 'I am the daughter of Laban'. And Jacob told (to) her that he (was) the son of her father's sister. (8) Joseph saw the gift which Jacob his father sent and he took (it) from their hand and he said unto them, 'In the evening you shall eat with me'.

72. LAMED GUTTURAL VERBS

Bearing in mind the peculiarities of the gutturals, a verb whose third root-letter is a guttural—i.e. a Lamed Guttural verb—is pointed thus:

	Qal			Niphal		
Perf.:	he (hath) heard &c. (regular)		שָׁמַע	he was heard &c. (regular)		נִשְׁמַע
Imperf.:	he will hear		יִשְׁמַע	he will be heard		יִשָּׁמַע
	she	„	תִּשְׁמַע	she	„	תִּשָּׁמַע
	thou (m.) wilt	„	תִּשְׁמַע	thou (m.) wilt	„	תִּשָּׁמַע
	thou (f.)	„	תִּשְׁמְעִי	thou (f.)	„	תִּשָּׁמְעִי
	I (c.) shall	„	אֶשְׁמַע	I (c.) shall	„	אֶשָּׁמַע
	they (m.) will	„	יִשְׁמְעוּ	they (m.) will	„	יִשָּׁמְעוּ
	they (f.)	„	תִּשְׁמַעְנָה	they (f.)	„	תִּשָּׁמַעְנָה
	ye (m.)	„	תִּשְׁמְעוּ	ye (m.)	„	תִּשָּׁמְעוּ
	ye (f.)	„	תִּשְׁמַעְנָה	ye (f.)	„	תִּשָּׁמַעְנָה
	we (c.) shall	„	נִשְׁמַע	we (c.) shall	„	נִשָּׁמַע

[a] Use the imperf. for continued action.

Cohort.: let me (c.) hear אֶשְׁמְעָה   let me (c.) be heard אֶשָּׁמְעָה

Imperf. with suffix: יִשְׁמָעֵ֫נִי
     he will hear me

Imper.: hear thou (m.) שְׁמַע   be thou (m.)   ,,   הִשָּׁמַע

     ,,   (f.)   שִׁמְעִי   ,,   (f.)   ,,   הִשָּׁמְעִי

     ,,   ye   (m.)   שִׁמְעוּ   ,,   ye (m.)   ,,   הִשָּׁמְעוּ

     ,,   (f.)   שְׁמַ֫עְנָה   ,,   (f.)   ,,   הִשָּׁמַ֫עְנָה

Imper. with suffix: שְׁמָעֵ֫נִי
     hear thou (m.) me

Part.

   active: hearing (m. sg.) שֹׁמֵ֫עַ

     ,,   (f. sg.) שֹׁמַ֫עַת &c.

   passive: heard (m. sg.) שָׁמ֫וּעַ &c.   being heard (m. sg.) נִשְׁמָע
                                               &c.

Inf. absolute: שָׁמ֫וֹעַ   נִשְׁמֹ֫עַ

   construct: שְׁמֹ֫עַ   הִשָּׁמַע

In the Imperfect and the Imperative of Qal and Niphal the guttural requires the vowel Pathaḥ before it (pp. 19 f.); when a suffix is attached, the short vowel Pathaḥ is in an open syllable which is unaccented and lengthened to Qameṣ. In the Qal Infinitives and active Participle the guttural takes a Furtive Pathaḥ after the full accented vowel (pp. 19 f.).

HIPHIL

Perf.:   *Imperf.*:

   he (hath) caused to hear הִשְׁמִ֫יעַ   he will cause to hear יַשְׁמִ֫יעַ

     she   ,,   הִשְׁמִ֫יעָה   she   ,,   תַּשְׁמִ֫יעַ

   thou (m.) hast   ,,   הִשְׁמַ֫עְתָּ   thou (m.) wilt   ,,   תַּשְׁמִ֫יעַ

       &c. (regular)   thou (f.)   ,,   תַּשְׁמִ֫יעִי

                                       I (c.) shall   ,,   אַשְׁמִ֫יעַ

Imper.:   they (m.) will   ,,   יַשְׁמִ֫יעוּ

   cause thou (m.) to hear הַשְׁמַע   they (f.)   ,,   תַּשְׁמַ֫עְנָה

     ,,   (f.)   ,,   הַשְׁמִ֫יעִי   ye (m.)   ,,   תַּשְׁמִ֫יעוּ

     ,,   ye   (m.)   ,,   הַשְׁמִ֫יעוּ   ye (f.)   ,,   תַּשְׁמַ֫עְנָה

     ,,   (f.)   ,,   הַשְׁמַ֫עְנָה   we (c.) shall   ,,   נַשְׁמִ֫יעַ

Part.:

causing to hear (m. sg.)	מַשְׁמִיעַ
,, (f. sg.)	מַשְׁמִיעָה
&c.	
Inf. absolute:	הַשְׁמֵעַ
construct:	הַשְׁמִיעַ

Shortened Imperf. Jussive:
let him cause to hear יַשְׁמַע

Imperf. with Waw Consec.:
and he caused to hear וַיַּשְׁמַע

N.B. The Hophal הָשְׁמַע (Perf.), יָשְׁמַע (Imperf.), &c. is regular.

For the Piel and Hithpael the verb בָּקַע ('to divide') will serve:

	Piel		Hithpael	
Perf.:	he (hath) split	בִּקַּע	he (hath) split himself	הִתְבַּקַּע
	she ,,	בִּקְּעָה &c.	she ,, herself	הִתְבַּקְּעָה &c.
Imperf.:	he will split	יְבַקַּע	he will split himself	יִתְבַּקַּע
	she ,,	תְּבַקַּע &c.	she ,, herself	תִּתְבַּקַּע &c.
Imper.:	split thou (m.)	בַּקַּע &c.	split thyself (m.)	הִתְבַּקַּע &c.
Part.:	splitting (m. sg.)	מְבַקֵּעַ &c.	splitting himself	מִתְבַּקֵּעַ &c.
Inf. absolute:		בַּקֵּעַ	*absolute* and *construct*:	הִתְבַּקֵּעַ
construct:		בַּקַּע		

N.B. Pual בֻּקַּע (Perf.), יְבֻקַּע (Imperf.), &c. is regular.

EXERCISE 31

Reuben	רְאוּבֵן	garment	בֶּגֶד
Canaanite	כְּנַעֲנִי	,, (with suffix)[a]	בִּגְדִי
beast	חַיָּה	,, (pl.)	בְּגָדִים
		,, (pl. constr.)	בִּגְדֵי

kingdom מַמְלָכָה (מַמְלֶכֶת cons.)

to tear, rend	קָרַע
to send away, to let go שלח in Piel	שִׁלַּח
to swear שבע in Niphal	נִשְׁבַּע

[a] See p. 84 (*c*).

(1) שָׁב רְאוּבֵן הַבּ֫וֹרָה, כִּי אָמַר בְּלִבּוֹ אַצִּ֫ילָה אֶת־יוֹסֵף מִיַּד־
אַחַי וְשִׁלַּחְתִּ֫י אֹתוֹ הַבַּ֫יְתָה בְּשָׁלוֹם אֶל־אָבִיו, וְלֹא מָצָא אֶת־
יוֹסֵף בַּבּוֹר: וַיִּשְׁאַל רְאוּבֵן אֶת־אֶחָיו לֵאמֹר אַיֵּה הַנַּ֫עַר, כִּי אֵינֶ֫נּוּ
בַּבּוֹר, וַיַּגִּ֫ידוּ לוֹ לֵאמֹר מְכַרְנ֫וּהוּ לְעֶ֫בֶד מִצְרַ֫יְמָה: וַיְהִי כִּשְׁמֹ֫עַ
רְאוּבֵן אֶת־דִּבְרֵיהֶם וַיִּפֹּל עַל־פָּנָיו אַ֫רְצָה וַיִּקְרַע אֶת־בְּגָדָיו
וַיִּצְעַק בְּקוֹל גָּדוֹל, וּמַה נַּגִּיד לְאָבִ֫ינוּ: וַיִּקְחוּ אֶת־בִּגְדֵי־יוֹסֵף
אֲשֶׁר נָפְלוּ מֵעָלָיו וַיִּקְרְעוּ אֹתָם וַיִּשְׁפְּכוּ עֲלֵיהֶם דָּם וַיֹּאמְרוּ,
כִּי יִרְאֶה[a] יַעֲקֹב אָבִ֫ינוּ אֶת־הַבְּגָדִים הַקְּרוּעִים הָאֵ֫לֶּה וְדָם
עֲלֵיהֶם, אָמוֹר יֹאמַר בִּגְדֵי־בְנִי הֵ֫מָּה, חַיָּה רָעָה מְצָאַ֫תְהוּ בַּדֶּ֫רֶךְ
וַתֹּאכַל אֹתוֹ (2) וַיִּשְׁמַע הַכְּנַעֲנִי הַיֹּשֵׁב בָּהָר אֵת כָּל־אֲשֶׁר עָשָׂה
יְהוֹשֻׁ֫עַ לְעֵ֫בֶר־הַיַּרְדֵּן, וַיִּשְׁלַח מַלְאָכִים אֶל־כָּל־מַלְכֵי הָאָ֫רֶץ
לֵאמֹר אַתֶּם יְדַעְתֶּם כִּי בָא עַם־יִשְׂרָאֵל מֵהַמִּדְבָּר וַיִּלָּ֫חֶם
בְּעֵ֫בֶר־הַיַּרְדֵּן וַיִּלְכֹּד אֹתָן וַיִּשְׂרֹף אֹתָן בָּאֵשׁ וְאֶת־כָּל־יֹשְׁבֵיהֶן
לָקַח לוֹ לַעֲבָדִים: וְעַתָּה שִׁמְעוּ־נָא בְקוֹלִי וְהִתְקַבְּצוּ אֵלַי
וְנִלָּחַמְנוּ אִתּוֹ וְהֶאֱבַ֫דְנוּ אֹתוֹ מֵעַל־פְּנֵי־הָאֲדָמָה, הֲלֹא אַחַי
וְאַנְשֵׁי־בְרִיתִי אַתֶּם: וַיִּמְצְאוּ הַדְּבָרִים הָאֵ֫לֶּה חֵן בְּעֵינֵי־הַמְּלָכִים
וַיִּתְקַבְּצוּ אֵלָיו, וְעִמָּהֶם עַם רַב כְּכוֹכְבֵי הַשָּׁמָ֫יִם: וַיַּגִּ֫ידוּ לִיהוֹשֻׁ֫עַ
לֵאמֹר הִנֵּה בָּ֫אוּ כָּל מַלְכֵי־הָאָ֫רֶץ לְהִלָּחֵם בָּ֫נוּ, וְעַתָּה הִתְפַּלֵּל
לַיהוה אֱלֹהֵ֫ינוּ לְהַצִּילֵ֫נוּ מִיָּדָם: וַיִּתְפַּלֵּל יְהוֹשֻׁ֫עַ לֵאמֹר אַל־נָא
תִּתְּנֵ֫נוּ בְּיַד־אֹיְבֵ֫ינוּ כִּי בְךָ לְבַדְּךָ בָּטָ֫חְנוּ: וַיְהִי בָּעֶ֫רֶב, וּמַלְכֵי־
כְּנַעַן אֹכְלִים[b] בַּמַּחֲנֶה, וַיִּשְׁמַע אֱלֹהִים קוֹל כְּקוֹל־סוּסִים רַבִּים,
וַתִּפֹּל עֲלֵיהֶם יִרְאַת־יִשְׂרָאֵל וַיֹּאמְרוּ אָבוֹד אָבַ֫דְנוּ כִּי נִמְכַּ֫רְנוּ
בְּיַד־יִשְׂרָאֵל, וַיִּתְּנוּ אִישׁ[c] אֶת־חַרְבּוֹ בְּלֵב־רֵעֵ֫הוּ[c] וַיַּהַרְגוּ אִישׁ

[a] Imperfect. [b] (Were) eating.
[c] 'One . . . the other', p. 158, footnote *b*.

אֶת־רֵעֵהוּ כָּל־הַלָּֽיְלָה׃ (3) וַיֹּ֫אמֶר יהוה אֶל־שְׁלֹמֹה, כִּי לֹא
הָיָה לְבָבְךָ שָׁלֵם אִתִּי כִּלְבַב־דָּוִד אָבִ֫יךָ וַתִּקַּח לְךָ נָשִׁים רַבּוֹת
מִבְּנוֹת־הַגּוֹיִם וַתַּעֲבֹד אֶת־אֱלֹהֵיהֶן וַתִּשְׁכַּח אֶת־מִצְוֹתַי, קָר֫וֹעַ
אֶקְרַע אֶת־הַמַּמְלָכָה מִמְּךָ וּנְתַתִּיהָ לְרֵעֲךָ הַטּוֹב מִמֶּֽךָּ׃ רַק
לְמַעַן דָּוִד עַבְדִּי לֹא יִהְיֶה הַדָּבָר הַזֶּה בְּיָמֶיךָ, כִּי מִיַּד־בִּנְךָ
הַיֹּשֵׁב עַל־כִּסְאֲךָ אֶקְרָעֶנָּה (4) וַיַּעֲמֹד מֹשֶׁה לִפְנֵי־פַרְעֹה וַיֹּ֫אמֶר
אֵלָיו, כֹּה אָמַר יהוה אֱלֹהֵי־יִשְׂרָאֵל, שַׁלַּח אֶת־עַמִּי וְיַעַבְדוּנִי
בַּמִּדְבָּר, וְאִם אֵינְךָ מְשַׁלֵּחַ אֹתָם, הִנְנִי שֹׁלֵ֫חַ אֶת־כָּל־מַגֵּפוֹתַי
בְּךָ וּבַעֲבָדֶ֫יךָ וְיָדַעְתָּ כִּי אֵין כָּמוֹנִי בְּכָל־הָאָֽרֶץ׃ וַיֹּ֫אמֶר פַּרְעֹה
מִי יהוה כִּי אֶשְׁמַע בְּקוֹלוֹ וְשִׁלַּחְתִּי אֶת־הָעָם מֵעֲבָדָ֫נִי, לֹא
יָ֫דַעְתִּי אֹתוֹ וְאֶת־יִשְׂרָאֵל לֹא אֲשַׁלֵּֽחַ[a] (5) זֹאת הָאָרֶץ אֲשֶׁר
נִשְׁבַּ֫עְתִּי לַאֲבוֹתֵיכֶם לָתֵת לְזַרְעָם (6) וַיֹּ֫אמֶר דָּוִד אֶל־שָׁאוּל,
הִשָּׁבַע לִי בַּיהוה אִם[b] תִּרְדֹּף אַחֲרָי וַיִּשָּׁבַע לוֹ שָׁם שָׁאוּל
(7) לָ֫מָּה לִי כָּל־מִנְחוֹתֵיכֶם, אָמַר יהוה׃ קִרְעוּ אֶת־לְבַבְכֶם
וְלֹא אֶת־בִּגְדֵיכֶם וְעִבְדוּנִי בֶּאֱמֶת (8) בַּקֵּשׁ אֶת־יהוה וְהוּא
יַצִּילֶךָ בְּטַח בּוֹ וְלֹא יַעַזְבֶךָ (9) כִּי יִהְיֶה מֵת בְּבֵית־כֹּהֵן, לֹא
יִקְרַע אֶת־בְּגָדָיו, כִּי קָדוֹשׁ הוּא לַיהוה (10) שְׁמַע יִשְׂרָאֵל,
יהוה אֱלֹהֵינוּ יהוה אֶחָד (11) וַיֹּ֫אמֶר יוֹסֵף אֶל־פַּרְעֹה, אָבִי
הִשְׁבִּ֫יעַ אֹתִי לִפְנֵי־מוֹתוֹ לֵאמֹר קָבְרֵנִי בְּקֶבֶר אֲבוֹתָי (12) לֹא
תִשְׁכַּח אֶת־חַסְדֵי־יהוה אֲשֶׁר עָשָׂה אִתְּךָ מִמִּצְרַיִם וְעַד־עָֽתָּה

(1) And it came to pass when the prophet read these words in the book which the priest had found in the house of God that (ẃaw consec.) the king rent his garments and he cried, 'This people hath indeed sinned before the Lord our God'. And he made all the people swear (in) that day, from great to ('and until')

[a] Pausal. [b] 'Swear if thou wilt' means 'swear that thou wilt not'.

small to serve the Lord and to forsake the gods of the land. (2) Pharaoh called (to) his servants and he said unto them, 'Why have we sent away this people from serving us (inf. constr. with prefixed preposition and suffix)?'; and his warriors said unto him, 'Let us pursue after them, for they are in the wilderness'. (3) And Jacob blessed his sons before his death and he said: 'Reuben, thou art my firstborn, thine enemies shall fall before thee and thy hand shall rule over them'. (4) There dwelt in the land of Israel a people who served not the Lord, and the Lord sent amongst them the beasts of the wilderness and they consumed their sheep and their cattle. And the ruler sent unto the king saying: 'Let the king send (to) us a priest from the children of Israel to whose voice ("who to his voice") we will hearken according to ("as") all that he shall say unto us.' (5) The woman sat under a tree and the boy with her, and she cried unto the Lord and she said: 'Save, Lord, the life ("soul") of the boy'. And she opened her eyes and behold a river (was) before her. (6) And it came to pass as Jacob was crossing (inf. const.) the river that (waw consec.) a man fought with him all the night until the light of the morning. And the man said unto him, 'Let me go (Piel of שׁלח), for I am an angel of God'; and Jacob said, 'I will not let thee go until [עַד־אֲשֶׁר] thou hast blessed me'. And the angel blessed him and Jacob let him go. (7) The prophet said to the king in the hearing[a] of all Israel: 'If thou shalt not hearken to the words of this law and thou shalt go after thy heart and after thine eyes, behold the Lord will surely tear the kingdom from thee, as I have torn thy garment from (upon) thee.' (8) Blessed is the man who shall trust in the Lord. (9) Thus shall ye say unto the king, 'Send thou not messengers unto me saying, "Pray for us to the Lord, for we are as (the) sheep upon whom ('which . . . upon them') the beasts of the wilderness have fallen", for behold in the morning the Lord will cause a great sound to be heard and the enemy will return to his land'. (10) Unto Thee, my God, I shall cry, for *Thou* (pronoun) wilt hear my voice and Thou wilt not forget Thy servant who seeketh Thee with a broken heart.

[a] 'The ears'.

73. LAMED 'ALEP VERBS

As explained on pp. 161 ff. the letter א is a guttural which is often quiescent. A verb whose *third* root-letter is א is classified as Lamed 'Alep.

	QAL			NIPHAL		
Perf.:	he (hath) found		מָצָא	he was found		נִמְצָא
	she	,,	מָצְאָה	she	,,	נִמְצְאָה
	thou (m.) hast	,,	מָצָאתָ	thou (m.) wast	,,	נִמְצֵאתָ
	thou (f.)	,,	מָצָאת	thou (f.)	,,	נִמְצֵאת
	I (c) (have)	,,	מָצָאתִי	I (c.) was	,,	נִמְצֵאתִי
	they (c.)	,,	מָצְאוּ	they (c.) were	,,	נִמְצְאוּ
	ye (m.)	,,	מְצָאתֶם	ye (m.)	,,	נִמְצֵאתֶם
	ye (f.)	,,	מְצָאתֶן	ye (f.)	,,	נִמְצֵאתֶן
	we (c.)	,,	מָצָאנוּ	we (c.)	,,	נִמְצֵאנוּ
Imperf.:	he will find		יִמְצָא	he will be found		יִמָּצֵא
	she	,,	תִּמְצָא	she	,,	תִּמָּצֵא
	thou (m.) wilt	,,	תִּמְצָא	thou (m.) wilt	,,	תִּמָּצֵא
	thou (f.)	,,	תִּמְצְאִי	thou (f.)	,,	תִּמָּצְאִי
	I (c.) shall	,,	אֶמְצָא	I (c.) shall	,,	אִמָּצֵא
	they (m.) will	,,	יִמְצְאוּ	they (m.) will	,,	יִמָּצְאוּ
	they (f.)	,,	תִּמְצֶאנָה	they (f.)	,,	תִּמָּצֶאנָה
	ye (m.)	,,	תִּמְצְאוּ	ye (m.)	,,	תִּמָּצְאוּ
	ye (f.)	,,	תִּמְצֶאנָה	ye (f.)	,,	תִּמָּצֶאנָה
	we (c.) shall	,,	נִמְצָא	we (c.) shall	,,	נִמָּצֵא
Cohort.:	let me (c.) find		אֶמְצְאָה	let me (c.)	,,	אִמָּצְאָה

Imperf. with suffix:

he will find me	יִמְצָאֵנִי

Imper.: find thou (m.)	מְצָא	be thou (m.) found	הִמָּצֵא
,, (f.)	מִצְאִי	,, (f.) ,,	הִמָּצְאִי
,, ye (m.)	מִצְאוּ	,, ye (m.) ,,	הִמָּצְאוּ
,, (f.)	מְצֶאנָה	,, (f.) ,,	הִמָּצֶאנָה
Part. active: finding (m. sg.) &c.	מֹצֵא		
passive: found (m. sg.) &c.	מָצוּא	being found (m. sg.) &c.	נִמְצָא
Inf. absolute:	מָצוֹא		נִמְצֹא
construct:	מְצֹא		הִמָּצֵא

The main point about the Lameḏ 'Alep̱ verb is that the א loses its power as a consonant. *In the Perfect Qal* of the normal verb (שָׁמַר, שָׁמַ֫רְתָּ) the third root-letter closes the syllable, but in the (hypothetical) corresponding forms מָצַא, מָצַ֫אְתָּ the א is inaudible and has no force as a consonant, so that the syllable is really open. Since open syllables have long vowels the Pathaḥ is lengthened to Qameṣ—מָצָא, מָצָאתָ (and the Dagheš Lene falls away after the vowel): מְצַאְתֶּם becomes מְצָאתֶם &c.

If the א were merely a guttural the *Imperfect Qal* would be יִמְצַא, but since the א has no consonantal value and the syllable is therefore open the vowel in it is lengthened—יִמְצָא. The 2nd and 3rd pl. fem. form תִּמְצֶ֫אנָה has Seghol in the second syllable (and likewise the Niphal Imperfect). In the Niphal *Perfect* 1st and 2nd person the vowel in the second syllable is Ṣere. These are due, very likely, to analogy with the Lameḏ He verb (pp. 216 ff.) which has the same characteristic of a mute third root-letter.

NOTE: The Stative Lameḏ 'Alep̱ verb is pointed as follows:

		('to fear', 'be afraid')	('to be full')		
QAL: *Perfect*	3. m. sg.	יָרֵא	מָלֵא	3. c. pl.	יָֽרְאוּ
	2. m. sg.	יָרֵ֫אתָ	מָלֵ֫אתָ	2. m. pl.	יְרֵאתֶם
	1. c. sg.	יָרֵ֫אתִי	מָלֵ֫אתִי	1. c. pl.	יָרֵ֫אנוּ

HIPHIL

Perf.:		*Imperf.*:	
he (hath) caused to find	הִמְצִיא	he will cause to find	יַמְצִיא
she ,,	הִמְצִיאָה	she ,,	תַּמְצִיא
thou (m.) hast ,,	הִמְצֵאתָ	thou (m.) wilt ,,	תַּמְצִיא
thou (f.) ,,	הִמְצֵאת	thou (f.) ,,	תַּמְצִיאִי
I (c.) (have) ,,	הִמְצֵאתִי	I (c.) shall ,,	אַמְצִיא
		they (m.) will ,,	יַמְצִיאוּ
they (c.) ,,	הִמְצִיאוּ	they (f.) ,,	תַּמְצֶאנָה
ye (m.) ,,	הִמְצֵאתֶם	ye (m.) ,,	תַּמְצִיאוּ
ye (f.) ,,	הִמְצֵאתֶן	ye (f.) ,,	תַּמְצֶאנָה
we (c.) ,,	הִמְצִינוּ	we (c.) shall ,,	נַמְצִיא

Shortened Imperf. Jussive:
let him cause to find יַמְצֵא

Imper.:		*Imperf. with Waw Consec.*:	
cause thou (m.) to find	הַמְצֵא	and he caused to find	וַיַּמְצֵא
,, (f.) ,,	הַמְצִיאִי	*Part.*: causing to find (m. sg.) &c.	מַמְצִיא
,, ye (m.) ,,	הַמְצִיאוּ	*Inf. absolute*:	הַמְצֵא
,, (f.) ,,	הַמְצֶאנָה	*construct*:	הַמְצִיא

For the Piel, Pual, and Hithpael the verb רִפֵּא ('to heal') will serve:

	PIEL		PUAL		HITHPAEL	
Perf.:	he (hath) healed	רִפֵּא	he was healed	רֻפָּא	he (hath) healed himself	הִתְרַפֵּא
	thou (m.) hast healed &c.	רִפֵּאתָ	thou (m.) wast healed &c.	רֻפֵּאתָ	thou (m.) hast healed thyself &c.	הִתְרַפֵּאתָ
Imperf.:	he will heal	יְרַפֵּא	he will be healed	יְרֻפָּא	he will heal himself	יִתְרַפֵּא
	she ,, &c.	תְּרַפֵּא	she will be healed &c.	תְּרֻפָּא	she will heal herself &c.	תִּתְרַפֵּא

Imper.:	heal thou (m.) רַפֵּא &c.		heal thyself (m.) הִתְרַפֵּא &c.
Part.:	healing (m. sg.) מְרַפֵּא &c.	being healed (m. sg.) מְרֻפָּא &c.	healing himself מִתְרַפֵּא &c.
Inf. absolute:	רַפֵּא		הִתְרַפֵּא
construct:	רַפֵּא		

EXERCISE 32

Eli עֵלִי	therefore לָכֵן / עַל־כֵּן	a (pace), time (f.) פַּ֫עַם
		twice (dual) פַּעֲמַ֫יִם

(1) וַיְהִי בַּלַּ֫יְלָה הַהוּא, וּשְׁמוּאֵל שֹׁכֵב[a] בְּהֵיכַל־יהוה אֲשֶׁר שָׁם אֲרוֹן הָאֱלֹהִים, וַיִּקְרָא יהוה אֶל־שְׁמוּאֵל, וַיֹּ֫אמֶר הַנַּ֫עַר אֶל־עֵלִי, הִנְנִי כִּי קָרָ֫אתָ לִי, וַיֹּ֫אמֶר עֵלִי לֹא קָרָ֫אתִי לָךְ: וַיִּקְרָא יהוה עוֹד אֶל־שְׁמוּאֵל, וַיֹּ֫אמֶר הַנַּ֫עַר עוֹד אֶל־עֵלִי הֲלֹא זֶה פַּעֲמַ֫יִם קָרָ֫אתָ לִי: אָז יָדַע עֵלִי כִּי יהוה הוּא הַקֹּרֵא לַנָּ֫עַר: וַיֹּ֫אמֶר אֵלָיו עֵלִי, שְׁכַב בְּנִי וְהָיָה כִּי יִקְרָא אֵלֶ֫יךָ וְאָמַרְתָּ, דַּבֵּר יהוה כִּי שֹׁמֵ֫עַ עַבְדֶּ֫ךָ: וַיִּשְׁכַּב הַנַּ֫עַר וַיִּשְׁמַע וְהִנֵּה קוֹל קֹרֵא שְׁמוּאֵל שְׁמוּאֵל, וַיֹּאמַר דַּבֶּר־נָא כִּי שֹׁמֵ֫עַ עַבְדֶּ֫ךָ: וַיֹּ֫אמֶר אֵלָיו, הִנֵּה אָנֹכִי שֹׁפֵט אֶת־עֵלִי וְאֶת־בֵּיתוֹ, כִּי עָשׂוּ בָנָיו אֶת־הָרַע בְּעֵינַי וְהוּא יָדַע וְלֹא כִבְּדֻ֫נִי לְעֵינֵיהֶם, לָכֵן יִפְּלוּ בָנָיו בַּחֶ֫רֶב וְנִכְרַת בֵּית־עֵלִי מִיִּשְׂרָאֵל: וַיְהִי בַבֹּ֫קֶר, וּשְׁמוּאֵל יָרֵא[a] לְהַגִּיד אֶת אֲשֶׁר דִּבֶּר אֵלָיו יהוה, וַיִּקְרָא אֵלָיו עֵלִי וַיֹּאמַר שְׁמוּאֵל בְּנִי, הַגִּ֫ידָה לִי אֶת־הַדָּבָר אֲשֶׁר דִּבֶּר אֵלֶ֫יךָ יהוה, אַל־תַּסְתֵּר מִמֶּנִּי: וַיַּגֵּד לוֹ אֶת־דִּבְרֵי־יהוה: וַיֹּ֫אמֶר עֵלִי, צַדִּיק יהוה וְאָנֹכִי הָרָשָׁע, מִשְׁפָּטוֹ צֶ֫דֶק וְכָל־דְּבָרָיו אֱמֶת, יְהִי שֵׁם־יהוה מְבֹרָךְ (2) כִּי תִמְצָא אֶת־צֹאן־אֹיִבְךָ[b] בַּדֶּ֫רֶךְ, אַל תַּסְתֵּר

[a] The clause containing the participle is subsidiary and, if put in parentheses, does not break the continuity of the main theme. Hence the subsidiary clause, not being part of the continuous narrative, does not employ the waw consecutive. With the participle in this connexion supply in English 'was'.

[b] For a hypothetical אֹיִבְךָ.

אֶת־עֵינֶ֫יךָ מֵהֶם כִּי קַבֵּץ תְּקַבְּצֵם אֶל־בֵּיתְךָ וְהַאֲכַלְתָּ֫ אֹתָם
וְשִׁלַּחְתָּ֫ לְהַגִּיד לוֹ, וְיָרֵאתָ מֵיהוה אֱלֹהֶיךָ (3) וַיְהִי בַּעֲמֹד מֹשֶׁה
עַל־רֹאשׁ־הָהָר וַיֹּ֫אמֶר אֵלָיו יהוה, זֹאת הָאָ֫רֶץ. אֲשֶׁר נָשָׂ֫אתִי
אֶת־[a]יָדִי לְאַבְרָהָם לָתֵת לְזַרְעוֹ (4) לָקַח הַמֶּ֫לֶךְ בְּיָדוֹ אֶת־
סֵ֫פֶר הַתּוֹרָה וַיִּקְרָא בְּאָזְנֵי־הָעָם אֶת־הַמִּצְוֹת וְאֶת־הַמִּשְׁפָּטִים
אֲשֶׁר צִוָּה מֹשֶׁה אֶת־יִשְׂרָאֵל, וַיִּקְרַע אֶת־בְּגָדָיו וַיֹּאמַר, חָטָ֫אנוּ
לַיהוה אֱלֹהֵי־אֲבוֹתֵינוּ כִּי לֹא שָׁמַ֫רְנוּ אֶת־מִצְוֹתָיו כְּכֹל הַכָּתוּב
בַּסֵּ֫פֶר הַזֶּה, לָכֵן בָּ֫אָה עָלֵ֫ינוּ הַצָּרָה הַזֹּאת (5) כֹּה דִבֶּר אֵלַי
יהוה, הִנְנִי שֹׁלֵ֫חַ אֹתְךָ אֶל־הָעָם הַזֶּה וְהָלַכְתָּ֫ וְקָרָ֫אתָ בְאָזְנֵיהֶם
לֵאמֹר, הִנֵּה מָצָ֫אתִי אֶתְכֶם בְּאֶ֫רֶץ מִצְרָיִם: וָאֶשְׁלַח אֲלֵיכֶם
אֶת־מֹשֶׁה עַבְדִּי לְהַצִּיל אֶתְכֶם מֵעֲבוֹדַת מִצְרַ֫יִם וָאֶגֹּף אֶת־
פַּרְעֹה וְאֶת־עֲבָדָיו עַד־אֲשֶׁר שִׁלַּח אֶתְכֶם מֵאַרְצוֹ: וַתַּעַמְדוּ
עַל־הַר־קָדְשִׁי[b] וַתִּשְׁמְעוּ אֶת־קוֹלִי בְּדַבְּרִי אֲלֵיכֶם מִתּוֹךְ־הָאֵשׁ
וַתֹּאמְרוּ בְּקוֹל אֶחָד, אֹתְךָ לְבַדְּךָ נַעֲבֹד: וְעַתָּה לֹא יְרֵאתֶם
לַעֲבֹד אֶת־אֱלֹהֵי־כְנַ֫עַן אֲשֶׁר עָשׂוּ אֹתָם יְדֵי־אָדָם וַתִּשְׁכְּחוּ
אֹתִי: לָכֵן אָנֹכִי אֶשְׁכַּח אֶתְכֶם וְהַסְתֵּר אַסְתִּיר אֶת־פָּנַי מִכֶּם
(6) צִוָּה יְהוֹשֻׁעַ וַיְבַקְשׁוּ וַיִּמְצְאוּ אֶת־הָאִישׁ אֲשֶׁר גָּנַב אֶת־הַזָּהָב
וַיַּגִּ֫ישׁוּ אֹתוֹ לַמִּשְׁפָּט: וַיֹּ֫אמֶר אֵלָיו יְהוֹשֻׁעַ הִנְּךָ בֶן־מָ֫וֶת[c] כִּי חָטָא
חַטָּ֫את לַיהוה וַתִּקַּח מִזְּהַב־הָעִיר וְלֹא יָרֵ֫אתָ לַעֲבֹר עַל־מִצְוַת־
יהוה (7) רָאָה דָוִד אֶת־הָאִשָּׁה וַתִּמְצָא חֵן בְּעֵינָיו, וַיְהִי אַחֲרֵי
מוֹת־אִישָׁהּ וַיִּשְׁלַח אֵלֶ֫יהָ דָוִד לֵאמֹר הִנֵּה מָצָאת חֵן בְּעֵינַי
מְאֹד וָאֶשְׁלַח לָקַ֫חַת אֹתָךְ לִי לְאִשָּׁה (8) רָאָה אַבְרָהָם אֶת־
הָאֲנָשִׁים עֹמְדִים לְפָנָיו וַיִּגַּשׁ אֲלֵיהֶם וַיֹּאמַר, אֲדוֹנַי אִם־נָא
מָצָ֫אתִי חֵן בְּעֵינֵיכֶם אַל־נָא־תַעַבְרוּ עַד־אֲשֶׁר אֲכַלְתֶּם לֶחֶם

(1) Sarah the wife of Abraham bore (to) him a son and she called his name Isaac, as the word which the angel spoke to

[a] The raising of the hand accompanies the taking of an oath and therefore 'to raise the hand' means 'to take an oath'.

[b] 'My mountain of holiness'—i.e. 'my holy mountain'. See Appendix 5, p. 253.

[c] 'Worthy of death'.

Abraham her husband. (2) Behold I (was) walking in the way and I found the old prophet and I gave (to) him to eat, for he was hungry, and I hid him with me in the house and I saved his life ('soul') from death. (3) Hear thou the word of God which he hath spoken against [עַל] thee. Behold I have made thee king over Israel and thou wast not afraid to forget the Lord and thou didst serve strange gods. (4) The king sought to take the woman to him(self) for a wife and she said unto him, 'My lord, I am the wife of a man'. And the king asked the name of her husband and she told (to) him. And he took a book and he wrote in it and he called (to) the husband of the woman and he said unto him, 'Take now this book and give it to the judge whom thou wilt find before the palace'. And the man took the book and he gave (it) to the judge. And the judge read the command of the king which (was) written in the book, saying, 'Send this man away to the wilderness and he shall die there'. And the judge hearkened to the voice of the king—according to ('as') all that he commanded him, so he did. And it was told to the king that the husband of the woman was dead and he took the woman to himself for a wife. And it came to pass in that time that the prophet called unto the king and he was very angry and he said, 'Thou whom the Lord hath chosen ("who, the Lord hath chosen thee") for a righteous judge[a] over His people, thou hast sinned before Him and He hath judged thee the judgement of death'. (5) I told not (to) thee that she is my wife for I was afraid lest thou shouldst (impf.) kill me. (6) *Thou* (pronoun) hast created the heavens and the earth and the seas and all that is in them. (7) The sons of Reuben drew near unto Moses and they said unto him, 'If we have found grace in thine eyes, give (to) us, we pray thee [נָא] these cities and we shall dwell in them'. (8) I have lifted up my hand to the Lord my God and I have sworn that I will not take[b] a thing from you. (9) The priest said to the woman, 'Behold thou art bearing a son and thou shalt call his name Samuel'. (10) Unto Thee, my God, I shall call and from Thy heavens Thou wilt hear my voice.

[a] 'A judge of righteousness'. See p. 136. **63.**

[b] In Hebrew 'I have sworn *if I shall take*', see p. 176, footnote *b*.

74. SOME DOUBLY WEAK VERBS

There are many verbs which have more than one peculiar root-letter, as נָגַע 'to touch', which is both a Pe Nun and Lamed Guttural, requiring two sets of adjustments to be made. A few doubly weak verbs are given below:

(*a*) נָגַע 'to touch'—Pe Nun and Lamed Guttural verb.

QAL: Perfect נָגַע; Imperfect יִגַּע (for יִנְגַּע); Imperative גַּע; Infinitive construct נְגֹעַ and גַּעַת (for גֶּעֶת).

In the Imperfect the *Nun* is assimilated and the *Guttural* has the vowel Pathaḥ. The alternative Infinitive construct has Pathaḥ before and under the guttural.

HIPHIL: Perfect הִגִּיעַ (for הִנְגִּיעַ 'to cause to touch', 'to reach'); Imperfect יַגִּיעַ (for יַנְגִּיעַ); Participle מַגִּיעַ (for מַנְגִּיעַ).

PIEL: Perfect נִגַּע (for נִגֵּעַ 'to plague'); Imperfect יְנַגַּע (for יְנַגֵּעַ). The explanations of the Qal hold also for the Hiphil and Piel.

Other types of Pe Nun and Lamed Guttural verbs are:

'to breathe' QAL: *Perfect* נָפַח; *Imperfect* יִפַּח

'to journey' ,, נָסַע; ,, יִסַּע

(HIPHIL *Perfect*: הִסִּיעַ 'to cause to journey')

'to plant' QAL: *Perfect* נָטַע; *Imperfect* יִטַּע.

(*b*) חבא (in Niphal and Hithpael 'to hide oneself' and in Hiphil 'to hide'—transitive)—Pe Guttural and Lamed 'Alep verb.

Similarly חָטָא 'to sin'

	QAL		HIPHIL	
Perf.:	he hath sinned	חָטָא	he hath caused to sin	הֶחֱטִיא
	thou (m.) hast ,,	חָטָאתָ	thou (m.) hast ,,	הֶחֱטֵאתָ
Imperf.:	he will sin	יֶחֱטָא	he will cause to sin	יַחֲטִיא
Inf. construct:		חֲטֹא		הַחֲטִיא
	with לְ	לַחֲטֹא		

NIPHAL: Perfect נֶחְבָּא; Imperfect יֵחָבֵא (for יִחָּבֵא); Participle נֶחְבָּא.

In the Perfect of Niphal the נ has Seghol (as all *Pe Guttural* verbs) and the second syllable has Qameṣ (as all *Lameḏ 'Alep̱* verbs). So also the participle.

HIPHIL: Perfect הֶחְבִּיא; Imperfect יַחְבִּיא &c.

HITHPAEL: Perfect הִתְחַבֵּא; Imperfect יִתְחַבֵּא &c.

(*c*) נָשָׂא 'to lift up', 'raise', 'bear'—Pe Nun and Lameḏ 'Alep̱ verb.

QAL: Perfect נָשָׂא; Imperfect יִשָּׂא; Imperative שָׂא; Infinitive construct נְשׂא and שְׂאֵת (for שֶׂ֫אֶת); with ל, לָשֵׂאת.

In the Imperfect the *Nun* is assimilated (as יִגַּשׁ) and the second syllable has Qameṣ because of the *Lameḏ 'Alep̱* (as יִמְצָא). The alternative form of the Infinitive construct is (first a theoretical שֶׂ֫אֶת since it is Pe Nun—as גֶּ֫שֶׁת—which easily becomes) שְׂאֵת and with a prefixed ל the א quiesces and its vowel is taken by the preceding letter—לָשֵׂאת.

NIPHAL: Perfect נִשָּׂא (for נִנְשָׂא); Imperfect יִנָּשֵׂא; Imperative הִנָּשֵׂא.

HIPHIL: Perfect הִשִּׂיא (for הִנְשִׂיא; Imperfect יַשִּׂיא (for יַנְשִׂיא); Participle מַשִּׂיא (for מַנְשִׂיא) &c.

The changes in these conjugations are obvious from the remarks above about the Qal. The Piel, Pual, and Hithpael, having a Dagheš Forte in the *second* root-letter, do not affect the first root-letter נ, so that they are simply Lameḏ Guttural or Lameḏ 'Alep̱ verbs in these conjugations.

EXERCISE 33

Eden	עֵ֫דֶן	vanity, falsehood	שָׁוְא	to flee	בָּרַח
knowledge	דַּ֫עַת	living, alive (adj.)	חַי	Edom	אֱדוֹם

(1) וַיִּבְרָא אֱלֹהִים אֶת־הָאָדָם, עָפָר מִן־הָאֲדָמָה, וַיִּפַּח בּוֹ רוּחַ
חַיִּים וַיְהִי הָאָדָם לְנֶ֫פֶשׁ חַיָּה: וַיִּטַּע יהוה גַּן בְּעֵ֫דֶן וַיִּתֵּן לָאָדָם

לְעָבְדָהּ וּלְשָׁמְרָהּ, וַיֹּאמֶר אֵלָיו, מִכֹּל עֲצֵי־הַגָּן אָכוֹל תֹּאכֵל,
רַק מֵעֵץ־הַדַּעַת אֲשֶׁר בְּתוֹךְ־הַגָּן לֹא־תֹאכַל מִמֶּנּוּ וְלֹא תִגַּע
בּוֹ, כִּי בְּיוֹם עָבְרְךָ אֶת־הַמִּצְוָה הַזֹּאת, מָוֶת יִהְיֶה מִשְׁפָּטֶךָ
(2) וַיֹּאמֶר מֹשֶׁה אֶל־אַהֲרֹן, כֹּה תְבָרֵךְ אֶת־בְּנֵי־יִשְׂרָאֵל, אָמֹר
אֲלֵיהֶם, יְבָרֶכְךָ יהוה וְיִשְׁמְרֶךָ יִשָּׂא יהוה אֶת־פָּנָיו אֵלֶיךָ וְנָתַן
לְךָ שָׁלוֹם (3) לֹא תִשָּׂא אֶת־שֵׁם־אֱלֹהֶיךָ לַשָּׁוְא (4) וַתֹּאמֶר
אֵשֶׁת אֲדוֹן־יוֹסֵף אֶל־כָּל־הָעֹמְדִים לְפָנֶיהָ, בָּא אֵלַי הָעֶבֶד
הָעִבְרִי הַזֶּה, וְאֵין אִישׁ אִתָּנוּ בַּבַּיִת, וַיַּחֲזֵק[a] בִּי, וָאֶשָּׂא אֶת־קוֹלִי
וָאֶקְרָא: וַיְהִי כְּשָׁמְעוֹ אֶת־קוֹלִי וַיִּבְרַח מִפָּנַי וַיַּעֲזֹב אֶת־בִּגְדוֹ
אִתִּי: וַיְהִי בָעֶרֶב וַתַּגֵּד לְאִישָׁהּ כַּדְּבָרִים הָאֵלֶּה וַיִּקְצֹף עַד־
מְאֹד וַיִּתֵּן אֶת־יוֹסֵף בַּבּוֹר (5) כִּי יְדַבֵּר אֵלֶיךָ רֵעֲךָ לֵאמֹר
שָׁוְא עֲבֹד אֶת־יהוה וְעַתָּה נַעַבְדָה אֶת־אֱלֹהֵי־כְנַעַן, וְהָלַכְתָּ
וְהִגַּדְתָּ לְשֹׁפְטֵי־עִירְךָ וְשָׁפְטוּ אֹתוֹ כַּכָּתוּב בַּתּוֹרָה הַזֹּאת
(6) וַיִּשְׁמַע יַעֲקֹב בְּקוֹל־יהוה וַיִּקַּח אֶת־נָשָׁיו וְאֶת־כָּל־בְּנֵי בֵיתוֹ
וַיִּסַּע אַרְצָה כְּנָעַן (7) יִרְאַת־אֱלֹהִים חָכְמָה וָדַעַת וְשָׁוְא עֲבוֹדַת
עֵץ וָאֶבֶן (8) וַיְהִי אַחֲרֵי הַדְּבָרִים הָאֵלֶּה וַיִּסְעוּ בְנֵי־יִשְׂרָאֵל
דֶּרֶךְ הַמִּדְבָּר הַיַּרְדֵּנָה: וַיִּשְׁלַח מֹשֶׁה מַלְאָכִים אֶל־מֶלֶךְ אֱדוֹם
לֵאמֹר נַעְבְּרָה־נָּא בְאַרְצְךָ אֶל־הָאָרֶץ אֲשֶׁר נִשְׁבַּע אֱלֹהֵינוּ
לַאֲבוֹתֵינוּ לָתֵת לָנוּ, וְהָיָה בְּתֵת אַתָּה יהוה בְּיָדֵנוּ וְזָכַרְנוּ אֶת־
הַחֶסֶד הַזֶּה וְכָרַתְנוּ אִתְּךָ בְּרִית־שָׁלוֹם: וַיֹּאמֶר מֶלֶךְ־אֱדוֹם,
לֹא תַעֲבֹר בְּאַרְצִי וְאִם לֹא תִשְׁמַע אֵלַי וְיָצָאתִי לְנֶגְדְּךָ בְּיָד
חֲזָקָה (9) בַּיּוֹם הַהוּא, אָמַר יהוה, לֹא יִשָּׂא גוֹי אֶל־גּוֹי חֶרֶב
וְלֹא תִהְיֶה עוֹד מִלְחָמָה וְלֹא יִשְׁפְּכוּ עוֹד דָּמִים, וְיָשְׁבוּ כָל־
הָעַמִּים בְּשָׁלוֹם עַל־אַדְמָתָם (10) שָׂא־נָא אֶת־עֵינֶיךָ מִן הַמָּקוֹם
אֲשֶׁר אַתָּה שָׁם, כִּי אֶת־כָּל־הָאָרֶץ הַזֹּאת לְךָ אֶתְּנֶנָּה (11) וַיְהִי
בִּנְסֹעַ הָעָם וַיִּשְׂאוּ בְנֵי־אַהֲרֹן הַכֹּהֲנִים אֶת־אֲרוֹן־הַבְּרִית
(12) צִוָּה מֹשֶׁה אֶת־הָעָם לֵאמֹר לֹא תִגְּשׁוּ אֶל־הָהָר וְלֹא תִגְּעוּ[b]
בּוֹ, כִּי יהוה יֹרֵד עָלָיו וְהָיָה הָהָר קֹדֶשׁ

[a] The Hiphil of this verb means 'to take hold of', 'seize'.

[b] נָגַע does not take an object—it is usually followed by בְּ.

(1) The sons of Reuben drew near unto Moses and they spoke unto him saying: 'Behold this land is good for our sheep, and now if we have found grace in thine eyes let us plant (cohortat.) trees, and let us work the land, and our wives and our children shall dwell there, and we will pass over with our brethren unto the land which the Lord hath sworn to our fathers to give to their seed, and we will fight for them'. And Moses said: 'I will ask of the Lord, if it is good in His eyes'. (2) And it came to pass after many days that we journeyed (waw consec.) in the wilderness to the mountain of God to hear the words of the Lord and ye said, 'All our days we will serve the Lord'. (3) The prophet said, 'All thy words are falsehood, for there is not in them the fear of the Lord and the knowledge of His law'. (4) Joshua commanded the people saying, 'When you hear (inf. constr. with suff.) my voice calling, "It is a war for the Lord and for Joshua!" then (waw consec.) shall ye call, even ye, so'. (5) All the warriors of David came unto him and they swore to him saying: 'Thee alone we will serve and no man shall touch (in) thee'. (6) Flee to the land of Egypt, for the king hath sworn to take thy life,[a] and thou shalt dwell there until the death of thine enemy and thou shalt deliver thy life from death. (7) And it came to pass when Jacob heard the words of his sons that he cried in a great voice, 'My son Joseph liveth and he hath sent to take me unto him to Egypt. Blessed be the Lord, the God of my fathers, who hath done kindness with me.' (8) My voice I will raise unto the Lord and from all my troubles He will deliver me. (9) Moses saw the serpent before him and he fled (from) before it; and the Lord said unto him, 'Why fleest thou? Take it in thy hand.' (10) Give (to) me wisdom and knowledge, in order that I may rule over Thy people with righteousness.

75. PE YOḎ AND PE WAW VERBS

There are two distinct types of weak verbs which have י as the first root-letter in the Perfect Qal. The one, represented by יָטַב ('to be good') is in Hebrew a true Pe Yoḏ; while the other, represented by יָשַׁב ('to sit, dwell') comes, as will be

[a] נֶ֫פֶשׁ.

shown, from an original וָשַׁב and is therefore a Pe Waw verb. The distinction between the Pe Yoḏ and the Pe Waw verbs, though not apparent in Qal, is quite clear in some of the derived conjugations. For example:

(*a*) The Hiphil of יָטַב is הֵיטִיב ('to cause to be good, to do good'). Note the original י (after the ה of Hiphil); but

(*b*) the Hiphil of יָשַׁב (originally וָשַׁב) is הוֹשִׁיב ('to cause to sit, dwell'). Note the original ו (though quiescent, after the ה of Hiphil).

It was noted on p. 157 that the regular Hiphil הִגְדִּיל comes from an earlier form הַגְדִּיל (hagdîl); so that:

(*a*) The Hiphil of the true Pe Yoḏ יָטַב was originally הַיְטִיב (haytîḇ) which became הֵיטִיב (hēytîḇ, hêtîḇ), just as the absolute עַ֫יִן and בַּ֫יִת became עֵין and בֵּית in the construct (pp. 47, 72).

(*b*) The Hiphil of the original Pe Waw verb וָשַׁב was first הַוְשִׁיב (hawšîḇ) which became הוֹשִׁיב (hôšîḇ), in the same way as מָוֶת became (מָוְת and then) מוֹת in the construct (p. 97, footnote *a*).

We now give Tables of the Pe Yoḏ and Pe Waw together, so that the differences between them may be seen.

Qal

	PE YOḎ		PE WAW	
Perf.:	(he hath been good	יָטַב)	he (hath) sat	יָשַׁב
	(*regular : not used*)		(*regular*)	
Imperf.:	he will be good	יִיטַב	he will sit	יֵשֵׁב
	she ,,	תִּיטַב	she ,,	תֵּשֵׁב
	thou (m.) wilt ,,	תִּיטַב	thou (m.) wilt ,,	תֵּשֵׁב
	thou (f.) ,,	תִּיטְבִי	thou (f.) ,,	תֵּשְׁבִי
	I (c.) shall ,,	אִיטַב	I (c.) shall ,,	אֵשֵׁב
	they (m.) will ,,	יִיטְבוּ	they (m.) will ,,	יֵשְׁבוּ
	they (f.) ,,	תִּיטַ֫בְנָה	they (f.) ,,	תֵּשַׁ֫בְנָה
	ye (m.) ,,	תִּיטְבוּ	ye (m.) ,,	תֵּשְׁבוּ
	ye (f.) ,,	תִּיטַ֫בְנָה	ye (f.) ,,	תֵּשַׁ֫בְנָה
	we (c.) shall ,,	נִיטַב	we (c.) shall ,,	נֵשֵׁב

Cohort.:	let me (c.) be good	אֵיטְבָה	let me (c.) sit	אֵשְׁבָה
Imperf. with Waw Consecutive:	and he was good	וַיִּיטַב	and he sat	וַיֵּשֶׁב [a]
Imper.:			sit thou (m.)	שֵׁב (שְׁבָה)
			,, (f.)	שְׁבִי
			,, ye (m.)	שְׁבוּ
			,, (f.)	שֵׁבְנָה
Part.:		(יֹטֵב)	sitting (m. sg.) &c.	יֹשֵׁב
Inf. absolute:		יָטוֹב		יָשׁוֹב
construct:		(יְטֹב)		שֶׁבֶת
,, *with* ל				לָשֶׁבֶת
,, ,, *suffixes*:				שִׁבְתִּי

The Pe Yod̲ verb retains the first root-letter quiescent in the Imperfect Qal—יִיְטַב (Stative, as יִשְׁכַּב) becomes יִיטַב (p. 18, 2).

The Pe Waw verb in Qal discards the first root-letter in the Imperfect יֵשֵׁב, the Imperative שֵׁב, and the Infinitive Construct שֶׁבֶת, the latter resembling that of the Pe Nun type. The Waw Consecutive with the Imperfect retards the accent one place, so that the last syllable וַיֵּ[שֵׁב] is now closed and unaccented and its vowel is thus shortened—וַיֵּשֶׁב.

NOTE: Some of these verbs have become mixed, partaking of the peculiarities of each other; e.g. the verb יָרַשׁ ('to inherit') is a Pe Waw Verb, but the Imperfect Qal is יִירַשׁ, as if it were a Pe Yod̲. Similarly in cognate languages the verb יָדַע ('to know') appears as a Pe Yod̲, but in Hebrew it takes the peculiarities of a Pe Waw (see p. 210 (*a*)).

In order to show the difference between the (true) Pe Yod̲ and the (original) Pe Waw the Hiphil is first given.

[a] But וָאֵשֵׁב 'and I sat'—no shortening for 1st sing. (p. 114 (*b*), N.B.).

Hiphil

	PE YOD		PE WAW	
Perf.:	he hath done good	הֵיטִיב	he hath caused to sit, dwell	הוֹשִׁיב
	she ,,	הֵיטִ֫יבָה	she ,,	הוֹשִׁ֫יבָה
	thou (m.) hast ,,	הֵיטַ֫בְתָּ	thou (m.) hast ,,	הוֹשַׁ֫בְתָּ
	thou (f.) ,,	הֵיטַבְתְּ	thou (f.) ,,	הוֹשַׁבְתְּ
	I have (c.) ,,	הֵיטַ֫בְתִּי	I (c.) have ,,	הוֹשַׁ֫בְתִּי
	they (c.) ,,	הֵיטִ֫יבוּ	they (c.) ,,	הוֹשִׁ֫יבוּ
	ye (m.) ,,	הֵיטַבְתֶּם	ye (m.) ,,	הוֹשַׁבְתֶּם
	ye (f.) ,,	הֵיטַבְתֶּן	ye (f.) ,,	הוֹשַׁבְתֶּן
	we (c.) ,,	הֵיטַ֫בְנוּ	we (c.) ,,	הוֹשַׁ֫בְנוּ
Imperf.:	he will do good	יֵיטִיב	he will cause to sit, dwell	יוֹשִׁיב
	she ,,	תֵּיטִיב	she ,,	תּוֹשִׁיב
	thou (m.) wilt ,,	תֵּיטִיב	thou (m.) wilt ,,	תּוֹשִׁיב
	thou (f.) ,,	תֵּיטִ֫יבִי	thou (f.) ,,	תּוֹשִׁ֫יבִי
	I (c.) shall ,,	אֵיטִיב	I (c.) shall ,,	אוֹשִׁיב
	they (m.) will ,,	יֵיטִ֫יבוּ	they (m.) will ,,	יוֹשִׁ֫יבוּ
	they (f.) ,,	תֵּיטַ֫בְנָה	they (f.) ,,	תּוֹשַׁ֫בְנָה
	ye (m.) ,,	תֵּיטִ֫יבוּ	ye (m.) ,,	תּוֹשִׁ֫יבוּ
	ye (f.) ,,	תֵּיטַ֫בְנָה	ye (f.) ,,	תּוֹשַׁ֫בְנָה
	we (c.) shall ,,	נֵיטִיב	we (c.) shall ,,	נוֹשִׁיב
Cohort.:	let me (c.) ,, I *will* ,,	אֵיטִ֫יבָה	let me (c.) ,, I *will* ,,	אוֹשִׁ֫יבָה
Jussive:	let him ,,	יֵיטֵב	let him ,,	יוֹשֵׁב
Imperf. with Waw Consecutive:	and he did good	וַיֵּ֫יטֶב	and he caused to sit	וַיּ֫וֹשֶׁב

Imper.:				
	do thou (m.) good	הֵיטֵב	cause thou (m.) to sit	הוֹשֵׁב
		(הֵיטִ֫יבָה) [a]		(הוֹשִׁ֫יבָה) [a]
	„ (f.) „	הֵיטִ֫יבִי	„ (f.) „	הוֹשִׁ֫יבִי
	„ ye (m.) „	הֵיטִ֫יבוּ	„ ye (m.) „	הוֹשִׁ֫יבוּ
	„ (f.) „	הֵיטֵ֫בְנָה	„ (f.) „	הוֹשֵׁ֫בְנָה
Part.:				
	doing good (m. sg.) &c.	מֵיטִיב	causing to sit (m. sg.) &c.	מוֹשִׁיב
Inf. absolute:		הֵיטֵב		הוֹשֵׁב
construct:		הֵיטִיב		הוֹשִׁיב

In the Hiphil the original first root-letter has remained; הֵיטִיב shows the original Yoḏ and הוֹשִׁיב the original Waw. Note that the Imperfect Hiphil has a shortened form (יוֹשֵׁב from יוֹשִׁיב, יֵיטֵב from יֵיטִיב) for the Jussive. Waw Consecutive is attached to the shortened form of the Imperfect and when this occurs the accent is retarded one place, leaving a closed unaccented syllable which must, consequently, shorten its vowel.

Pe Waw

	NIPHAL		HOPHAL	
Perf.:	he was inhabited	נוֹשַׁב	he was made to sit, dwell	הוּשַׁב
	she „	נֽוֹשְׁבָה	she „	הֽוּשְׁבָה
	thou (m.) wast „ &c.	נוֹשַׁ֫בְתָּ	thou (m.) wast „ &c.	הוּשַׁ֫בְתָּ
Imperf.:				
	he will be inhabited	יִוָּשֵׁב	he will be made to sit, dwell	יוּשַׁב
	she „	תִּוָּשֵׁב	she „	תּוּשַׁב
	I (c.) „ &c.	אִוָּשֵׁב	I (c.) „ &c.	אוּשַׁב
Imper.:				
	be thou (m.) inhabited &c.	הִוָּשֵׁב		
Part.:				
	being inhabited (m. sg.)	נוֹשָׁב	being made to sit (m. sg.) &c.	מוּשָׁב
	„ (f. sg.) &c.	נוֹשָׁבָה		
Infinitives:		הִוָּשֵׁב		הוּשַׁב

[a] Emphatic imperative, p. 88 (*b*).

NIPHAL: Since the Niphal Perfect נִשְׁמַר (nišmar) was originally נַשְׁמַר (našmar) (see note on Niphal of Pe Guttural verb, p. 156), the Niphal Perfect of the original וָשַׁב was נַוְשַׁב (nawšab̲) which became נוֹשַׁב (nôšab̲). The original initial ו has survived in the Niphal Imperfect as a full consonant and so this part of the conjugation is normal.

HOPHAL: It will be remembered that the Hophal of the Pe Nun verb has Qibbuṣ instead of Qameṣ-Ḥaṭuph (p. 144). The Hophal of the Pe Waw verb follows this tendency and the (hypothetical form) הֻוְשַׁב (huwšab̲) becomes הוּשַׁב (hûšab̲); the waw quiesces.

NOTE: A special type of the above verbs is one whose second root-letter is a sibilant (S-sound), since this behaves like a Pe Nun verb:

'to pour out'	Qal:	*Perfect* יָצַק;	*Imperfect* יִצֹּק
'to burn'	Qal:	„ יָצַת	„ יִצַּת
	Hiphil:	„ הִצִּית	„ יַצִּית

EXERCISE 34

maidservant אָמָה — door דֶּלֶת

three (m.) שְׁלֹשָׁה[a], (f.) שָׁלֹשׁ — wall (of a city) חוֹמָה

sister אָחוֹת, pl. (irreg.) אֲחָיוֹת; with suffix אֲחוֹתִי, pl. (with suffix) אַחְיוֹתַי

to go down, descend יָרַד (Imperf. יֵרֵד)

to cause to go down, to bring down ירד in Hiphil הוֹרִיד

to go out, go forth יָצָא (Imperf. יֵצֵא)

to cause to go out, to bring out, bring forth יצא in Hiphil הוֹצִיא

(1) צִוָּה יהוה אֶת־אַבְרָהָם לֵאמֹר צֵא מֵאַרְצְךָ וּמִבֵּית־אָבִיךָ
אֶל־הָאָרֶץ אֲשֶׁר אֹמַר אֵלֶיךָ׃ וַיִּקַּח אַבְרָהָם אֶת־שָׂרָה אִשְׁתּוֹ
וְאֶת־לוֹט בֶּן־אָחִיו וַיֵּצְאוּ אַרְצָה כְּנַעַן וַיֵּשְׁבוּ שָׁם׃ וַיְהִי רָעָב
בָּאָרֶץ וַיֹּאמֶר אַבְרָהָם אֶל־שָׂרָה נֵרְדָה־נָּא מִצְרַיְמָה, וַיֵּרְדוּ

[a] It is interesting to note (pp. 243–4 (*b*)) that the numerals from 3 to 10 end in הָ when in connexion with a masc. noun.

שָׁמָּה (2) עָשָׂה יהוה לְשָׂרָה כַּאֲשֶׁר אָמַר וַתֵּ֫לֶד שָׂרָה בֵּן וַתִּקְרָא
אֶת־שְׁמוֹ יִצְחָק׃ וַיִּגְדַּל הַנַּ֫עַר וַיְהִי אֱלֹהִים אִתּוֹ׃ וַתֹּ֫אמֶר שָׂרָה
אֶל־אַבְרָהָם אִישָׁהּ, לֹא יִירַשׁ בֶּן־הָאָמָה הַזֹּאת עִם־בְּנִי עִם־
יִצְחָק (3) וַיְהִי כִּשְׁמֹעַ יֹשְׁבֵי־הָעִיר כִּי בָ֫אוּ שְׁנֵי[a]־אֲנָשִׁים אֶל־
בֵּית־לוֹט וַיִּתְקַבְּצוּ לִפְנֵי־בֵיתוֹ וַיִּקְרְאוּ אֵלָיו לֵאמֹר אַיֵּה הָאֲנָשִׁים
אֲשֶׁר בָּ֫אוּ אֵלֶ֫יךָ הַלַּ֫יְלָה הוֹצִיאָה[b] אֹתָם אֵלֵינוּ׃ וַיֵּצֵא אֲלֵיהֶם
לוֹט וַיֹּ֫אמֶר אֲלֵיהֶם, אַל־נָא תִשְׁפְּכוּ דָמִים׃ וְלֹא שָׁמְעוּ אֵלָיו
וַיִּגְּשׁוּ לִשְׁבּוֹר אֶת־הַדֶּ֫לֶת וַיִּגֹּף אֹתָם יהוה וְלֹא רָאוּ וַיְבַקְשׁוּ אֶת־
הַדֶּ֫לֶת וְלֹא מָצָאוּ׃ וַיֹּאמְרוּ הַמַּלְאָכִים אֶל־לוֹט, צֵא מִן הָעִיר
אַתָּה וְכָל־בְּנֵי בֵיתֶ֫ךָ כִּי מַשְׁחִיתִים אֲנַ֫חְנוּ אֶת־הַמָּקוֹם׃ וַיִּשְׁמַע
לוֹט בְּקוֹלָם וַיֵּצֵא הוּא וְאִשְׁתּוֹ וּשְׁתֵּי[c]־בְנוֹתָיו וַיִּמָּלְטוּ לְנַפְשָׁם
הָהָ֫רָה׃ וַתֵּ֫רֶד אֵשׁ־אֱלֹהִים מִשָּׁמַ֫יִם וַתֹּאכַל אֶת־הָעִיר וְאֶת־כָּל־
אֲשֶׁר בָּהּ (4) וַיֹּ֫אמֶר יוֹסֵף אֶל־אֶחָיו, הוֹרִ֫ידוּ אֵלַי אֶת־אֲחִיכֶם
הַקָּטֹן וְיָדַ֫עְתִּי כִּי אֱמֶת דִּבַּרְתֶּם׃ וַיְהִי כְּשָׁמְעָם אֶת־דִּבְרֵי־יוֹסֵף
וַיִּירְאוּ מְאֹד וַיֹּאמְרוּ אִישׁ אֶל־רֵעֵ֫הוּ, חָטוֹא חָטָ֫אנוּ לַיהוה
בִּדְבַר־אָחִינוּ, לָכֵן בָּ֫אָה עָלֵ֫ינוּ הַצָּרָה הַזֹּאת׃ וְלֹא יָכֹל יוֹסֵף
לַעֲמֹד בִּפְנֵי־אֶחָיו וַיֵּצֵא (5) וַיַּגֵּד בְּאָזְנֵי־פַרְעֹה לֵאמֹר הִנֵּה
אֲבִי־יוֹסֵף וְאֶחָיו וּנְשֵׁיהֶם וּבְנֵיהֶם בָּאִים מִצְרַ֫יְמָה׃ וַיִּקְרָא
פַּרְעֹה אֶל־יוֹסֵף וַיֹּ֫אמֶר אֵלָיו, הִנֵּה אֶ֫רֶץ מִצְרַ֫יִם לְפָנֶ֫יךָ הִיא,
הוֹשֵׁב אֶת־בְּנֵי בֵית־אָבִ֫יךָ בַּמָּקוֹם אֲשֶׁר יִיטַב בְּעֵינֶ֫יךָ, וְהֵיטֵב
אֵיטִיב עִמָּם (6) וַיְהִי רָעָב בָּאָ֫רֶץ וַיֵּ֫רֶד יַעֲקֹב מִצְרַ֫יְמָה וַיֵּ֫שֶׁב
שָׁם וַיְהִי לְגוֹי גָּדוֹל חָזָק וָרָב׃ וַיִּירְאוּ מִפָּנָיו הַמִּצְרִים וַיֹּאמְרוּ
הִנֵּה בְּתוֹכֵ֫נוּ עַם גָּדוֹל וְחָזָק וְהָיָה כִּי תִהְיֶה מִלְחָמָה וְנִלְחַם גַּם
הוּא בָּנוּ׃ וַיַּעֲבִ֫ידוּהוּ וַיִּתְּנוּ עָלָיו עֲבוֹדָה וַיִּצְעַק יִשְׂרָאֵל אֶל־
יהוה מֵעֲבוֹדָתוֹ (7) וַיֹּ֫אמֶר אֱלֹהִים תּ֫וֹצֵא[d] הָאָ֫רֶץ עֲצֵי־פְרִי אֲשֶׁר
זַרְעָם בָּם, וַיְהִי־כֵן (8) וַיִּשְׁכַּב שָׁם יַעֲקֹב בַּלַּ֫יְלָה הַהוּא וַיַּחֲלֹם

[a] Lit. 'a pair of', i.e. 'two'. See p. 243 (*b*). [b] Longer form of Imperative.

[c] Fem. constr. of שְׁתַּ֫יִם, lit. 'a pair of'. See p. 243 (*b*).

[d] Jussive—shortened form.

וְהִנֵּה יהוה מְדַבֵּר אֵלָיו לֵאמֹר אָנֹכִי אֱלֹהֵי־אַבְרָהָם וֵאלֹהֵי־
יִצְחָק אָבִיךָ וְהֵיטֵב[a] אֵיטִיב עִמְּךָ, כִּי מָצָאתָ חֵן בְּעֵינַי (9) כִּי
תֵצֵא לַמִּלְחָמָה עַל־אֹיְבֶיךָ וּנְתָנָם יהוה בְּיָדֶךָ וְהָיוּ לָכֶם
לַעֲבָדִים: וְכִי תִשָּׂא[b] אַחַת מִבְּנוֹתֵיהֶם חֵן[c] לְפָנֶיךָ וְלָקַחְתָּ אֹתָהּ
לְךָ לְאִשָּׁה וְיָשְׁבָה בְּבֵיתֶךָ וְהָיָה אַחֲרֵי יָמִים רַבִּים וְלֹא תִמְצָא
עוֹד חֵן בְּעֵינֶיךָ, לֹא תִמְכֹּר אֹתָהּ לְאָמָה כִּי שַׁלֵּחַ תְּשַׁלַּח אֹתָהּ
כַּמִּשְׁפָּט הַזֶּה (10) שָׁמְעוּ הַמְרַגְּלִים בְּקוֹל הָאִשָּׁה וַיֵּשְׁבוּ אִתָּהּ
בַּבַּיִת וַיִּשְׁכְּבוּ שָׁם: וַיְהִי בַבֹּקֶר, וְאֵין אִישׁ בָּעִיר, וַתִּקַּח הָאִשָּׁה
אֶת־הָאֲנָשִׁים וַתּוֹרֶד אֹתָם מֵעַל־הַחוֹמָה, וַיִּמָּלְטוּ לְנַפְשָׁם הָהָרָה
וַיִּהְיוּ שָׁם שְׁלֹשָׁה יָמִים עַד־אֲשֶׁר שָׁבוּ הָרֹדְפִים הָעִירָה
(11) עֲבָדִים הָיוּ אֲבוֹתֵינוּ לְפַרְעֹה בְּמִצְרַיִם וַיּוֹצִיאֵם יהוה
אֱלֹהֵינוּ מִשָּׁם בְּיָד חֲזָקָה וּבְאֹתוֹת גְּדוֹלוֹת (12) בָּא הַנָּבִיא
לִפְנֵי־הַמֶּלֶךְ וַיֹּאמֶר אֵלָיו, הֲלֹא יָדַעְתָּ כִּי הִמְלִיכוּ בְנֵי־יִשְׂרָאֵל
עֲלֵיהֶם מֶלֶךְ, וְאַתָּה אָמַרְתָּ כִּי שְׁלֹמֹה בִנְךָ יֵשֵׁב עַל־כִּסְאֲךָ
אַחֲרֶיךָ (13) וַתְּדַבֵּר הָאִשָּׁה הַחֲכָמָה מֵעַל הַחוֹמָה לֵאמֹר תִּמְצָא־
נָא אֲמָתְךָ חֵן בְּעֵינֵי־אֲדוֹנִי וְהַגִּידָה לָּנוּ אֶת־מִי אַתָּה מְבַקֵּשׁ
וְהוֹרַדְנוּ אֹתוֹ אֵלֶיךָ, וְלָמָּה נִפֹּל אֲנַחְנוּ בֶחָרֶב: וַיִּיטְבוּ דְבָרֶיהָ
בְּעֵינָיו מְאֹד וַיֹּאמֶר אֵלֶיהָ, בְּרוּכָה אַתְּ לַיהוה אֲשֶׁר נָתַן חָכְמָה
בְּלִבֵּךְ, כִּי הִצַּלְתְּ אֶת־כָּל־יֹשְׁבֵי הָעִיר מִמָּוֶת (14) וַיִּשְׁלַח
מֶלֶךְ יִשְׂרָאֵל מַלְאָכִים אֶל־הַנָּבִיא לֵאמֹר כֹּה אָמַר הַמֶּלֶךְ, רֵד
אֵלָי: וַיֹּאמֶר אֲלֵיהֶם הַנָּבִיא לֹא אֵרֵד, וְאִם אִישׁ־אֱלֹהִים אָנֹכִי
תֵּרֶד אֵשׁ־אֱלֹהִים מִשָּׁמַיִם וְאָכְלָה אֶתְכֶם: וַיְהִי כְּדַבֵּר הַנָּבִיא
אֶת־הַדְּבָרִים הָאֵלֶּה וַתֵּרֶד אֵשׁ מִשָּׁמַיִם וַתֹּאכַל אֹתָם

(1) The sons of Jacob returned unto their father and they told (to) him the words of Joseph which he (had) commanded them, saying: 'Thus said thy son Joseph, "Come down unto me to Egypt, thou and all thy house(hold) and I will make thee dwell

[a] Inf. abs. before the finite verb, for emphasis. [b] Fem. sg. 3rd.
[c] Idiomatic—'to bear grace' = 'to have grace', meaning 'to please'.

with me, for the famine is very heavy in the land of Canaan".' And it came to pass, as Jacob heard these words that (waw consec.) he cried in a loud voice, 'My son Joseph is yet alive; blessed be the Lord who hath done kindness with His servant'. And Jacob went down to Egypt, he and all his house(hold) and they dwelt there. (2) And Sarah drew near unto Abraham her husband and she said unto him: 'Behold I am old (perfect) and the Lord hath not given (to) me a son; and now hearken in my voice according to ("as") all which I shall say unto thee, and take my handmaid unto thee for a wife.' And the words of Sarah were good in his eyes and he took her handmaid to him for a wife. And it came to pass after many days that (waw consec.) the handmaid bore (to) him a son. (3) And Moses heard that Pharaoh (was) seeking his life and he fled from (before) him and he went forth to the wilderness and he escaped from the hand of Pharaoh. (4) The servant of Abraham returned and the girl (was) with him and she was good in the eyes of Isaac and she bore [נָשָׂא] grace before him and she became his wife ('to him for a wife'). (5) And it came to pass when Judah heard that the wife of his son had gone in the evil way that (waw consec.) he was exceedingly angry and he said unto his servants, 'Bring her forth that she may be burnt in (the) fire'. And they brought her forth and she stood before him and she said, 'To the man to whom these belong ("to the man who these are to him") I have borne a son.' (6) The brothers of Joseph saw him and they said, one to the other, 'Behold the dreamer of dreams cometh'. And they took him and they rent his garments from (upon) him and they made him go down into the pit, and they sat (down) to eat. (7) Thus said the Lord unto me, 'Go forth and speak unto this people and thou shalt say unto them, "Your fathers went after strange gods and they forgot the Lord who brought them forth from the land of Egypt with a strong hand and who made them dwell in the land of their enemies whom He (had) destroyed before them".' (8) Moses spoke unto the children of Israel saying, 'Ye shall not fear the nations against whom[a] ye shall fight, for the Lord is in our midst and He will bring down upon them stones of fire from the heavens and He will utterly destroy (inf.

[a] 'Who . . . against them'; see p. 135.

abs. with finite verb) them from (upon) the face of the earth.' (9) If thy brother shall be sold to thee for a slave and he shall serve thee; with thee he shall dwell in thy house and thou shalt indeed deal kindly (Hiph. of יָטַב) with him, and thou shalt remember that I am the Lord thy God. (10) Solomon commanded him, saying, 'Dwell in thy house and go not forth (use the negative אַל, p. 77) from the city, for in the day that thou transgressest[a] (inf. const. with suff.) my commandment thy blood shall be on thy head.' And one of his servants fled from him to the land of Edom; and he took his men and he pursued after him and he found him. And the king heard that his enemy had transgressed his commandment and had gone forth from the city, and he sent unto him saying: 'Because thou hast transgressed my word and thou didst go forth from Jerusalem, behold death will be thy judgement.'

76. ʻAYIN WAW AND ʻAYIN YOḎ VERBS

We now come to the type of verb whose medial root-letter is a ו or י which quiesces, i.e. The *ʻAyin Waw and ʻAyin Yoḏ* verb. The original form of the verb 'to rise' was קָוַם (qāwam) in Perfect Qal, but the feeble ו not only lost its power as a consonant but disappeared, leaving the form קָם. Since the normal Imperfect Qal יִשְׁמֹר (yišmōr) comes from an original יַשְׁמֻר (yašmur—see note on Imperfect Qal of Pe Guttural verb, p. 155), the early form of our verb was יַקְוֻם (yaqwum) which became יָקוּם (yāqûm); the ו lost its consonantal power and became the vowel Šureq (see p. 18, 3).[b] In the same way, the Perfect Qal of the verb 'to place' was originally שָׂיַם (sāyam) and the medial י disappeared, leaving שָׂם. In the Imperfect the vowel in the second syllable was of the *i* class יַשְׂיִם (yasyim) instead of the *u* class (cf. Imperfect of נָתַן, p. 148 f.) and this form developed into יָשִׂים (yāsîm).

[a] The verb עָבַר.

[b] There are two other branches of the ʻAyin Waw verb of the *e* and *o* types (מֵת and בּוֹשׁ) corresponding to the Statives (pp. 95 ff.) but, for the sake of clearness, they are dealt with separately in the next chapter.

QAL

	'AYIN WAW			'AYIN YODH	
Perf.:	he hath risen	קָם		he (hath) placed	שָׂם
	she ,,	קָ֫מָה		she ,,	שָׂ֫מָה
	thou (m.) hast ,,	קַ֫מְתָּ		thou (m.) hast ,,	שַׂ֫מְתָּ
	thou (f.) ,,	קַמְתְּ		thou (f.) ,,	שַׂמְתְּ
	I (c.) have ,,	קַ֫מְתִּי		I (c.) have ,,	שַׂ֫מְתִּי
	they (c.) ,,	קָ֫מוּ		they (c.) ,,	שָׂ֫מוּ
	ye (m.) ,,	קַמְתֶּם		ye (m.) ,,	שַׂמְתֶּם
	ye (f.) ,,	קַמְתֶּן		ye (f.) ,,	שַׂמְתֶּן
	we (c.) ,,	קַ֫מְנוּ		we (c.) ,,	שַׂ֫מְנוּ
Imperf.:	he will arise	יָקוּם		he will place	יָשִׂים
	she ,,	תָּקוּם		she ,,	תָּשִׂים
	thou (m.) wilt ,,	תָּקוּם		thou (m.) wilt ,,	תָּשִׂים
	thou (f.) ,,	תָּקוּמִי		thou (f.) ,,	תָּשִׂ֫ימִי
	I (c.) shall ,,	אָקוּם		I (c.) shall ,,	אָשִׂים
	they (m.) will ,,	יָק֫וּמוּ		they (m.) will ,,	יָשִׂ֫ימוּ
	they (f.) ,,	תְּקוּמֶ֫נָה		they (f.) ,,	תְּשִׂימֶ֫נָה
	ye (m.) ,,	תָּק֫וּמוּ		ye (m.) ,,	תָּשִׂ֫ימוּ
	ye (f.) ,,	תְּקוּמֶ֫נָה		ye (f.) ,,	תְּשִׂימֶ֫נָה
	we (c.) shall ,,	נָקוּם		we (c.) shall ,,	נָשִׂים
Cohort.:	let me (c.) ,, I (c.) *will* ,,	אָק֫וּמָה		let me (c.) ,, I (c.) *will* ,,	אָשִׂ֫ימָה

Shortened Imperf.
  Jussive:

| | let him arise | יָקֹם | | let him ,, | יָשֵׂם |

Imperf. with Waw
  Consecutive:

| | and he arose | וַיָּ֫קָם | | and he placed | וַיָּ֫שֶׂם [b] |
| | (wayyáqom) [a] | | | | |

  [a] But וָאָקוּם 'and I arose' (p. 114 (*b*), N.B.).
  [b] But וָאָשִׂים 'and I set' (p. 114 (*b*), N.B.).

Imper.: arise thou (m.)	(קֽוּמָה)[a] קוּם	place thou (m.)	(שִֽׂימָה)[a] שִׂים
„ (f.)	קֽוּמִי	„ (f.)	שִֽׂימִי
„ ye (m.)	קֽוּמוּ	„ ye (m.)	שִֽׂימוּ
„ (f.)	קֹֽמְנָה	„ (f.)	[שֵֽׂמְנָה]
Part.: arising (m. sg.)	קָם	placing (m. sg.)	שָׂם
„ (f. sg.)	קָמָ֫ה	„ (f. sg.)	שָׂמָ֫ה
	&c.		&c.
Inf. absolute:	קוֹם		שׂוֹם
construct:	קוּם		שִׂים
„ *with* לְ	לָקוּם		לָשִׂים

(*a*) There is no difference in form between the 'Ayin Waw and the 'Ayin Yoḏ in the Perfect Qal, but in the Imperfect, Imperative, and Infinitive construct the original medial root-letter reappears as a vowel: יָקוּם, יָשִׂים, &c. The Imperfect (יָקוּם and יָשִׂים) has a shortened form for the Jussive (יָקֹם and יָשֵׂם). When the waw consecutive is attached to the shortened form of the Imperfect the accent recedes one syllable, so that the final syllable (־קֹם and ־שֵׂם) is now closed and unaccented and the vowel in it must consequently be shortened (to ־קָם -qom and ־שֶׂם). Note carefully that וַיָּ֫קָם is read wayyáqom—the vowel in the last syllable is Qameṣ-Ḥaṭuph.

(*b*) The f. sg. Perf. (of קָם) is קָ֫מָה and (of שָׂם) שָׂ֫מָה—accent Mil'el (p. 8).

The f. sg. Part. (of קָם) is קָמָ֫ה and (of שָׂם) שָׂמָ֫ה—accent Milra' (p. 8).

NIPHAL

The normal Niphal Perfect נִשְׁמַר (nišmar) comes from an earlier נַשְׁמַר (našmar—see Niphal of Pe Guttural verb, p. 156) so that the Niphal Perfect of קוּם was נַקְוַם (naqwam) which became נָקוֹם (nāqôm)—its present form. The normal Imperfect Niphal יִשָּׁמֵר comes from an earlier יִנְשָׁמֵר (yinšamar) יִשָּׁמֵר (yiššamar),

[a] Longer form of Imperative.

so that in our verb it was יִנְקַוָם (yinqawam), then יִקַּוָם (yiqqawam), and finally יִקּוֹם (yiqqôm)—its present form.

(N.B. Since קָם is an intransitive verb and has no passive or reflexive meaning in Niphal, we may take the verb כּוּן, which in Niphal means 'to be ready, prepared', as the example illustrating the form of the Niphal.)

Perf.:	he was prepared	נָכוֹן	*Imperf.*:	he will be prepared	יִכּוֹן
	she ,,	נָכוֹנָה		she ,,	תִּכּוֹן
	thou (m.) wast ,,	נְכוּנוֹתָ		thou (m.) wilt ,,	תִּכּוֹן
	thou (f.) ,,	נְכוּנוֹת		thou (f.) ,,	תִּכּוֹנִי
	I (c.) was ,,	נְכוּנוֹתִי		I (c.) shall ,,	אֶכּוֹן
	they (c.) were ,,	נָכוֹנוּ		they (m.) will ,,	יִכּוֹנוּ
				they (f.) ,,	——
	ye (m.) ,,	נְכוֹנֹתֶם [a]		ye (m.) ,,	תִּכּוֹנוּ
	ye (f.) ,,	נְכוֹנֹתֶן [a]		ye (f.) ,,	——
	we (c.) ,,	נְכוּנוֹנוּ		we (c.) shall ,,	נִכּוֹן
Imper.:			*Part.*:	being prepared (m. sg.)	נָכוֹן
	be thou (m.) prepared	הִכּוֹן		,, (f. sg.)	נְכוֹנָה
	,, (f.) ,,	הִכּוֹנִי			&c.
	,, ye (m.) ,,	הִכּוֹנוּ			
	,, (f.) ,,	——	*Inf.*:		הִכּוֹן

N.B. Distinguish carefully between the 3rd f. sg. Perfect נָכֹוֹנָה (with accent Mil'el) and the f. sg. Participle נְכוֹנָה (with accent Milra'). The context determines whether הִכּוֹן is an Imperative or Infinitive.

Hiphil and Hophal

The Hiphil Perfect is הֵקִים ('he caused to rise, he raised, he set up') and the Hophal Perfect is הוּקַם. After noting the changes in the foregoing forms due to the ו it will not be difficult to see how a hypothetical Hiphil הִקְוִים became הֵקִים and how the Hophal הָקְוַם became הוּקַם.

[a] Note ô vowel instead of û found in the 2nd pl.

	Hiphil		Hophal	
Perf.:	he (hath) raised	הֵקִים	he was raised	הוּקַם
	she ,,	הֵקִ֫ימָה	she ,,	הוּקְמָה
	thou (m.) hast ,,	הֲקִימ֫וֹתָ	thou (m.) wast ,,	הוּקַ֫מְתָּ
	thou (f.) ,,	הֲקִימוֹת	thou (f.) ,,	הוּקַמְתְּ
	I (c.) have ,,	הֲקִימ֫וֹתִי	I (c.) was ,,	הוּקַ֫מְתִּי
	they (c.) ,,	הֵקִ֫ימוּ	they (c.) were ,,	הוּקְמוּ
	ye (m.) ,,	הֲקִימוֹתֶם	ye (m.) ,,	הוּקַמְתֶּם
	ye (f.) ,,	הֲקִימוֹתֶן	ye (f.) ,,	הוּקַמְתֶּן
	we (c.) ,,	הֲקִימ֫וֹנוּ	we (c.) ,,	הוּקַ֫מְנוּ
Imperf.:	he will raise	יָקִים	he will be raised	יוּקַם
	she ,,	תָּקִים	she ,,	תּוּקַם
	thou (m.) wilt ,,	תָּקִים	thou (m.) wilt ,,	תּוּקַם
	thou (f.) ,,	תָּקִ֫ימִי	thou (f.) ,,	תּוּקְמִי
	I (c.) shall ,,	אָקִים	I (c.) shall ,,	אוּקַם
	they (m.) will ,,	יָקִ֫ימוּ	they (m.) will ,,	יוּקְמוּ
	they (f.) ,,	תָּקֵ֫מְנָה תְּקִימֶ֫נָה	they (f.) ,,	תּוּקַ֫מְנָה
	ye (m.) ,,	תָּקִ֫ימוּ	ye (m.) ,,	תּוּקְמוּ
	ye (f.) ,,	תָּקֵ֫מְנָה	ye (f.) ,,	תּוּקַ֫מְנָה
	we (c.) shall ,,	נָקִים	we (c.) shall ,,	נוּקַם

Shortened Imperf.
Jussive:

let him raise יָקֵם

Imperf. with Waw Consecutive:

and he raised וַיָּ֫קֶם[a]

[a] But וָאָקִים = 'and I raised' (p. 114 (*b*), N.B.).

Imper.: raise thou (m.)	הָקֵם		
	(הָקִ֫ימָה)[a]		
,, (f.)	הָקִ֫ימִי		
,, ye (m.)	הָקִ֫ימוּ		
,, (f.)	הָקֵ֫מְנָה		
Part.: raising (m. sg.)	מֵקִים	being raised (m. sg.)	מוּקָם
,, (f. sg.)	מְקִימָה	,, (f. sg.)	מוּקָמָה
	&c.		&c.
Inf. absolute:	הָקֵם		הוּקֵם
construct:	הָקִים		

The Imperfect Hiphil יָקִים has a shortened form יָקֵם. When waw consecutive is attached to this shortened form of the Imperfect the accent recedes one syllable, so that the final syllable (in יָקֵם) is now closed and unaccented and its vowel is therefore shortened (וַיָּ֫קָם).

The Intensives and Reflexive

Except for a few cases in the later books of the Bible (indicating late Hebrew) there is no Piel, Pual, or Hithpael in 'Ayin Waw verbs. The normal Intensives and the Reflexive are expressed by doubling the middle root-letter (or, failing that, by lengthening the preceding vowel instead); but since the medial ו (is so feeble that it) not only becomes a vowel but in many cases disappears—in other words since the medial ו has no status as a consonant at all—it cannot be doubled. However, there are intensives and a reflexive expressed by repeating the *third* root-letter, giving rise to the following forms:

קוֹמֵם: called Polel because the Lameḏ (3rd root-letter) is repeated: active intensive.

[a] Longer form of Imperative.

קוֹמַם: called Polal because the Lameḏ (3rd root-letter) is repeated: passive intensive.

הִתְקוֹמֵם: called Hithpolel because the Lameḏ (3rd root-letter) is repeated: reflexive.

These derived forms receive the normal prefixes and suffixes.

Note: It is to be understood that what is meant by an 'Ayin Waw verb is one whose medial root-letter is a ו *which quiesces and disappears.* A verb of the type גָּוַע ('to perish') whose medial radical ו remains a full consonant throughout (and does not quiesce or disappear), thus: יִגְוַע ('he will perish') is not weak in its medial ו, and therefore is *not* an 'Ayin Waw verb at all.

EXERCISE 35

Elijah	אֵלִיָּהוּ
wealth, possessions	רְכוּשׁ
four (m.)	אַרְבָּעָה[a]
four (f.)	אַרְבַּע

to be high, lofty רוּם in Qal	רָם
to cause to be high, to lift up, raise up רוּם in Hiphil	הֵרִים
to return, come back שׁוּב in Qal	שָׁב
to cause to return, to bring back, restore שׁוּב in Hiphil	הֵשִׁיב
to flee נוּס in Qal	נָס

(1) וַיֵּצְאוּ הַמְרַגְּלִים אַרְצָה כְּנַעַן וַיִּהְיוּ שָׁם יָמִים רַבִּים׃ וַיָּשׁוּבוּ
אֶל־הַמַּחֲנֶה וַיְדַבְּרוּ אֶל־הָעָם לֵאמֹר הִנֵּה עָרֵי־כְנַעַן חֲזָקוֹת
מְאֹד הֵנָּה וְחוֹמוֹתֵיהֶן עַד־הַשָּׁמָיִם׃ וַיֹּאמְרוּ בְנֵי־יִשְׂרָאֵל אִישׁ
אֶל־רֵעֵהוּ, לָמָּה יָצָאנוּ מִמִּצְרַיִם לִנְפֹּל בַּחֶרֶב לִפְנֵי־אֹיְבֵינוּ,
כִּי מִי יִלָּחֵם לָנוּ בְּיֹשְׁבֵי־כְנָעַן וְעַתָּה נָשִׂימָה לָנוּ רֹאשׁ וְנָשׁוּבָה
מִצְרָיְמָה׃ וַיְהִי כְּדַבְּרָם כַּדְּבָרִים הָאֵלֶּה וַיֵּרֶד כְּבוֹד־יהוה
בַּמַּחֲנֶה וַיִּפֹּל מֹשֶׁה עַל־פָּנָיו אַרְצָה (2) רָאָה אֵלִיָּהוּ אֶת־הָאִשָּׁה
עֹמֶדֶת לְפָנָיו וַיִּשְׁאַל אֹתָהּ לֵאמֹר מַה־תְּבַקְשִׁי, הַגִּידִי־נָא לִי׃

[a] See footnote, p. 192.

וַתֹּאמֶר אֵלָיו הָאִשָּׁה, הֲשָׁאַלְתִּי בֵן מֵאֵת[a] אֲדֹנִי כִּי הִנּוֹ מֵת׃
וַיְהִי כִּשְׁמֹעַ אֵלִיָּהוּ אֶת־דִּבְרֶיהָ וַיָּקָם וַיָּשָׁב אֶל־בֵּיתָהּ׃ וַיִּשְׁכַּב
עַל־הַיֶּלֶד הַמֵּת, פָּנָיו עַל־פָּנָיו וְיָדָיו עַל־יָדָיו, וַיִּתְפַּלֵּל אֶל־
יהוה וַיֹּאמַר הָשֵׁב נָא אֶת־נֶפֶשׁ הַיֶּלֶד׃ וַיִּשְׁמַע יהוה אֶל־תְּפִלַּת־
אֵלִיָּהוּ, וַתָּשָׁב אֵלָיו רוּחַ הַיֶּלֶד וַיִּפְקַח אֶת־עֵינָיו׃ וַיִּקְרָא אֵלִיָּהוּ
אֶל־הָאִשָּׁה וַיֹּאמֶר אֵלֶיהָ, הִנֵּה חַי בְּנֵךְ׃ וַתֹּאמֶר אֵלָיו הָאִשָּׁה
עַתָּה יָדַעְתִּי כִּי נְבִיא־אֱלֹהִים אָתָּה וַתִּשָּׂא אֶת־בְּנָהּ וַתֵּצֵא
(3) וַיְהִי אַחֲרֵי הַדְּבָרִים הָאֵלֶּה וַיִּלָּחֲמוּ אַרְבָּעָה מְלָכִים בְּמֶלֶךְ
סְדֹם וַיִּלְכְּדוּ אֶת־הָעִיר וַיִּקְחוּ אֶת־הָעָם וְאֶת־כָּל־רְכוּשָׁם,
וְגַם אֶת־לוֹט בֶּן־אֲחִי־אַבְרָהָם לָקְחוּ אִתָּם וַיֵּצְאוּ לָשׁוּב אֶל־
עָרֵיהֶם׃ וַיִּמָּלֵט אֶחָד מֵעַבְדֵי־לוֹט וַיִּבְרַח אֶל־אַבְרָהָם וַיַּגֵּד לוֹ
אֶת־כָּל־אֲשֶׁר רָאָה׃ וַיָּקָם אַבְרָהָם וַיִּקַּח אֶת־אֲנָשָׁיו אִתּוֹ וַיִּרְדֹּף
אַחֲרֵי־הַמְּלָכִים וַיִּמְצָאֵם שֹׁכְבִים בַּמַּחֲנֶה וַיִּפֹּל עֲלֵיהֶם וַיִּרְאוּ
מִפָּנָיו וַיָּנוּסוּ הַמִּדְבָּרָה׃ וַיָּשֶׁב אַבְרָהָם אֶת־יֹשְׁבֵי־סְדֹם וְאֶת־
רְכוּשָׁם, וְגַם אֶת־לוֹט בֶּן־אָחִיו וְאֶת־רְכוּשׁוֹ הֵשִׁיב׃ וַיֹּאמֶר
אֵלָיו מֶלֶךְ סְדֹם תֶּן לִי אֶת־הַנֶּפֶשׁ[b] וְאֶת־הָרְכוּשׁ קַח לָךְ׃
וַיֹּאמֶר אַבְרָהָם נִשְׁבַּעְתִּי בַּיהוה אֲשֶׁר עָשָׂה אֶת־הַשָּׁמַיִם וְאֶת־
הָאָרֶץ אִם[c] אֶקַּח מִכֹּל[d] אֲשֶׁר לָךְ, וְלֹא תֹאמַר הִנֵּה רְכוּשׁ־
אַבְרָהָם לִי הוּא׃ רַק הָאֲנָשִׁים אֲשֶׁר הָלְכוּ אִתִּי הֵמָּה יִקְחוּ
כַּטּוֹב בְּעֵינֵיהֶם׃ וַיֵּצֵא כֹּהֵן־הָעִיר וַיְבָרֶךְ אֶת־אַבְרָהָם וַיֹּאמַר
בָּרוּךְ אַבְרָהָם לֵאלֹהִים וּבָרוּךְ אֱלֹהֶיךָ אֲשֶׁר נָתַן אֶת־אֹיְבֶיךָ
בְּיָדֶךָ (4) וַיֹּאמֶר יהוה אֶל־מֹשֶׁה לָמָּה תִּצְעַק אֵלָי הָרֵם אֶת־
יָדְךָ עַל־הַיָּם וְשָׁבוּ הַמַּיִם לִמְקוֹמָם׃ וַיָּרֶם מֹשֶׁה אֶת־יָדוֹ
כְּמִצְוַת־יהוה וַיָּשׁוּבוּ הַמַּיִם עַל־הַמִּצְרִים וַיֵּרְדוּ הַמִּצְרִים בְּלֵב
הַיָּם (5) הֲשִׁיבֵנוּ יהוה אֵלֶיךָ וְנָשׁוּבָה, וּזְכָר[e]־לָנוּ אֶת־דְּבָרֶיךָ

[a] 'From (with)'.
[b] Sing. collective.
[c] See special note on oath, p. 176.
[d] 'From anything'.
[e] The imperative זְכֹר, when joined to the next word by Maqqeph becomes זְכָר־ (zeḵor).

אֲשֶׁר דִּבַּרְתָּ לֵאמֹר שׁוּבוּ אֵלַי בֵּית־יַעֲקֹב וְאָשׁוּבָה אֲלֵיכֶם׃
קוּמָה יהוה לִישׁוּעָתֵנוּ וְאַל־תִּתְּנֵנוּ בְּיַד־אֹיְבֵינוּ, כִּי בְךָ לְבַדְּךָ
בָטָחְנוּ (6) עָשָׂה מֹשֶׁה כַּאֲשֶׁר צִוָּה אֹתוֹ יהוה וַיִּקְרָא לִיהוֹשֻׁעַ
וַיָּשֶׂם אֶת־יָדָיו עַל־רֹאשׁוֹ וַיְבָרְכֵהוּ לְעֵינֵי עֲדַת־יִשְׂרָאֵל׃ וַתֵּרֶד
רוּחַ אֱלֹהִים עַל־יְהוֹשֻׁעַ וַיִּתְנַבֵּא לִפְנֵיהֶם (7) כִּי יָקוּם בְּעִירְךָ
נָבִיא וְדִבֶּר אֲלֵיכֶם לֵאמֹר נַעַבְדָה אֱלֹהִים אֲחֵרִים, וְנָתַן לְךָ
אוֹת וּבָא הָאוֹת׃ לֹא תִשְׁמַע אֶל־דְּבָרָיו (8) מִפְּנֵי זָקֵן תָּקוּם
וְכִבַּדְתָּ אֶת־פְּנֵי־הֶחָכָם (9) בְּדֶרֶךְ אֶחָד תֵּצְאוּ לַמִּלְחָמָה
וּבִדְרָכִים רַבִּים תָּנוּסוּ לִפְנֵי־אֹיְבֵיכֶם (10) קְחוּ לָכֶם אֲבָנִים
וַהֲקִימוּ אֹתָן בְּתוֹךְ הַנָּהָר, לְמַעַן יֵדְעוּ בְנֵיכֶם כִּי כָּרַת יהוה
אֶת־מֵי־הַיַּרְדֵּן לִפְנֵיכֶם, וְהָיוּ הָאֲבָנִים הָאֵלֶּה לְאוֹת־עוֹלָם
(11) לְפָנָיו לֹא הָיָה כָמֹהוּ מֶלֶךְ בְּיִשְׂרָאֵל אֲשֶׁר שָׁב אֶל־יהוה
בְּכָל־לְבָבוֹ, וְאַחֲרָיו לֹא קָם כָּמֹהוּ

(1) And it shall come to pass in that day that ye shall seek (waw consec.) Me in the land of your enemies and ye shall cry unto Me with a perfect heart and in truth and ye shall return unto Me with all your heart and with all your soul. Even I (pronoun) will return to you and I will bring you back to the land of your fathers and I will let you dwell (Hiphil) there again and ye shall plant gardens and ye shall eat their fruit as in the days of David My servant and your afflictions will be forgotten and they will be remembered no more. (2) Evil men have risen up against me and they have sought to take my life and they placed not God before them; but [ו] Thou, Lord, Thou wilt bring back their evil upon their head. (3) Moses spoke unto them, saying: 'Go ye forth to the land of Canaan and take ye from the fruit of the trees which are in it and return ye to the camp'. And the men went forth to the land of Canaan and they took from the fruit of the land and they returned to the camp. (4) Joseph said unto his father, 'Behold my two sons ("the two-of my sons") are with me; place, I pray thee, thy

hands upon them and bless them'. And Jacob arose and he placed his hands upon their heads and he blessed them. (5) And one of the servants drew near unto Elijah and he said, 'Come down, I pray thee, from the mountain and return to the city and no man shall raise his hand before thee, for now we indeed know that the word of the Lord thou hast spoken'. And the prophet said unto him, 'I (pronoun) will return to the city.' And he arose and he came down from the mountain and he returned with them. (6) Arise thou (f.), daughter of Israel, why dost thou sit (impf., expressing continued action) in the dust? For the Lord hath heard thy cry and He will bring thee back unto Him. (7) There arose not in Israel a prophet like Moses who knew the Lord face to face, as a man who knoweth his neighbour. (8) When ye shall go forth to (the) battle and your enemies shall have many horses, ye shall not fear them, and ye shall not flee from before them, for the Lord, He is with you, and He will fight for you. (9) And the priest prayed and he said: 'Bring back, Lord, Thy sons from the lands of the nation whither ("which—thither") Thou hast scattered them, for unto Thee alone are their eyes'. (10) 'I have sent My plagues in you and ye have not yet returned unto Me', said the Lord. (11) The Hebrew said unto Moses, 'Who hath placed thee for a judge over us? Thinkest ('sayest') thou to slay me as thou hast slain the Egyptian?' And it came to pass as Moses heard these words that (waw consec.) he arose and he fled from the land of Egypt.

77. 'AYIN WAW VERBS CONTINUED

It was shown on pp. 95 ff. that there are three types of regular verb distinguished by the second vowel in the Perfect Qal, thus: *a* (as in שָׁמַר), *e* (as in כָּבֵד), and *o* (as in קָטֹן) types. These three types are found in the 'Ayin Waw verb, thus: *a* in קָם (from the root קום), *e* in מֵת (from the root מות), and *o* in בּוֹשׁ. The first type was given in the preceding chapter; the other two, which are rarer, are given in the table on the next page.

QAL

Perf.:	he (hath) died	מֵת		he was ashamed	בּוֹשׁ
	she ,,	מֵ֫תָה		she ' ,,	בּוֹ֫שָׁה
	thou (m.) hast ,,	מַ֫תָּה		thou (m.) wast ,,	בֹּ֫שְׁתָּ
	(for מַתְתָּ)ᵃ				
	thou (f.) ,,	מַתְּ		thou (f.) ,,	בֹּשְׁתְּ
	(for מַתְתְּ)				
	I (c.) (have) ,,	מַ֫תִּי		I (c.) was ,,	בֹּ֫שְׁתִּי
	(for מָ֫תְתִּי)				
	they (c.) ,,	מֵ֫תוּ		they (c.) were ,,	בֹּ֫שׁוּ
	ye (m.) ,,	מַתֶּם		ye (m.) ,,	בָּשְׁתֶּם
	(for מַתְתֶּם)			(boštem)	
	ye (f.) ,,	מַתֶּן		ye (f.) ,,	בָּשְׁתֶּן
	(for מַתְתֶּן)			(bošten)	
	we (c.) ,,	מַ֫תְנוּ		we (c.) ,,	בֹּ֫שְׁנוּ
Imperf.:	he will die	יָמוּת		he will be ashamed	יֵבוֹשׁ
	she ,,	תָּמוּת		she ,,	תֵּבוֹשׁ
	I (c.) shall ,,	אָמוּת		I (c.) shall ,,	אֵבוֹשׁ
	&c.			&c.	

Cohort.:
let me (c.) die / I *will* ,, — אָמ֫וּתָה
let me (c.) ,, / I (c.) *will* ,, — אֵבוֹ֫שָׁה

Shortened Imperf.
Jussive:
let him die — יָמֹת

Imperf. with Waw Consecutive:
and he died — וַיָּ֫מָת
(wayyā́moṭ)

Imper.:	die thou (m.)	מוּת		be thou (m.) ashamed	בּוֹשׁ
	,, (f.)	מ֫וּתִי		,, (f.) ,,	בּ֫וֹשִׁי
	&c.			&c.	

ᵃ Cf. כָּרַ֫תְתָּ which becomes כָּרַ֫תָּ.

Part.: dying (m. sg.)	מֵת	being ashamed (m. sg.)	בּוֹשׁ
,, (f. sg.)	מֵתָה	,, (f. sg.)	בּוֹשָׁה
	&c.		&c.
Inf. absolute:	מוֹת		בּוֹשׁ
construct:	מוּת		
,, with ל	לָמוּת		

The other derived forms follow the קָם type:

HIPHIL—*Perf.*: הֵמִית 'he caused to die, he put to death'

Imperf.: יָמִית 'he will cause to die, he will put to death'

HOPHAL—*Perf.*: הוּמַת 'he was put to death'

Imperf.: יוּמַת 'he will be put to death'.

EXERCISE 36

generation	דּוֹר	to depart, turn סוּר in Qal	סָר
(pl.)	דּוֹרוֹת	to cause to depart, to remove סוּר in Hiphil	הֵסִיר
Philistine	פְּלִשְׁתִּי		
Levi, Levite	לֵוִי	cry	צְעָקָה

(1) וַיְדַבֵּר יהוה אֶל־מֹשֶׁה לֵאמֹר הִנֵּה אָנֹכִי יֹצֵא בְּתוֹךְ־אֶ֫רֶץ
מִצְרַ֫יִם וְהָרַגְתִּ֫י אֶת־כָּל־בְּכוֹרֵיהֶם, מִבְּכוֹר־פַּרְעֹה הַיֹּשֵׁב עַל־
כִּסְאוֹ עַד־בְּכוֹר־הָאָמָה, וְהִבְדַּלְתִּי בֵּין יִשְׂרָאֵל וּבֵין מִצְרָיִם׃
וַיְהִי בַּלַּ֫יְלָה הַהוּא וַיָּ֫מוּתוּ כֹּל בְּכוֹרֵי־מִצְרַ֫יִם וַתְּהִי[a] צְעָקָה
גְדוֹלָה בָּאָ֫רֶץ, כִּי לֹא הָיָה בַ֫יִת אֲשֶׁר לֹא הָיָה שָׁם מֵת׃ וַיָּ֫קָם
פַּרְעֹה הוּא וַעֲבָדָיו וַיִּקְרָא אֶל־מֹשֶׁה וְאֶל־אַהֲרֹן וַיֹּ֫אמֶר אֲלֵיהֶם,
ק֫וּמוּ צְאוּ מִתּוֹךְ עַמִּי, גַּם[b] אַתֶּם גַּם[b] כָּל־הָעָם אֲשֶׁר אִתְּכֶם, גַּם[b]
צֹאנְכֶם גַּם[b] בְּקַרְכֶם קְחוּ אִתְּכֶם, וְעִבְדוּ אֶת־אֱלֹהֵיכֶם כַּאֲשֶׁר
דִּבַּרְתֶּם (2) וַיְהִי אַחֲרֵי הַדְּבָרִים הָאֵ֫לֶּה וַיָּ֫מָת יוֹסֵף וְכָל־הַדּוֹר
הַהוּא׃ וַיָּ֫קָם מֶ֫לֶךְ עַל־מִצְרַ֫יִם אֲשֶׁר לֹא יָדַע אֶת־יוֹסֵף

[a] Fem. prefix.

[b] 'Also . . . also' means 'both . . . and'.

(3) וַיֹּ֫אמֶר יהוה אֶל־מֹשֶׁה, רֵד מִן הָהָר כִּי סָ֫רוּ בְנֵי־יִשְׂרָאֵל
מִן־הַדֶּ֫רֶךְ וְגַם עָשׂוּ לָהֶם אֱלֹהֵי־זָהָב וַיִּקְרְאוּ לִפְנֵיהֶם, אֵ֫לֶּה
אֱלֹהֶ֫יךָ יִשְׂרָאֵל אֲשֶׁר הוֹצִ֫יאוּ אֹתְךָ מֵאֶ֫רֶץ מִצְרַ֫יִם מִבֵּית־
עֲבָדִים: וַיֵּ֫רֶד מֹשֶׁה מִן הָהָר, וּבְיָדוֹ שְׁנֵי־לוּחוֹת הַבְּרִית וַיְשַׁבֵּר
אֹתָם עַל־הָאֲדָמָה: וַיִּקְרָא מֹשֶׁה בְּקוֹל גָּדוֹל, מִי לַיהוה אֵלָי
וַיָּ֫סוּרוּ אֵלָיו כָּל־בְּנֵי־לֵוִי: וַיֹּ֫אמֶר אֲלֵיהֶם מֹשֶׁה, קְחוּ אִישׁ[a] אֶת־
חַרְבּוֹ וְהָמִ֫יתוּ אֶת־אֲחֵיכֶם הָעֹבְדִים אֶת־אֱלֹהֵי־הַזָּהָב, פֶּן־יִגֹּף
יהוה בָּעָם (4) וַיִּצְעֲקוּ בְנֵי־יִשְׂרָאֵל אֶל־מֹשֶׁה, לָ֫מָּה נָמוּת בָּרָעָב
אֲנַ֫חְנוּ וְנָשֵׁ֫ינוּ וּבָנֵינוּ: וַיִּתְפַּלֵּל מֹשֶׁה אֶל־יהוה וַיּ֫וֹרֶד לָהֶם יהוה
לֶ֫חֶם מִשָּׁמַ֫יִם וַיֹּאכַל הָעָם (5) הִשָּׁמְרוּ[b] מְאֹד פֶּן־תִּשְׁכְּחוּ אֶת־
מִצְוֹת־יהוה וּפֶן־יָ֫סוּרוּ מִלְּבַבְכֶם: וְהָאִישׁ אֲשֶׁר לֹא יִשְׁמֹר אֶת־
הַתּוֹרָה הַזֹּאת וְסָר לְבָבוֹ מֵעִם[c] יהוה אֱלֹהָיו מוֹת[d] יָמוּת הָאִישׁ
הַהוּא (6) כִּי יִגְנֹב אִישׁ אֶת־רֵעֵ֫הוּ וּמָכַר אֹתוֹ לְעֶ֫בֶד, הוּמַת[d]
יוּמַת הָאִישׁ הַזֶּה, וְזָכַרְתָּ֫ כִּי אֲנִי יהוה אֱלֹהֶ֫יךָ (7) לֹא תָ֫סוּרוּ
אַחֲרֵי לְבַבְכֶם וְאַחֲרֵי עֵינֵיכֶם, כִּי בְּדֶ֫רֶךְ יהוה תִּבְחָרוּ, לְמַ֫עַן
יִיטַב לָכֶם בָּאָ֫רֶץ אֲשֶׁר אַתֶּם בָּאִים שָׁ֫מָּה (8) וַיֹּ֫אמֶר דָּוִד אֶל־
שָׁאוּל, יֵצֵא־נָא עַבְדְּךָ וְנִלְחַם עִם־הַפְּלִשְׁתִּי הַזֶּה: וַיֹּ֫אמֶר אֵלָיו
שָׁאוּל, הֲלֹא נַ֫עַר אַתָּה וְהוּא אִישׁ גִּבּוֹר־מִלְחָמָה, שׁוּב אֶל־
בֵּית־אָבִ֫יךָ וְלָ֫מָּה תָמוּת לְנֶ֫גֶד עֵינָי: וַיֹּ֫אמֶר דָּוִד, רֹעֶה הָיָה
עַבְדְּךָ וָאֶשְׁמֹר אֶת־צֹאן־אָבִי, וְהִנֵּה חַיָּה רָעָה בָּ֫אָה מֵהַמִּדְבָּר
וַתִּפֹּל עַל־הַצֹּאן, וָאָקוּם וָאֶקַּח אֶת־חַרְבִּי בְּיָדִי וָאָמִית אֶת־הַחַיָּה
לְבַדִּי, כִּי לֹא הָיָה אִישׁ אִתִּי: וְעַתָּה אִם טוֹב בְּעֵינֵי־הַמֶּ֫לֶךְ
אָנֹכִי אֶלָּחֵם עִם־הַפְּלִשְׁתִּי הַזֶּה וְהָסֵר אָסִ֫ירָה אֶת־רֹאשׁוֹ מֵעָלָיו,
וְיָדַע כָּל־הַקָּהָל הַזֶּה כִּי יֵשׁ אֱלֹהִים בְּיִשְׂרָאֵל: וַיֹּ֫אמֶר שָׁאוּל,
צֵא אֵלָיו בְּנִי וְיִתֵּן[e]־יהוה אֶת־אֹיִבְךָ בְּיָדֶךָ (9) סוּר מֵרָע וּבַקֵּשׁ
טוֹב (10) וַיְהִי בִּנְסֹ֫עַ הָאָרוֹן וַיֹּ֫אמֶר מֹשֶׁה קֽוּמָה יהוה וְיָנ֫וּסוּ

[a] 'Every man'. [b] 'Take heed'. [c] 'From (with)'.
[d] Inf. abs. before verb expresses emphasis. [e] Jussive effect.

אֹיְבֶ֫יךָ מִפָּנֶיךָ (11) לֹא תֵבֹ֫ושִׁי בַּת־יִשְׂרָאֵל, קֹ֫ומִי מִן־הֶעָפָר
וְשִׂ֫ימִי עָלַ֫יִךְ אֶת־בִּגְדֵי כְבוֹדֵךְ׃[a]

(1) If thou shalt say in thy heart, 'Let me place over me a king as all the nations'; from among thy brethren shalt thou choose for thyself a king. He shall not have many horses, lest he shall bring back the people to Egypt, and he shall not take unto himself many wives, lest his heart shall be high and he shall depart from the words of this law. (2) The prophet came unto the king and he said unto him: 'The Lord hath heard thy prayer; thou shalt not die, for thou hast walked before Him in truth.' (3) Aaron commanded the people saying: 'Remove from (upon) you all the gold and all the silver and give (it) to me.' And the children of Israel removed all the gold and all the silver from (upon) them(selves) and they gave (it) to him. (4) A generation goeth and another generation cometh, and the world endureth ('standeth') for ever. (5) As I have torn this garment from (upon) thee, so hath the Lord removed the kingdom from thee and He hath given it to thy neighbour who is better than thee. (6) The Lord spoke unto Moses saying: 'Let not the people journey (by) the way of the Philistines, lest there shall be a battle and they shall be afraid and they shall return to Egypt'. (7) Hearken unto me, (ye) sons of Levi; hath not the Lord chosen you from the midst of your brethren to serve His service and why will ye depart from the way of the Lord? (8) In the dungeon where Joseph was there were two of the servants of Pharaoh; and they dreamed dreams and they told their dreams to Joseph. And Joseph said unto the one: 'In the morning thou shalt return to thy place and thou shalt serve Pharaoh.' And unto his neighbour he said: 'In the morning Pharaoh will remove thy head from (upon) thee'. (9) The king said, to him: 'Sell (to) me thy garden and I will give (to) thee another garden which is greater than it'. And the man said: 'I will not sell (to) thee my garden which I have inherited from mine ancestors'. And the king was exceedingly angry and he said unto him: 'Thou shalt indeed die'. And the man arose and he fled (from) before the king. And the king sent his servants and they pursued (after) him and they put

[a] 'Thy garments of glory', i.e. 'thy glorious garments'. See Appendix 5, p. 253.

him to death and they buried him in one of the mountains. (10) And it came to pass after these things that (waw consec.) Samuel, the prophet of God, died and he was buried in his house. (11) The Philistines saw that their warrior (was) dead and they fled from (before) the children of Israel. (12) Ye shall not depart after your eyes and after your heart, but the Lord your God shall ye fear and Him shall ye serve.

78. MORE DOUBLY WEAK VERBS

Note how two sets of adjustments are made in verbs doubly weak:

(*a*) יָדַע ('to know')—Pe Waw and Lame<u>d</u> Guttural verb:

N.B. In Hebrew יָדַע may be treated as a Pe Waw verb, since it behaves as such, even though it is a Pe Yo<u>d</u> in cognate languages.

	Qal		Niphal	
Perf.:	he knew	יָדַע	he was known	נוֹדַע
	she ,,	יָֽדְעָה	she ,,	נוֹדְעָה
		&c. (regular)		&c. (regular)
Imperf.:	he will know	יֵדַע	he will be known	יִוָּדַע
	she ,,	תֵּדַע	she ,,	תִּוָּדַע
		&c.		&c.
Imper.:	know thou (m.)	דַּע	be thou (m.) ,,	הִוָּדַע
	,, (f.)	דְּעִי	,, (f.) ,,	הִוָּֽדְעִי
		&c.		&c.
Part. active:				
	knowing (m. sg.)	יֹדֵעַ		
	,, (f. sg.)	יֹדַעַת		
		&c.		
passive:				
	known (m. sg.)	יָדוּעַ	being known (m. sg.)	נוֹדָע
	,, (f. sg.)	יְדוּעָה	,, (f. sg.)	נוֹדָעָה
				&c. (regular)
Inf. absolute:		יָדוֹעַ		
onstruct:		דַּעַת		הִוָּדַע
	,, with ל: to know	לָדַעַת	to be known	לְהִוָּדַע

	Hiphil		Hithpael	
Perf.:				
he (hath) made known	הוֹדִיעַ		he (hath) made himself known	הִתְוַדַּע
she ,,	הוֹדִיעָה		she herself ,,	הִתְוַדְּעָה
	&c.			
Imperf.:				
he will make ,,	יוֹדִיעַ		he will make himself ,,	יִתְוַדַּע
she ,,	תּוֹדִיעַ		she herself ,,	תִּתְוַדַּע
	&c.			
Imper.:				
make thou (m.) ,,	הוֹדַע		make thyself (m.) ,,	הִתְוַדַּע
,, (f.) ,,	הוֹדִיעִי		,, (f.) ,,	הִתְוַדְּעִי
	&c.			&c.
Part.:				
making known (m. sg.)	מוֹדִיעַ		making oneself known (m. sg.)	מִתְוַדַּע
,, (f. sg.)	מוֹדִיעָה			&c.
Inf. absolute:	הוֹדֵעַ			הִתְוַדַּע
construct:	הוֹדִיעַ			
,, with לְ: to make known	לְהוֹדִיעַ		to make oneself known	לְהִתְוַדַּע

Similarly the root ישע which in Niphal נוֹשַׁע means 'to be delivered, saved'
and in Hiphil הוֹשִׁיעַ ,, 'to deliver, save'.

(*b*) יָרֵא 'to fear', 'to be afraid'—Pe Yoḏ and Lameḏ 'Alep̄ verb; also stative:

Qal

Perf.:	he (hath) feared	יָרֵא	*Imperf.*:	he will fear	יִירָא
	thou (m.) hast ,,	יָרֵאתָ		thou (m.) wilt ,,	תִּירָא
	I (c.) have ,,	יָרֵאתִי		I (c.) shall ,,	אִירָא
Part.:	fearing (m. sg.)	יָרֵא	*Imper.*:	fear thou (m.)	יְרָא
	,, (m. pl.)	יְרֵאִים		,, ye (m.)	יִרְאוּ
Inf. absolute:		יָרוֹא	*construct*:		יִרְאָה (noun)
				,, with לְ: to fear	לְיִרְאָה

(c) יָצָא 'to go forth'—Pe Waw and Lamed 'Alep verb:

	Qal		Hiphil[a]	
Perf.:	he hath gone forth	יָצָא	he hath brought forth	הוֹצִיא
	thou (m.) hast ,,	יָצָ֫אתָ	thou (m.) hast ,,	הוֹצֵ֫אתָ
		&c.		&c.
Imperf.:	he will go forth	יֵצֵא	he will bring ,,	יוֹצִיא
	she ,,	תֵּצֵא	she ,,	תּוֹצִיא
		&c.		&c.
Shortened Imperf. Jussive:		—	let him ,,	יוֹצֵא
Imperf. with Waw Consecutive:	and he went forth	וַיֵּצֵא	and he brought ,,	וַיּוֹצֵא
Imper.:	go thou (m.) forth	צֵא	bring thou (m.) ,,	הוֹצֵא
	,, (f.) ,,	צְאִי	,, (f.) ,,	הוֹצִ֫יאִי
		&c.		&c.
Part.:	going forth (m. sg.)	יֹצֵא	bringing forth (m. sg.)	מוֹצִיא
	,, (f. sg.)	יֹצֵאת	,, (f. sg.)	מוֹצִיאָה
		&c.		&c.
Inf. absolute:		יָצוֹא		הוֹצֵא
construct:		צֵאת (for צֵ֫אֶת)		הוֹצִיא
	,, with ל	לָצֵאת (to go forth)		לְהוֹצִיא (to bring forth)

(d) בָּא (root בּוֹא) 'to come' 'to go in'—'Ayin Waw and Lamed 'Alep verb:

	Qal		Hiphil[b]	
Perf.:	he hath come	בָּא	he hath brought	הֵבִיא
	thou (m.) hast ,,	בָּ֫אתָ	thou (m.) hast ,,	הֵבֵ֫אתָ
	ye (m.) have ,,	בָּאתֶם	ye (m.) have ,,	הֲבֵאתֶם
		&c.		&c.

[a] 'To cause to go forth, to bring forth'.
[b] 'To cause to come', i.e. 'to bring'.

Imperf.: he will come	יָבוֹא or יָבֹא	he will bring	יָבִיא
she "	תָּבוֹא &c. &c.	she "	תָּבִיא &c.
Shortened Imperf. Jussive:	—	let him "	יָבֵא
Imperf. with Waw Consecutive:			
and he came	וַיָּבוֹא	and he brought	וַיָּבֵא
Imper.: come thou (m.)	בּוֹא or בֹּא	bring thou (m.)	הָבֵא
" (f.)	בּ֫וֹאִי &c. &c.	" (f.)	הָבִ֫יאִי &c.
Part.: coming (m. sg.)	בָּא	bringing (m. sg.)	מֵבִיא
" (m. pl.)	בָּאִים	" (m. pl.)	מְבִיאִים
Inf. absolute:	בּוֹא		הָבֵא
construct:	בֹּא		הָבִיא
" with ל	לָבֹא (to come)		לְהָבִיא (to bring)

(*e*) רוע used in Hiphil—הֵרִ֫יעַ—'to shout'—'Ayin Waw and Lamed Guttural verb:

HIPHIL

Perf.: he hath shouted	הֵרִ֫יעַ	*Imperf.*: he will shout	יָרִ֫יעַ
Part.: shouting (m. sg.)	מֵרִ֫יעַ	*Imper.*: shout thou (m.)	הָרֵ֫עַ
" (m. pl.)	מְרִ֫יעִים	" ye (m.)	הָרִ֫יעוּ
Inf. absolute:	הָרֵ֫עַ	*construct*:	הָרִ֫יעַ

EXERCISE 37

towards, to meet	לִקְרַאת־	to learn	לָמַד in Qal
" (with suffix)	לִקְרָאתִי	to teach למד in Piel	לִמֵּד
without	בְּלִי	to wash, bathe (used of washing the body)	רָחַץ

(1) וַיָּשֻׁ֫בוּ הַמַּלְאָכִים אֶל־יַעֲקֹב וַיֹּאמְרוּ אֵלָיו, בָּ֫אנוּ אֶל־עֵשָׂו
אָחִ֫יךָ וַנְּדַבֵּר אֵלָיו כְּכֹל אֲשֶׁר אָמַרְתָּ וְהִנֵּה הוּא הֹלֵךְ לִקְרָאתְךָ

וְעַם רַב עִמּוֹ: וַיִּירָא יַעֲקֹב מְאֹד וַיִּתְפַּלֵּל אֶל־יהוה וַיֹּאמַר
יהוה אֱלֹהַי הָאֹמֵר אֵלַי, שׁוּב אֶל־אַרְצְךָ וְאֶל־בֵּית־אָבִיךָ
וְאֵיטִיבָה עִמְּךָ, הַצִּילֵנִי נָא מִיַּד־אָחִי מִיַּד־עֵשָׂו, כִּי יָרֵא אָנֹכִי
אֹתוֹ, פֶּן־יָבֹא עָלַי וְהֵמִית אֹתִי וְאֶת־כָּל־בְּנֵי בֵיתִי: וַיֹּאמֶר
אֵלָיו יהוה, אַל־תִּירָא יַעֲקֹב, אָנֹכִי עִמְּךָ וּשְׁמַרְתִּיךָ מִכָּל־רָע
(2) וַיֵּצֵא מֹשֶׁה מֵאֵת[a] פְּנֵי־פַרְעֹה וַיִּצְעַק אֶל־יהוה לֵאמֹר לָמָּה
שְׁלַחְתַּנִי אֶל־פַּרְעֹה, כִּי מִיּוֹם בּוֹאִי לְפָנָיו הִכְבִּיד אֶת־הָעֲבוֹדָה
עַל־בְּנֵי־יִשְׂרָאֵל, וְהַצֵּל לֹא הִצַּלְתָּ אֶת־עַמֶּךָ: וַיֹּאמֶר אֵלָיו
יהוה שָׁמַעְתִּי אֶת־צַעֲקַת בְּנֵי־יִשְׂרָאֵל אֲשֶׁר מִצְרַיִם[b] מַעֲבִידִים
אֹתָם, וְהוֹצֵא אוֹצִיא אֹתָם מֵאֶרֶץ מִצְרַיִם וְהִצַּלְתִּי אֹתָם
מֵעֲבוֹדָתָם וְלָקַחְתִּי אֹתָם לִי לְעָם, וְהֵבֵאתִי אֹתָם אֶל־הָאָרֶץ
אֲשֶׁר נָשָׂאתִי אֶת־יָדִי לַאֲבוֹתָם לָתֵת לָהֶם (3) כִּי תָבֹאוּ אֶל־
הָאָרֶץ אֲשֶׁר אָנֹכִי מֵבִיא אֶתְכֶם שָׁמָּה וִירַשְׁתֶּם אֹתָהּ וִישַׁבְתֶּם
בָּהּ, וְהִבְדַּלְתֶּם לָכֶם שָׁלֹשׁ עָרִים אֲשֶׁר יָנוּס שָׁמָּה הָאִישׁ הַהֹרֵג
אֶת־רֵעֵהוּ בִּבְלִי־דַעַת וְהוּא לֹא אֹיֵב לוֹ: וְנָס הָאִישׁ הַהוּא אֶל־
אַחַת־הֶעָרִים הָאֵלֶּה, וְשָׁפְטוּ אֹתוֹ זִקְנֵי־הָעִיר, וְיָשַׁב שָׁם עַד
מוֹת־הַכֹּהֵן הַגָּדוֹל (4) כִּי יִמָּצֵא אִישׁ הָרוּג עַל־הָאֲדָמָה וְלֹא יִוָּדַע
מִי הֲרָגוֹ, וְיָצְאוּ זִקְנֵי־הָעִיר וְשֹׁפְטֶיהָ וְלָקְחוּ אֶת־הַמֵּת וְהוֹרִידוּ
אֹתוֹ אֶל־הַנָּהָר וְרָחֲצוּ אֶת־יְדֵיהֶם בְּמֵי־הַנָּהָר וְאָמְרוּ, יָדֵינוּ
לֹא שָׁפְכוּ אֶת־הַדָּם הַזֶּה וְעֵינֵינוּ לֹא רָאוּ: וְקָבְרוּ שָׁם אֶת־הַמֵּת
כַּמִּשְׁפָּט הַזֶּה (5) הִנֵּה נָתַתִּי לָכֶם אֶת־הַמִּצְוֹת וְאֶת־הַמִּשְׁפָּטִים
הָאֵלֶּה, וְהוֹדַעְתֶּם אֶת־בְּנֵיכֶם לְמַעַן יִלְמְדוּ לִשְׁמֹר אֹתָם כְּכֹל
הַכָּתוּב בְּסֵפֶר הַתּוֹרָה הַזֶּה[c], וְהֵבִיא עֲלֵיהֶם יהוה אֶת־הַבְּרָכוֹת
הָאֵלֶּה (6) זָכוֹר תִּזְכֹּר אֶת־חַסְדֵי־יהוה אֲשֶׁר עָשָׂה אִתְּךָ מִיּוֹם־
צֵאתְךָ מֵאֶרֶץ מִצְרַיִם וְעַד־עָתָּה: וְלִמַּדְתָּ אֶת־בָּנֶיךָ אֶת־

[a] Lit. 'from (with)'.

[b] Egypt—collect. for Egyptians; hence pl. verb.

[c] 'This' is masc. since it refers to the 'book'—'this book of the law'

דִּבְרֵי־הַתּוֹרָה הַזֹּאת, לְמַ֫עַן יִיטַב לָהֶם בָּאָ֫רֶץ אֲשֶׁר הֵ֫מָּה בָאִים
שָׁ֫מָּה לְרִ֫שְׁתָּהּ אֹתָהּ: אֲנִי יהוה הַמּוֹצִיא אֶתְכֶם מִבֵּית־עֲבָדִים
(7) וַיְהִי הַיּוֹם וַיְבַקְשׁוּ שְׁנֵי־אֲנָשִׁים לַהֲרֹג אֶת־הַמֶּ֫לֶךְ בַּהֵיכָל:
וַיִּוָּדַע הַדָּבָר לְאֶחָד מֵעֲבָדָיו וַיַּגֵּד לַמֶּ֫לֶךְ וַיְבֻקַּשׁ הַדָּבָר וַיִּמָּצֵא
וְהִנֵּה אֱמֶת דְּבַר עַבְדּוֹ: וַיּוּמְתוּ שְׁנֵי־הָאֲנָשִׁים הָאֵ֫לֶּה וַיִּכָּתֵב
הַדָּבָר בְּסֵ֫פֶר דִּבְרֵי־הַיָּמִים[a] לִפְנֵי־הַמֶּ֫לֶךְ

(1) And the Lord spoke unto Moses and unto Aaron in the land of Egypt saying: 'Go ye in unto Pharaoh and ye shall say unto him: "Let go (Piel of שׁלח) my people Israel a journey ('way') of three days in the wilderness to serve the Lord our God".' And Moses and Aaron came and they stood before Pharaoh and they spoke these words unto him. And Pharaoh said unto them: 'Why have ye come unto me? Know ye (perf.) not that the children of Israel are servants to me? I will indeed not let them go.' And Moses said: 'Thou shalt surely know that if thou transgressest (imperf.) the commandment of the Lord our God, behold He will send plagues against thee and against thy people, and He will bring the beasts of the wilderness in(to) the land and they will eat all the fruit of the ground and they will come in(to) thy house and in(to) the houses of thy servants, in order that thou shalt know that there is none like Him.' And it came to pass as they spoke (inf. const. with suff.) these words that (waw consec.) they went forth from (with) the presence ('face') of Pharaoh. (2) Abraham did according to ('as') all which the Lord (had) commanded him and he took his wife and the son of his brother and all the wealth which he had and he went forth to the land of Canaan. And Abraham was very old when he went forth ('in his going forth', inf. const. with suff.) from his land. (3) And it came to pass as they heard the words of the spies that (waw consec.) they cried unto Moses, saying: 'Why didst thou bring us forth from the land of Egypt to slay ("put to death") all this congregation? For behold the inhabitants of Canaan are mighty men of war and we are not able (perf.) to go forth against them for (the) war. Why went we forth from Egypt?' (4) And the old man sat in the dust before his friends

[a] i.e. chronicles.

[רֵעַ] and he lifted up his voice and he cried: 'Naked went I forth unto the world and naked shall I return to the earth. The Lord I have feared all the days of my life and why hath He brought upon me all these?' And one of ('from') his friends rose and he said: 'Who art thou that thou shouldst judge (imperf.) the Lord? Art thou not flesh and blood? Will the Lord bring trouble upon a man who sinned not against ('to') Him?' (5) I said that she (was)[a] my sister, for there is not the fear of God in this place and I was afraid lest they would (imperf.) put me to death. (6) And the fame ('name') of Solomon went forth in all the world; and the kings of the land came to Jerusalem and they brought with them (every) man his present to Solomon.

79. LAMED HE VERBS (Lamed Yod and Lamed Waw)

The verb גָּלָה ('to uncover, reveal' and also 'to go into exile') is weak, since its third root-letter is a silent ה. Most ל״ה verbs were originally ל״י and some ל״ו. The verb גָּלָה, for example, comes from an original גָּלַי, *gālay*, which evolved into גָּלָה, *gālâ*, but the original third root-letter י has survived in many of the verb-forms:

	Qal			Niphal		
Perf.:	he (hath) uncovered		גָּלָה	he was uncovered		נִגְלָה
	she	,,	גָּלְתָה[b]	she	,,	נִגְלְתָה
	thou (m.) hast	,,	גָּלִיתָ	thou (m.) wast	,,	נִגְלֵיתָ נִגְלִיתָ
	thou (f.)	,,	גָּלִית	thou (f.)	,,	נִגְלֵית
	I (c.) (have)	,,	גָּלִיתִי	I (c.) was	,,	נִגְלֵיתִי
	they (c.)	,,	גָּלוּ	they (c.) were	,,	נִגְלוּ
	ye (m.)	,,	גְּלִיתֶם	ye (m.)	,,	נִגְלֵיתֶם
	ye (f.)	,,	גְּלִיתֶן	ye (f.)	,,	נִגְלֵיתֶן
	we (c.)	,,	גָּלִינוּ	we (c.)	,,	נִגְלֵינוּ
Perf. with suffix:						
	he hath uncovered me		גָּלַנִי			

[a] In Hebrew 'I said that she *is* my sister'.

[b] The 3rd f. sg. perf. was originally גָּלַת (reduced from גָּלָיַת) but it strangely received another f. sg. termination, as if גָּלַת itself had been the root.

Imperf.:	he will uncover	יִגְלֶה	he will be uncovered	יִגָּלֶה
	she ,,	תִּגְלֶה	she ,,	תִּגָּלֶה
	thou (m.) wilt ,,	תִּגְלֶה	thou (m.) wilt ,,	תִּגָּלֶה
	thou (f.) ,,	תִּגְלִי	thou (f.) ,,	תִּגָּלִי
	I (c.) shall ,,	אֶגְלֶה	I (c.) shall ,,	אֶגָּלֶה
	they (m.) will ,,	יִגְלוּ	they (m.) will ,,	יִגָּלוּ
	they (f.) ,,	תִּגְלֶינָה	they (f.) ,,	תִּגָּלֶינָה
	ye (m.) ,,	תִּגְלוּ	ye (m.) ,,	תִּגָּלוּ
	ye (f.) ,,	תִּגְלֶינָה	ye (f.) ,,	תִּגָּלֶינָה
	we (c.) shall ,,	נִגְלֶה	we (c.) shall ,,	נִגָּלֶה
Imperf. with suffix:	he will uncover me	יִגְלֵנִי		
Shortened Imperf. *Jussive*:	let him uncover	יִגֶל	let him be ,,	יִגָּל
Imperf. with Waw Consecutive:	and he uncovered	וַיִּגֶל	and he was	וַיִּגָּל
Imper.:	uncover thou (m.)	גְּלֵה	be thou (m.) ,,	הִגָּלֵה
	,, (f.)	גְּלִי	,, (f.) ,,	הִגָּלִי
	,, ye (m.)	גְּלוּ	,, ye (m.) ,,	הִגָּלוּ
	,, (f.)	גְּלֶינָה	,, (f.) ,,	הִגָּלֶינָה
Part. (*active*):	uncovering (m. sg.)	גֹּלֶה		
	,, (f. sg.)	גֹּלָה		
	,, (m. pl.)	גֹּלִים		
	,, (f. pl.)	גֹּלוֹת		
(*passive*):	uncovered (m. sg.) [N.B. gālûy]	גָּלוּי	being uncovered (m. sg.)	נִגְלֶה
			,, (f. sg.)	נִגְלָה
	,, (f. sg.)	גְּלוּיָה	,, (m. pl.)	נִגְלִים
	,, (m. pl.)	גְּלוּיִם	,, (f. pl.)	נִגְלוֹת
	,, (f. pl.)	גְּלוּיוֹת		
Inf. absolute:		גָּלֹה		נִגְלֹה
construct:		גְּלוֹת		הִגָּלוֹת
,, with ל:		לִגְלוֹת		לְהִגָּלוֹת

In the passive Participle Qal the third root-letter י has survived as a full consonant—גָּלוּי, גְּלוּיָה &c. In the 2nd and 1st Perf. of the Qal (גָּלִ֫יתָ, גָּלִ֫יתִי, גְּלִיתֶם &c.) and of the Niphal (נִגְלֵ֫יתָ, נִגְלֵיתֶם &c.) the original third root-letter י has survived as a silent letter: the original גָּלַ֫יְתָ (galáytâ) became גָּלֵ֫יתָ (galḗyṯâ) and finally גָּלִ֫יתָ (galiyṯâ—galîṯâ), and likewise the original נִגְלַ֫יְתָ (niḡláytâ) became נִגְלֵ֫יתָ (niḡlḗyṯâ, niḡlêṯâ). In the 3rd Perf. of the Qal and Niphal the third root-letter י has disappeared: גָּֽלְיוּ (gāl^{e}yû) became גָּלוּ (gālû) and נִגְלְיוּ (niḡl^{e}yû) became נִגְלוּ (niḡlû).

Note carefully the shortened form of the Imperfect: the Qal יִגְלֶה is shortened to (יִגְל, and then) יִ֫גֶל and the Niphal יִגָּלֶה to יִגָּל.

The Infinitive construct assumes an וֹת ending (cf. the assumption of a ת by the inf. const. Qal of Pe Nun and Pe Waw verbs).

The Piel and Pual have the same terminations as the Qal and Niphal:

	Piel		Pual	
Perf.:	he (hath) revealed	גִּלָּה	he was revealed	גֻּלָּה
	she ,,	גִּלְּתָה	she ,,	גֻּלְּתָה
	thou (m.) hast ,,	גִּלִּ֫יתָ גִּלֵּ֫יתָ	thou (m.) wast ,,	גֻּלֵּ֫יתָ &c.
	I (c.) have ,,	גִּלִּ֫יתִי &c.		
Imperf.:	he will reveal	יְגַלֶּה	he will be revealed	יְגֻלֶּה
	she ,,	תְּגַלֶּה &c.	she ,,	תְּגֻלֶּה &c.
Shortened Imperf. *Jussive*:	let him reveal	יְגַל		
Imperf. with Waw Consecutive:	and he revealed	וַיְגַל	and he was ,,	וַיְגֻלֶּה
Imper.:	reveal thou (m.)	גַּלֵּה		
	,, (f.)	גַּלִּי &c.		

Part.:	revealing (m. sg.)	מְגַלֶּה &c.	being revealed (m. sg.)	מְגֻלֶּה &c.
Inf. absolute:		גַּלֵּה		גֻּלֵּה
construct:		גַּלּוֹת		גֻּלּוֹת

The other derived forms follow the same pattern as the preceding ones. To make the Hiphil intelligible גלה has been taken in its other meaning 'to go into exile' which in Hiphil is 'to cause to go into exile—to exile'.

	Hiphil		Hophal	
Perf.:	he (hath) exiled	הִגְלָה	he was exiled	הָגְלָה
	she ,,	הִגְלְתָה	she ,,	הָגְלְתָה
	thou (m.) hast ,,	הִגְלִיתָ הִגְלֵיתָ	thou (m.) wast ,,	הָגְלֵיתָ &c.
	I (c.) have ,,	הִגְלִיתִי הִגְלֵיתִי		
Imperf.:	he will exile	יַגְלֶה	he will be ,,	יָגְלֶה
	she ,,	תַּגְלֶה &c.	she ,,	תָּגְלֶה &c.
Shortened Imperf. Jussive:	let him ,,	יֶגֶל[a]		
Imperf. with Waw Consecutive:	and he exiled	וַיֶּגֶל		
Imper.:	exile thou (m.)	הַגְלֵה		
	,, (f.)	הַגְלִי &c.		
Part.:	exiling (m. sg.)	מַגְלֶה &c.	being exiled (m. sg.)	מָגְלֶה &c.
Inf. absolute:		הַגְלֵה		הָגְלֵה
construct:		הַגְלוֹת		הָגְלוֹת

[a] The shortened Imperfect יַגְל is a Segholate form which evolves into יֶגֶל (as מַלְךְ into מֶלֶךְ, pp. 82 ff.).

Hithpael

Perf.:	he (hath) revealed himself	הִתְגַּלָּה
	she ,, herself	הִתְגַּלְּתָה
	thou (m.) hast ,, thyself	הִתְגַּלִּיתָ
	I (c.) have ,, myself	הִתְגַּלִּיתִי
Imperf.:	he will ,, himself	יִתְגַּלֶּה
	she ,, herself	תִּתְגַּלֶּה &c.
Shortened Imperf. Jussive:	let him reveal himself	יִתְגַּל
Imperf with Waw Consecutive:	and he revealed himself	וַיִּתְגַּל
Imper.:	reveal thyself (m.)	הִתְגַּלֵּה &c.
Part.:	revealing oneself (m. sg.)	מִתְגַּלֶּה &c.
Inf. absolute: הִתְגַּלֵּה	*construct*:	הִתְגַּלּוֹת

N.B. The Imperfects in all forms of the Lamed He verb terminate in ֶה, the Infinitives construct all terminate in וֹת, and there is a shortened Imperfect (Jussive) in Qal, Niphal, Piel, and Hithpael, as well as in the Hiphil.

EXERCISE 38

Gilead	גִּלְעָד	to build	בָּנָה
cattle	מִקְנֶה	to command צוה in Piel	צִוָּה
Tyre	צֹר	to see	רָאָה
		to appear ראה in Niphal	נִרְאָה
here	פֹּה	to cause to see, to show ראה in Hiphil	הֶרְאָה

(1) וְלִבְנֵי־רְאוּבֵן הָיָה צֹאן וּבָקָר רַב עַד־מְאֹד, וַיִּרְאוּ אֶת־
אֶרֶץ־הַגִּלְעָד וְהִנֵּה הַמָּקוֹם מְקוֹם־מִקְנֶה: וַיִּגְּשׁוּ אֶל־מֹשֶׁה
וַיְדַבְּרוּ אֵלָיו לֵאמֹר הָאָרֶץ אֲשֶׁר נָתַן יהוה בְּיָדֵנוּ אֶרֶץ מִקְנֶה
הִיא, וְלַעֲבָדֶיךָ מִקְנֶה: וְעַתָּה אִם־נָא מָצָאנוּ חֵן בְּעֵינֶיךָ, תְּנָה

לָ֫נוּ אֶת־הָאָ֫רֶץ הַזֹּאת וְאַל־תַּעֲבִרֵ֫נוּ אֶת־הַיַּרְדֵּן אַ֫רְצָה כְּנָֽעַן׃
וַיֹּ֫אמֶר אֲלֵיהֶם מֹשֶׁה, הַ[a]אֲחֵיכֶם יַעַבְרוּ אֶת־הַיַּרְדֵּן לַמִּלְחָמָה
וְאַתֶּם תֵּשְׁבוּ פֹה׃ וַיֹּאמְרוּ בְנֵי־רְאוּבֵן, בָּתִּים נִבְנֶה לְנָשֵׁינוּ
וּלְבָנֵ֫ינוּ וְיָשְׁבוּ בָהֶם, וַאֲנַ֫חְנוּ נַעֲבֹר עִם־אַחֵ֫ינוּ לְהִלָּחֵם בְּיֹשְׁבֵי־
כְנָ֫עַן׃ לֹא נָשׁוּב אֶל־בָּתֵּ֫ינוּ עַד־אֲשֶׁר נָתַן יהוה אֶת־כָּל־הָאָ֫רֶץ
בְּיַד־יִשְׂרָאֵל׃ אָז נָשׁוּב אֶל־הֶעָרִים אֲשֶׁר בָּנִ֫ינוּ וְיָשַׁ֫בְנוּ שָׁם׃
וַיִּיטְבוּ דִבְרֵיהֶם בְּעֵינֵי־מֹשֶׁה, וַיִּקְרָא אֶת־יְהוֹשֻׁעַ וְאֶת־רָאשֵׁי־
הָעָם וַיְצַו אֹתָם לֵאמֹר אִם יַעַבְרוּ בְנֵי־רְאוּבֵן אִתְּכֶם אֶת־
הַיַּרְדֵּן לְהִלָּחֵם בְּאֹיְבֵיכֶם, וְהָיָה בְּתֵת יהוה בְּיֶדְכֶם[b] אֶת־אֶ֫רֶץ
כְּנַ֫עַן, וּנְתַתֶּם לָהֶם אֶת־כָּל־אֶ֫רֶץ הַגִּלְעָד (2) אַתֶּם רְאִיתֶם אֶת־
כָּל־אֲשֶׁר עָשָׂה לָכֶם יהוה בְּמִצְרַ֫יִם וְעַל־הַיָּם וּבַמִּדְבָּר הַגָּדוֹל
הַזֶּה׃ וְעַתָּה שָׁמוֹר תִּשְׁמְרוּ אֶת־מִצְוֹתָיו כְּכֹל אֲשֶׁר צִוִּ֫יתִי אֶתְכֶם
וִהְיִיתֶם קְדוֹשִׁים לַיהוה אֱלֹהֵיכֶם אֲשֶׁר הוֹצִיא אֶתְכֶם מִבֵּית־
עֲבָדִים לִהְיוֹת לָכֶם לֵאלֹהִים (3) וַיְהִי אַחֲרֵי מוֹת־מֹשֶׁה וַיְדַבֵּר
יהוה אֶל־יְהוֹשֻׁעַ וַיֹּ֫אמֶר אֵלָיו קוּם עֲבֹר אֶת־הַיַּרְדֵּן, אַתָּה
וְכָל־הָעָם אִתְּךָ אֶל־הָאָ֫רֶץ אֲשֶׁר נִשְׁבַּ֫עְתִּי לַאֲבוֹתָם לָתֵת
לָהֶם׃ אַל־תִּירָא מִפְּנֵי־יֹשְׁבֶ֫יהָ, כִּי כַּאֲשֶׁר הָיִ֫יתִי עִם מֹשֶׁה כֵּן
אֶהְיֶה עִמָּךְ׃ לֹא אֶעֱזָבְךָ עַד־אֲשֶׁר עָשִׂ֫יתִי כְּכֹל אֲשֶׁר דִּבַּ֫רְתִּי
אֶל־מֹשֶׁה עַבְדִּי (4) וַיֵּצֵא הַגִּבּוֹר הַפְּלִשְׁתִּי וַיַּעֲמֹד עַל־הָהָר
נֶ֫גֶד מַחֲנֵה־יִשְׂרָאֵל וַיִּקְרָא אֲלֵיהֶם בְּקוֹל גָּדוֹל וַיֹּ֫אמֶר בַּחֲרוּ
לָכֶם אִישׁ מִבֵּין גִּבּוֹרֵיכֶם וְיָבֹא עָלַי לְהִלָּחֵם בִּי׃ וְהָיָה אִם הוּא
יְמִיתֵ֫נִי וְהָיִ֫ינוּ לָכֶם לַעֲבָדִים וְאִם אָנֹכִי אֲמִיתֵ֫הוּ וִהְיִיתֶם לָ֫נוּ
לַעֲבָדִים׃ וַיַּגִּ֫ידוּ לְשָׁאוּל אֶת־דִּבְרֵי־הַפְּלִשְׁתִּי׃ (5) וַיִּשְׁלַח
שְׁלֹמֹה מַלְאָכִים אֶל־מֶ֫לֶךְ צֹר לֵאמֹר אַתָּה יָדַ֫עְתָּ אֶת־דָּוִד
אָבִי כִּי לֹא יָכֹל לִבְנוֹת בַּ֫יִת לְשֵׁם־יהוה אֱלֹהָיו, כִּי מִלְחָמוֹת
רַבּוֹת הָיוּ לוֹ׃ וְעַתָּה הִנְנִי יֹשֵׁב עַל כִּסֵּא־יִשְׂרָאֵל, וֵאלֹהִים נָתַן
שָׁלוֹם בְּאַרְצִי, וְאֹמַר אָנֹכִי אֶבְנֶה הֵיכָל לַיהוה אֱלֹהָי׃ וְעַתָּה

[a] He Interrogative.

[b] Note יֶדְכֶם [for יַדְכֶם]—with this [heavy] suffix the Pathaḥ has been weakened into S^e^ghol.

אִם טוֹב בְּעֵינֶיךָ וְעָשִׂיתָ חֶסֶד אִתִּי, צַוֵּה־נָא וְיִכְרְתוּ לִי עֵצִים
מֵהֶהָרִים אֲשֶׁר בְּאַרְצֶךָ וַעֲבָדַי יִהְיוּ עִם עֲבָדֶיךָ וְהוֹרִידוּ אֶת־
הָעֵצִים אֵלַי יְרוּשָׁלַ֫יְמָה וּבָנִיתִי אֶת־הֵיכַל־יהוה שָׁם: וַיִּזְכֹּר
מֶלֶךְ צֹר אֶת־חַסְדֵי־דָוִד אֲשֶׁר עָשָׂה אִתּוֹ וְאֶת־הַבְּרִית אֲשֶׁר
כָּרַת אִתּוֹ וַיִּשְׁמַע בְּקוֹל־שְׁלֹמֹה: וַיְצַו אֶת־עֲבָדָיו וַיִּכְרְתוּ עֵצִים
וַיָּבִיאוּ אֹתָם עַבְדֵי־שְׁלֹמֹה יְרוּשָׁלַ֫יְמָה וַיִּבֶן שָׁם שְׁלֹמֹה הֵיכָל
אֲשֶׁר לְפָנָיו לֹא הָיָה כָּמוֹהוּ: וַיָּבֹאוּ כֹּל מַלְכֵי־הַגּוֹיִם לִרְאוֹת
אֶת־הֵיכַל־שְׁלֹמֹה אֲשֶׁר בָּנָה לֵאלֹהָיו, וַיָּבִיאוּ בְיָדָם זָהָב וָכֶסֶף
וַיִּתְּנוּ בְּבֵית־יהוה: וַיֵּצֵא שֵׁם־הַמֶּלֶךְ שְׁלֹמֹה בְּכָל־הָאָרֶץ וַיְהִי
מְכֻבָּד מְאֹד בְּעֵינֵי כָל־הַמְּלָכִים (6) אַתָּה נִגְלֵיתָ אֵלֵינוּ בִּכְבוֹדְךָ
עַל הַר־סִינַי, וַתְּדַבֵּר אֵלֵינוּ מִתּוֹךְ הָאֵשׁ, וַתְּלַמְּדֵנוּ מִשְׁפְּטֵי־
צֶדֶק וְתוֹרַת־אֱמֶת,[a] וַתְּצַוֵּנוּ לִהְיוֹת מַמְלֶכֶת כֹּהֲנִים וְגוֹי קָדוֹשׁ
לְפָנֶיךָ: וְעַתָּה עָשִׂיתִי כְּכֹל אֲשֶׁר צִוִּיתָנוּ וָאָבִיא מִפְּרִי־אַדְמָתִי
מִנְחָה לַיהוה: שְׁלַח־נָא אֶת־בִּרְכָתְךָ בִּפְרִי־אַדְמָתִי וְשָׁמְרֵנִי
מִכָּל־רָע (7) וַיְהִי בְּצֵאת יִשְׂרָאֵל מִמִּצְרַיִם וַיִּקְרָא פַרְעֹה אֶל־
עֲבָדָיו וַיֹּאמֶר אֲלֵיהֶם, מַה־זֹּאת עָשִׂינוּ כִּי שִׁלַּחְנוּ אֶת־הָעָם
מֵעָבְדֵנוּ, נִרְדְּפָה אַחֲרֵיהֶם וְנָשִׁיבָה אֹתָם מִצְרַ֫יְמָה

(1) And the Lord spoke unto Moses in the land of Egypt, saying: 'Thus shalt thou say unto the children of Israel, "The Lord, God of your fathers, hath appeared unto me in the wilderness and He spoke unto me from the midst of (the) fire and He said: 'I have indeed seen (inf. abs. with finite verb) the affliction of My people Israel and I will indeed deliver them from the hand of Pharaoh and I will bring them forth from the land of Egypt and I will bring them into the land which I have sworn to their fathers, to Abraham, to Isaac, and to Jacob, to give to their seed, and they shall be to Me (for) a people and *I* (pronoun) shall be to them (for) a God'." And it shall come to pass if they will not hearken unto thee and they shall say "Give (to) us a sign that the Lord hath appeared unto thee and that He hath sent thee unto us," then (waw consec.) thou shalt do all these signs,

[a] See p. 136. 63.

as I have commanded thee.' (2) And it came to pass in the morning that (waw consec.) the king called (to) all his wise (men) and he related in their ears the dream which he (had) dreamed. And he said: 'Behold in my dream I saw a man standing over me and in his hand (was) a sword. And I said unto him, "Who art thou, and why hast thou come unto me and why is there a sword in thy hand?" And he said unto me, "Thou shalt indeed know that the Lord hath sent me to slay (Hiphil of מות) thee, for thou hast built for thyself a great house and thou didst not set thy heart to the ark of God which hath not a house". And I was afraid exceedingly and I said unto him, "Slay me not, my lord, for I shall indeed build a temple for the ark of the Lord my God like which there was not yet ('which there was not like it yet')." And the man who appeared (part. with art., pp. 65 f.) unto me said, "Behold I have hearkened to thy voice, but (conjunction) I shall indeed return if thou shalt not keep thy word; and now, command thy servants to build a temple for the Lord thy God upon the mount of Jerusalem".' And all the wise men said unto the king in one voice, 'Let the king command his servants and let them build a temple upon the holy mount ("mount of holiness") as the king hath sworn'. (3) And Joshua said unto the elders of the people: 'Pass ye (through) in the camp and command the people saying, "Leave ye your wives and your children and your cattle and your old (men) and the camp and pass ye (over) to (the) battle opposite the city, for the Lord will indeed give in(to) our hand the city and its inhabitants. Fear ye not them, for the Lord, He will fight for us".' And the elders passed (through) the camp and they commanded the people as Joshua (had) commanded them. (4) And the heads of the people sought and they found the man who had taken from the gold and the silver and they brought him near unto Joshua for (the) judgement. And Joshua asked him saying: 'Why hast thou done this thing? Tell (to) me, my son.' And the man said, 'Behold thy servant was among those who were fighting (part. with art.[a]) against the inhabitants of the city; and it came to pass, when the wall of the city fell (inf. const.) that I came into the palace of the king and I saw all the gold and the

[a] 'Among the (ones) fighting'.

silver and I took from it and I hid (it) in the ground.' (5) And David sent messengers to the king of Tyre saying: 'Let us make a covenant I and thou in order that there shall be peace between my people and between thy people.' And the messengers came and they brought a present to the king of Tyre and they spoke unto him as these words. And the servants of the king said unto him: 'Send away these men, for they are spies, for they have come to see the land.'

80. MORE DOUBLY WEAK VERBS

(*a*) נָטָה—Pe Nun and Lameḏ He verb:

'to turn, incline' (intrans.); 'to stretch, pitch (a tent)'.

	QAL		HIPHIL	
Perf.: he (hath) turned	נָטָה		he (hath) caused to turn	הִטָּה
she „	נָטְתָה &c.		she „	הִטְּתָה &c.
Imperf.: he will turn	יִטֶּה		he will cause to turn	יַטֶּה
she „	תִּטֶּה &c.		she „	תַּטֶּה &c.
Shortened Imperf. Jussive:				
let him „	יֵט		let him „	יַט
Imperf. with Waw Consecutive:				
and he turned	וַיֵּט		and he caused to turn	וַיַּט
Imper.: turn thou (m.)	נְטֵה &c.		cause thou (m.) to turn	הַטֵּה / הַט &c.
Part. active:				
turning (m. sg.)	נֹטֶה		causing to turn (m. sg.)	מַטֶּה &c.
passive:				
turned (m. sg.)	נָטוּי			
Inf. absolute:	נָטֹה			הַטֵּה
construct:	נְטוֹת			הַטּוֹת

NOTE: The Imperfects (as in all Lameḏ He verbs) have shortened forms for tne Jussive. In Qal the Imperf. יִטֶּה is first shortened to יְטּ but, since the final letter of a word cannot be doubled, the preceding vowel is prolonged, producing יֵט. It will, of course, be noted how the peculiarities of both the Pe Nun and Lamed He operate together.

The doubly weak verb נכה of the above type, found only in Hiphil ('to smite') and in Hophal, occurs very frequently in Scripture, and the student is advised to familiarize himself with its main parts.

	Hiphil		Hophal	
Perf.:	he hath smitten	הִכָּה	he was smitten	הֻכָּה
	she ,,	הִכְּתָה	she ,,	הֻכְּתָה
Imperf.:	he will smite	יַכֶּה	he will be ,,	יֻכֶּה
	she ,,	תַּכֶּה	she ,,	תֻּכֶּה
Shortened Imperf. Jussive:	let him smite	יַךְ		
Imperf. with Waw Consecutive:	and he smote	וַיַּךְ	and he was ,,	וַיֻּכֶּה
Imper.:	smite thou (m.)	הַכֵּה הַךְ		
Part.:	smiting (m. sg.)	מַכֶּה	being smitten (m. sg.)	מֻכֶּה
Inf. absolute:		הַכֵּה		הֻכֵּה
construct:		הַכּוֹת		הֻכּוֹת

(*b*) עָלָה—Pe Guttural and Lamed He: 'to go up, ascend'.
עָשָׂה— ,, ,, 'to do, make, perform'.

	Qal			
Perf.:	he hath gone up	עָלָה	he (hath) made	עָשָׂה
	she ,,	עָלְתָה	she ,,	עָשְׂתָה
	ye (m.) have ,,	עֲלִיתֶם	ye (m.) have ,,	עֲשִׂיתֶם
		&c.		&c.

Imperf.:	he will go up	יַעֲלֶה	he will make		יַעֲשֶׂה
	she ,,	תַּעֲלֶה	she	,,	תַּעֲשֶׂה
Shortened Imperf. Jussive:					
	let him go ,,	יַ֫עַל	let him	,,	יַ֫עַשׂ
Imperf. with Waw Consecutive:					
	and he went ,,	וַיַּ֫עַל	and he made		וַיַּ֫עַשׂ
Imper.:	go thou (m.) ,,	עֲלֵה &c.	make thou (m.)		עֲשֵׂה &c.
Part. active:					
	going up (m. sg.)	עֹלֶה	making (m. sg.)		עֹשֶׂה
	passive:		made (m. sg.)		עָשׂוּי
Inf. absolute:		עָלֹה			עָשֹׂה
construct:		עֲלוֹת			עֲשׂוֹת
	,, with ל:	לַעֲלוֹת	with ל:		לַעֲשׂוֹת

The terminations of this doubly weak verb are those of the Lameḏ He, while the initial guttural takes composite shewa instead of the simple shewa, and attracts the vowel Pathaḥ under it and before it.

	Niphal		Hiphil		
Perf.:	he was made	נַעֲשָׂה	he (hath) brought up		הֶעֱלָה
	she ,,	נֶעֶשְׂתָה	she	,,	הֶעֶלְתָה
	they (c.) were ,,	נַעֲשׂוּ	they (have)	,,	הֶעֱלוּ
Imperf.:	he will be ,,	יֵעָשֶׂה	he will bring	,,	יַעֲלֶה
	she ,,	תֵּעָשֶׂה	she	,,	תַּעֲלֶה
Shortened Imperf. Jussive:					
	let him be ,,	יֵעָשׂ	let him bring	,,	יַ֫עַל
Imperf. with Waw Consecutive:					
	and he was ,,	וַיֵּעָשׂ	and he brought	,,	וַיַּ֫עַל

Imper.: be thou (m.) made	הֵעָשֵׂה	bring thou (m.) up	הַעֲלֵה הַעַל
Part.: being made (m. sg.)	נַעֲשֶׂה	bringing up (m. sg.)	מַעֲלֶה
Inf. absolute:	נַעֲשׂה		הַעֲלֵה
construct:	הֵעָשׂוֹת		הַעֲלוֹת

NOTE how the Guttural determines the beginnings and the He the terminations. The Imperfects of the Qal and the Hiphil (and following them the Jussives too) have evolved into the same form through different processes; so that the context is relied upon to indicate which is meant.

(*c*) אָפָה—Pe 'Alep̱ and Lameḏ He verb—'to bake'.

QAL		NIPHAL	
Perf.: he (hath) baked	אָפָה	he (hath) been baked	נֶאֱפָה
Imperf.: he will bake	יֹאפֶה	he will be baked	יֵאָפֶה

Since the Pe 'Alep̱ verb diverges from the Pe Guttural in the Qal Imperfect, this type of doubly weak verb differs from the preceding type in this respect too.

(*d*) רָאָה 'to see' is a peculiar verb, since the first root-letter cannot be doubled, there is a medial 'Alep̱, and a third root-letter He.

QAL Imperfect, 'he will see' יִרְאֶה, but with Waw Consecutive וַיַּרְא 'and he saw'; 'and she saw' is וַתֵּרֶא.

NIPHAL Imperfect, 'he will be seen, appear' יֵרָאֶה, but with Waw Consecutive it is וַיֵּרָא 'and he was seen, and he appeared'.

EXERCISE 39

border	גְּבוּל	to answer	עָנָה
mouth	פֶּה	to afflict ענה in Piel	עִנָּה
,, (const.)	פִּי־	ox, bull	פַּר
,, (pl.)	פִּיּוֹת	,, (with art.)	הַפָּר

(1) וַיְהִי אַחֲרֵי הַדְּבָרִים הָאֵלֶּה וַיִּשְׁלַח מֹשֶׁה מַלְאָכִים אֶל־מֶלֶךְ אֱדוֹם לֵאמֹר׃ כֹּה אָמַר אָחִיךָ יִשְׂרָאֵל, אַתָּה יָדַעְתָּ כִּי

יָמִים רַבִּים יָשַׁבְנוּ בְמִצְרָיִם וַיַּעֲבִידוּ אֹתָנוּ הַמִּצְרִים וַיְעַנּוּ אֹתָנוּ
עַד־מְאֹד׃ וַנִּצְעַק אֶל־יהוה אֱלֹהֵינוּ וַיִּשְׁמַע אֶת־קוֹלֵנוּ וַיּוֹצִיאֵנוּ
מִשָּׁם בְּיָד חֲזָקָה לְהָבִיא אֹתָנוּ אֶל־הָאָרֶץ אֲשֶׁר נִשְׁבַּע לַאֲבוֹתֵינוּ
לָתֶת לָנוּ׃ וְהִנֵּה אֲנַחְנוּ עֹמְדִים עַל־גְּבוּלֶךָ לָבוֹא אַרְצָה כְנָעַן׃
וְעַתָּה נַעְבְּרָה־נָּא בְאַרְצֶךָ וְעָשִׂיתָ עִמָּנוּ חָסֶד׃ וַיַּעַן מֶלֶךְ אֱדוֹם
לֵאמֹר לֹא תַעַבְרוּ בְאַרְצִי, פֶּן־בַּחֶרֶב אֵצֵא לִקְרָאתְכֶם׃ וַיֵּצֵא
לִקְרַאת־יִשְׂרָאֵל, וְעַם כָּבֵד מְאֹד אִתּוֹ וַיֵּט יִשְׂרָאֵל מִמֶּנּוּ וַיָּשֶׂם
אֶת־פָּנָיו הַמִּדְבָּרָה, כִּי לֹא נָתַן[a] לוֹ מֶלֶךְ אֱדוֹם לַעֲבֹר בְּאַרְצוֹ
(2) וַיְהִי כִּרְאוֹת שָׁאוּל אֶת־גִּבּוֹר־הַפְּלִשְׁתִּים וַיִּשָּׁבַע לֵאמֹר
הָאִישׁ אֲשֶׁר יַעֲלֶה וְהִכָּה אֶת־הַפְּלִשְׁתִּי הַזֶּה, לוֹ אֶתֵּן אֶת־בִּתִּי
לְאִשָּׁה׃ וַיָּבֹא דָוִד וַיַּעֲמֹד לִפְנֵי־שָׁאוּל וַיֹּאמֶר אָנֹכִי אֶעֱלֶה
וְהִכִּיתִי אֹתוֹ וְהֵבֵאתִי אֵלֶיךָ אֶת־רֹאשׁוֹ׃ וַיֹּאמֶר אֵלָיו שָׁאוּל,
עֲלֵה בְנִי, וִיהִי יהוה עִמְּךָ וְנָתַן אֶת־אֹיִבְךָ בְּיָדֶךָ׃ וַיַּעַל דָּוִד
וַיִּגַּשׁ אֶל־הַגִּבּוֹר וַיַּךְ אֶת־הַפְּלִשְׁתִּי אַרְצָה וַיִּקַּח אֶת־חַרְבּוֹ
מֵעָלָיו וַיִּכְרֹת בָּהּ אֶת־רֹאשׁוֹ וַיָּבֵא אֶל־שָׁאוּל׃ וְכָל־יִשְׂרָאֵל
עֹמְדוּ עַל־הָהָר מִנֶּגֶד וַיִּרְאוּ כִּי הִכָּה דָוִד אֶת־אֹיְבוֹ וַיִּקְרְאוּ
בְקוֹל אֶחָד, לֹא נִמְצָא בָאָרֶץ גִּבּוֹר כְּדָוִד׃ וַיִּשְׁמַע שָׁאוּל אֶת־
דִּבְרֵי־הָעָם וַיִּקְצֹף עַד־מְאֹד וַתָּבֹא עָלָיו הָרוּחַ הָרָעָה וַיְבַקֵּשׁ
לְהָמִית אֶת־דָּוִד (3) וַיְהִי אַחֲרֵי מוֹת־הַשֹּׁפֵט וַיָּשׁוּבוּ בְנֵי־יִשְׂרָאֵל
אֶל־דַּרְכֵי־הַגּוֹיִם אֲשֶׁר יָשְׁבוּ בְתוֹכָם וַיַּעֲשׂוּ אֶת־הָרַע בְּעֵינֵי־
יהוה וַיַּעַבְדוּ אֶת־אֱלֹהֵי הָאָרֶץ וַיִּשְׁכְּחוּ אֶת־תּוֹרַת־יהוה׃ וַיִּתְּנֵם
יהוה בְּיַד־מֶלֶךְ אֱדוֹם וַיְעַנֵּם, וְלֹא הָיָה בָהֶם עוֹד רוּחַ לַעֲמֹד
לִפְנֵי־אֹיְבֵיהֶם וַיִּצְעֲקוּ אֶל־יהוה לֵאמֹר חָטֹא חָטָאנוּ לְפָנֶיךָ
וַנַּעֲבֹר אֶת־בְּרִיתְךָ אֲשֶׁר כָּרַתָּ[b] אִתָּנוּ׃ הַצִּילֵנוּ נָא יהוה מִיַּד־
אֹיְבֵינוּ וְאַל־נָא תַעַזְבֵנוּ, אִם לֹא לְמַעֲנֵנוּ לְמַעַן מֹשֶׁה עַבְדְּךָ
הוֹשִׁיעֵנוּ׃ וַיִּשְׁלַח אֲלֵיהֶם יהוה אִישׁ נָבִיא וַיְדַבֵּר אֲלֵיהֶם לֵאמֹר

[a] Here = 'to permit, allow'.
[b] For כָּרַתְתָּ, see footnote, p. 206.

כֹּה אָמַר יהוה, אָנֹכִי הֶעֱלֵיתִי אֶתְכֶם מֵאֶרֶץ מִצְרַיִם וָאוֹצִיא
אֶתְכֶם מִבֵּית־עֲבָדִים וָאָבִיא אֶתְכֶם אַרְצָה כְּנַעַן וָאֶתֵּן לָכֶם
אֶת־הָאָרֶץ׃ וָאֲצַוֶּה עֲלֵיכֶם לֵאמֹר לֹא תִירְאוּ אֶת־אֱלֹהֵי הַגּוֹיִם
אֲשֶׁר אַתֶּם יֹשְׁבִים בְּאַרְצָם׃ וְלֹא שְׁמַרְתֶּם אֶת־מִצְוֺתַי אֲשֶׁר
צִוִּיתִי אֶתְכֶם וַתַּעַבְדוּ אֶת־אֱלֹהֵיהֶם וַתַּקְצִיפוּ אֹתִי עַד־מְאֹד׃
וְעַתָּה אִם בֶּאֱמֶת אַתֶּם שָׁבִים אֵלַי, הָסִירוּ מִבָּתֵּיכֶם אֶת־אֱלֹהֵי
הַזָּהָב וְאֶת־אֱלֹהֵי הַכֶּסֶף אֲשֶׁר עֲשִׂיתֶם לָכֶם וְשִׂרְפוּ אֹתָם בָּאֵשׁ׃
וַיַּעֲנוּ בְנֵי־יִשְׂרָאֵל וַיֹּאמְרוּ, כֹּל אֲשֶׁר צִוָּה אֹתָנוּ יהוה נַעֲשֶׂה
(4) וַיְהִי כַּעֲבֹר כָּל־הָעָם אֶת־הַיָּם וַיְצַו יהוה אֶת־מֹשֶׁה לֵאמֹר
נְטֵה אֶת־יָדְךָ עַל־הַיָּם וְשָׁבוּ הַמַּיִם לִמְקוֹמָם׃ וַיַּעַשׂ מֹשֶׁה כַּאֲשֶׁר
צִוָּהוּ יהוה וַיֵּט אֶת־יָדוֹ עַל־הַיָּם וַיָּשׁוּבוּ הַמַּיִם לִמְקוֹמָם׃ וַיִּרְאוּ
בְנֵי־יִשְׂרָאֵל אֶת־הַיְשׁוּעָה הַגְּדוֹלָה אֲשֶׁר עָשָׂה לָהֶם יהוה וַיְהַלְלוּ
אֶת־שְׁמוֹ׃ (5) וַיְהִי בַבֹּקֶר וַיִּקְרָא יַעֲקֹב אֶל־שְׁתֵּי נָשָׁיו וַיֹּאמֶר
אֲלֵיהֶן, יהוה אֱלֹהֵי אָבִי נִרְאָה אֵלַי בַּחֲלוֹם וַיְדַבֵּר אֵלַי לֵאמֹר
רָאֹה רָאִיתִי אֶת־כָּל־אֲשֶׁר עָשָׂה לְךָ לָבָן וָאֶשְׁמֹר עָלֶיךָ וְלֹא
נְתַתִּי[a] לוֹ לִנְגֹּעַ בְּךָ, וְעַתָּה קוּם שׁוּב אֶל־אַרְצְךָ וְאֶל־בֵּית־
אָבִיךָ, אַל־תִּירָא יַעֲקֹב, כִּי אָנֹכִי אֶהְיֶה אִתְּךָ וּבֵרַכְתִּיךָ׃
וַתַּעַן רָחֵל וַתֹּאמַר עֲשֵׂה כְּכֹל אֲשֶׁר צִוְּךָ אֱלֹהֶיךָ כִּי כְאָמָה
אָנֹכִי בְּבֵית אָבִינוּ׃ וַיַּעַשׂ יַעֲקֹב כֵּן, וַיִּקַּח אֶת־נָשָׁיו וְאֶת־בָּנָיו
וְאֶת־בְּנוֹתָיו וְאֶת־כָּל־רְכוּשׁוֹ וַיִּסַּע אַרְצָה כְנָעַן׃ וַיְהִי בְּשׁוּב
לָבָן הַבַּיְתָה וַיִּשְׁמַע כִּי בָרַח יַעֲקֹב וַיִּקְצֹף עַד־מְאֹד וַיִּקַּח אֶת־
אֲנָשָׁיו אִתּוֹ וַיִּרְדֹּף אַחֲרֵיהֶם וַיָּבֹא עֲלֵיהֶם בַּלָּיְלָה׃ וַיֵּרָא מַלְאַךְ־
אֱלֹהִים אֶל־לָבָן וַיֹּאמֶר אֵלָיו, אַל־תִּגַּע בְּעַבְדֵי יַעֲקֹב
פֶּן־תָּמוּת׃ וַיְהִי בַבֹּקֶר וַיִּירָא לָבָן עַד־מְאֹד וַיִּכְרֹת בְּרִית
עִם־יַעֲקֹב וַיָּקָם וַיָּשָׁב אֶל־בֵּיתוֹ

(1) And it came to pass after these things that the Lord commanded (waw consec.) Moses saying: 'Make thou for

[a] Here = 'to permit, allow'.

thyself two tablets of stone and come up unto me upon this mountain and I shall write upon them the judgements which thou shalt set before the children of Israel.' And Moses did as the Lord commanded him and he made for himself two tablets of stone and he went up on the mountain of Sinai and he was there many days. And Israel saw that Moses came not down from the mountain and they cried unto Aaron and they said: 'Where is thy brother Moses, for he hath gone up on the mountain of the Lord and hath not returned unto us. Make for us therefore a god'. And Aaron took their gold and he made for them a bull; and it came to pass when they saw the bull of gold that they cried, 'This is thy God, O Israel, who brought thee forth from the land of Egypt'. And the Lord spoke unto Moses, saying: 'Go thou down from the mountain, for thy people hath corrupted his way upon the earth and they have made for themselves a bull of gold and they cried before it, "This is thy God, O Israel".' And it came to pass as Moses heard the words of the Lord that he took the tablets and he broke them upon the ground. (2) And the sons of Jacob returned unto their father and they told (to) him all the words which Joseph their brother (had) commanded them. And Jacob answered and said: 'Blessed is the Lord who hath shown me this day, for my son Joseph liveth, and I shall go down to Egypt and I shall see him, face to face, before I die.' And the Lord appeared unto Jacob in a dream of the night and he said unto him: 'Go thou down to Egypt and thou shalt see thy son Joseph and thou shalt dwell there with him' (3) And it came to pass as the elders of Israel heard the words of Joshua which he spoke unto them that they answered (waw consec.) and they said: 'All that thou hast commanded us we will do; we will not depart from it. Only let the Lord thy God be with thee. As we hearkened unto Moses, so will we hearken unto thee.' (4) In that day the Lord gave a great salvation[a] to Israel and they pursued the inhabitants of the city unto the wilderness and they smote them and they took all the gold and the silver and their sheep and their cattle which was found in the city and they went up into the city and they dwelt in it. (5) And the prophet came before the king and

[a] 'Victory'.

he said unto him: 'Thus said the Lord, "Because thou hast transgressed My commandments and thou hast taken to thyself many wives from the daughters of the nations and thou hast not kept My word which I commanded thee and thou hast gone up upon the mountains to serve the gods of the nations and thou hast done these (things) to anger[a] Me, behold I will raise up against thee an enemy who shall smite thee and all thy house and all thy priests".'

81. DOUBLE 'AYIN VERBS

We now consider the type of weak verb which instead of having three root-letters, has its second root-letter (i.e. its 'Ayin) duplicated—the Double 'Ayin Verb:

QAL

Perf.:	ACTIVE		STATIVE		
he hath gone round		סַב , סָבַב	he was light		קַל [קָלַל]
she	,,	סַבָּה , סָבְבָה	she	,,	קַלָּה
thou (m.) hast	,,	סַבּוֹתָ	thou (m.) wast	,,	קַלּוֹתָ
thou (f.)	,,	סַבּוֹת	thou (f.)	,,	קַלּוֹת
I (c.) have	,,	סַבּוֹתִי	I (c.) was	,,	קַלּוֹתִי
they (c.)	,,	סַבּוּ , סָבְבוּ	they (c.) were	,,	קַלּוּ
ye (m.)	,,	סַבּוֹתֶם	ye (m.)	,,	קַלּוֹתֶם
ye (f.)	,,	סַבּוֹתֶן	ye (f.)	,,	קַלּוֹתֶן
we (c.)	,,	סַבּוֹנוּ	we (c.)	,,	קַלּוֹנוּ
Imperf.:					
he will go round		יִסֹּב , יָסֹב	he will be light		יֵקַל
she	,,	תִּסֹּב , תָּסֹב	she	,,	תֵּקַל
thou (m.) wilt	,,	תִּסֹּב , תָּסֹב	thou (m.) wilt	,,	תֵּקַל
thou (f.)	,,	תִּסְּבִי , תָּסֹבִּי	thou (f.)	,,	תֵּקַלִּי
I (c.) shall	,,	אֶסֹּב , אָסֹב	I (c.) shall	,,	אֵקַל
they (m.) will	,,	יִסְּבוּ , יָסֹבּוּ	they (m.) will	,,	יֵקַלּוּ
they (f.)	,,	תִּסֹּבְנָה , תְּסֻבֶּנָה	they (f.)	,,	תְּקַלֶּינָה
ye (m.)	,,	תִּסְּבוּ , תָּסֹבּוּ	ye (m.)	,,	תֵּקַלּוּ
ye (f.)	,,	תִּסֹּבְנָה , תְּסֻבֶּנָה	ye (f.)	,,	תְּקַלֶּינָה
we (c.) shall	,,	נִסֹּב , נָסֹב	we (c.) shall	,,	נֵקַל

[a] Hiphil of קצף or כעס.

Imperf. with Waw Consecutive:

and he turned round וַיָּ֫סָב (wayyásobh), וַיִּסֹּב — and he was light וַיֵּ֫קַל

Imper.: go thou (m.) round סֹב

„ (f.) „ סֹ֫בִּי

„ ye (m.) „ סֹ֫בּוּ

„ (f.) „ סֻבֶּ֫ינָה

Part. active:

going round (m. sg.) סֹבֵב &c. — being light (m. sg.) קַל &c.

passive:

surrounded (m. sg.) סָבוּב

Inf. absolute: סָבוֹב — קָלוֹל

construct: סֹב — קַל and קֹל

„ with לְ: לָסֹב

In the Perfect Qal the 3rd person has two forms: סָבַב, סָבְבוּ and סַב, סַ֫בּוּ—the former being transitive and the latter intransitive. These meanings of the two forms are well shown by the verb צָרַר = 'to make strait, oppress' with its intransitive form צַר = 'to be in a strait'.

The Imperfect Qal has two alternative forms. The one, יָסֹב, seems to have been influenced by the 'Ayin Waw verb (which resembles in many respects the Double 'Ayin verb). Like the 'Ayin Waw verb, it has the (original) *a* vowel under the prefix. The other type, יִסֹּב, strangely resembles the Pe Nun verb.

The Imperative follows the Imperfect of the first type.

NIPHAL

Perf.: he hath surrounded		נָסַב
she	,,	נָסַבָּה
thou (m.) hast	,,	נְסַבּוֹתָ
thou (f.)	,,	נְסַבּוֹת
I (c.) have	,,	נְסַבּוֹתִי
they (c.)	,,	נָסַבּוּ
ye (m.)	,,	נְסַבּוֹתֶם
ye (f.)	,,	נְסַבּוֹתֶן
we (c.)	,,	נְסַבּוֹנוּ

Imperf.: he will surround		יִסַּב
she	,,	תִּסַּב
thou (m.) wilt	,,	תִּסַּב
thou (f.)	,,	תִּסַּבִּי
I (c.) shall	,,	אֶסַּב
they (m.) will	,,	יִסַּבּוּ
they (f.)	,,	[תִּסַּבֶּינָה]
ye (m.)	,,	תִּסַּבּוּ
ye (f.)	,,	[תִּסַּבֶּינָה]
we (c.) shall	,,	נִסַּב

Part.: surrounding (m. sg.)		נָסָב
,,	(f. sg.)	נְסַבָּה
		&c.

Inf. absolute:	הִסּוֹב
construct:	הִסֵּב

Imper.: surround thou (m.)		הִסַּב
,,	(f.)	הִסַּבִּי
,, ye	(m.)	הִסַּבּוּ
,,	(f.)	הִסַּבֶּינָה

HIPHIL

Perf.:

he (hath) turned[a]		הֵסֵב (הֵסַב)
she	,,	הֵסַבָּה
thou (m.) hast	,,	הֲסִבּוֹתָ
thou (f.)	,,	הֲסִבּוֹת
I (c.) have	,,	הֲסִבּוֹתִי
they (c.)	,,	הֵסַבּוּ
ye (m.)	,,	הֲסִבּוֹתֶם
ye (f.)	,,	הֲסִבּוֹתֶן
we (c.)	,,	הֲסִבּוֹנוּ

Imperf.:

he will turn[b]		יָסֵב (יַסֵּב)
she	,,	תָּסֵב
thou (m.) wilt	,,	תָּסֵב
thou (f.)	,,	תָּסֵבִּי
I (c.) shall	,,	אָסֵב
they (m.) will	,,	יָסֵבּוּ (יַסֵּבּוּ)
they (f.)	,,	תְּסִבֶּינָה
ye (m.)	,,	תָּסֵבּוּ
ye (f.)	,,	תְּסִבֶּינָה
we (c.) shall	,,	נָסֵב

[a] Literally: he (hath) caused to go round.

[b] Literally: he will cause to go round.

Imper.: turn thou (m.)	הָסֵב	*Jussive*: let him turn	יָסֵב
,, (f.)	הָסֵ֫בִּי	*Imperf. with Waw Consecutive*:	
,, ye (m.)	הָסֵ֫בּוּ	and he turned	וַיָּ֫סֶב
,, (f.)	[הֲסִבֶּ֫ינָה]	*Part.*: turning (m. sg.)	מֵסֵב
		,, (f. sg.)	מְסִבָּה
Inf. absolute and construct:	הָסֵב		&c.

EXERCISE 40

to-morrow	מָחָר	festival	חַג
dawn	שַׁ֫חַר	,, (with art.)	הֶחָג
Passover	פֶּ֫סַח	,, (pl.)	חַגִּים
Jericho	יְרִיחוֹ	to bespoil, to take as spoil	בָּזַז
		to celebrate	חָגַג

(1) וַיְהִי בְּהִוָּדַע לְיֹשְׁבֵי־הָעִיר כִּי בָ֫אוּ אֲנָשִׁים אֶל בֵּית־לוֹט
וַיִּתְקַבְּצוּ לִפְנֵי בֵיתוֹ וַיְבַקְשׁוּ לְהוֹצִיא אֶת־הַמַּלְאָכִים מִשָּׁם:
וַיַּכּוּ אֹתָם הַמַּלְאָכִים וְלֹא יָֽכְלוּ לִרְאוֹת, וַיָּ֫סֹבּוּ אֶת־הַבַּ֫יִת,
וְאֶת־הַדֶּ֫לֶת לֹא מָצָֽאוּ: (2) וַיְדַבֵּר יהוה אֶל־מֹשֶׁה לֵּאמֹר בֹּא
אֶל־פַּרְעֹה וְאָמַרְתָּ֫ אֵלָיו: כֹּה אָמַר יהוה אֱלֹהֵי־יִשְׂרָאֵל, שַׁלַּח
אֶת־עַמִּי וְיָחֹ֫גּוּ לִי בַּמִּדְבָּר, וְאִם אֵינְךָ מְשַׁלֵּחַ אֹתָם הִנְנִי נֹגֵף
אֹתְךָ וְאֶת־עֲבָדֶ֫יךָ: וְכִי יִשְׁאַל אֹתְךָ פַּרְעֹה לֵאמֹר אַיֵּה הַצֹּאן
וְהַבָּקָר כִּי תָחֹ֫גּוּ לֵאלֹהֵיכֶם, וְאָמַרְתָּ֫ אֵלָיו, גַּם אַתָּה תִּתֵּן בְּיָדֵ֫נוּ,
וּמִמְּךָ נִקַּח לַעֲבֹד אֶת־יהוה אֱלֹהֵ֫ינוּ, כִּי חַג לָ֫נוּ עַל־הַר־
הָאֱלֹהִים בַּמִּדְבָּר (3) וַיְהִי בַבֹּ֫קֶר כַּעֲלוֹת הַשַּׁ֫חַר, וְכָל־הָעָם
עֹמְדִים לִפְנֵי הַר־סִינַי, וַיְצַו אֹתָם מֹשֶׁה לֵאמֹר סֹ֫בּוּ אֶת־הָהָר
פַּ֫עַם אַחַת, וְאַל־יַ֫עַל אִישׁ עַל־הָהָר, פֶּן־יִגֹּף בּוֹ יהוה וָמֵת
הָאִישׁ הַהוּא: וּבִרְאוֹתְכֶם אֶת־הָאֵשׁ בְּרֹאשׁ־הָהָר וּנְפַלְתֶּם עַל־
פְּנֵיכֶם אָֽרְצָה כִּי יֵרֵד יהוה עַל־הָהָר וְנִגְלָה אֲלֵיכֶם וְדִבֶּר
אֲלֵיכֶם מִתּוֹךְ־הָאֵשׁ: וַיִּשְׁמְעוּ בְנֵי־יִשְׂרָאֵל אֶת־דִּבְרֵי מֹשֶׁה
וַיִּֽירְאוּ עַד־מְאֹד (4) וַיַּקְהֵל יְהוֹשֻׁ֫עַ אֶת־בְּנֵי־יִשְׂרָאֵל וַיְדַבֵּר

אֲלֵיהֶם לֵאמֹר יהוה אֱלֹהֵינוּ הֶעֱבִירָנוּ אֶת־הַיַּרְדֵּן הַזֶּה לָתֵת
לָנוּ אֶת־הָאָרֶץ הַזֹּאת כַּאֲשֶׁר נִשְׁבַּע לַאֲבוֹתֵינוּ׃ וְהִנֵּה אֲנַחְנוּ
עֹמְדִים נֶגֶד הָעִיר יְרִיחוֹ אֲשֶׁר תִּנָּתֵן בְּיָדֵנוּ מָחָר׃ וְעַתָּה שִׁמְעוּ־
נָא אֵת אֲשֶׁר אָנֹכִי מְצַוֶּה אֶתְכֶם וְנִשְׁמַרְתֶּם מְאֹד לַעֲשׂוֹת כְּכֹל
אֲשֶׁר אָנֹכִי מְדַבֵּר אֲלֵיכֶם׃ וְהָיָה בַבֹּקֶר וְקַמְתֶּם וִירַדְתֶּם
הַיַּרְדֵּנָה וּרְחַצְתֶּם בְּמֵי־הַנָּהָר וַעֲלִיתֶם הָעִירָה וְסַבֹּתֶם אֶת־
חוֹמוֹתֶיהָ כָּל־הַיּוֹם עַד־הָעָרֶב׃ וְרָאוּ יֹשְׁבֵי־יְרִיחוֹ וְאָמְרוּ אִישׁ
אֶל־רֵעֵהוּ, הֵן רַבִּים בְּנֵי־יִשְׂרָאֵל כְּכוֹכְבֵי־הַשָּׁמַיִם וְכַעֲפַר־
הָאֲדָמָה, וּמִי יָכֹל לַעֲמֹד בִּפְנֵיהֶם׃ וְנָפְלָה עֲלֵיהֶם יִרְאַתְכֶם[a]
וְלֹא תִהְיֶה בָהֶם רוּחַ לַעֲמֹד בְּפָנֵינוּ, הֲלֹא שְׁמַעְתֶּם אֶת־דִּבְרֵי
הַמְרַגְּלִים אֲשֶׁר דִּבְּרוּ אֲלֵיכֶם בְּשׁוּבָם מִן־הָעִיר יְרִיחוֹ׃ וְהָיָה
אִם יֵצְאוּ לִקְרָאתֵנוּ בְּשָׁלוֹם, אַל־תִּשְׁפְּכוּ דָמִים כִּי[b] זָכוֹר תִּזְכְּרוּ
אֶת־מִצְוַת־מֹשֶׁה וַעֲשִׂיתֶם עִמָּהֶם חֶסֶד׃ וְאִם[c] לֹא יֵצְאוּ לִקְרָאתֵנוּ
בְּשָׁלוֹם וְקָרְאוּ עָלֵינוּ לַמִּלְחָמָה, וּקְרָאתֶם אַתֶּם בְּקוֹל גָּדוֹל
לַיהוה וְלִיהוֹשֻׁעַ, וַעֲלִיתֶם הָעִירָה וְהִכִּיתֶם אֹתָם לְפִי־חֶרֶב
מִגָּדוֹל וְעַד־קָטוֹן׃ וְהָיָה בְּתֵת יהוה אֶת־הָעִיר בְּיֶדְכֶם, אַל־
תִּקְחוּ לָכֶם מִן־הַזָּהָב וּמִן־הַכֶּסֶף אֲשֶׁר יִמָּצֵא בָהּ, כִּי[b] בְהֵיכַל־
יהוה תָּבִיאוּ אֹתָם, וְאֶת[c]־בְּקָרָם וְאֶת־צֹאנָם תָּבֹזּוּ לָכֶם׃ הִשָּׁמְרוּ
מְאֹד לַעֲשׂוֹת כְּכֹל אֲשֶׁר צִוִּיתִי אֶתְכֶם וְאַל־תָּסוּרוּ מִמֶּנּוּ, פֶּן־
תִּהְיֶה מַגֵּפָה בָעָם׃ וַיִּשְׁמְעוּ בְנֵי־יִשְׂרָאֵל אֶל־יְהוֹשֻׁעַ וַיַּעֲשׂוּ כְּכֹל
אֲשֶׁר צִוָּם, וַיָּסֹבּוּ אֶת־הָעִיר כָּל־הַיּוֹם מֵהַבֹּקֶר עַד־הָעָרֶב׃
וַיְהִי בָעֶרֶב וַיֵּצְאוּ יֹשְׁבֵי־יְרִיחוֹ לַמִּלְחָמָה וַיִּקְרְאוּ בְנֵי־יִשְׂרָאֵל
בְּקוֹל גָּדוֹל מְאֹד לַיהוה וְלִיהוֹשֻׁעַ וַיַּעֲלוּ הָעִירָה׃ וַתֶּחֱזַק עֲלֵיהֶם
יַד־יִשְׂרָאֵל וַיָּנוּסוּ אַנְשֵׁי־יְרִיחוֹ מִפְּנֵי־יִשְׂרָאֵל הַיַּרְדֵּנָה׃ וַיְצַו
יְהוֹשֻׁעַ וַיִּרְדְּפוּ בְנֵי־יִשְׂרָאֵל אַחֲרֵיהֶם וַיַּכּוּ אֹתָם לְפִי־חָרֶב׃
וַיָּשׁוּבוּ אֶל־יְרִיחוֹ וַיָּבֹזּוּ לָהֶם אֶת־הַצֹּאן וְאֶת־הַבָּקָר וּמִן[c]־הַכֶּסֶף

[a] 'Fear of you'—objective.

[b] 'But'.

[c] 'But'. The conjunction ו takes this meaning from the context.

וּמִן־הַזָּהָב אֲשֶׁר מָצְאוּ בָעִיר לֹא לָקְחוּ לָהֶם כִּי[a] בְהֵיכַל־יהוה
הֵבִ֫יאוּ, כַּאֲשֶׁר צִוָּה אֹתָם יְהוֹשֻׁעַ (5) וַיְהִי אַחֲרֵי־הַדְּבָרִים הָאֵ֫לֶּה
וַיְצַו יְהוֹשֻׁ֫עַ אֶת־הָעָם לֵאמֹר זִכְרוּ אֶת־יוֹם צֵאתְכֶם מֵאֶ֫רֶץ
מִצְרַ֫יִם וְחַגֹּתֶם אֶת־חַג־הַפֶּ֫סַח כַּאֲשֶׁר צִוָּה אֶתְכֶם מֹשֶׁה עֶ֫בֶד
יהוה: וַיַּעֲשׂוּ בְנֵי־יִשְׂרָאֵל אֶת־הַפֶּ֫סַח נֶ֫גֶד עִיר־יְרִיחוֹ

(1) And it came to pass after these things that the Lord sent a great darkness upon the land of Egypt and a man saw not his neighbour. And Pharaoh called unto Moses and unto Aaron and he said unto them: 'Arise ye and go ye forth from my land, ye and all Israel with you, and celebrate the festival to the Lord your God in the wilderness; both your cattle and your sheep take ye with you and pray to the Lord that he may remove (Imperfect Jussive with conjunction) from me this death.' And Moses answered and said: 'To-morrow the Lord will do this thing, in order that thou shalt know that there is none like Him.' (2) The dawn came up and the people sanctified themselves and they went round the mountain twice, as Moses commanded them, and they were exceedingly afraid and they said unto Moses: 'All that the Lord shall command us we will do'. (3) And there was found a man who had taken from the gold which (was) in the city of Jericho and the elders of Israel brought him before Joshua for (the) judgement. And Joshua said unto him: 'Why hast thou taken from the gold? Didst thou not hear my commandment which I commanded the people, saying, "Take ye for yourselves the cattle and the sheep, but (conjunction) from the gold and (from) the silver ye shall not take-as-spoil", and why hast thou transgressed my word?' And the man answered and said: 'I have indeed sinned to the Lord our God, and now, behold I am in thy hand, do to me as is good in thine eyes'. And Joshua commanded and they took that man and they brought him up upon the top of the mountain and they burned him in (the) fire, him and all that he had, before ('to the eyes of') the children of Israel. (4) And the king stood before the people and he prayed unto the Lord and he said:

[a] 'But'.

'Thou hast chosen us from all the nations and Thou hast commanded us to celebrate this festival of the Passover, as it is written in the Law of Moses Thy servant, in order that we may not forget the kindness which Thou hadst done with our fathers in the day they went forth ('their going-forth'—inf. const. with suff.) from the land of Egypt, from the house of slaves. And now, we have done according to all which Thou hast commanded us and we have celebrated the festival of the Passover this day. Remember, Lord, Thy people Israel and hear their prayer, for unto Thee alone are our eyes. Deliver us, Lord, from the hand of our enemies who have come to fight against us and have surrounded the walls of our city, in order that they may know that there is none like Thee and in Thee is our salvation.' And the prophet came and he stood before the king and he said: 'The Lord hath heard thy prayer which thou hast prayed unto Him with a broken heart. Fear not! for to-morrow thine enemies will hear that their king hath died and they will return unto their land.' And the king answered and said: 'Blessed is the Lord who hath not forsaken His kindness (from) with His servants.'

82. DEFECTIVE VERBS

A few of the weak verbs are *defective*, i.e. they are not complete but function only in part. It is found, however, that two kindred defective verbs, having two root-letters in common and differing only in the third root-letter, often supplement each other, so that together they make up one complete verb. The more frequently used defective verbs are:

A. 'To go, walk': the *Qal* Perfect is הָלַךְ &c., the Participle הֹלֵךְ &c., and the Infinitive absolute הָלוֹךְ: but the Imperfect, Imperative, and the Infinitive construct apparently come from the Pe Waw root יָלַךְ, thus:

Imperf.: he will go יֵלֵךְ she will go תֵּלֵךְ I shall go אֵלֵךְ &c.

Cohort.: I *will* go, let me go אֵלְכָה

Imperf. with Waw Consecutive: and he went וַיֵּלֶךְ

Imper.: go thou (m.) לֵךְ, לְכָה go thou (f.) לְכִי &c.

Inf. construct: לֶכֶת with ל: לָלֶכֶת with suffix: לֶכְתִּי

The *Hiphil*, too, apparently comes from the Pe Waw root יָלַךְ, thus:

Perf.: he (hath) caused to go	הוֹלִיךְ	she (hath) caused to go	הוֹלִיכָה
Imperf.: he will cause to go	יוֹלִיךְ	she will cause to go	תּוֹלִיךְ
Jussive: let him cause to go	יוֹלֵךְ	*Imperf. and Waw Consec.*: and he caused to go	וַיּוֹלֶךְ

B. 'To be good': the *Qal* Perfect, Participle, and Infinitive come from the 'Ayin Waw root טוֹב; but the Imperfect is from the Pe Yod root יָטַב i.e. יִיטַב, 'he will be good'. The *Hiphil* also comes from the Pe Yod יָטַב, i.e. הֵיטִיב 'he hath done good' (Perf.); יֵיטִיב 'he will do good' (Impf.).

C. 'To drink': all parts of the *Qal* come from the root שָׁתָה, but the *Hiphil* comes from the root שָׁקָה, thus: 'he (hath) caused to drink' הִשְׁקָה (Perfect): 'he will cause to drink' יַשְׁקֶה (Imperfect); 'let him cause to drink' יַשְׁקְ (Jussive); 'and he caused to drink' וַיַּשְׁקְ (Imperfect with Waw Consecutive).

D. 'To be able', 'to prevail'. Perfect יָכֹל (as קָטֹן on pp. 95 ff.), but the Imperfect is יוּכַל &c. Some regard this form as a Hophal, meaning 'to be enabled' and therefore think that this verb comes under the category of Defectives. It is likely, however, that the Imperfect יוּכַל is an arrested form from an original יַוְכַל, yawkal, yaukal, and then yûkal for the expected yôkal (יוֹכַל).

The Infinitive absolute is יָכוֹל, and the Infinitive construct יְכֹלֶת has a feminine termination.

EXERCISE 41

feast	מִשְׁתֶּה
,, (const.)	מִשְׁתֵּה
camel	גָּמָל
,, (pl.)	גְּמַלִּים
master, lord, husband	בַּעַל
Eliezer	אֱלִיעֶזֶר
pitcher	כַּד
spring, well	עַיִן
wine	יַיִן
beautiful (m.)	יָפֶה
,, (f.)	יָפָה
or	אוֹ

(1) וַיַּ֫עַן אֱלִיעֶ֫זֶר וַיֹּאמַר הִנֵּה אָנֹכִי עֹמֵד[a] עַל[b]־עֵין־הַמַּ֫יִם לְעֵת־
עֶ֫רֶב וָאֶשָּׂא אֶת־עֵינַי וָאֶרְאֶה אֶת־הַיַּלְדָּה יֹצֵאת לְהַשְׁקוֹת אֶת־
הַצֹּאן וְכַדָּהּ עַל־רֹאשָׁהּ׃ וַתִּמְצָא חֵן בְּעֵינַי מְאֹד וָאֶגַּשׁ אֵלֶ֫יהָ
וָאֹמַר הַשְׁקִ֫ינִי נָא מָ֫יִם׃ וַתּ֫וֹרֶד אֶת־כַּדָּהּ מֵעַל רֹאשָׁהּ וַתֹּ֫אמֶר
אֵלַי שְׁתֵה אֲדוֹנִי, וְגַם אֶת־גְּמַלֶּ֫יךָ אַשְׁקֶה׃ וַתַּ֫עַשׂ כַּאֲשֶׁר אָמְרָה
וַתִּתֵּן לִי לִשְׁתּוֹת וְגַם אֶת־גְּמַלַּי הִשְׁקָ֫תָה[c] וַתַּגֵּד לִי אֶת־שְׁמָהּ
וְאֶת־שֵׁם־אָבִיהָ׃ וַיְהִי כְּשָׁמְעִי אֶת־שְׁמָהּ וָאֶפֹּל עַל־פָּנַי וָאֲהַלֵּל
אֶת־שֵׁם־יהוה אֲשֶׁר לֹא עָזַב אֶת־חַסְדּוֹ מֵעִם אֲדוֹנִי אַבְרָהָם
וַיּוֹלִיכֵ֫נִי אֶל־הַמָּקוֹם הַזֶּה׃ וְעַתָּה אִם טוֹב בְּעֵינֵיכֶם תֵּ֫לֶךְ[d] הַיַּלְדָּה
אַחֲרַי וּתְהִי[d] אִשָּׁה לְבֶן־אֲדוֹנִי לְיִצְחָק, וְאִם לֹא, הַגִּ֫ידוּ לִי
וְאָס֫וּרָה מֵעֲלֵיכֶם׃ וַיַּ֫עֲנוּ אֲבִי־הַיַּלְדָּה וְאָחִ֫יהָ וַיֹּאמְרוּ לֹא נוּכַל
דַּבֵּר אֵלֶ֫יךָ טוֹב אוֹ רָע נִקְרָאָה לַיַּלְדָּה וְנִשְׁאֲלָה אֶת־פִּ֫יהָ[e]׃
וַיִּקְרְאוּ לָהּ וַיַּגִּ֫ידוּ לָהּ אֶת־דִּבְרֵי אֱלִיעֶ֫זֶר וַיִּשְׁאֲלוּ אֹתָהּ לֵאמֹר
הֲתֵלְכִי אַחֲרֵי הָאִישׁ הַזֶּה לִהְיוֹת לְיִצְחָק לְאִשָּׁה, וַתֹּ֫אמֶר אֵלֵךְ׃
וַיְהִי בַבֹּ֫קֶר וַיֹּ֫אמֶר אֱלִיעֶ֫זֶר שַׁלְּחֻ֫נִי נָא לְבֵית־אֲדוֹנִי, וַיֹּאמְרוּ
אֵלָיו כַּטּוֹב בְּעֵינֶ֫יךָ עֲשֵׂה׃ וַיָּ֫קָם אֱלִיעֶ֫זֶר וַיָּ֫שֶׂם אֶת־הַיַּלְדָּה
עַל־הַגָּמָל וַיֵּצְאוּ לָלֶ֫כֶת אַ֫רְצָה כְּנָ֫עַן׃ (2) וַיְהִי אַחֲרֵי יָמִים
רַבִּים וַיַּ֫עַשׂ הַמֶּ֫לֶךְ מִשְׁתֶּה גָדוֹל לְכָל־עֲבָדָיו אֲשֶׁר בְּאַרְצוֹת־
מַמְלַכְתּוֹ׃ וַיָּ֫בֹאוּ כָּל־עֲבָדָיו אֶל מִשְׁתֵּה־הַמֶּ֫לֶךְ וַיֹּאכְלוּ וַיִּשְׁתּוּ
אִתּוֹ כָּל־הַלַּ֫יְלָה עַד־עֲלוֹת הַשָּׁ֫חַר׃ וַיְהִי כְּטוֹב לֵב־הַמֶּ֫לֶךְ[f] בַּיַּ֫יִן
וַיְצַו אֶת־שֹׁמֵר־הַנָּשִׁים לְהָבִיא אֶת־הַמַּלְכָּה לְפָנָיו לְהַרְאוֹתָהּ
לַעֲבָדָיו כִּי יָפָה הִיא[a] עַד־מְאֹד׃ וַיֵּ֫לֶךְ שֹׁמֵר־הַנָּשִׁים וַיַּגֵּד
לַמַּלְכָּה אֶת־מִצְוַת־הַמֶּ֫לֶךְ, וַתֹּ֫אמֶר אֵלָיו לֹא אֵלֵךְ׃ וַיְהִי כִּשְׁמֹ֫עַ
הַמֶּ֫לֶךְ אֶת־דִּבְרֵי־הַמַּלְכָּה וַיִּקְצֹף עַד־מְאֹד, וַיִּקְרָא לַחֲכָמָיו
וַיִּשְׁאַל אֹתָם מַה־לַּעֲשׂוֹת לַמַּלְכָּה, כִּי לֹא עָשְׂתָה כְּמִצְוַת־הַמֶּ֫לֶךְ
וְלֹא בָ֫אָה לְפָנָיו׃ וַיַּ֫עַן אֶחָד מֵחֲכָמָיו וַיֹּאמַר לֹא לַמֶּ֫לֶךְ לְבַדּוֹ

[a] Understand 'was'. [b] 'By'. [c] Pausal. [d] Jussive.
[e] 'Her mouth', for 'her word' or 'her opinion'.
[f] Meaning that he was merry.

חָטְאָה הַמַּלְכָּה כִּי לְכָל־עֲבָדָיו׃ כִּי עַתָּה תֹּאמַרְנָה נְשֵׁי־עֲבָדֶיךָ
אֶל־בַּעֲלֵיהֶן, הִנֵּה הַמַּלְכָּה לֹא עָשְׂתָה כְּמִצְוַת־הַמֶּלֶךְ וְלָמָּה
נִשְׁמַע אֲנַחְנוּ בְּקוֹלְכֶם׃ וְעַתָּה אִם טוֹב בְּעֵינֵי־הַמֶּלֶךְ יְשַׁלַּח
אֶת־הַמַּלְכָּה וְלֹא תָבֹא עוֹד לְפָנָיו, וּבָחַר הַמֶּלֶךְ בְּאִשָּׁה אַחֶרֶת
אֲשֶׁר תִּמְלֹךְ תַּחַת הַמַּלְכָּה׃ וְשָׁמְעוּ נְשֵׁי־עֲבָדֶיךָ וְיָרְאוּ וְנָתְנוּ
כָּבוֹד לְבַעֲלֵיהֶן׃ וַיִּיטַב הַדָּבָר בְּעֵינֵי־הַמֶּלֶךְ וַיְצַו לַעֲשׂוֹת כֵּן׃
(3) וַיְהִי אַחַר הַדְּבָרִים הָאֵלֶּה וַיִּקְרָא יִצְחָק אֶל־יַעֲקֹב בְּנוֹ
וַיֹּאמֶר אֵלָיו הִנֵּה עֵשָׂו אָחִיךָ מְבַקֵּשׁ אֶת נַפְשֶׁךָ כִּי לָקַחְתָּ אֶת־
בִּרְכוֹתָיו מִמֶּנּוּ׃ וְעַתָּה שְׁמַע בְּקוֹלִי כְּכֹל אֲשֶׁר אֲצַוֶּךָּ וְקוּם
בְּרַח־לְךָ אֶל־לָבָן אֲחִי־אִמְּךָ וְיָשַׁבְתָּ שָׁם׃ וַיְבָרְכֵהוּ יִצְחָק
וַיֹּאמַר יְהִי יהוה אֱלֹהֵי־אָבִי אִתְּךָ וְהֵשִׁיבְךָ אֵלַי בְּשָׁלוֹם׃ וַיַּעַשׂ
יַעֲקֹב כַּאֲשֶׁר צִוָּה אֹתוֹ אָבִיו וַיָּקָם וַיֵּלֶךְ אֶל־לָבָן אֲחִי־אִמּוֹ
וַיֵּשֶׁב אִתּוֹ׃ (4) וַיִּשְׁמַע יִתְרוֹ[a] אֶת־כָּל־אֲשֶׁר עָשָׂה יהוה לְיִשְׂרָאֵל
כִּי הוֹצִיא אֹתָם מֵאֶרֶץ מִצְרָיִם׃ וַיִּקַּח אֶת־אֵשֶׁת מֹשֶׁה וְאֶת־
שְׁנֵי־בָנֶיהָ וַיָּקָם וַיֵּלֶךְ אִתָּם אֶל־מַחֲנֵה־יִשְׂרָאֵל נֶגֶד הַר־הָאֱלֹהִים׃
וַיֵּצֵא מֹשֶׁה לִקְרָאתָם הוּא וְזִקְנֵי־הָעָם אִתּוֹ וַיָּבֵא אֹתָם אֶל־
הַמַּחֲנֶה׃ וַיֹּאמֶר יִתְרוֹ בָּרוּךְ יהוה אֲשֶׁר הִצִּיל אֶתְכֶם מִיַּד־
מִצְרַיִם וּמִיַּד־פַּרְעֹה, עַתָּה יָדַעְתִּי כִּי גָדוֹל יהוה מִכָּל־אֱלֹהִים
וְאֵין כָּמוֹהוּ׃ וַיְהִי בַבֹּקֶר וַיֵּשֶׁב מֹשֶׁה לִשְׁפֹּט אֶת־הָעָם, וְכָל־
הָעָם עֹמְדִים לְפָנָיו מִן־הַבֹּקֶר וְעַד־הָעָרֶב׃ וַיֹּאמֶר יִתְרוֹ אֶל־
מֹשֶׁה, לֹא טוֹב הַדָּבָר אֲשֶׁר אַתָּה עֹשֶׂה, לֹא תוּכַל לִשְׁפֹּט
אֶת־כָּל־הָעָם לְבַדֶּךָ׃ וְעַתָּה שְׁמַע בְּקוֹלִי כְּכֹל אֲשֶׁר אֹמַר
אֵלֶיךָ וּבְחַר לְךָ מֵרָאשֵׁי־הָעָם אַנְשֵׁי־אֱמֶת יִרְאֵי[b]־אֱלֹהִים וְשָׁפְטוּ
הֵמָּה אֶת־הָעָם, וְכָל־דָּבָר גָּדוֹל יָבִיאוּ אֵלֶיךָ׃ וַתִּיטַב עֲצַת־
יִתְרוֹ בְּעֵינֵי־מֹשֶׁה וַיִּשְׁמַע בְּקוֹלוֹ וַיַּעַשׂ כְּכֹל אֲשֶׁר אָמַר

[a] 'Jethro', Moses' father-in-law.

[b] M. pl. const. of יָרֵא.

(1) And it came to pass after these things that the Lord remembered Sarah and she bare a son and she called his name Isaac. And Sarah saw the handmaid and her son and she was exceedingly afraid, and she said unto Abraham her husband, 'Send them away to the wilderness, for the son of this handmaid shall not inherit with my son, with Isaac'. And Abraham did as Sarah said and he took bread and a pitcher of water and he gave (them) to the handmaid and he sent her away with her son. And it came to pass in the evening that there was no(t) water in the pitcher and she placed the child under a tree and she went and she sat opposite and she lifted up her voice and she cried unto the Lord. And an angel of God called unto her and he said, 'Fear not, for the Lord hath heard thy voice'. And she opened her eyes and she saw and behold a spring of water (was) before her, and she took from the water and she gave the child to drink. And the Lord was with the lad and he grew [√גָּדַל] and became a man, and his mother took a wife for him from the land of Egypt. (2) And it came to pass after these things that the king made a great feast and he commanded to bring the gold and the silver which he had taken from the house of the Lord to show his servants. And it came to pass, while (use conjunction) they (were) eating flesh and drinking wine, that they saw and behold a hand (was) writing upon the wall of the palace, and they were exceedingly afraid. And the king called all his wise (men) and he said unto them: 'Tell (to) me the words which are written upon the wall, and if ye are not able (imperf.) to tell (to) me, death will be your judgement'. And the wise men answered and said: 'Behold there is among the servants of the king a prophet from the Hebrews whom the king hath brought to exile.[a] And now if it is good in the eyes of the king, let us call him, and he will read the words which are written upon the wall'; and the king commanded to do so. And they went and they brought the prophet before the king and he read the words which (were) written upon the wall and he said unto the king: 'Because thou hast lifted up thy heart and thou wast not afraid to sin against the Lord God of Israel, behold He hath removed thee from being king[b] over this people and He hath

[a] Hiphil of גָּלָה. See p. 219. [b] The verb מָלַךְ—'to reign', 'to be king'.

given thy throne to another'. And the prophet went forth from (before) the king. (3) And it came to pass after the death of the judge that the children of Israel did that which was evil in the eyes of the Lord and he delivered them [√מָכַר] into the hands of the king of Canaan and they served him many days and they cried unto the Lord from their afflictions and He heard their voice. And there (there was) a woman a prophetess who judged Israel in that time; and she sent and she called Barak [בָּרָק] and she said unto him: 'Hear thou the word of the Lord which he hath spoken concerning [עַל] thee. Go and gather together all the mighty men of Israel upon the top of this mountain and thou shalt fight against [בְּ] the enemies of Israel, for the Lord hath given them into thy hand.' And Barak answered and said: 'If thou wilt go with me then (waw consecutive) I will go, but [וְ] if thou wilt not go with me I will not go.' And the prophetess said unto him: 'I will indeed go with thee', and she arose and she went with him. And all the mighty men of Israel gathered together upon the mountain and they came down from the mountain and they fought with their enemies and the Lord gave them salvation[a] in that day and they smote all the camp of Canaan and they pursued them to the wilderness. And the king of Canaan saw that his warriors had fallen and he took his sword in his hand and he arose and he fled (he) alone (from) before the children of Israel.

83. THE NUMERALS

1. The Cardinal Numbers are:

	With the Masculine		*With the Feminine*	
	Absolute	*Construct*	*Absolute*	*Construct*
1	אֶחָד	אַחַד	אַחַת	אַחַת
2	שְׁנַיִם	שְׁנֵי	שְׁתַּיִם	שְׁתֵּי
3	שְׁלֹשָׁה	שְׁלֹשֶׁת	שָׁלֹשׁ	שְׁלֹשׁ
4	אַרְבָּעָה	אַרְבַּעַת	אַרְבַּע	אַרְבַּע
5	חֲמִשָּׁה	חֲמֵשֶׁת	חָמֵשׁ	חֲמֵשׁ
6	שִׁשָּׁה	שֵׁשֶׁת	שֵׁשׁ	שֵׁשׁ

[a] 'Victory'.

7	שִׁבְעָה	שִׁבְעַת	שֶׁ֫בַע	שְׁבַע
8	שְׁמֹנָה	שְׁמֹנַת	שְׁמֹנֶה	שְׁמֹנֶה
9	תִּשְׁעָה	תִּשְׁעַת	תֵּ֫שַׁע	תְּשַׁע
10	עֲשָׂרָה	עֲשֶׂ֫רֶת	עֶ֫שֶׂר	עֶ֫שֶׂר
11	אַחַד עָשָׂר		אַחַת עֶשְׂרֵה	
	עַשְׁתֵּי עָשָׂר		עַשְׁתֵּי עֶשְׂרֵה	
12	שְׁנֵים עָשָׂר		שְׁתֵּים עֶשְׂרֵה	
	שְׁנֵי עָשָׂר		שְׁתֵּי עֶשְׂרֵה	
13	שְׁלֹשָׁה עָשָׂר		שְׁלֹשׁ עֶשְׂרֵה	
14	אַרְבָּעָה עָשָׂר		אַרְבַּע עֶשְׂרֵה	
	&c.		&c.	

20	עֶשְׂרִים	60	שִׁשִּׁים
30	שְׁלֹשִׁים	70	שִׁבְעִים
40	אַרְבָּעִים	80	שְׁמֹנִים
50	חֲמִשִּׁים	90	תִּשְׁעִים

100 מֵאָה fem.; constr. מְאַת; pl. מֵאוֹת ('hundreds')

200 מָאתַ֫יִם (dual, reduced from מְאָתַיִם)

300 שְׁלֹשׁ מֵאוֹת 400 אַרְבַּע מֵאוֹת 500 חֲמֵשׁ מֵאוֹת &c.

1,000 אֶ֫לֶף 2,000 אַלְפַּ֫יִם (dual)

3,000 שְׁלֹ֫שֶׁת אֲלָפִים 4,000 אַרְבַּ֫עַת אֲלָפִים

10,000 רְבָבָה 20,000 רִבּוֹתַ֫יִם (dual)

(*a*) The numeral 'one' is considered an adjective; it follows its noun and agrees with it in gender: 'one man' אִישׁ אֶחָד; 'one woman' אִשָּׁה אַחַת. It may be used in the construct state, thus: 'one of the prophets' אַחַד הַנְּבִיאִים.

(*b*) The numeral 'two' is a noun which, as a construct, precedes the word numbered, שְׁנֵי־בָנִים ('a pair-of sons') or, as an absolute, stands *after* it in apposition, בָּנִים שְׁנַ֫יִם ('sons, a pair').

The feminine of שְׁנַיִם is curiously שְׁתַּיִם; both are dual forms. The numerals 3 to 10 are feminine nouns which, as constructs, precede the word numbered, שְׁלֹשֶׁת בָּנִים ('a triad-of sons'), but the appositional construction came to be extended by using the numeral in the absolute not only *after* the word numbered, בָּנִים שְׁלֹשָׁה ('sons, a triad') but even *before* it, שְׁלֹשָׁה בָּנִים ('a triad, sons'). These numerals (3 to 10) though feminines, remained in use with masculine nouns and a special shortened form came to be used with feminine nouns by way of differentiation (שָׁלֹשׁ &c.).

(*c*) The numerals 11 to 19 are formed by placing the unit before the ten (the latter being עָשָׂר for the masculine and עֶשְׂרֵה for the feminine). The plural noun is generally used with the numerals 11 to 19, with the exception of a few which follow them in the singular. These nouns are אִישׁ ('man'), יוֹם ('day'), שָׁנָה ('year'), נֶפֶשׁ ('soul, person'), and a few more; e.g. '11 days' אַחַד עָשָׂר יוֹם; '11 men' אַחַד עָשָׂר אִישׁ; '11 years' אַחַת עֶשְׂרֵה שָׁנָה.[a]

(*d*) With the exception of the numeral 20 עֶשְׂרִים (which is derived from עֶשֶׂר) the tens are denoted by the plural forms of the units, thus: שְׁלֹשִׁים 30; אַרְבָּעִים 40; חֲמִשִּׁים 50; שִׁשִּׁים 60; &c.

(*e*) The tens and the units are connected by the conjunction; 77 is שִׁבְעִים וְשִׁבְעָה (i.e. 70 and 7), &c.

(*f*) Some numerals can take suffixes; e.g. שְׁנֵינוּ 'we two'; שְׁנֵיהֶם 'they two'; שְׁנֵיכֶם 'you two'; שְׁלָשְׁתֵּנוּ 'we three'; &c.

2. The Ordinals are:

	Masculine	*Feminine*
first	רִאשׁוֹן[b]	רִאשׁוֹנָה[b]
second	שֵׁנִי[c]	שֵׁנִית[c]
third	שְׁלִישִׁי	שְׁלִישִׁית

[a] As in English we say '11 thousand' (not 11 thousands).

[b] From רֹאשׁ 'a head'.

[c] From 2 to 10 the Ordinals are from the same roots as the Cardinals—the masculines ending in ִי and the feminines in ִית.

fourth	רְבִיעִי	רְבִיעִית
fifth	חֲמִישִׁי	חֲמִישִׁית
sixth	שִׁשִּׁי	שִׁשִּׁית
seventh	שְׁבִיעִי	שְׁבִיעִית
eighth	שְׁמִינִי	שְׁמִינִית
ninth	תְּשִׁיעִי	תְּשִׁיעִית
tenth	עֲשִׂירִי	עֲשִׂירִית

The Ordinal numbers from 1 to 10 are adjectives, following the noun and agreeing with it in gender. From 11 upwards the Cardinal numbers serve as Ordinals. 'On the second day' בַּיּוֹם הַשֵּׁנִי; 'in the second year' בַּשָּׁנָה הַשֵּׁנִית; 'on the fifteenth day' בַּחֲמִשָּׁה עָשָׂר יוֹם; &c.

EXERCISE 42

month	חֹדֶשׁ	to lift up, to forgive	נָשָׂא
work	מְלָאכָה	to approach, draw near	קָרַב
,, (cons.)	מְלֶאכֶת	to rebel	מָרַד
,, (with suffix)	מְלַאכְתִּי [a]	perhaps	אוּלַי
year	שָׁנָה	because of, on account of	בַּעֲבוּר
,, (pl.)	שָׁנִים	for the sake of, in order that	לְמַעַן

בֶּן־ / בַּת with שָׁנִים '... years old' in Hebrew is 'a son or daughter of ... years'.

(1) וַיֹּאמֶר יהוה אֶל־אַבְרָהָם רָאֹה רָאִיתִי אֶת־כָּל־אֲשֶׁר עָשׂוּ
אַנְשֵׁי סְדֹם וְהִנְנִי מַשְׁחִיתָם מֵעַל פְּנֵי־הָאֲדָמָה כִּי אֲנָשִׁים רִשְׁעֵי־
לֵב הֵמָּה: וַיִּתְפַּלֵּל אַבְרָהָם וַיֹּאמַר הֲגַם תָּמִית צַדִּיק עִם רָשָׁע,
אוּלַי יֵשׁ חֲמִשִּׁים צַדִּיקִים בְּתוֹךְ־הָעִיר, הֲלֹא תִשָּׂא[b] לַמָּקוֹם
לְמַעַן חֲמִשִּׁים הַצַּדִּיקִים אֲשֶׁר בָּהּ, הֲשֹׁפֵט כָּל־הָאָרֶץ לֹא
יַעֲשֶׂה מִשְׁפָּט: וַיֹּאמֶר יהוה אִם אֶמְצָא בִסְדֹם חֲמִשִּׁים צַדִּיקִים

[a] The construct is a Segholate noun, and it is to this form that suffixes are attached.

[b] Extended meaning 'to forgive'.

וְנָשָׂאתִי לְכָל־הַמָּקוֹם בַּעֲבוּרָם׃ וַיַּעַן אַבְרָהָם וַיֹּאמַר אוּלַי
יִמָּצְאוּ שָׁם אַרְבָּעִים וַיֹּאמֶר יהוה לֹא אַשְׁחִית בַּעֲבוּר הָאַרְבָּעִים׃
וַיְדַבֵּר אַבְרָהָם עוֹד וַיֹּאמַר אַל־נָא יִקְצֹף יהוה וַאֲדַבְּרָה, אוּלַי
יִמָּצְאוּ שָׁם שְׁלֹשִׁים׃ וַיֹּאמֶר יהוה לֹא אֶעֱשֶׂה אִם יִהְיוּ שָׁם רַק
עֲשָׂרָה צַדִּיקִים וְנָשָׂאתִי לְכָל־הָעִיר בַּעֲבוּרָם (2) וַיִּסְעוּ[a] בְּנֵי־
יִשְׂרָאֵל וַיָּבֹאוּ אֶל־מִדְבַּר־סִינַי בַּחֲמִשָּׁה עָשָׂר יוֹם לַחֹדֶשׁ הַשֵּׁנִי
לְצֵאתָם מֵאֶרֶץ מִצְרָיִם׃ וַיְדַבֵּר מֹשֶׁה אֶל־הָעָם לֵאמֹר זְכוֹר
אֶת־יוֹם הַשַּׁבָּת לְקַדְּשׁוֹ׃ שֵׁשֶׁת יָמִים תַּעֲבֹד וְעָשִׂיתָ אֶת־כָּל־
מְלַאכְתֶּךָ וְהַיּוֹם הַשְּׁבִיעִי שַׁבָּת לַיהוה אֱלֹהֶיךָ׃ לֹא תַעֲשֶׂה כָּל[b]־
מְלָאכָה, אַתָּה וּבִנְךָ וּבִתֶּךָ וְעַבְדְּךָ וַאֲמָתְךָ׃ (3) וַיְדַבֵּר יהוה
אֶל־יְהוֹשֻׁעַ לֵאמֹר קַח לְךָ מִן־הָעָם שְׁנֵים־עָשָׂר אִישׁ וְצַוֵּה
אֹתָם לֵאמֹר׃ שְׂאוּ לָכֶם שְׁתֵּים־עֶשְׂרֵה אֲבָנִים וְהַעֲבַרְתֶּם אֹתָם
עִמָּכֶם, וְהָיָה בְּהִכָּרֵת מֵי־הַיַּרְדֵּן לְפָנֵינוּ וְעָבַר כָּל־הָעָם
וְשַׂמְתֶּם אֶת־הָאֲבָנִים בְּתוֹךְ־הַיַּרְדֵּן׃ וְהָיוּ הָאֲבָנִים הָאֵלֶּה לִבְנֵי־
יִשְׂרָאֵל לְאוֹת־עוֹלָם, וְיָדְעוּ בְנֵיכֶם וּבְנֵי־בְנֵיכֶם כִּי בַּמָּקוֹם
הַזֶּה נִכְרְתוּ מֵי־הַיַּרְדֵּן לְפָנֵינוּ בְּעָבְרֵנוּ אַרְצָה כְּנָעַן (4) וַיִּקְרְבוּ
יְמֵי־דָוִד לָמוּת וַיִּקְרָא אֶת־שְׁלֹמֹה בְנוֹ וַיְצַו אֹתוֹ לֵאמֹר אָנֹכִי
הֹלֵךְ בְּדֶרֶךְ כָּל־הָאָרֶץ וְחָזַקְתָּ וְהָיִיתָ לְאִישׁ׃ וַיִּשְׁכַּב דָּוִד
עִם־אֲבֹתָיו[c] וַיִּקָּבֵר בְּעִיר־דָּוִד׃ וְהַיָּמִים אֲשֶׁר מָלַךְ דָּוִד עַל־
יִשְׂרָאֵל אַרְבָּעִים שָׁנָה בְּחֶבְרוֹן[d] מָלַךְ שֶׁבַע שָׁנִים וּבִירוּשָׁלַיִם
מָלַךְ שָׁלֹשׁ שָׁנִים וּשְׁלֹשִׁים[e] שָׁנָה׃ (5) וַיְהִי אַחֲרֵי הַדְּבָרִים הָאֵלֶּה
וַיָּמָת מֶלֶךְ יְהוּדָה וַיִּמְלֹךְ חִזְקִיָּה[f] בְנוֹ תַּחְתָּיו׃ בֶּן־עֶשְׂרִים וְחָמֵשׁ
שָׁנָה הָיָה בְמָלְכוֹ, וְעֶשְׂרִים וָתֵשַׁע שָׁנָה מָלַךְ בִּירוּשָׁלָיִם׃ וַיַּעַשׂ
אֶת־הַטּוֹב בְּעֵינֵי־יהוה וַיֵּלֶךְ בִּדְרָכָיו וַיִּשְׁמֹר אֶת־מִצְוֹתָיו בְּלֵב

[a] For וַיִּסְעוּ from √נָסַע. Dagheš Forte is often omitted when the letter has shewa. Cf. p. 150, first note.

[b] Any.

[c] 'He slept with his fathers' means 'he died'.

[d] 'Hebron'.

[e] This order is often used in the Bible.

[f] 'Hezekiah'.

שָׁלֵם, וַיְהִי יהוה אִתּוֹ בְּכֹל אֲשֶׁר עָשָׂה: וַיְהִי בְּאַרְבַּע עֶשְׂרֵה
שָׁנָה לְמָלְכוֹ וַיִּמְרֹד חִזְקִיָּה בְּמֶלֶךְ אַשּׁוּר[a]: וַיַּעַל מֶלֶךְ אַשּׁוּר
עַל־כָּל־עָרֵי יְהוּדָה וַיִּלְכְּדֵם וַיָּבֹא יְרוּשָׁלַיְמָה וְאִתּוֹ מֵאָה
וּשְׁמֹנִים אֶלֶף אִישׁ מַחֲנֶה גָּדוֹל מְאֹד: וַיִּשְׁלַח מַלְאָכִים לְפָנָיו
אֶל־חִזְקִיָּה וַיָּבֹאוּ וַיַּעַמְדוּ עַל־הָהָר נֶגֶד הָעִיר וַיִּקְרְאוּ בְקוֹל
גָּדוֹל: כֹּה אָמַר הַמֶּלֶךְ הַגָּדוֹל מֶלֶךְ אַשּׁוּר עַל־מִי בָטַחְתָּ כִּי
מָרַדְתָּ בִּי: וְכִי תֹאמַר בַּיהוה אֱלֹהֵינוּ בָּטָחְנוּ לֹא יוּכַל לְהַצִּיל
אֶתְכֶם מִיָּדִי: אַיֵּה אֱלֹהֵי[b] כָל־הַגּוֹיִם הָעֹבְדִים אֹתִי, וּמִי בְּכָל־
אֱלֹהֵי[b]־הָאֲרָצוֹת אֲשֶׁר הִצִּילוּ אֶת־אַרְצָם מִיָּדִי כִּי יַצִּיל יהוה
אֶת־יְרוּשָׁלַיִם מִיָּדִי: וַיְהִי כִּשְׁמֹעַ חִזְקִיָּה אֶת־דִּבְרֵי מֶלֶךְ אַשּׁוּר
וַיִּקְרַע אֶת־בְּגָדָיו וַיֵּשֶׁב בֶּעָפָר וְלֹא אָכַל לֶחֶם כָּל־הַיּוֹם:
וַיִּשְׁלַח אֶל־הַנָּבִיא לֵאמֹר הִתְפַּלֵּל לָנוּ אֶל־יהוה אֱלֹהֵינוּ, אוּלַי
יִשְׁמַע אֶת־דִּבְרֵי־מֶלֶךְ אַשּׁוּר וְיוֹשִׁיעֵנוּ מִיָּדוֹ: וַיָּבֹא הַנָּבִיא לִפְנֵי
הַמֶּלֶךְ וַיֹּאמֶר אֵלָיו אַל־תִּירָא מִפְּנֵי־הַדְּבָרִים אֲשֶׁר שָׁמָעְתָּ:
כִּי כֹה אָמַר יהוה, לֹא יָבֹא מֶלֶךְ אַשּׁוּר אֶל־הָעִיר הַזֹּאת
וְהוֹשַׁעְתִּי אֹתָהּ לְמַעַן חִזְקִיָּה עַבְדִּי: וַיְהִי בַּלַּיְלָה הַהוּא וַיֵּצֵא
מַלְאַךְ־אֱלֹהִים וַיַּךְ בְּמַחֲנֵה־אַשּׁוּר וַתַּעַל צַעֲקָתָם כָּל־הַלַּיְלָה
עַד־אוֹר־הַבֹּקֶר: וַיְהִי בַבֹּקֶר וַיֵּצְאוּ בְנֵי־יִשְׂרָאֵל עַל־הַחוֹמָה
וַיִּרְאוּ וְהִנֵּה כֻלָּם מֵתִים וַיֵּרְדוּ אֶל־הַמַּחֲנֶה וַיִּקְחוּ אֶת־כָּל־
הַכֶּסֶף וְאֶת־כָּל־הַזָּהָב וַיָּבִיאוּ הָעִירָה וַיִּתְּנוּ בְּבֵית־יהוה

(1) And it came to pass in those days that the king of Sodom rebelled against the king of Edom. Thirteen years he served him and in the fourteenth year he rebelled and in the fifteenth year the king of Edom came to Sodom and with him (were) ten thousand men. And he fought against Sodom and he captured it and he burnt it in (the) fire and he took the men of Sodom with him and in the midst of them was Lot the son of Abraham's brother and he went (away) unto his land. And it

[a] 'Assyria'.

[b] Here 'gods', referring to the nations.

came to pass when Abraham heard (inf. constr. with prefixed prepos.) this thing that he took his servants with him, three hundred and eighteen men, and he pursued (after) the king of Edom (in) that night and he fought with him and he smote him and he brought back Lot and also all the men of Sodom. (2) And the Lord said unto Moses on the seventh day: 'Go up on the mountain and abide on the top of it, and I shall give (to) thee the tables of the stones and the Law and the commandments which thou shalt teach the children of Israel'. And Moses went up on the holy mountain, as the Lord had commanded him, and he was there forty days and forty nights; bread he ate not and water he drank not all the days that he was there. (3) And Moses spoke unto the children of Israel, saying: 'In the second year of the departure of (inf. constr. of יָצָא with prep. לְ) Israel from the land of Egypt in the third month we were in the wilderness of Sinai. And ye drew near unto me and ye said: "Let us send (Cohortative) spies to the land of Canaan to see the cities against which we shall fight ('which we shall fight against them')". And the thing was good in mine eyes and I chose from the heads of the people twelve men and I sent them to the land of Canaan. And the spies returned to the camp and they said: "We shall not be able to fight against the inhabitants of Canaan, for their cities are exceedingly strong". And ye said unto me: "Why hath the Lord brought us forth from the land of Egypt to slay us? Let us return to Egypt." And the Lord was exceedingly angry and he swore, saying: "Because they have not trusted (in) me, behold they shall not see the land which I have sworn to their fathers to give to their seed. Forty years they shall be in this great wilderness and they shall die there. And their sons who come after them, *they* (pronoun) shall come thither and they shall inherit the land."' (4) And Jeroboam [יָרָבְעָם] the king of Israel built the city Shechem and he dwelt there. And he was afraid lest the people[a] go up to Jerusalem to serve the Lord there and they[a] see the glory of the House of the Lord and their heart[a] turn [וְשָׁב] back to the king of Judah. And he made gods of gold and he said unto the people: 'These

[a] Understand 'will' for the Hebrew.

are thy gods, O Israel, and them shall ye serve.' And he made a festival in the eighth month on [בְּ] the fifteenth day of [לְ] the month and he commanded them (to) keep the festival. (5) These are the words which Jeremiah [יִרְמְיָהוּ] the prophet spoke unto the elders of Israel whom the king of Babylon [בָּבֶל] had exiled to Babylon. 'Build ye houses and dwell in them and take unto you(rselves) wives and beget children, and seek ye the peace of the city whither I have exiled you ("which I have exiled you thither") in order that it shall be well with you. For I will not forget you there and when ye pray ("in your praying", inf. constr.) unto Me I will hear your voice. And in another [בְּעוֹד] seventy years I will indeed bring you back to the land of your fathers and ye shall (re)build the cities which the king of Babylon hath thrown down (Hiph. of נָפַל) and My glory shall return to the city which I have chosen and ye shall be My people as in the days of David My servant and ye shall dwell in peace upon your land unto eternity.'

APPENDIX

1. The Hebrew letters are:

אָ֫לֶף, בֵּית, גִּ֫מֶל, דָּ֫לֶת, הֵא, וָו, זַ֫יִן, חֵית, טֵית, יוֹד, כַּף, לָ֫מֶד,
מֵים, נוּן, סָ֫מֶךְ, עַ֫יִן, פֵּא, צָ֫דֵי, קוֹף, רֵישׁ, שִׁין, תָּו.

The Hebrew alphabet in use is generally known as the 'Square Character', as distinct from the 'archaic' Hebrew writing found in inscriptions: the square script being a development from the archaic. It seems that the names of the Hebrew letters denoted the objects which the archaic forms crudely represented, thus: 𐤀 (אָ֫לֶף) means 'a bull', o (עַ֫יִן) 'an eye', w (שִׁין) 'a tooth'.

2. The *accents* are of two kinds—*Disjunctive* ('stops') and *Conjunctive* ('continuation marks'). The main Disjunctive accents are:

(*a*) (ֽ) *Sillûq* (סִלּוּק), always in the tone-syllable of the *last* word in a verse and followed by the sign (:) *Sôph*[a] *Pāsûq* (סוֹף פָּסוּק 'end of verse') thus: ׃ הָאָֽרֶץ . . . . . .

(*b*) (֑) *'Athnāḥ* (אַתְנָח), in the tone-syllable of the word which divides the verse into logical parts, thus:

׃ ֽ. . . . הָאָ֑רֶץ . . . .

(*c*) (֒) *S^eghôltâ* (סְגוֹלְתָּא) divides the clause before 'Athnaḥ and is usually found in long verses. It stands *above* the word and *on the last letter*, so that it does not necessarily mark the tone-syllable, thus: ׃ ֽ. . . . ֑. . . . הָאָ֫רֶץ֒[b] . . . .

(*d*) (֔) *Zāqēph Qāṭōn* (זָקֵף קָטֹן) subdivides a clause between 'Athnaḥ and Silluq, between the beginning of a verse and 'Athnaḥ (when Segholta is absent), and sometimes even between Segholta and 'Athnaḥ, thus:

׃ ֽ. . . . ֔. . . . ֑. . . . ֔. . . .

[a] See p. 4, footnote *a*.

[b] This is a Mil'el word, but Segholta is on the last letter.

When not preceded by a Conjunctive accent the form it takes is

(*e*) (֔) and it is called Zāqēph Gādhôl (זָקֵף גָּדוֹל).

(*f*) (֖) *Ṭiphḥâ* (טִפְחָה) usually comes before Silluq and 'Athnah, thus: : ֽ . . . . ֖ . . . . ֑ . . . . ֖ . . . .

Other Disjunctive accents are: (֓) *Šalšé.eth* (שַׁלְשֶׁלֶת), (֗) *R^ebhî'a* (רְבִיעַ), (֮) *Zarqâ*[a] (זַרְקָא), (֙) *Paštâ* (פַּשְׁטָא), (֚) *Y^ethîbh* (יְתִיב), (֛) *T^ebhîr* (תְּבִיר), (֡) *Pāzēr* (פָּזֵר), (֜) *Géreš* (גֶּרֶשׁ) and (֞) *Double Gereš* (גֵּרְשַׁיִם), (֠) *T^elîšâ G^edhôlâ* (תְּלִישָׁא גְדוֹלָה), (֟) *Qarnê Phārâ* (קַרְנֵי פָרָה) or *Pāzēr Gādhôl* (פָּזֵר גָּדוֹל).

The Conjunctive accents are:

(֥) *Mêr^ekhâ* (מֵירְכָא), (֣) *Mûnaḥ* (מוּנַח), (֤) *Mahpakh* (מַהְפַּךְ), (֧) *Dargâ* (דַּרְגָּא), (֨) *Qadhmâ* (קַדְמָא) or *'Azlâ* (אַזְלָא) when followed by Gereš,[b] (֩) *T^elîšâ Q^eṭannâ* (תְּלִישָׁא קְטַנָּה).

Note: The foregoing system of accents is used in the books of the Bible with the exception of Psalms (תְּהִלִּים), Proverbs (מִשְׁלֵי), and Job (אִיּוֹב), where there are certain combinations of accents which make the accentuation system of these books somewhat different.

3. *Quadriliteral Verbs.* There are a number of verbs in Hebrew which have four root-letters as their basis, an additional letter having been inserted. In Psalm lxxx, verse 14 we find the form יְכַרְסְמֶנָּה ('he will ravage it')—an Imperfect of the Pi'el כִּרְסֵם which is an extension of the root כָּסַם.

4. The following note has kindly been supplied by Professor G. R. Driver, M.A., Fellow of Magdalen College, Oxford. He explains the 'Waw Consecutive' construction, thus:

'All attempts to explain this at first sight strange phenomenon, whereby two tenses apparently exchange functions, on logical grounds, have failed, but the historical development of the Hebrew language readily accounts for it. When it is remembered that this is a composite language containing elements drawn from

[a] On the last letter of the word. [b] (֜).

all the Semitic languages, it is at once seen why it has two pronouns for the first person, namely אָנֹכִי and אֲנִי: for the former is the same word as the Accadian *anāku* (cf. Phoenician אנך), the latter as the Aramaean אֲנָא (cf. Arabic *'anâ*). So there are two different systems, drawn from different sources, merged in the Hebrew scheme of tenses. The "consecutive" וְקָטַלְתָּ "and thou shalt kill" (with the accent on the last syllable but a counter-tone, representing the primitive accent, on the first syllable) corresponds to the Acc. Permansive *qátil* "he is, has been, will be killed" and less often "he has killed, kills, will kill" (for this primitive form had a universal sense, i.e. denoted merely a killing state whether active or passive, past or present or future, and only gradually came to be restricted to present or future time when a preterite tense was devised) while the simple קָטַלְתָּ "thou hast killed" corresponds with the Aram. קְטַל "he has killed". Similarly the "consecutive" וַיִּקְטֹל "and he killed" (whose accent has been assimilated to that of the imperfect יִקְטֹל "he was killing, kills, will kill" but whose true accent is preserved in such forms as וַיָּקָם "and he arose") corresponds with the Acc. preterite *íqtul* "he killed" (cf. Acc. *íbni* "he built" with Hebr. וַיִּבֶן "and he built"), while the imperfect יִקְטֹל "he kills, was killing, will kill" corresponds with the Aram. יִקְטֻל "he was killing, kills, will kill". Thus the consecutive constructions are connected with the East-Semitic (Accadian) and the ordinary construction with the West-Semitic (Aramaean) verbal system, and the two have survived side by side in the classical language.'

5. *The Construct–Genitive Relationship.* When two nouns stand together in the construct–genitive arrangement and the second noun (as genitive) limits or qualifies the first one (in the construct) adjectivally (p. 137. **63**), then the suffix, denoting a possessive, is attached to the second noun, but applies to the whole compound concept. For example, אֱלֹהֵי־יִשְׁעָתִי is (not 'God of my salvation', but) 'my God of salvation', i.e. 'my saving God'. Similarly הַר־קָדְשׁוֹ is (not 'the mount of His holiness', but) 'His mount of holiness', i.e. 'His holy mount'.

THE REGULAR VERB[1]

	Qal Active	Qal Stative	Qal Stative	Niph'al	Pi'el	Pu'al	Hiph'il	Hoph'al	Hithpa'el
Perf. sg. 3. m.	קָטַל	כָּבֵד	קָטֹן	נִקְטַל	קִטֵּל[6]	קֻטַּל	הִקְטִיל	הָקְטַל	הִתְקַטֵּל[9]
3. f.	קָֽטְלָה	כָּֽבְדָה	קָֽטְנָה	נִקְטְלָה	קִטְּלָה	קֻטְּלָה	הִקְטִילָה	הָקְטְלָה	הִתְקַטְּלָה
2. m.	קָטַלְתָּ	כָּבַדְתָּ	קָטֹנְתָּ	נִקְטַלְתָּ	קִטַּלְתָּ	קֻטַּלְתָּ	הִקְטַלְתָּ	הָקְטַלְתָּ	הִתְקַטַּלְתָּ
2. f.	קָטַלְתְּ	כָּבַדְתְּ	קָטֹנְתְּ	נִקְטַלְתְּ	קִטַּלְתְּ	קֻטַּלְתְּ	הִקְטַלְתְּ	הָקְטַלְתְּ	הִתְקַטַּלְתְּ
1. c.	קָטַלְתִּי	כָּבַדְתִּי	קָטֹנְתִּי	נִקְטַלְתִּי	קִטַּלְתִּי	קֻטַּלְתִּי	הִקְטַלְתִּי	הָקְטַלְתִּי	הִתְקַטַּלְתִּי
pl. 3. c.	קָֽטְלוּ	כָּֽבְדוּ	קָֽטְנוּ	נִקְטְלוּ	קִטְּלוּ	קֻטְּלוּ	הִקְטִילוּ	הָקְטְלוּ	הִתְקַטְּלוּ
2. m.	קְטַלְתֶּם	כְּבַדְתֶּם	קְטָנְתֶּם	נִקְטַלְתֶּם	קִטַּלְתֶּם	קֻטַּלְתֶּם	הִקְטַלְתֶּם	הָקְטַלְתֶּם	הִתְקַטַּלְתֶּם
2. f.	קְטַלְתֶּן	כְּבַדְתֶּן	קְטָנְתֶּן	נִקְטַלְתֶּן	קִטַּלְתֶּן	קֻטַּלְתֶּן	הִקְטַלְתֶּן	הָקְטַלְתֶּן	הִתְקַטַּלְתֶּן
1. c.	קָטַלְנוּ	כָּבַדְנוּ	קָטֹנּוּ[4]	נִקְטַלְנוּ	קִטַּלְנוּ	קֻטַּלְנוּ	הִקְטַלְנוּ	הָקְטַלְנוּ	הִתְקַטַּלְנוּ
Imperf. sg. 3. m.	יִקְטֹל	יִכְבַּד	יִקְטַן	יִקָּטֵל	יְקַטֵּל	יְקֻטַּל	יַקְטִיל	יָקְטַל	יִתְקַטֵּל
3. f.	תִּקְטֹל	תִּכְבַּד		תִּקָּטֵל	תְּקַטֵּל	תְּקֻטַּל	תַּקְטִיל	תָּקְטַל	תִּתְקַטֵּל
2. m.	תִּקְטֹל	תִּכְבַּד		תִּקָּטֵל	תְּקַטֵּל	תְּקֻטַּל	תַּקְטִיל	תָּקְטַל	תִּתְקַטֵּל
2. f.	תִּקְטְלִי	תִּכְבְּדִי		תִּקָּֽטְלִי	תְּקַטְּלִי	תְּקֻטְּלִי	תַּקְטִילִי	תָּקְטְלִי	תִּתְקַטְּלִי
1. c.	אֶקְטֹל	אֶכְבַּד		אֶקָּטֵל[5]	אֲקַטֵּל	אֲקֻטַּל	אַקְטִיל	אָקְטַל	אֶתְקַטֵּל
pl. 3. m.	יִקְטְלוּ	יִכְבְּדוּ		יִקָּֽטְלוּ	יְקַטְּלוּ	יְקֻטְּלוּ	יַקְטִילוּ	יָקְטְלוּ	יִתְקַטְּלוּ
3. f.	תִּקְטֹלְנָה	תִּכְבַּדְנָה		תִּקָּטַלְנָה	תְּקַטֵּלְנָה	תְּקֻטַּלְנָה	תַּקְטֵלְנָה	תָּקְטַלְנָה	תִּתְקַטֵּלְנָה

2. m.	תִּקְטְלוּ	תִּכְבְּדוּ		תִּקָּטְלוּ	תְּקַטְּלוּ	תְּקֻטְּלוּ	תַּקְטִילוּ	תָּקְטְלוּ	תִּתְקַטְּלוּ
2. f.	תִּקְטֹלְנָה	תִּכְבַּדְנָה		תִּקָּטַלְנָה	תְּקַטֵּלְנָה	תְּקֻטַּלְנָה	תַּקְטֵלְנָה	תָּקְטַלְנָה	תִּתְקַטֵּלְנָה
1. c.	נִקְטֹל	נִכְבַּד		נִקָּטֵל	נְקַטֵּל	נְקֻטַּל	נַקְטִיל	נָקְטַל	נִתְקַטֵּל
Cohort. sg. 1. c.	אֶקְטְלָה	אֶכְבְּדָה		אִקָּטְלָה	אֲקַטְּלָה		אַקְטִילָה		אֶתְקַטְּלָה
Jussive sg. 3. m.	יִקְטֹל	יִכְבַּד		יִקָּטֵל	יְקַטֵּל	יְקֻטַּל	יַקְטֵל [8]	יָקְטַל	יִתְקַטֵּל
Impf. & ו *consec*.	וַיִּקְטֹל	וַיִּכְבַּד		וַיִּקָּטֵל	וַיְקַטֵּל [7]	וַיְקֻטַּל [7]	וַיַּקְטֵל [8]	וַיָּקְטַל	וַיִּתְקַטֵּל
Perf. ,,	וְקָטַלְתָּ [2]			וְנִקְטַלְתָּ [2]	וְקִטַּלְתָּ [2]		וְהִקְטַלְתָּ [2]		
Imper. sg. 2. m.	קְטֹל (קָטְלָה)[3]	כְּבַד		הִקָּטֵל	קַטֵּל	wanting	הַקְטֵל	wanting	הִתְקַטֵּל
2. f.	קִטְלִי	כִּבְדִי		הִקָּטְלִי	קַטְּלִי		הַקְטִילִי		הִתְקַטְּלִי
pl. 2. m.	קִטְלוּ	כִּבְדוּ		הִקָּטְלוּ	קַטְּלוּ		הַקְטִילוּ		הִתְקַטְּלוּ
2. f.	קְטֹלְנָה	כְּבַדְנָה		הִקָּטַלְנָה	קַטֵּלְנָה		הַקְטֵלְנָה		הִתְקַטֵּלְנָה
Part. (*act*.) sg. m.	קֹטֵל	כָּבֵד	קָטֹן		מְקַטֵּל		מַקְטִיל		מִתְקַטֵּל
,, (*pass*.) ,,	קָטוּל			נִקְטָל		מְקֻטָּל		מָקְטָל	
Inf. *absolute*	קָטוֹל	כָּבוֹד		הִקָּטֹל, נִקְטֹל	קַטֹּל, קַטֵּל	קֻטֹּל	הַקְטֵל	(הָקְטֵל)	הִתְקַטֵּל
,, *construct*	קְטֹל	כְּבַד		הִקָּטֵל	קַטֵּל		הַקְטִיל	(הָקְטַל)	

[1] Refer to the chapters dealing with each section of this table. [2] Accent moves forward, p. 92. (*c*), and p. 253.
[3] Emphatic Imperative, p. 88, § **48** (*b*). [4] For קְטֹנּוּ. [5] Sometimes אֲקַטֵּל. [6] Sometimes קַטֵּל.
[7] Dagheš Forte absent in יְ, pp. 17–18, § **10**. [8] Shortened Imperfect, p. 114. (*b*), (*c*). [9] Sometimes הִתְקַטֵּל.

THE REGULAR VERB WITH VERBAL SUFFIXES [1]

	Qal								Pi'el	Hiph'il
	Perfect								Perfect	Perfect
	3. m. sg.	3. f. sg.	2. m. sg.	2. f. sg.	1. c. sg.	3. c. pl.	2. pl. m. & f.	1. c. pl.	3. m. sg.	3. m. sg.
suff.	קָטַל	קָֽטְלָה	קָטַ֫לְתָּ	קָטַלְתְּ	קָטַלְתִּי	קָֽטְלוּ	קְטַלְתֶּם, ־תֶּן	קָטַ֫לְנוּ	קִטֵּל	הִקְטִיל
sg. 1. c.	קְטָלַ֫נִי	קְטָלַ֫תְנִי	קְטַלְתַּ֫נִי	קְטַלְתִּ֫ינִי	—	קְטָלוּ֫נִי	קְטַלְתּוּ֫נִי	—	קִטְּלַ֫נִי	הִקְטִילַ֫נִי
2. m.	קְטָלְךָ	קְטָלַ֫תְךָ	—	—	קְטַלְתִּ֫יךָ	קְטָלוּ֫ךָ	—	קְטַלְנ֫וּךָ	קִטֶּלְךָ	הִקְטִילְךָ
2. f.	קְטָלֵךְ	קְטָלָ֫תֶךְ	—	—	קְטַלְתִּיךְ	קְטָלוּךְ	—	קְטַלְנוּךְ	קִטְּלֵךְ	&c.
3. m.	קְטָלוֹ קְטָלָ֫הוּ	קְטָלַ֫תְהוּ קְטָלַ֫תּוּ	קְטַלְתָּ֫הוּ קְטַלְתּוֹ	קְטַלְתִּיהוּ	קְטַלְתִּ֫יהוּ קְטַלְתִּיו	קְטָלוּהוּ	קְטַלְתּוּ֫הוּ &c.	קְטַלְנ֫וּהוּ &c.	קִטְּלוֹ	
3. f.	קְטָלָהּ	קְטָלַ֫תָּה	קְטַלְתָּהּ	קְטַלְתִּיהָ	קְטַלְתִּ֫יהָ	קְטָלוּהָ			קִטְּלָהּ	
pl 1. c.	קְטָלָ֫נוּ	קְטָלַ֫תְנוּ	קְטַלְתָּ֫נוּ	קְטַלְתִּ֫ינוּ	—	קְטָלוּ֫נוּ			קִטְּלָ֫נוּ	
2. m.	—	—	—	—	קְטַלְתִּיכֶם	—			&c.	
2. f.	—	—	—	—	קְטַלְתִּיכֶן	—				
3. m.	קְטָלָם	קְטָלָ֫תַם	קְטַלְתָּם	קְטַלְתִּים	קְטַלְתִּים	קְטָלוּם				
3. f.	קְטָלָן	קְטָלָ֫תַן	קְטַלְתָּן	קְטַלְתִּין	קְטַלְתִּין	קְטָלוּן				

	Imperfect 3. m. sg.	(with נ energic)	3. m. pl.	Imperative sg.	pl.	Infinitive Construct (subj.)		(obj.)	Imperfect 3. m. sg.	Imperfect 3. m. sg.
	יִקְטֹל		יִקְטְלוּ	קְטֹל	קִטְלוּ		קְטֹל		יְקַטֵּל	יַקְטִיל
sg. 1. c.	יִקְטְלֵנִי	יִקְטְלֶנִּי	יִקְטְלוּנִי	קָטְלֵנִי	קִטְלוּנִי	קָטְלִי		קָטְלֵנִי	יְקַטְּלֵנִי	יַקְטִילֵנִי
2. m.	יִקְטָלְךָ		יִקְטְלוּךָ	—	—		{ קָטָלְךָ קָטְלְךָ		יְקַטֶּלְךָ	יַקְטִילְךָ
2. f.	יִקְטְלֵךְ		יִקְטְלוּךְ	—	—		קָטְלֵךְ		יְקַטְּלֵךְ	יַקְטִילֵךְ
3. m.	[2]יִקְטְלֵהוּ	יִקְטְלֶנּוּ	יִקְטְלוּהוּ	קָטְלֵהוּ	קִטְלוּהוּ		קָטְלוֹ		יְקַטְּלֵהוּ	&c.
3. f.	[2]יִקְטְלֶהָ	יִקְטְלֶנָּה	יִקְטְלוּהָ	קָטְלֶהָ	&c.		קָטְלָהּ		&c.	
pl. 1. c.	יִקְטְלֵנוּ		יִקְטְלוּנוּ	קָטְלֵנוּ			קָטְלֵנוּ			
2. m.	יִקְטָלְכֶם		יִקְטְלוּכֶם	—			קָטָלְכֶם			
2. f.	יִקְטָלְכֶן		יִקְטְלוּכֶן	—			קָטָלְכֶן			
3. m.	יִקְטְלֵם		יִקְטְלוּם	קָטְלֵם			קָטְלָם			
3. f.	יִקְטְלֵן		יִקְטְלוּן				קָטְלָן			

[1] See pp. 123 ff.

[2] Rarely יִקְטְלָה, יִקְטְלוֹ.

PE NUN VERB[1]

	Qal		Niph'al	Hiph'il	Hoph'al	Qal		Niph'al	
Perf. sg. 3. m.	[נָגַשׁ]	נָפַל	נִגַּשׁ	הִגִּישׁ	הֻגַּשׁ	נָתַן	לָקַח	נִתַּן	נִלְקַח
3. f.			נִגְּשָׁה	הִגִּישָׁה	הֻגְּשָׁה	נָֽתְנָה		נִתְּנָה	
2. m.			נִגַּשְׁתָּ	הִגַּשְׁתָּ	הֻגַּשְׁתָּ	נָתַתָּ		נִתַּתָּ	
2. f.			נִגַּשְׁתְּ	הִגַּשְׁתְּ	הֻגַּשְׁתְּ	נָתַתְּ	(regular)		
1. c.	(regular)		נִגַּשְׁתִּי	הִגַּשְׁתִּי	הֻגַּשְׁתִּי	נָתַתִּי		&c. (regular)	
pl. 3. c.			נִגְּשׁוּ	הִגִּישׁוּ	הֻגְּשׁוּ	נָֽתְנוּ			
2. m.			נִגַּשְׁתֶּם	הִגַּשְׁתֶּם	הֻגַּשְׁתֶּם	נְתַתֶּם			
2. f.			נִגַּשְׁתֶּן	הִגַּשְׁתֶּן	הֻגַּשְׁתֶּן	נְתַתֶּן			
1. c.			נִגַּשְׁנוּ	הִגַּשְׁנוּ	הֻגַּשְׁנוּ	נָתַנּוּ			
Imperf. sg. 3. m.	יִגַּשׁ	יִפֹּל	[יִנָּגֵשׁ]	יַגִּישׁ	יֻגַּשׁ	יִתֵּן	יִקַּח[7]	יִנָּתֵן	יִלָּקַח
3. f.	תִּגַּשׁ	תִּפֹּל		תַּגִּישׁ	תֻּגַּשׁ	תִּתֵּן	תִּקַּח		
2. m.	תִּגַּשׁ	תִּפֹּל		תַּגִּישׁ	תֻּגַּשׁ	תִּתֵּן	תִּקַּח	&c.	
2. f.	תִּגְּשִׁי	תִּפְּלִי		תַּגִּישִׁי	תֻּגְּשִׁי	תִּתְּנִי	תִּקְחִי		
1. c.	אֶגַּשׁ	אֶפֹּל	(regular)	אַגִּישׁ	אֻגַּשׁ	אֶתֵּן	אֶקַּח		
pl. 3. m.	יִגְּשׁוּ	יִפְּלוּ		יַגִּישׁוּ	יֻגְּשׁוּ	יִתְּנוּ	יִקְחוּ	(regular as Lamed Guttural)	
3. f.	תִּגַּשְׁנָה	תִּפֹּלְנָה		תַּגֵּשְׁנָה	תֻּגַּשְׁנָה	(תִּתֵּנָּה)	תִּקַּחְנָה		

2. m.	תִּגְּשׁוּ	תִּפְּלוּ		תַּגִּישׁוּ	תֻּגְּשׁוּ	תִּתְּנוּ	תִּקְחוּ		
2. f.	תִּגַּשְׁנָה	תִּפֹּלְנָה		תַּגֵּשְׁנָה	תֻּגַּשְׁנָה	(תִּתֵּנָּה)	תִּקַּחְנָה		
1. c.	נִגַּשׁ	נִפֹּל		נַגִּישׁ	נֻגַּשׁ	נִתֵּן	נִקַּח		
Cohort. sg. 1. c.	אֶגְּשָׁה	אֶפְּלָה		אַגִּישָׁה		אֶתְּנָה	אֶקְחָה		
Jussive sg. 3. m.	יִגַּשׁ	יִפֹּל		יַגֵּשׁ[5]	יֻגַּשׁ	יִתֵּן	יִקַּח		
Impf. & ו *consec*.	וַיִּגַּשׁ	וַיִּפֹּל		וַיַּגֵּשׁ	וַיֻּגַּשׁ	וַיִּתֵּן	וַיִּקַּח		
Perf. ,,		וְנָפַלְתָּ				וְנָתַתָּ			
Imper. sg. 2. m.	גַּשׁ (גְּשָׁה)[2]	נְפֹל	הִנָּגֵשׁ	הַגֵּשׁ		תֵּן (תְּנָה)[2]	קַח (קְחָה)[2]	הִנָּתֵן	הִלָּקַח
2. f.	גְּשִׁי	נִפְלִי	הִנָּגְשִׁי	הַגִּישִׁי	wanting	תְּנִי	קְחִי	&c.	&c.
pl. 2. m.	גְּשׁוּ	נִפְלוּ	הִנָּגְשׁוּ	הַגִּישׁוּ		תְּנוּ	קְחוּ		
2. f.	גַּשְׁנָה	נְפֹלְנָה	הִנָּגַשְׁנָה	הַגֵּשְׁנָה		(תֵּנָּה)	(קַחְנָה)		
Part. (*act*.) sg. m.	[נֹגֵשׁ]	נֹפֵל		מַגִּישׁ		נֹתֵן	לֹקֵחַ[7]		
,, (*pass*.) ,,	[נָגוּשׁ]		נִגָּשׁ		מֻגָּשׁ	נָתוּן	לָקוּחַ[7]	נִתָּן	נִלְקָח
Inf. *absolute*	נָגוֹשׁ	נָפוֹל		הַגֵּשׁ	הֻגֵּשׁ	נָתוֹן	לָקוֹחַ[7]	הִנָּתֹן	הִלָּקֹחַ[7]
,, *construct*	גֶּשֶׁת[3]	נְפֹל[4]	הִנָּגֵשׁ	הַגִּישׁ	הֻגַּשׁ	תֵּת[6]	קַחַת[8]	הִנָּתֵן	הִלָּקַח[7]

[1] See pp. 141 ff. [2] Long form of Imperative. [3] With ל לָגֶשֶׁת; with suff. גִּשְׁתִּי &c. [4] With ל לִנְפֹּל. [5] Shortened Imperfect.
[6] With ל לָתֵת; with suff. תִּתִּי &c. [7] לָקַח is also a Lamed Guttural, pp. 172 ff. [8] With ל לָקַחַת; with suff. קַחְתִּי &c.

PE GUTTURAL VERBS [1] | PE 'ALEP̱ VERBS [2]

	Qal Active	Qal Stative	Niph'al	Hiph'il	Hoph'al	Pe 'Alep̱: Qal
Perf. sg. 3. m.	עָמַד	חָזֵק	נֶֽעֱמַד [5]	הֶֽעֱמִיד	הָֽעֳמַד	אָכַל
3. f.	עָֽמְדָה		נֶֽעֶמְדָה	הֶֽעֱמִ֫ידָה	הָֽעָמְדָה	
2. m.	עָמַ֫דְתָּ	&c.	נֶֽעֱמַ֫דְתָּ	הֶֽעֱמַ֫דְתָּ	הָֽעֳמַ֫דְתָּ	
2. f.	עָמַדְתְּ		נֶֽעֱמַדְתְּ	הֶֽעֱמַדְתְּ	הָֽעֳמַדְתְּ	&c.
1. c.	עָמַ֫דְתִּי		נֶֽעֱמַ֫דְתִּי	הֶֽעֱמַ֫דְתִּי	הָֽעֳמַ֫דְתִּי	
pl. 3. c.	עָֽמְדוּ		נֶֽעֶמְדוּ	הֶֽעֱמִ֫ידוּ	הָֽעָמְדוּ	
2. m.	עֲמַדְתֶּם		נֶֽעֱמַדְתֶּם	הֶֽעֱמַדְתֶּם	הָֽעֳמַדְתֶּם	
2. f.	עֲמַדְתֶּן		נֶֽעֱמַדְתֶּן	הֶֽעֱמַדְתֶּן	הָֽעֳמַדְתֶּן	
1. c.	עָמַ֫דְנוּ		נֶֽעֱמַ֫דְנוּ	הֶֽעֱמַ֫דְנוּ	הָֽעֳמַ֫דְנוּ	
Imperf. sg. 3. m.	יַֽעֲמֹד [3]	יֶֽחֱזַק [4]	יֵֽעָמֵד	יַֽעֲמִיד	יָֽעֳמַד	יֹאכַל
3. f.	תַּֽעֲמֹד	תֶּֽחֱזַק	תֵּֽעָמֵד	תַּֽעֲמִיד	תָּֽעֳמַד	תֹּאכַל
2. m.	תַּֽעֲמֹד	תֶּֽחֱזַק	תֵּֽעָמֵד	תַּֽעֲמִיד	תָּֽעֳמַד	תֹּאכַל
2. f.	תַּֽעַמְדִי	תֶּֽחֶזְקִי	תֵּֽעָמְדִי	תַּֽעֲמִ֫ידִי	תָּֽעָמְדִי	תֹּֽאכְלִי
1. c.	אֶֽעֱמֹד	אֶֽחֱזַק	אֵֽעָמֵד	אַֽעֲמִיד	אָֽעֳמַד	אֹכַל
pl. 3. m.	יַֽעַמְדוּ	יֶֽחֶזְקוּ	יֵֽעָמְדוּ	יַֽעֲמִ֫ידוּ	יָֽעָמְדוּ	יֹֽאכְלוּ
3. f.	תַּֽעֲמֹ֫דְנָה	תֶּֽחֱזַ֫קְנָה	תֵּֽעָמַ֫דְנָה	תַּֽעֲמֵ֫דְנָה	תָּֽעֳמַ֫דְנָה	תֹּאכַ֫לְנָה

2. m.	תַּעַמְדוּ	תֶּחֶזְקוּ	תֵּעָמְדוּ	תַּעֲמִידוּ	תָּעָמְדוּ	תֹּאכְלוּ
2. f.	תַּעֲמֹדְנָה	תֶּחֱזַקְנָה	תֵּעָמַדְנָה	תַּעֲמֵדְנָה	תָּעֳמַדְנָה	תֹּאכַלְנָה
1. c.	נַעֲמֹד	נֶחֱזַק	נֵעָמֵד	נַעֲמִיד	נָעֳמַד	נֹאכַל
Cohort. sg. 1. c.	אֶעֶמְדָה			אַעֲמִידָה		אֹכְלָה
Jussive sg. 3. m.	יַעֲמֹד	יֶחֱזַק		יַעֲמֵד[6]		יֹאכַל
Impf. & ו *consec.*	וַיַּעֲמֹד	וַיֶּחֱזַק		וַיַּעֲמֵד		וַיֹּאכַל[8]
Perf. ,,	וְעָמַדְתָּ			וְהֶעֱמַדְתָּ		וְאָכַלְתָּ
Imper. sg. 2. m.	עֲמֹד	חֲזַק	הֵעָמֵד	הַעֲמֵד	wanting	אֱכֹל
2. f.	עִמְדִי	חִזְקִי	הֵעָמְדִי	הַעֲמִידִי		אִכְלִי
pl. 2. m.	עִמְדוּ	חִזְקוּ	הֵעָמְדוּ	הַעֲמִידוּ		אִכְלוּ
2. f.	עֲמֹדְנָה	חֲזַקְנָה	הֵעָמַדְנָה	הַעֲמֵדְנָה		אֱכֹלְנָה
Part. (*act.*) sg. m.	עֹמֵד			מַעֲמִיד		אֹכֵל
,, (*pass.*) ,,	עָמוּד		נֶעֱמָד[5]		מָעֳמָד	אָכוּל
Inf. absolute	עָמוֹד		נַעֲמֹד	הַעֲמֵד	הָעֳמַד	אָכוֹל
,, *construct*	עֲמֹד with ל לַעֲמֹד		הֵעָמֵד	הַעֲמִיד		אֱכֹל with ל לֶאֱכֹל

[1] See pp. 154 ff.

[2] See pp. 161 ff.

[3] But from חָמַד the Imperfect is יַחְמֹד, p. 156, special note.

[4] But from חָשַׁךְ the Imperfect is יֶחְשַׁךְ, p. 156.

[5] חָמַד Niph'al Perfect is נֶחְמַד and Participle נֶחְמָד.

[6] Shortened Imperfect.

[7] Pausal יֹאכֵל.

[8] But וַיֹּאמֶר, p. 162 (*a*) and (*b*).

ʿAYIN GUTTURAL VERBS[1]

	Qal	Niph'al	Pi'el	Pu'al	Hithpa'el
Perf. sg. 3. m.	בָּחַר	נִבְחַר	בֵּרַךְ[2]	בֹּרַךְ[6]	הִתְבָּרֵךְ[7]
3. f.	בָּחֲרָה	נִבְחֲרָה	בֵּרְכָה[3]	בֹּרְכָה[3]	הִתְבָּרְכָה[3]
2. m.	בָּחַרְתָּ	נִבְחַרְתָּ	בֵּרַכְתָּ	בֹּרַכְתָּ	הִתְבָּרַכְתָּ
2. f.	בָּחַרְתְּ	נִבְחַרְתְּ	בֵּרַכְתְּ	בֹּרַכְתְּ	הִתְבָּרַכְתְּ
1. c.	בָּחַרְתִּי	נִבְחַרְתִּי	בֵּרַכְתִּי	בֹּרַכְתִּי	הִתְבָּרַכְתִּי
pl. 3. c.	בָּחֲרוּ	נִבְחֲרוּ	בֵּרְכוּ[3]	בֹּרְכוּ[3]	הִתְבָּרְכוּ[3]
2. m.	בְּחַרְתֶּם	נִבְחַרְתֶּם	בֵּרַכְתֶּם	בֹּרַכְתֶּם	הִתְבָּרַכְתֶּם
2. f.	בְּחַרְתֶּן	נִבְחַרְתֶּן	בֵּרַכְתֶּן	בֹּרַכְתֶּן	הִתְבָּרַכְתֶּן
1. c.	בָּחַרְנוּ	נִבְחַרְנוּ	בֵּרַכְנוּ	בֹּרַכְנוּ	הִתְבָּרַכְנוּ
Imperf. sg. 3. m.	יִבְחַר	יִבָּחֵר	יְבָרֵךְ[2]	יְבֹרַךְ[6]	יִתְבָּרֵךְ[7]
3. f.	תִּבְחַר	תִּבָּחֵר	תְּבָרֵךְ	תְּבֹרַךְ	תִּתְבָּרֵךְ
2. m.	תִּבְחַר	תִּבָּחֵר	תְּבָרֵךְ	תְּבֹרַךְ	תִּתְבָּרֵךְ
2. f.	תִּבְחֲרִי	תִּבָּחֲרִי	תְּבָרְכִי[3]	תְּבֹרְכִי[3]	תִּתְבָּרְכִי[3]
1. c.	אֶבְחַר	אֶבָּחֵר	אֲבָרֵךְ	אֲבֹרַךְ	אֶתְבָּרֵךְ
pl. 3. m.	יִבְחֲרוּ	יִבָּחֲרוּ	יְבָרְכוּ[3]	יְבֹרְכוּ[3]	יִתְבָּרְכוּ[3]
3. f.	תִּבְחַרְנָה	תִּבָּחַרְנָה	תְּבָרֵכְנָה[4]	תְּבֹרַכְנָה	תִּתְבָּרֵכְנָה

2. m.	תִּבְחֲרוּ	תִּבָּחֲרוּ	תְּבָרְכוּ[3]	תְּבֹרְכוּ[3]	תִּתְבָּרְכוּ[3]
2. f.	תִּבְחַ֫רְנָה	תִּבָּחַ֫רְנָה	תְּבָרֵ֫כְנָה[4]	תְּבֹרַ֫כְנָה	תִּתְבָּרַ֫כְנָה
1. c.	נִבְחַר	נִבָּחֵר	נְבָרֵךְ	נְבֹרַךְ	נִתְבָּרֵךְ
Cohort. sg. 1. c.	אֶבְחֲרָה	אִבָּחֲרָה	אֲבָרְכָה[3]		
Jussive sg. 3. m.	יִבְחַר	יִבָּחֵר	יְבָרֵךְ		
Impf. & ו *consec.*	וַיִּבְחַר	וַיִּבָּחֵר	וַיְבָ֫רֶךְ[5]		
Perf. ,,	וּבָחַרְתָּ֫	וְנִבְחַרְתָּ֫			
Imper. sg. 2. m.	בְּחַר	הִבָּחֵר	בָּרֵךְ		הִתְבָּרֵךְ
2. f.	בַּחֲרִי	הִבָּחֲרִי	בָּרְכִי[3]	wanting	הִתְבָּרְכִי[3]
pl. 2. m.	בַּחֲרוּ	הִבָּחֲרוּ	בָּרְכוּ[3]		הִתְבָּרְכוּ[3]
2. f.	בְּחַ֫רְנָה	הִבָּחַ֫רְנָה	בָּרֵ֫כְנָה		הִתְבָּרַ֫כְנָה
Part. (*act.*) sg. m.	בֹּחֵר		מְבָרֵךְ		
,, (*pass.*) ,,	בָּחוּר	נִבְחָר		מְבֹרָךְ	מִתְבָּרֵךְ
Inf. absolute	בָּחוֹר	נִבְחוֹר	בָּרֵךְ	בֹּרֵךְ	
,, *construct*	בְּחֹר	הִבָּחֵר			

[1] See pp. 166 ff. [2] Or בֵּרֵךְ, but נִחַם &c., Imperfect יְנַחֵם &c. [3] Medial guttural would have composite shewa. [4] Medial guttural would have Pathaḥ. [5] Accent is retarded one syllable; hence vowel in final closed unaccented syllable is shortened. [6] But נֻחַם &c., Imperfect יְנֻחַם &c. [7] But הִתְנַחֵם &c., Imperfect יִתְנַחֵם &c.

LAMEḎ GUTTURAL VERBS[1]

	Qal	Niph'al	Pi'el	Pu'al	Hiph'il	Hoph'al	Hithpa'el
Perf. sg. 3. m.	שָׁלַח	נִשְׁלַח	שִׁלַּח	שֻׁלַּח	הִשְׁלִיחַ	הָשְׁלַח	הִשְׁתַּלַּח[4]
3. f.	שָֽׁלְחָה	נִשְׁלְחָה	שִׁלְּחָה	שֻׁלְּחָה	הִשְׁלִ֫יחָה	הָשְׁלְחָה	הִשְׁתַּלְּחָה
2. m.	שָׁלַ֫חְתָּ	נִשְׁלַ֫חְתָּ	שִׁלַּ֫חְתָּ	שֻׁלַּ֫חְתָּ	הִשְׁלַ֫חְתָּ	הָשְׁלַ֫חְתָּ	הִשְׁתַּלַּ֫חְתָּ
2. f.	שָׁלַ֫חַתְּ	נִשְׁלַ֫חַתְּ	שִׁלַּ֫חַתְּ	שֻׁלַּ֫חַתְּ	הִשְׁלַ֫חַתְּ	הָשְׁלַ֫חַתְּ	הִשְׁתַּלַּ֫חַתְּ
1. c.	שָׁלַ֫חְתִּי	נִשְׁלַ֫חְתִּי	שִׁלַּ֫חְתִּי	שֻׁלַּ֫חְתִּי	הִשְׁלַ֫חְתִּי	הָשְׁלַ֫חְתִּי	הִשְׁתַּלַּ֫חְתִּי
pl. 3. c.	שָֽׁלְחוּ	נִשְׁלְחוּ	שִׁלְּחוּ	שֻׁלְּחוּ	הִשְׁלִ֫יחוּ	הָשְׁלְחוּ	הִשְׁתַּלְּחוּ
2. m.	שְׁלַחְתֶּם	נִשְׁלַחְתֶּם	שִׁלַּחְתֶּם	שֻׁלַּחְתֶּם	הִשְׁלַחְתֶּם	הָשְׁלַחְתֶּם	הִשְׁתַּלַּחְתֶּם
2. f.	שְׁלַחְתֶּן	נִשְׁלַחְתֶּן	שִׁלַּחְתֶּן	שֻׁלַּחְתֶּן	הִשְׁלַחְתֶּן	הָשְׁלַחְתֶּן	הִשְׁתַּלַּחְתֶּן
1. c.	שָׁלַ֫חְנוּ	נִשְׁלַ֫חְנוּ	שִׁלַּ֫חְנוּ	שֻׁלַּ֫חְנוּ	הִשְׁלַ֫חְנוּ	הָשְׁלַ֫חְנוּ	הִשְׁתַּלַּ֫חְנוּ
Imperf. sg. 3. m.	יִשְׁלַח[2]	יִשָּׁלַח	יְשַׁלַּח	יְשֻׁלַּח	יַשְׁלִיחַ	יָשְׁלַח	יִשְׁתַּלַּח
3. f.	תִּשְׁלַח	תִּשָּׁלַח	תְּשַׁלַּח	תְּשֻׁלַּח	תַּשְׁלִיחַ	תָּשְׁלַח	תִּשְׁתַּלַּח
2. m.	תִּשְׁלַח	תִּשָּׁלַח	תְּשַׁלַּח	תְּשֻׁלַּח	תַּשְׁלִיחַ	תָּשְׁלַח	תִּשְׁתַּלַּח
2. f.	תִּשְׁלְחִי	תִּשָּֽׁלְחִי	תְּשַׁלְּחִי	תְּשֻׁלְּחִי	תַּשְׁלִ֫יחִי	תָּשְׁלְחִי	תִּשְׁתַּלְּחִי
1. c.	אֶשְׁלַח	אֶשָּׁלַח	אֲשַׁלַּח	אֲשֻׁלַּח	אַשְׁלִיחַ	אָשְׁלַח	אֶשְׁתַּלַּח
pl. 3. m.	יִשְׁלְחוּ	יִשָּֽׁלְחוּ	יְשַׁלְּחוּ	יְשֻׁלְּחוּ	יַשְׁלִ֫יחוּ	יָשְׁלְחוּ	יִשְׁתַּלְּחוּ
3. f.	תִּשְׁלַ֫חְנָה	תִּשָּׁלַ֫חְנָה	תְּשַׁלַּ֫חְנָה	תְּשֻׁלַּ֫חְנָה	תַּשְׁלַ֫חְנָה	תָּשְׁלַ֫חְנָה	תִּשְׁתַּלַּ֫חְנָה

2. m.	תִּשְׁלְחוּ	תִּשָּׁלְחוּ	תְּשַׁלְּחוּ	תְּשֻׁלְּחוּ	תַּשְׁלִיחוּ	תָּשְׁלְחוּ	תִּשְׁתַּלְּחוּ
2. f.	תִּשְׁלַחְנָה	תִּשָּׁלַחְנָה	תְּשַׁלַּחְנָה	תְּשֻׁלַּחְנָה	תַּשְׁלַחְנָה	תָּשְׁלַחְנָה	תִּשְׁתַּלַּחְנָה
1. c.	נִשְׁלַח	נִשָּׁלַח	נְשַׁלַּח	נְשֻׁלַּח	נַשְׁלִיחַ	נָשְׁלַח	נִשְׁתַּלַּח
Cohort. sg. 1. c.	אֶשְׁלְחָה	אִשָּׁלְחָה	אֲשַׁלְּחָה		אַשְׁלִיחָה		
Jussive sg. 3. m.	יִשְׁלַח	יִשָּׁלַח	יְשַׁלַּח		יַשְׁלַח[3]		
Impf. & ו *consec*.	וַיִּשְׁלַח	וַיִּשָּׁלַח	וַיְשַׁלַּח		וַיַּשְׁלַח		
Perf. ,,	וְשָׁלַחְתָּ						
Imper. sg. 2. m.	שְׁלַח	הִשָּׁלַח	שַׁלַּח		הַשְׁלַח		הִשְׁתַּלַּח
2. f.	שִׁלְחִי	הִשָּׁלְחִי	שַׁלְּחִי	wanting	הַשְׁלִיחִי	wanting	הִשְׁתַּלְּחִי
pl. 2. m.	שִׁלְחוּ	הִשָּׁלְחוּ	שַׁלְּחוּ		הַשְׁלִיחוּ		הִשְׁתַּלְּחוּ
2. f.	שְׁלַחְנָה	הִשָּׁלַחְנָה	שַׁלַּחְנָה		הַשְׁלַחְנָה		הִשְׁתַּלַּחְנָה
Part. (*act*.) sg. m.	שֹׁלֵחַ		מְשַׁלֵּחַ		מַשְׁלִיחַ		
,, (*pass*.) ,,	שָׁלוּחַ	נִשְׁלָח		מְשֻׁלָּח		מָשְׁלָח	מִשְׁתַּלֵּחַ
Inf. *absolute*	שָׁלוֹחַ	נִשְׁלֹחַ	שַׁלֵּחַ		הַשְׁלֵחַ	הָשְׁלֵחַ	הִשְׁתַּלַּח
,, *construct*	שְׁלֹחַ	הִשָּׁלַח	שַׁלַּח		הַשְׁלִיחַ		

[1] See pp. 172 ff.

[2] With suffix יִשְׁלָחֵנִי.

[3] Shortened Imperfect.

[4] Transposition of sibilant first root-letter שׁ with ת of Hithpa'el prefixed particle: p. 120, Note.

LAMED 'ALEP VERBS [1]

	Qal Active	Qal Stative	Niph'al	Pi'el	Pu'al	Hiph'il	Hoph'al	Hithpa'el
Perf. sg. 3. m.	מָצָא	מָלֵא	נִמְצָא	מִצֵּא	מֻצָּא	הִמְצִיא	הֻמְצָא	הִתְמַצֵּא
3. f.	מָצְאָה	מָלְאָה	נִמְצְאָה	מִצְּאָה	מֻצְּאָה	הִמְצִיאָה	הֻמְצְאָה	הִתְמַצְּאָה
2. m.	מָצָאתָ	מָלֵאתָ	נִמְצֵאתָ	מִצֵּאתָ	מֻצֵּאתָ	הִמְצֵאתָ	הֻמְצֵאתָ	הִתְמַצֵּאתָ
2. f.	מָצָאת	מָלֵאת	נִמְצֵאת	מִצֵּאת	מֻצֵּאת	הִמְצֵאת	הֻמְצֵאת	הִתְמַצֵּאת
1. c.	מָצָאתִי	מָלֵאתִי	נִמְצֵאתִי	מִצֵּאתִי	מֻצֵּאתִי	הִמְצֵאתִי	הֻמְצֵאתִי	הִתְמַצֵּאתִי
pl. 3. c.	מָצְאוּ	מָלְאוּ	נִמְצְאוּ			הִמְצִיאוּ		
2. m.	מְצָאתֶם	מְלֵאתֶם	נִמְצֵאתֶם	&c. as Niph'al	&c. as Niph'al	הִמְצֵאתֶם	&c. as Niph'al	&c. as Niph'al
2. f.	מְצָאתֶן	מְלֵאתֶן	נִמְצֵאתֶן			הִמְצֵאתֶן		
1. c.	מָצָאנוּ	מָלֵאנוּ	נִמְצֵאנוּ			הִמְצֵאנוּ		
Imperf. sg. 3. m.	יִמְצָא [2]		יִמָּצֵא	יְמַצֵּא	יְמֻצָּא	יַמְצִיא	יֻמְצָא	יִתְמַצֵּא
3. f.	תִּמְצָא		תִּמָּצֵא	תְּמַצֵּא	תְּמֻצָּא	תַּמְצִיא	תֻּמְצָא	תִּתְמַצֵּא
2. m.	תִּמְצָא		תִּמָּצֵא	תְּמַצֵּא	תְּמֻצָּא	תַּמְצִיא	תֻּמְצָא	תִּתְמַצֵּא
2. f.	תִּמְצְאִי		תִּמָּצְאִי	תְּמַצְּאִי	תְּמֻצְּאִי	תַּמְצִיאִי	תֻּמְצְאִי	תִּתְמַצְּאִי
1. c.	אֶמְצָא		אֶמָּצֵא	אֲמַצֵּא	אֲמֻצָּא	אַמְצִיא	אֻמְצָא	אֶתְמַצֵּא
pl. 3. m.	יִמְצְאוּ		יִמָּצְאוּ	&c. as Niph'al	&c. as Qal	יַמְצִיאוּ	&c. as Qal	&c. as Niph'al
3. f.	תִּמְצֶאנָה		תִּמָּצֶאנָה			תַּמְצֶאנָה		

2. m.	תִּמְצְאוּ	תִּמָּצְאוּ			תַּמְצִיאוּ		
2. f.	תִּמְצֶאנָה	תִּמָּצֶאנָה			תַּמְצֶאנָה		
1. c.	נִמְצָא	נִמָּצֵא			נַמְצִיא		
Cohort. sg. 1. c.	אֶמְצְאָה	אִמָּצְאָה			אַמְצִיאָה		
Jussive sg. 3. m	יִמְצָא	יִמָּצֵא			יַמְצֵא[4]		
Impf. & ו *consec*.	וַיִּמְצָא	וַיִּמָּצֵא			וַיַּמְצֵא		
Perf. ,,	וּמָצָאתָ						
Imper. sg. 2. m.	מְצָא	הִמָּצֵא	מַצֵּא	wanting	הַמְצֵא	wanting	הִתְמַצֵּא
2. f.	מִצְאִי	הִמָּצְאִי	מַצְּאִי		הַמְצִיאִי		הִתְמַצְּאִי
pl. 2. m.	מִצְאוּ	הִמָּצְאוּ	&c. as Niph'al		הַמְצִיאוּ		&c. as Niph'al
2. f.	מְצֶאנָה	הִמָּצֶאנָה			הַמְצֶאנָה		
Part. (*act*.) sg. m.	מֹצֵא[3]		מְמַצֵּא		מַמְצִיא		מִתְמַצֵּא
,, (*pass*.) ,,	מָצוּא	נִמְצָא		מְמֻצָּא		מֻמְצָא	
Inf. *absolute*	מָצוֹא	נִמְצֹא	מַצֹּא	wanting	הַמְצֵא	הָמְצָא	הִתְמַצֵּא
,, *construct*	מְצֹא	הִמָּצֵא	מַצֵּא		הַמְצִיא		

[1] See pp. 178 ff.

[2] With suffix יִמְצָאֻנִי, יִמְצָאֲךָ, יִמְצָאֵהוּ &c.

[3] Participle Active of the Stative is מָלֵא.

[4] Shortened Imperfect.

PE WAW AND PE YOD̲ VERBS [1]

	ORIGINAL PE WAW				ORIGINAL PE YOD̲	
	QAL	NIPH'AL	HIPH'IL	HOPH'AL	QAL	HIPH'IL
Perf. sg. 3. m.	יָשַׁב	נוֹשַׁב	הוֹשִׁיב	הוּשַׁב	יָטַב	הֵיטִיב
3. f.	יָֽשְׁבָה	נוֹשְׁבָה	הוֹשִׁיבָה	הוּשְׁבָה		הֵיטִיבָה
2. m.	יָשַׁבְתָּ	נוֹשַׁבְתָּ	הוֹשַׁבְתָּ	הוּשַׁבְתָּ		הֵיטַבְתָּ
2. f.		נוֹשַׁבְתְּ	הוֹשַׁבְתְּ	הוּשַׁבְתְּ		הֵיטַבְתְּ
1. c.		נוֹשַׁבְתִּי	הוֹשַׁבְתִּי	הוּשַׁבְתִּי		הֵיטַבְתִּי
pl. 3. c.	&c. (regular)	נוֹשְׁבוּ	הוֹשִׁיבוּ	הוּשְׁבוּ	&c. (regular)	הֵיטִיבוּ
2. m.		נוֹשַׁבְתֶּם	הוֹשַׁבְתֶּם	הוּשַׁבְתֶּם		הֵיטַבְתֶּם
2. f.		נוֹשַׁבְתֶּן	הוֹשַׁבְתֶּן	הוּשַׁבְתֶּן		הֵיטַבְתֶּן
1. c.		נוֹשַׁבְנוּ	הוֹשַׁבְנוּ	הוּשַׁבְנוּ		הֵיטַבְנוּ
Imperf. sg. 3. m.	יֵשֵׁב [2]	יִוָּשֵׁב	יוֹשִׁיב	יוּשַׁב	יִיטַב	יֵיטִיב
3. f.	תֵּשֵׁב	תִּוָּשֵׁב	תּוֹשִׁיב	תּוּשַׁב	תִּיטַב	תֵּיטִיב
2. m.	תֵּשֵׁב	תִּוָּשֵׁב	תּוֹשִׁיב	תּוּשַׁב	תִּיטַב	תֵּיטִיב
2. f.	תֵּשְׁבִי	תִּוָּשְׁבִי	תּוֹשִׁיבִי	תּוּשְׁבִי	תִּיטְבִי	תֵּיטִיבִי
1. c.	אֵשֵׁב	אִוָּשֵׁב	אוֹשִׁיב	אוּשַׁב	אִיטַב	אֵיטִיב
pl. 3. m.	יֵשְׁבוּ	יִוָּשְׁבוּ	יוֹשִׁיבוּ	יוּשְׁבוּ	יִיטְבוּ	יֵיטִיבוּ
3. f.	תֵּשַׁבְנָה	תִּוָּשַׁבְנָה	(תּוֹשֵׁבְנָה)	תּוּשַׁבְנָה	תִּיטַבְנָה	תֵּיטַבְנָה

2. m.	תֵּשְׁבוּ	תִּוָּשְׁבוּ	תּוֹשִׁיבוּ	תּוּשְׁבוּ	תִּיטְבוּ	תֵּיטִיבוּ
2. f.	תֵּשַׁבְנָה	תִּוָּשַׁבְנָה	(תּוֹשֵׁבְנָה)	תּוּשַׁבְנָה	תִּיטַבְנָה	תֵּיטֵבְנָה
1. c.	נֵשֵׁב	נִוָּשֵׁב	נוֹשִׁיב	נוּשַׁב	נִיטַב	נֵיטִיב
Cohort. sg. 1. c.	אֵשְׁבָה					
Jussive sg. 3. m.	יֵשֵׁב		יוֹשֵׁב [7]		יִיטַב	יֵיטֵב [7]
Impf. & ו *consec.*	וַיֵּשֶׁב [3]		וַיּוֹשֶׁב [3]		וַיִּיטַב	וַיֵּיטֶב [3]
Perf. ,,	וְיָשַׁבְתָּ					
Imper. sg. 2. m.	שֵׁב [4] (שְׁבָה)[5]	הִוָּשֵׁב	הוֹשֵׁב	wanting		הֵיטֵב
2. f.	שְׁבִי	הִוָּשְׁבִי	הוֹשִׁיבִי			הֵיטִיבִי
pl. 2. m.	שְׁבוּ	הִוָּשְׁבוּ	הוֹשִׁיבוּ			הֵיטִיבוּ
2. f.	שֵׁבְנָה	הִוָּשַׁבְנָה	הוֹשֵׁבְנָה			הֵיטֵבְנָה
Part. (*act.*) sg. m.	יֹשֵׁב		מוֹשִׁיב		יֹטֵב	מֵיטִיב
,, (*pass.*) ,,	יָשׁוּב	נוֹשָׁב		מוּשָׁב	יָטוּב	
Inf. absolute	יָשׁוֹב	הִוָּשֵׁב	הוֹשֵׁב	הוּשַׁב	יָטוֹב	הֵיטֵב
,, *construct*	שֶׁבֶת[6]		הוֹשִׁיב		(יְטֹב)	הֵיטִיב

[1] See pp. 187 ff. [2] But from יָרַשׁ the Imperfect is יִירַשׁ, תִּירַשׁ &c. [3] Accent is retarded, hence the last syllable, being closed and now unaccented, shortens its vowel. [4] But from יָרַשׁ the Imperative is רַשׁ. [5] Long form of Imperative. [6] With ל לָשֶׁבֶת. [7] Shortened Imperfect.

'AYIN WAW AND 'AYIN YOD VERBS[1]

	'AYIN WAW						'AYIN YOD
	QAL			NIPH'AL	HIPH'IL	HOPH'AL	QAL
	Active	*Stative*					
Perf. sg. 3. m.	קָם	מֵת	בּוֹשׁ	נָקוֹם	הֵקִים	הוּקַם	שָׂם
3. f.	קָמָה	מֵתָה	בּוֹשָׁה	נָקוֹמָה	הֵקִימָה	הוּקְמָה	שָׂמָה
2. m.	קַמְתָּ	מַתָּה [2]	בֹּשְׁתָּ	נְקוּמוֹתָ	הֲקִימוֹתָ [7]	הוּקַמְתָּ	שַׂמְתָּ
2. f.	קַמְתְּ	מַתְּ	בֹּשְׁתְּ	נְקוּמוֹת	הֲקִימוֹת	הוּקַמְתְּ	
1. c.	קַמְתִּי	מַתִּי	בֹּשְׁתִּי	נְקוּמוֹתִי	הֲקִימוֹתִי	הוּקַמְתִּי	
pl. 3. c.	קָמוּ	מֵתוּ	בּוֹשׁוּ	נָקוֹמוּ	הֵקִימוּ	הוּקְמוּ	&c. as קָם
2. m.	קַמְתֶּם	מַתֶּם	בָּשְׁתֶּם	נְקוּמוֹתֶם [6]	הֲקִימוֹתֶם	הוּקַמְתֶּם	
2. f.	קַמְתֶּן	מַתֶּן	בָּשְׁתֶּן	נְקוּמוֹתֶן	הֲקִימוֹתֶן	הוּקַמְתֶּן	
1. c.	קַמְנוּ	מַתְנוּ	בֹּשְׁנוּ	נְקוּמוֹנוּ	הֲקִימוֹנוּ	הוּקַמְנוּ	
Imperf. sg. 3. m.	יָקוּם	יָמוּת	יֵבוֹשׁ	יִקּוֹם	יָקִים	יוּקַם	יָשִׂים [9]
3. f.	תָּקוּם		תֵּבוֹשׁ	תִּקּוֹם	תָּקִים	תּוּקַם	תָּשִׂים
2. m.	תָּקוּם		תֵּבוֹשׁ	תִּקּוֹם	תָּקִים	תּוּקַם	תָּשִׂים
2. f.	תָּקוּמִי	&c.	תֵּבוֹשִׁי	תִּקּוֹמִי	תָּקִימִי	תּוּקְמִי	תָּשִׂימִי
1. c.	אָקוּם		אֵבוֹשׁ	אֶקּוֹם	אָקִים	אוּקַם	אָשִׂים
pl. 3. m.	יָקוּמוּ		יֵבוֹשׁוּ	יִקּוֹמוּ	יָקִימוּ	יוּקְמוּ	יָשִׂימוּ
3. f.	תְּקוּמֶינָה		תֵּבֹשְׁנָה	—	תָּקֵמְנָה [8]	תּוּקַמְנָה	תְּשִׂימֶינָה [10]

2. m.	תְּקוּמוּ		תֵּבוֹשׁוּ	תִּקּוֹמוּ	תָּקִימוּ	תּוּקְמוּ	תָּשִׂימוּ
2. f.	תְּקוּמֶינָה		תֵּבֹשְׁנָה	—	תָּקֵמְנָה	תּוּקַמְנָה	תָּשִׂימֶינָה[10]
1. c.	נָקוּם		נֵבוֹשׁ	נִקּוֹם	נָקִים	נוּקַם	נָשִׂים
Cohort. sg. 1. c.	אָקוּמָה	אָמוּתָה	אֵבוֹשָׁה		אָקִימָה		אָשִׂימָה
Jussive sg. 3. m.	יָקֹם[3]	יָמֹת[3]	יֵבוֹשׁ		יָקֵם[3]		יָשֵׂם[3]
Impf. & ו *consec*.	וַיָּקָם[4]	וַיָּמָת[4]	וַיֵּבוֹשׁ		וַיָּקֶם[4]		וַיָּשֶׂם[4]
Perf. ,,	וְקַמְתָּ				וַהֲקִימֹתָ		וְשַׂמְתָּ
Imper. sg. 2. m.	קוּם	מוּת	בּוֹשׁ	הִקּוֹם	הָקֵם	wanting	שִׂים
2. f.	קוּמִי	&c.	בּוֹשִׁי	הִקּוֹמִי	הָקִימִי		שִׂימִי
pl. 2. m.	קוּמוּ		בּוֹשׁוּ	הִקּוֹמוּ	הָקִימוּ		שִׂימוּ
2. f.	קֹמְנָה		בֹּשְׁנָה	הִקֹּמְנָה	הָקֵמְנָה		
Part. (*act*.) sg. m.	קָם	מֵת	בּוֹשׁ	נָקוֹם	מֵקִים		שָׂם
,, (*pass*.) ,,	קוּם			(f. נְקוֹמָה)		מוּקָם	
Inf. *absolute*	קוֹם	מוֹת			הָקֵם	הוּקַם	שׂוֹם
,, *construct*	קוּם[5]	מוּת[5]	בּוֹשׁ	הִקּוֹם	הָקִים		שִׂים

[1] See pp. 196 ff. [2] For מַתְּתָּ &c. [3] Shortened Imperfect. [4] The accent is retarded, so that the last syllable, being closed and now unaccented, reduces its vowel. N.B. pausal וַיָּקֹם, וַיָּמֹת. [5] With ל לָמוּת, לָקוּם. [6] Found in the form נְקוֹמֹתֶם. [7] Also found as הֲקִימוֹתָ &c. [8] Also תְּקִימֶינָה. [9] Also found as יָשׂוּם. [10] Or תָּשֵׂמְנָה.

LAMED̲ HE VERB [1]

	Qal	Niph'al	Pi'el	Pu'al	Hiph'il	Hoph'al	Hithpa'el
Perf. sg. 3. m.	גָּלָה [2]	נִגְלָה	גִּלָּה	גֻּלָּה	הִגְלָה	הָגְלָה	הִתְגַּלָּה
3. f.	גָּלְתָה	נִגְלְתָה	גִּלְּתָה	גֻּלְּתָה	הִגְלְתָה	הָגְלְתָה	הִתְגַּלְּתָה
2. m.	גָּלִיתָ	נִגְלֵיתָ	גִּלִּיתָ [7]	גֻּלֵּיתָ	הִגְלִיתָ [7]	הָגְלֵיתָ	הִתְגַּלִּיתָ [7]
2. f.	גָּלִית	נִגְלֵית	גִּלִּית	&c.	&c.	&c.	&c.
1. c.	גָּלִיתִי	נִגְלֵיתִי	גִּלִּיתִי [7]				
pl. 3. c.	גָּלוּ	נִגְלוּ	&c.				
2. m.	גְּלִיתֶם	נִגְלֵיתֶם					
2. f.	גְּלִיתֶן	נִגְלֵיתֶן					
1. c.	גָּלִינוּ	נִגְלֵינוּ					
Imperf. sg. 3. m.	יִגְלֶה [3]	יִגָּלֶה	יְגַלֶּה	יְגֻלֶּה	יַגְלֶה	יָגְלֶה	יִתְגַּלֶּה
3. f.	תִּגְלֶה	תִּגָּלֶה	תְּגַלֶּה	תְּגֻלֶּה	תַּגְלֶה	תָּגְלֶה	תִּתְגַּלֶּה
2. m.	תִּגְלֶה	תִּגָּלֶה					
2. f.	תִּגְלִי	תִּגָּלִי	&c.	&c.	&c.	&c.	&c.
1. c.	אֶגְלֶה	אֶגָּלֶה					
pl. 3. m.	יִגְלוּ	יִגָּלוּ					
3. f.	תִּגְלֶינָה	תִּגָּלֶינָה					

2. m.	תִּגְלוּ	תִּגָּלוּ					
2. f.	תִּגְלֶינָה	תִּגָּלֶינָה					
1. c.	נִגְלֶה	נִגָּלֶה					
Jussive sg. 3. m.	יִגֶל [4]	יִגָּל [4]	יְגַל [4]		יֶגֶל [4]		יִתְגַּל [4]
Impf. & ו *consec.*	וַיִּגֶל	וַיִּגָּל	וַיְגַל	וַיְגֻלֶּה	וַיֶּגֶל		וַיִּתְגַּל
Perf. ,,	וְגָלִיתָ	וְנִגְלֵיתָ					
Imper. sg. 2. m.	גְּלֵה	הִגָּלֵה	גַּלֵּה [8]	wanting	הַגְלֵה	wanting	הִתְגַּלֵּה [9]
2. f.	גְּלִי	הִגָּלִי	גַּלִּי		הַגְלִי		הִתְגַּלִּי
pl. 2. m.	גְּלוּ	הִגָּלוּ	גַּלּוּ		&c.		&c.
2. f.	גְּלֶינָה	הִגָּלֶינָה	גַּלֶּינָה				
Part. (*act.*) sg. m.	גֹּלֶה [5]	נִגְלֶה	מְגַלֶּה		מַגְלֶה		מִתְגַּלֶּה
(*pass.*) ,,	גָּלוּי [6]			מְגֻלֶּה		מָגְלֶה	
Inf. absolute	גָּלֹה	נִגְלֹה	גַּלֵּה	גֻּלֹּה	הַגְלֵה	הָגְלֵה	הִתְגַּלֵּה
,, *construct*	גְּלוֹת	הִגָּלוֹת	גַּלּוֹת	גֻּלּוֹת	הַגְלוֹת	הָגְלוֹת	הִתְגַּלּוֹת

[1] Original Lamed Yod or Lamed Waw (see pp. 216 ff.).
[2] With suffix גָּלְנִי, גֵּלְךָ &c.
[3] With suffix יַגְלֵנִי.
[4] Shortened Imperfect.
[5] f. sg. גֹּלָה, m. pl. גֹּלִים.
[6] f. sg. גְּלוּיָה, m. pl. גְּלוּיִם.
[7] Often with *ê* in penultimate syllable.
[8] Sometimes גַּל.
[9] Sometimes הִתְגַּל.

DOUBLE 'AYIN VERB [1]

	Qal: Active		Qal: Stative	Niph'al	Hiph'il		Hoph'al	
Perf. sg. 3. m.	סַב	סָבַב	קַל	נָסַב		הֵסֵב		הוּסַב
3. f.	סַבָּה	סָבְבָה	קַלָּה	נָסַבָּה		הֵסֵבָּה		הוּסַבָּה
2. m.		סַבּוֹתָ	קַלּוֹתָ	נְסַבּוֹתָ		הֲסִבּוֹתָ		הוּסַבּוֹתָ
2. f.		סַבּוֹת	קַלּוֹת	נְסַבּוֹת		הֲסִבּוֹת		הוּסַבּוֹת
1. c.		סַבּוֹתִי	קַלּוֹתִי	נְסַבּוֹתִי		הֲסִבּוֹתִי		הוּסַבּוֹתִי
pl. 3. c.	סַבּוּ	סָבְבוּ	קַלּוּ	נָסַבּוּ		הֵסֵבּוּ		
2. m.		סַבּוֹתֶם	קַלּוֹתֶם	נְסַבּוֹתֶם		הֲסִבּוֹתֶם		&c.
2. f.		סַבּוֹתֶן	קַלּוֹתֶן	נְסַבּוֹתֶן		הֲסִבּוֹתֶן		
1. c.		סַבּוֹנוּ	קַלּוֹנוּ	נְסַבּוֹנוּ		הֲסִבּוֹנוּ		
Imperf. sg. 3. m.	יָסֹב [2]	יִסֹּב	יֵקַל [5]	יִסַּב	יַסֵּב	יָסֵב	יֻסַּב	יוּסַב
3. f.	תָּסֹב	תִּסֹּב	תֵּקַל	תִּסַּב		תָּסֵב		תּוּסַב
2. m.	תָּסֹב	תִּסֹּב	תֵּקַל	תִּסַּב		תָּסֵב		
2. f.	תָּסֹבִּי	תִּסְּבִי	תֵּקַלִּי	תִּסַּבִּי		תָּסֵבִּי		
1. c.	אָסֹב	אֶסֹּב	אֵקַל	אֶסַּב		אָסֵב		
pl. 3. m.	יָסֹבּוּ	יִסְּבוּ	יֵקַלּוּ	יִסַּבּוּ	יַסֵּבּוּ	יָסֵבּוּ		
3. f.	תְּסֻבֶּינָה	תִּסֹּבְנָה	תְּקַלֶּינָה	תִּסַּבֶּינָה		תְּסִבֶּינָה		&c.

2. m.	תָּסֹבּוּ	תִּסֹּבוּ	תֵּקַלּוּ	תִּסַּבּוּ	תָּסֵבּוּ	
2. f.	תְּסֻבֶּינָה	תִּסֹּבְנָה	תְּקַלֶּינָה	תִּסַּבֶּינָה	תְּסִבֶּינָה	
1. c.	נָסֹב	נִסֹּב	נֵקַל	נִסַּב	נָסֵב	
Cohort. sg. 1. c.	אָסֹבָּה	אֶסְּבָה				
Jussive sg. 3. m.	יָסֹב	יִסֹּב	יֵקַל	יִסַּב	יָסֵב	
Impf. & ו *consec*.	וַיָּסָב [3]	וַיִּסֹּב	וַיֵּקַל	וַיִּסַּב	וַיָּסֶב [3]	
Perf. ,,	וְסַבֹּתָ					
Imper. sg. 2. m.	סֹב			הִסַּב	הָסֵב	
2. f.	סֹבִּי			הִסַּבִּי	הָסֵבִּי	wanting
pl. 2. m.	סֹבּוּ			הִסַּבּוּ	הָסֵבּוּ	
2. f.	סֻבֶּינָה			הִסַּבֶּינָה	הֲסִבֶּינָה	
Part. (*act*.) sg. m.	סֹבֵב		קַל [6]	נָסָב [7]	מֵסֵב [8]	
,, (*pass*.) ,,	סָבוּב					מוּסָב
Inf. *absolute*	סָבוֹב			הִסּוֹב		
,, *construct*	סֹב [4]			הִסַּב	הָסֵב	הוּסַב

[1] See pp. 231 ff. [2] With suffix יְסֻבֵּנִי &c. [3] Accent is retarded; therefore the final syllable, being closed and now unaccented, shortens its vowel. [4] With ל לָסֹב. [5] But יִמַּל &c. [6] F. sg. קַלָּה. [7] F. sg. נְסַבָּה. [8] F. sg. מְסִבָּה.

DOUBLY WEAK VERBS

	PE NUN AND LAMEḎ GUTTURAL[1]				PE NUN AND LAMEḎ 'ALEP̱[2]		
	Qal	Niph'al	Hiph'il	Pi'el	Qal	Niph'al	Hiph'il
Perf.	נָגַע	נִגַּע	הִגִּיעַ	נִגַּע	נָשָׂא	נִשָּׂא	הִשִּׂיא
Imperf.	יִגַּע	&c. As Lameḏ Guttural	יַגִּיעַ	יְנַגַּע	יִשָּׂא	&c. As Lameḏ 'Alep̱	יַשִּׂיא
Short. Imperf.			יַגַּע	&c. As Lameḏ Guttural			
Imper.	גַּע		הַגַּע		שָׂא		הַשֵּׂא
Part.	נֹגֵעַ		מַגִּיעַ		נֹשֵׂא		מַשִּׂיא
Inf. absolute	נָגוֹעַ		הַגֵּעַ		נָשׂוֹא		הַשֵּׂא
Inf. construct	נְגֹעַ גַּעַת		הַגִּיעַ		שְׂאֵת[6]		הַשִּׂיא

	PE NUN AND LAMED HE[3]			PE GUTTURAL AND LAMED 'ALEP[4]		
	QAL	HIPH'IL	HOPH'AL	QAL	NIPH'AL	HIPH'IL
Perf.	נָטָה (נכה)[5]	הִכָּה הִטָּה	הֻכָּה הֻטָּה	חָטָא (חבא)[5]	נֶחְבָּא	הֶחְבִּיא הֶחֱטִיא
Imperf.	יִטֶּה	יַכֶּה יַטֶּה	יֻכֶּה	יֶחֱטָא	יֵחָבֵא	יַחְבִּיא יַחֲטִיא
Short. Imperf.	יֵט	יַךְ יַט				יַחֲטָא
Imper.	נְטֵה	הַכֵּה הַטֵּה		חֲטָא	הֵחָבֵא	הַחְבֵּא הַחֲטֵא
Part.	נֹטֶה	מַכֶּה מַטֶּה	מֻכֶּה	חֹטֵא	נֶחְבָּא	מַחְבִּיא מַחֲטִיא
Inf. absolute	נָטֹה	הַכֵּה הַטֵּה	הֻכֵּה	חָטוֹא		הַחְבֵּא הַחֲטֵא
Inf. construct	נְטוֹת	הַכּוֹת הַטּוֹת	הֻכּוֹת	חֲטֹא[7]	הֵחָבֵא	הַחְבִּיא הַחֲטִיא

1 See p. 184 (*a*).
2 See p. 185 (*c*).
3 See p. 224 (*a*).
4 See p. 184 f. B.
5 Not used in Qal.
6 With prefixed ל לָשֵׂאת.
7 With prefixed ל לַחֲטֹא.

DOUBLY WEAK VERBS (*continued*)

	PE GUTTURAL AND LAMEḎ HE[1]			PE 'ALEP̱ AND LAMEḎ HE[2]	
	QAL	NIPH'AL	HIPH'IL	QAL	NIPH'AL
Perf.	עָלָה עָשָׂה	נֶעֱלָה נֶעֱשָׂה	הֶעֱלָה	אָפָה	נֶאֱפָה
Imperf.	יַעֲלֶה יַעֲשֶׂה	יֵעָשֶׂה	יַעֲלֶה	יֹאפֶה	יֵאָפֶה
Short. Imperf.	יַ֫עַל[5] יַ֫עַשׂ	יֵעָשׂ	יַ֫עַל[5]		
Imper.	עֲלֵה עֲשֵׂה	הֵעָשֵׂה	הַ֫עַל הַעֲלֵה	אֱפֵה	
Part.	עֹלֶה עֹשֶׂה	נַעֲשֶׂה	מַעֲלֶה	אֹפֶה	
Inf. absolute	עָלֹה עָשׂה	נַעֲשׂה	הַעֲלֵה	אָפֹה	
Inf. construct	עֲלוֹת[6] עֲשׂוֹת[6]	הֵעָשׂוֹת	הַעֲלוֹת	אֱפוֹת	הֵאָפוֹת

PE WAW AND LAMED GUTTURAL[3] / PE WAW AND LAMED 'ALEP[4]

	Qal	Niph'al	Hiph'il	Hoph'al	Hithpa'el	Qal	Hiph'il	Hoph'al
Perf.	יָדַע	נוֹדַע	הוֹדִיעַ	הוֹדַע	הִתְוַדַּע	יָצָא	הוֹצִיא	הוּצָא
Imperf.	יֵדַע	יִוָּדַע	יוֹדִיעַ		יִתְוַדַּע	יֵצֵא	יוֹצִיא	יוּצָא
Short. Imperf.			יוֹדַע				יוֹצֵא	
Imper.	דַּע	הִוָּדַע	הוֹדַע		הִתְוַדַּע	צֵא	הוֹצֵא	
Part.	יֹדֵעַ	נוֹדָע	מוֹדִיעַ	מוּדָע	מִתְוַדַּע	יֹצֵא	מוֹצִיא	מוּצָא
Inf. absolute	יָדוֹעַ		הוֹדֵעַ			יָצוֹא	הוֹצֵא	
Inf. construct	דַּעַת [7]	הִוָּדַע	הוֹדִיעַ		הִתְוַדַּע	צֵאת [8]	הוֹצִיא	

'AYIN WAW AND LAMED 'ALEP[9]

	Qal	Hiph'il	Hoph'al		Qal	Hiph'il	Hoph'al
Perf.	בָּא	הֵבִיא	הוּבָא	*Part.*	בָּא	מֵבִיא	מוּבָא
Imperf.	יָבֹא	יָבִיא	יוּבָא	*Inf. absolute*	בּוֹא	הָבֵא	
Short. Imperf.		יָבֵא		*Inf. construct*	בֹּא [10]	הָבִיא	(הוּבָא)
Imper.	בֹּא	הָבֵא					

[1] See pp. 225 ff. (*b*). [2] See p. 227 (*c*). [3] See p. 210 f. (*a*). [4] See p. 212 (*c*).
[5] The context determines whether יַעֲל is Qal or Hiphil. [6] With prefixed ל לַעֲשׂוֹת, לַעֲלוֹת.
[7] With prefixed ל לָדַעַת. [8] With prefixed ל לָצֵאת. [9] See p. 212 (*d*). [10] With prefixed ל לָבֹא.

MASCULINE NOUNS

	I		II					III	
	UNCHANGEABLE VOWELS		CHANGEABLE QAMEṢ					CHANGEABLE ṢERE	
Sing.	(horse)	(just man)	(star)	(tower)	(overseer)	(word)	(wise man)	(heart)	(enemy)
abs.	סוּס [1]	צַדִּיק	כּוֹכָב	מִגְדָּל	פָּקִיד	דָּבָר	חָכָם [6]	לֵבָב	אֹיֵב
cons.	סוּס [1]	צַדִּיק	כּוֹכַב	מִגְדַּל	פְּקִיד [3]	דְּבַר	חֲכַם	לְבַב	אֹיֵב
my (c.)	סוּסִי	צַדִּיקִי	כּוֹכָבִי	מִגְדָּלִי	פְּקִידִי [4]	דְּבָרִי	חֲכָמִי	לְבָבִי	אֹיְבִי
thy (m.)	סוּסְךָ [2]	צַדִּיקְךָ	כּוֹכָבְךָ	&c.	פְּקִידְךָ	דְּבָרְךָ	חֲכָמְךָ	לְבָבְךָ	אֹיִבְךָ
thy (f.)	סוּסֵךְ	צַדִּיקֵךְ	כּוֹכָבֵךְ		פְּקִידֵךְ	דְּבָרֵךְ	חֲכָמֵךְ	לְבָבֵךְ	אֹיְבֵךְ
his	סוּסוֹ	צַדִּיקוֹ	כּוֹכָבוֹ		פְּקִידוֹ	דְּבָרוֹ	חֲכָמוֹ	לְבָבוֹ	אֹיְבוֹ
her	סוּסָהּ	צַדִּיקָהּ	כּוֹכָבָהּ		פְּקִידָהּ	דְּבָרָהּ	חֲכָמָהּ	לְבָבָהּ	אֹיְבָהּ
our (c.)	סוּסֵ֫נוּ	צַדִּיקֵ֫נוּ	כּוֹכָבֵ֫נוּ		פְּקִידֵ֫נוּ	דְּבָרֵ֫נוּ	חֲכָמֵ֫נוּ	לְבָבֵ֫נוּ	אֹיְבֵ֫נוּ
your (m.)	סוּסְכֶם [2]	צַדִּיקְכֶם	כּוֹכַבְכֶם	מִגְדַּלְכֶם	פְּקִידְכֶם	דְּבַרְכֶם	חֲכַמְכֶם	לְבַבְכֶם	אֹיִבְכֶם
your (f.)	סוּסְכֶן [2]	צַדִּיקְכֶן	כּוֹכַבְכֶן	&c.	פְּקִידְכֶן	דְּבַרְכֶן	חֲכַמְכֶן	לְבַבְכֶן	אֹיִבְכֶן
their (m.)	סוּסָם	צַדִּיקָם	כּוֹכָבָם		פְּקִידָם	דְּבָרָם	חֲכָמָם	לְבָבָם	אֹיְבָם
their (f.)	סוּסָן	צַדִּיקָן	כּוֹכָבָן		פְּקִידָן	דְּבָרָן	חֲכָמָן	לְבָבָן	אֹיְבָן

Plur.	(horses)	(just men)	(stars)	(towers)	(overseers)	(words)	(wise men)	(enemies)
abs.	סוּסִים	צַדִּיקִים	כּוֹכָבִים	מִגְדָּלִים	פְּקִידִים[5]	דְּבָרִים	חֲכָמִים	אֹיְבִים
cons.	סוּסֵי	צַדִּיקֵי	כּוֹכְבֵי	מִגְדְּלֵי	פְּקִידֵי	דִּבְרֵי	חַכְמֵי	אֹיְבֵי
my (c.)	סוּסַי	צַדִּיקַי	כּוֹכָבַי	מִגְדָּלַי	פְּקִידַי	דְּבָרַי	חֲכָמַי	אֹיְבַי
thy (m.)	סוּסֶיךָ	צַדִּיקֶיךָ	כּוֹכָבֶיךָ	&c.	פְּקִידֶיךָ	דְּבָרֶיךָ	חֲכָמֶיךָ	אֹיְבֶיךָ
thy (f.)	סוּסַיִךְ	צַדִּיקַיִךְ	כּוֹכָבַיִךְ		פְּקִידַיִךְ	דְּבָרַיִךְ	חֲכָמַיִךְ	אֹיְבַיִךְ
his	סוּסָיו	צַדִּיקָיו	כּוֹכָבָיו		פְּקִידָיו	דְּבָרָיו	חֲכָמָיו	אֹיְבָיו
her	סוּסֶיהָ	צַדִּיקֶיהָ	כּוֹכָבֶיהָ		פְּקִידֶיהָ	דְּבָרֶיהָ	חֲכָמֶיהָ	אֹיְבֶיהָ
our (c.)	סוּסֵינוּ	צַדִּיקֵינוּ	כּוֹכָבֵינוּ		פְּקִידֵינוּ	דְּבָרֵינוּ	חֲכָמֵינוּ	אֹיְבֵינוּ
your (m.)	סוּסֵיכֶם	צַדִּיקֵיכֶם	כּוֹכְבֵיכֶם	מִגְדְּלֵיכֶם	פְּקִידֵיכֶם	דִּבְרֵיכֶם	חַכְמֵיכֶם	אֹיְבֵיכֶם
your (f.)	סוּסֵיכֶן	צַדִּיקֵיכֶן	כּוֹכְבֵיכֶן	&c.	פְּקִידֵיכֶן	דִּבְרֵיכֶן	חַכְמֵיכֶן	אֹיְבֵיכֶן
their (m.)	סוּסֵיהֶם	צַדִּיקֵיהֶם	כּוֹכְבֵיהֶם		פְּקִידֵיהֶם	דִּבְרֵיהֶם	חַכְמֵיהֶם	אֹיְבֵיהֶם
their (f.)	סוּסֵיהֶן	צַדִּיקֵיהֶן	כּ כְבֵיהֶן		פְּקִידֵיהֶן	דִּבְרֵיהֶן	חַכְמֵיהֶן	אֹיְבֵיהֶן

[1] But רוּחַ (p. 19. 4).

[2] רוּחֲכֶם, רוּחֲךָ &c.

[3] But construct of אָסִיר is אֲסִיר.

[4] אָסִיר with suffix אֲסִירִי &c.

[5] Plural of אָסִיר אֲסִירִים.

[6] Same as דָּבָר but with initial guttural.

MASCULINE NOUNS (*continued*)

	IV					
	SEGHOLATES			GUTTURAL SEGHOLATES		
Sing.	(king)	(book)	(holiness)	(lad)	(eternity)	(work)
abs.	מֶ֫לֶךְ	סֵ֫פֶר	קֹ֫דֶשׁ	נַ֫עַר	נֵ֫צַח	פֹּ֫עַל
cons.	מֶ֫לֶךְ	סֵ֫פֶר	קֹ֫דֶשׁ	נַ֫עַר	נֵ֫צַח	פֹּ֫עַל
my (c.)	מַלְכִּי	סִפְרִי	קָדְשִׁי	נַעֲרִי	נִצְחִי	פָּעֳלִי
thy (m.)	מַלְכְּךָ	סִפְרְךָ	קָדְשְׁךָ	נַעַרְךָ	נִצְחֲךָ	פָּעָלְךָ
thy (f.)	מַלְכֵּךְ	סִפְרֵךְ	&c.	&c.	&c.	&c.
his	מַלְכּוֹ	סִפְרוֹ				
her	מַלְכָּהּ	&c.				
our (c.)	מַלְכֵּ֫נוּ					
your (m.)	מַלְכְּכֶם					
your (f.)	מַלְכְּכֶן					
their (m.)	מַלְכָּם					
their (f.)	מַלְכָּן					

Plur.	(kings)	(books)	(holinesses)	(lads)	(eternities)	(works)
abs.	מְלָכִים	סְפָרִים	קֳדָשִׁים	נְעָרִים	נְצָחִים	פְּעָלִים
cons.	מַלְכֵי	סִפְרֵי	קָדְשֵׁי	נַעֲרֵי	נִצְחֵי	פָּעֳלֵי
my (c.)	מְלָכַי	סְפָרַי	קֳדָשַׁי	נְעָרַי	נְצָחַי	פְּעָלַי
thy (m.)	מְלָכֶ֫יךָ	סְפָרֶ֫יךָ	קֳדָשֶׁ֫יךָ	נְעָרֶ֫יךָ	נְצָחֶ֫יךָ	פְּעָלֶ֫יךָ
thy (f.)	מְלָכַ֫יִךְ	&c.	&c.	&c.	&c.	
his	מְלָכָיו					
her	מְלָכֶ֫יהָ					
our (c.)	מְלָכֵ֫ינוּ					
your (m.)	מַלְכֵיכֶם	סִפְרֵיכֶם	קָדְשֵׁיכֶם	נַעֲרֵיכֶם	נִצְחֵיכֶם	פָּעֳלֵיכֶם
your (f.)	מַלְכֵיכֶן	סִפְרֵיכֶן	&c.	&c.	&c.	&c.
their (m.)	מַלְכֵיהֶם	&c.				
their (f.)	מַלְכֵיהֶן					

MASCULINE NOUNS (*continued*)

	V			VI		
	DOUBLE 'AYIN			LAMED HE, ending in הֶ		
Sing.	(people)	(arrow)	(statute)	(shepherd)	(field)	(deed)
abs.	עַם	חֵץ	חֹק	רֹעֶה	שָׂדֶה	מַעֲשֶׂה
cons.	עַם	חֵץ	חָק־	רֹעֵה	שְׂדֵה	מַעֲשֵׂה
my (c.)	עַמִּי	חִצִּי	חֻקִּי	רֹעִי	שָׂדִי	מַעֲשִׂי
thy (m.) &c.	עַמְּךָ	חִצְּךָ	חָקְךָ	(his) רֹעֵהוּ	שָׂדֵהוּ	מַעֲשֵׂהוּ
your (m.) &c.	עַמְּכֶם	חִצְּכֶם	חָקְכֶם	רֹעֲכֶם		
Plur.	(peoples)	(arrows)	(statutes)	(shepherds)	(reeds)[1]	(deeds)
abs.	עַמִּים	חִצִּים	חֻקִּים	רֹעִים	קָנִים	מַעֲשִׂים
cons.	עַמֵּי	חִצֵּי	חֻקֵּי	רֹעֵי	קְנֵי	מַעֲשֵׂי
my (c.)	עַמַּי	חִצַּי	חֻקַּי	רֹעַי	קָנַי	מַעֲשַׂי
thy (m.) &c.	עַמֶּיךָ	חִצֶּיךָ	חֻקֶּיךָ	רֹעֶיךָ	קָנֶיךָ	מַעֲשֶׂיךָ
your (m.) &c.	עַמֵּיכֶם	חִצֵּיכֶם	חֻקֵּיכֶם	רֹעֵיכֶם	קְנֵיכֶם	מַעֲשֵׂיכֶם

	VI Lamed Yod proper, ending in original Yod			VII Medial Waw and Yod	
Sing.	(vessel)	(half)	(sickness)	(death)	(olive)
abs.	כְּלִי [2]	חֲצִי [3]	חֳלִי [4]	מָוֶת	זַיִת
cons.	כְּלִי	חֲצִי	חֳלִי	מוֹת	זֵית
my (c.)	כֶּלְיִי	חֶצְיִי	חָלְיִי	מוֹתִי	זֵיתִי
thy (m.) &c.	כֶּלְיְךָ	חֶצְיְךָ	חָלְיְךָ	מוֹתְךָ	זֵיתְךָ
your (m.) &c.	כֶּלְיְכֶם			מוֹתְכֶם	זֵיתְכֶם
Plur.	(vessels)				(olives)
abs.	כֵּלִים		חֳלָיִים		זֵיתִים
cons.	כְּלֵי		חָלְיֵי		זֵיתֵי
my (c.)	כֵּלַי		חֳלָיַי		זֵיתַי
thy (m.) &c.	כֵּלֶיךָ		חֳלָיֶיךָ		זֵיתֶיךָ
your (m.) &c.	כְּלֵיכֶם		חָלְיֵיכֶם		זֵיתֵיכֶם

[1] The pl. of שָׂדֶה is שָׂדוֹת. [2] Pausal כֶּלִי. [3] Pausal חֵצִי. [4] Pausal חֹלִי.

FEMININE NOUNS

	I	II	III	IV	V
Sing.	(law)	(year)	(righteousness)	(queen)	(kingdom)
abs.	תּוֹרָה	שָׁנָה [1]	צְדָקָה [3]	מַלְכָּה	מַמְלָכָה
cons.	תּוֹרַת	שְׁנַת	צִדְקַת	מַלְכַּת	מַמְלֶכֶת
my (c.)	תּוֹרָתִי	שְׁנָתִי	צִדְקָתִי	מַלְכָּתִי	מַמְלַכְתִּי
thy (m.)	תּוֹרָתְךָ	שְׁנָתְךָ	צִדְקָתְךָ	מַלְכָּתְךָ	מַמְלַכְתְּךָ
thy (f.)	תּוֹרָתֵךְ	&c.	&c.	&c.	&c.
his	תּוֹרָתוֹ				
her	תּוֹרָתָהּ				
our (c.)	תּוֹרָתֵנוּ				
your (m.)	תּוֹרַתְכֶם	שְׁנַתְכֶם	צִדְקַתְכֶם	מַלְכַּתְכֶם	
your (f.)	תּוֹרַתְכֶן	&c.	&c.		
their (m.)	תּוֹרָתָם				
their (f.)	תּוֹרָתָן				

Plur.	(laws)	(years)	(righteousnesses)	(queens)	(kingdoms)
abs.	תּוֹרוֹת	שָׁנוֹת [2]	צְדָקוֹת	מְלָכוֹת	מַמְלָכוֹת
cons.	תּוֹרוֹת	שְׁנוֹת	צִדְקוֹת	מַלְכוֹת	מַמְלְכוֹת
my (c.)	תּוֹרוֹתַי	שְׁנוֹתַי	צִדְקוֹתַי	מַלְכוֹתַי	מַמְלְכוֹתַי
thy (m.)	תּוֹרוֹתֶ֫יךָ	שְׁנוֹתֶ֫יךָ	צִדְקוֹתֶ֫יךָ	מַלְכוֹתֶ֫יךָ	&c.
thy (f.)	תּוֹרוֹתַ֫יִךְ	&c.	&c.	&c.	
his	תּוֹרוֹתָיו				
her	תּוֹרוֹתֶ֫יהָ				
our (c.)	תּוֹרוֹתֵ֫ינוּ				
your (m.)	תּוֹרוֹתֵיכֶם	שְׁנוֹתֵיכֶם	צִדְקוֹתֵיכֶם	מַלְכוֹתֵיכֶם	
your (f.)	תּוֹרוֹתֵיכֶן	&c.	&c.	&c.	
their (m.)	תּוֹרוֹתֵיהֶם				
their (f.)	תּוֹרוֹתֵיהֶן				
	Unchangeable vowel before fem. termination; similarly בְּתוּלָה 'virgin'.	Changeable Qameṣ or Ṣere (שֵׁנָה 'sleep') before fem. termination.	Same as Col. II with shewa before changeable vowel.	From Segholate form: מַלְכָּה is the fem. of מֶ֫לֶךְ, originally מַלְךְ.	Suffixes are attached to Segholate form.

[1] With initial guttural עֵצָה 'counsel'; cons. עֲצַת; with suff. עֲצָתִי &c.

[3] With initial guttural אֲדָמָה 'ground'; cons. אַדְמַת; with suff. אַדְמָתִי.

[2] Usually שָׁנִים.

IRREGULAR NOUNS

Sing.	(father)	(brother)	(sister)	(son)	(daughter)	(mouth)	(house)
abs.	אָב	אָח	אָחוֹת	בֵּן	בַּת	פֶּה	בַּיִת
cons.	אַב אֲבִי	אֲחִי	אֲחוֹת	בֶּן־ [3]	בַּת	פִּי	בֵּית
my (c.)	אָבִי	אָחִי	אֲחוֹתִי	בְּנִי	בִּתִּי	פִּי	בֵּיתִי
thy (m.)	אָבִיךָ	אָחִיךָ	אֲחוֹתְךָ	בִּנְךָ	בִּתְּךָ	פִּיךָ	בֵּיתְךָ
thy (f.)	אָבִיךְ	אָחִיךְ	&c.	בְּנֵךְ	&c.	פִּיךְ	&c.
his	אָבִיו אָבִיהוּ	אָחִיו אָחִיהוּ		בְּנוֹ		פִּיו פִּיהוּ	
her	אָבִיהָ	אָחִיהָ		&c.		פִּיהָ	
our (c.)	אָבִינוּ	אָחִינוּ				פִּינוּ	
your (m.)	אֲבִיכֶם	אֲחִיכֶם		בִּנְכֶם	בִּתְּכֶם	פִּיכֶם	
your (f.)	אֲבִיכֶן	אֲחִיכֶן		&c.	&c.	&c.	
their (m.)	אֲבִיהֶם	אֲחִיהֶם		בְּנָם	בִּתָּם	פִּיהֶם	
their (f.)	אֲבִיהֶן	אֲחִיהֶן			&c.	&c.	

Plur.

abs.	אָבוֹת	אַחִים	(אֲחָיוֹת)	בָּנִים	בָּנוֹת	פִּיּוֹת	בָּתִּים[4]
cons.	אֲבוֹת	אֲחֵי	אַחְיוֹת	בְּנֵי	בְּנוֹת		בָּתֵּי
my (c.)	אֲבוֹתַי	אַחַי	אַחְיוֹתַי	בָּנַי	בְּנוֹתַי		בָּתַּי
thy (m.)	אֲבוֹתֶיךָ	אַחֶיךָ	&c.	בָּנֶיךָ	בְּנוֹתֶיךָ		&c.
thy (f.)	אֲבוֹתַיִךְ	אַחַיִךְ		&c.	&c.		
his	אֲבוֹתָיו	אֶחָיו[2]					
her	אֲבוֹתֶיהָ	אַחֶיהָ					
our (c.)	אֲבוֹתֵינוּ	אַחֵינוּ					
your (m.)	אֲבוֹתֵיכֶם	אֲחֵיכֶם	אַחְיוֹתֵיכֶם	בְּנֵיכֶם	בְּנוֹתֵיכֶם		בָּתֵּיכֶם
your (f.)	אֲבוֹתֵיכֶן	אֲחֵיכֶן	&c.	&c.	&c.		&c.
their (m.)	אֲבוֹתָם[1]	אֲחֵיהֶם					
their (f.)	אֲבוֹתָן	אֲחֵיהֶן					

[1] Rarer אֲבוֹתֵיהֶם.
[2] Note carefully.
[3] Rarely בֶּן־.
[4] Bātîm, see p. 13. 3. N.B.

VOCABULARIES

HEBREW — ENGLISH

א

אָב father: *cons.* אֲבִי; *pl.* אָבוֹת, *cons.* אֲבוֹת p. 288

אָבַד *in Qal* to perish, be lost: *imperf.* יֹאבַד pp. 161, 260; *in Hiph.* הֶאֱבִיד to destroy

אֶ֫בֶן *f.* stone: *pl.* אֲבָנִים, *cons.* אַבְנֵי (*segholate*)

אַבְרָהָם Abraham

אֱדוֹם Edom

אָדוֹן lord

אָדָם man

אֲדָמָה *f.* ground: *cons.* אַדְמַת

אַהֲרֹן Aaron

אוֹ *conj.* or

אוֹי *interj.* woe! alas!

אוּלַי *adv.* perhaps

אוֹר *m.* light

אָז *adv.* then

אֹ֫זֶן *f.* ear: *dual* אָזְנַ֫יִם (*segholate*)

אָח brother: *cons.* אֲחִי; *pl.* אַחִים, *cons.* אֲחֵי p. 288

אֶחָד *m.* one: *cons.* אַחַד p. 242

אָחוֹת sister: *cons.* אֲחוֹת; *pl.* אֲחָיוֹת, *cons.* אַחְיוֹת p. 288

אַחֵר another, other: *f.* אַחֶ֫רֶת; *pl. m.* אֲחֵרִים

אַחַר, אַחֲרֵי *prep.* after, behind: *with suff.* אַחֲרַי *&c.* p. 87

אֹיֵב *m.* enemy: *with suff.* אֹיְבִי; *pl.* אֹיְבִים

אַיֵּה *interrog.* where?

אַ֫יִן nothing, there is not: *cons.* אֵין, *with suff.* אֵינֶנִּי

אִישׁ man: *pl.* אֲנָשִׁים pp. 37, 70

אָכַל to eat: *imperf.* יֹאכַל pp. 161, 260

אַל no, not: *used with Jussive*

אֶל *prep.* unto: *with suff.* אֵלַי *&c.* p. 87

אֵל *m.* God (mighty one)

אֱלֹהִים *pl.* God: *also* gods

אֵ֫לֶּה *c. pl. demonstr. adj.* these

אֵלִיָּ֫הוּ Elijah

אֱלִיעֶ֫זֶר Eliezer

אִם *adv.* if: אִם . . . אִם whether . . . or

אֵם mother: *with suff.* אִמִּי; *pl.* אִמּוֹת p. 110

אָמָה handmaid: *with suff.* אֲמָתִי; *pl.* אֲמָהוֹת

אָמַר to say: *imperf.* יֹאמַר, *with waw consec.* וַיֹּ֫אמֶר p. 162

אֱמֶת *f.* truth: *with suff.* אֲמִתִּי

אֲנִי, אָנֹכִי *pers. pron.* I: *pl.* אֲנַ֫חְנוּ we

אָסַף to gather: *imperf.* יֶאֱסֹף; *Niph. and Hithp.* to assemble, be assembled

אָפָה to bake: *imperf.* יֹאפֶה p. 278

אַרְבַּע *f.*, אַרְבָּעָה *m.* four: אַרְבָּעִים *c.* forty: p. 242 f.

אָרוֹן ark, chest, coffin: *cons.* אֲרוֹן

אֲרִי lion

אֶרֶץ *f.* earth, land, world: *with art.* הָאָרֶץ, *with old acc. case-ending* אַרְצָה; *pl.* אֲרָצוֹת, *cons.* אַרְצוֹת (*segholate*)

ארר to curse: *imperf.* יָאֹר p. 274

אֵשׁ *f.* fire

אִשָּׁה woman, wife: *cons.* אֵשֶׁת, *with suff.* אִשְׁתִּי *&c.*; *pl.* נָשִׁים, *cons.* נְשֵׁי p. 72 [p. 135

אֲשֶׁר *rel. pron. indecl.* who, which:

אֵת, אֶת־ *mark of def. obj.*; *with suff.* אֹתִי me *&c.* pp. 52, 55 f.

אֵת, אֶת־ *prep.* with: *with suff.* אִתִּי *&c.* p. 84

אוֹת sign; *pl.* אֹתוֹת

אַתָּה *m.* thou: *f.* אַתְּ; *pl. m.* אַתֶּם, *f.* אַתֵּן ye

אָתוֹן she-ass

ב

בְּ *insep. prep.* in, with, by: p. 26 f.

בֶּגֶד *m.* garment: *with suff.* בִּגְדִי; *pl.* בְּגָדִים, *cons.* בִּגְדֵי (*segholate*)

בדל *in Hiph.* הִבְדִּיל to divide, distinguish

בוא to come, enter: *Qal perf.* בָּא, *imperf.* יָבוֹא, *imper.* בֹּא; *Hiph.* to cause to come, *i.e.* to bring; *perf.* הֵבִיא, *imperf.* יָבִיא p. 279

בּוֹר *m.* pit, dungeon: *pl.* בּוֹרוֹת

בוש to be ashamed: *imperf.* יֵבוֹשׁ pp. 205 f., 270

בָּזַז to plunder, bespoil: *imperf.* יָבֹז p. 274

בָּחַר to choose: *imperf.* יִבְחַר; *followed by* בְּ p. 262

בָּטַח to trust (in בְּ): *imperf.* יִבְטַח p. 264

בֵּין *prep.* between: *with suff.* בֵּינִי

בַּיִת *m.* house: *cons.* בֵּית; *pl.* בָּתִּים pp. 13. 3 N.B., 288

בְּכוֹר *m.* firstborn

בְּלִי *prep.* without

בֵּן son: *cons.* בֶּן־, *with suff.* בְּנִי; *pl.* בָּנִים, *cons.* בְּנֵי p. 288

followed by שָׁנִים . . . (years) . . . (years) old

בָּנָה to build: *imperf.* יִבְנֶה, *with waw consec.* וַיִּבֶן p. 272

בַּעֲבוּר for the sake of

בַּעַל *m.* lord, master, husband

בָּקָר *c. collect.* herd

בֹּקֶר *m.* morning

בקשׁ *in Pi.* בִּקֵּשׁ to seek: *imperf.* יְבַקֵּשׁ p. 105 f.

בָּרָא to create: *imperf.* יִבְרָא p. 266

בָּרַח to flee: *imperf.* יִבְרַח p. 264

בְּרִית *f.* covenant: כָּרַת בְּרִית to make a covenant

ברך *in Pi.* בֵּרֵךְ to bless: *imperf.* יְבָרֵךְ p. 262

בְּרָכָה *f.* blessing: *with suff.* בִּרְכָתִי pp. 61 f., 70

בָּשָׂר *m.* flesh

בַּת daughter: *pl.* בָּנוֹת p. 288

followed by שָׁנִים . . . (years) . . . (years) old

ג

גְּבוּל *m.* border

גִּבּוֹר hero, mighty man: גִּבּוֹר מִלְחָמָה mighty man of war, warrior

גָּדוֹל *adj.* great, elder

גָּדַל and גָּדֵל to be great, grow up: *imperf.* יִגְדַּל; *Pi.* גִּדֵּל and גִּדַּל to make great, magnify; to bring up (a child); *Hithp.* הִתְגַּדֵּל to make oneself great

גּוֹי *m.* nation: *pl.* גּוֹיִם, *cons.* גּוֹיֵי

גָּלָה to uncover, reveal; go into exile: p. 272

גִּלְעָד Gilead

גַּם also: גַּם . . . גַּם both . . . and

גָּמָל *c.* camel: *with suff.* גְּמַלַּי; *pl.* גְּמַלִּים

גַּן *c.* garden: *with art.* הַגָּן; *pl.* גַּנִּים

גָּנַב to steal

ד

דבר *in Pi.* דִּבֶּר to speak

דָּבָר *m.* word, thing

דָּוִד David

דּוֹר *m.* generation: *pl.* דּוֹרוֹת

דֶּ֫לֶת *f.* door

דָּם *m.* blood: *pl.* דָּמִים bloodshed

דַּ֫עַת *f.* knowledge (*inf. cons. of* יָדַע *used as noun*)

דֶּ֫רֶךְ *c.* way, journey (*segholate*)

ה

ה *art.* the: *pointed* · הַ הָ הֶ p. 23 f.

הֲ *interrogative prefix* p. 80

הוּא *pers. pron. m. sg.* he: *f.* הִיא she

הָיָה to be: *imperf.* יִהְיֶה, *with waw consec.* וַיְהִי p. 92

הֵיכָל *m.* palace, temple

הָלַךְ to go, walk: *imperf.* יֵלֵךְ, *with waw consec.* וַיֵּ֫לֶךְ; *Hiph.* הוֹלִיךְ to cause to go, to lead; *Hithp.* הִתְהַלֵּךְ to walk about. *See* p. 237 f.

הלל *in Pi.* הִלֵּל to praise

הֵם, הֵ֫מָּה *pers. pron. m. pl.* they: *f.* הֵ֫נָּה

הֵן, הִנֵּה behold, lo

הַר *m.* mountain: *with art.* הָהָר; *pl.* הָרִים, *with art.* הֶהָרִים

הָרַג to slay, kill: *imperf.* יַהֲרֹג p. 260

ו

ו *conj.* וּ וְ and: p. 40 f.

ז

זאת *f. sg. demonstr. adj.* this: *m.* זֶה

זֶ֫בַח *m.* sacrifice: *with suff.* זִבְחִי (*segholate*)

זֶה *m. sg. demonstr. adj.* this: *f.* זאת

זָהָב *m.* gold

זָכַר to remember

זָקֵן *vb. stative* to be old: *imperf.* יִזְקַן p. 95 f.

זָקֵן *adj.* old: *as noun* elder; *cons.* זְקַן; *pl.* זְקֵנִים, *cons.* זִקְנֵי

זֶ֫רַע *m.* seed: *with suff.* זַרְעִי (*segholate*)

ח

חבא *not used in Qal*; *Niph.* נֶחְבָּא to hide oneself: *Hiph.* הֶחְבִּיא to hide; *Hithp.* הִתְחַבֵּא to hide oneself: p. 277

חַג *m.* festival: *with art.* הֶחָג; *pl.* חַגִּים

חָגַג to celebrate, keep a feast: *imperf.* יָחֹג p. 274

חֹדֶשׁ *m.* month, new moon (*segholate*)

חוֹמָה *f.* wall (of a city)

חָזַק *vb. stative* to be strong: *imperf.* יֶחֱזַק pp. 155 f., 260; *Hiph.* הֶחֱזִיק to take hold of, to seize

חָזָק *adj.* strong

חָטָא to sin: *imperf.* יֶחֱטָא p. 277

חֵטְא *m.*, חַטָּאת *f.* sin

חַי *adj.* living: *f.* חַיָּה

חַיָּה *f.* living thing, beast

חַיִּים *pl.* life

חָכָם *adj.* wise: *pl.* חֲכָמִים, *cons.* חַכְמֵי

חָכְמָה *f.* wisdom

חֲלוֹם *m.* dream: *pl.* חֲלוֹמוֹת

חָלַם to dream: *imperf.* יַחֲלֹם p. 260

חֲמוֹר m. ass

חֲמִשָּׁה *m.*, חָמֵשׁ *f.* five: p. 242 f.

חֵן *m.* favour, grace: *with suff.* חִנִּי

חֶסֶד *m.* kindness: *with suff.* חַסְדִּי (*segholate*)

חֹק *m.* statute, law: *pl.* חֻקִּים

חֶרֶב *f.* sword: *with suff.* חַרְבִּי (*segholate*); לְפִי־חֶרֶב with the edge of the sword (*see* פֶּה)

חָשַׁךְ *vb. stative* to be dark: *imperf.* יֶחְשַׁךְ p. 156

חֹשֶׁךְ *m.* darkness

ט

טוֹב *vb.* to be good: *used in perf.*; *imperf.* (*from* יָטַב) יִיטַב; *Hiph.* הֵיטִיב pp. 238, 268

טוֹב *adj.* good

יָד *f.* hand: *cons.* יַד; *dual* יָדַיִם, *cons.* יְדֵי

יָדַע to know: *imperf.* יֵדַע, *imper.* דַּע, *inf. cons.* דַּעַת; *Hiph.* הוֹדִיעַ to make kown: p. 279

יְהוּדָה Judah

יהוה Yahweh, the Lord: (*pointed with the vowels of* אֲדֹנָי, *producing* יְהֹוָה p. 23); *with prefix* ליהוה (*representing* לַאדֹנָי) p. 28

יְהוֹשֻׁעַ Joshua

יוֹם *m.* day: *du.* יוֹמַיִם; *pl.* יָמִים, *cons.* יְמֵי

יוֹסֵף Joseph

יטב (*Qal perf. not used, for which* טוֹב *serves*) to be good: *imperf.* יִיטַב; *Hiph.* הֵיטִיב to do good: pp. 238, 268

יַיִן *m.* wine: *cons.* יֵין

יָכֹל to be able: *imperf.* יוּכַל p. 238

יָלַד bear (child): *imperf.* יֵלֵד; *Hiph.* הוֹלִיד to beget: p. 268

יֶלֶד *m.* child, boy (*segholate*)

יַלְדָּה *f.* child, girl

ילך (*perf. Qal not used, for which* הָלַךְ *serves*) to go, walk: *imperf.* יֵלֵךְ, *inf. cons.* לֶכֶת; *Hiph.* הוֹלִיךְ to lead. *See* p. 237 f.

יָם *m.* sea : *pl.* יַמִּים

יַעֲקֹב Jacob

יָפֶה *adj.* fair, beautiful : *f.* יָפָה

יָצָא to go out : *imperf.* יֵצֵא, *inf. cons.* צֵאת ; *Hiph.* הוֹצִיא to bring out : p. 279

יִצְחָק Isaac

יָרֵא to fear : *imperf.* יִירָא, *inf. cons.* יִרְאָה p. 211 ; *followed by* מִן, מִפְּנֵי, *or* אֶת־ p. 127 vocab.

יִרְאָה *f.* fear

יָרַד to go down : *imperf.* יֵרֵד, *imper.* רֵד, *inf. cons.* רֶדֶת ; *Hiph.* הוֹרִיד to bring down : p. 268

יַרְדֵּן Jordan

יְרוּשָׁלַיִם Jerusalem : *usually found in the Bible as* יְרוּשָׁלִַם *with vowels of former*

יְרִיחוֹ Jericho

יָרַשׁ to inherit : *imperf.* יִירַשׁ, *inf. cons.* רֶשֶׁת p. 189

יִשְׂרָאֵל Israel

יָשַׁב to sit, dwell, abide : *imperf.* יֵשֵׁב, *with waw consec.* וַיֵּשֶׁב, *imper.* שֵׁב, *inf. cons.* שֶׁבֶת ; *Hiph.* הוֹשִׁיב p. 268

יֹשֵׁב *part. Qal* dweller, inhabitant

יְשׁוּעָה *f.* salvation

יָשֵׁן *vb. stative* to sleep : *imperf.* יִישַׁן pp. 95, 188

ישׁע (*not used in Qal*) *Hiph.* הוֹשִׁיעַ to save, deliver : *Niph.* נוֹשַׁע to be saved, delivered : p. 211

יָשָׁר upright, righteous

כ

כּ *insep. prep.* (*see* p. 26 f.) as, like, according to

כַּאֲשֶׁר *prep. with rel.* as, when

כָּבֵד *vb. stative* to be heavy : *imperf.* יִכְבַּד p. 95 f. ; *Pi.* כִּבֵּד to harden, honour

כָּבֵד *adj.* heavy

כָּבוֹד *m.* honour, glory

כַּד *m.* jar, pitcher : *with suff.* כַּדִּי

כֹּה *adv.* thus

כֹּהֵן *m.* priest : *pl.* כֹּהֲנִים

כּוֹכָב *m.* star

כִּי *conj.* that, because, when : כִּי אִם except, only

כֹּל, כָּל־ all, every : *with suff.* כֻּלִּי all of me

כֵּן so, thus : לָכֵן, עַל־כֵּן therefore

כְּנַעַן Canaan

כְּנַעֲנִי *m.* Canaanite : *f.* כְּנַעֲנִית

כִּסֵּא throne, seat

כֶּסֶף *m.* silver, money (*segholate*)

כָּרַת to cut : כָּרַת בְּרִית to make a covenant

כָּתַב to write

ל

ל *insep. prep.* to, for : *see* p. 26 f.

לֹא not

לֵב *m.* heart : *with suff.* לִבִּי ; *pl.* לִבּוֹת

לֵבָב *m.* heart : *with suff.* לְבָבִי ; *pl.* לְבָבוֹת

לְבַד (√בדד) alone : *with suff.* לְבַדִּי

לָבָן Laban

לוּחַ tablet : *pl.* לוּחוֹת

לוֹט Lot

לחם *used in Niph.* נִלְחַם to fight: *followed by* בְּ

לֶ֫חֶם *c.* bread (*segholate*)

לַ֫יִל *m. usually* לַ֫יְלָה night: *pl.* לֵילוֹת

לָכַד to capture

לָכֵן therefore: *see* כֵּן (thus)

לָמַד to learn: *Pi.* לִמֵּד to teach

לָ֫מָּה why? wherefore? (ל + מָה)

לְמַ֫עַן *conj. and prep.* in order that, for the sake of: *with suff.* לְמַעֲנִי for my sake

לִפְנֵי (ל + פְּנֵי *prep. with cons. pl. of* פָּנִים face) before

לָקַח to take: *imperf.* יִקַּח, *inf. cons.* קַ֫חַת pp. 149, 258

לִקְרַאת towards, to meet (*prep. with inf. cons. of* קרא = קרה to meet): *with suff.* לִקְרָאתִי to meet me, towards me

מ

מְאֹד *adv., follows adj.* very, exceedingly

מֵאָה *f.* hundred: *dual* מָאתַ֫יִם

מַגֵּפָה *f.* plague (√נגף)

מִדְבָּר *m.* desert, wilderness: *cons.* מִדְבַּר

מַדּ֫וּעַ *interrog. adv.* why? wherefore?

מָה (מֶה, מַה) *interrog. pron.* what? p. 42

מות to die: *Qal perf.* מֵת, *imperf.* יָמוּת; *Hiph.* to put to death; *perf.* הֵמִית, *imperf.* יָמִית p. 205 f.

מָ֫וֶת *m.* death: *cons.* מוֹת, *with suff.* מוֹתִי

מַחֲנֶה camp: *cons.* מַחֲנֵה

מָחָר to-morrow

מִי *interrog. pron. indecl.* who?

מַ֫יִם *pl.* water: *cons.* מֵי

מָכַר to sell

מָלֵא *vb. stative* to be full (with), *takes direct obj.*; *Pi.* to fill (with): p. 179

מָלֵא *part.* full [מַלְאָךְ

מַלְאָךְ *m.* messenger, angel: *cons.*

מְלָאכָה *f.* work: *cons.* מְלֶ֫אכֶת, *with suff.* מְלַאכְתִּי

מִלְחָמָה *f.* war, battle (√לחם): *cons.* מִלְחֶ֫מֶת [escape

מלט (*Qal not used*) *Niph.* נִמְלַט to

מָלַךְ to reign: *Niph.* הִמְלִיךְ to make one king

מֶ֫לֶךְ *m.* king (*segholate*)

מַלְכָּה *f.* queen

מַמְלָכָה *f.* kingdom: *cons.* מַמְלֶ֫כֶת, *with suff.* מַמְלַכְתִּי

מִן *prep.* from: p. 29; *with suff.* מִמֶּ֫נִּי p. 63

מִנְחָה *f.* gift, present

מָצָא to find: *imperf.* יִמְצָא p. 266

מִצְוָה *f.* commandment: *pl.* מִצְוֹת (√צוה)

מִצְרִי *m.* Egyptian: *f.* מִצְרִית

מִצְרַ֫יִם Egypt

מָקוֹם *m.* place: *pl.* מְקוֹמוֹת (√קום)

מִקְנֶה *m.* cattle: *cons.* מִקְנֵה

מְרַגֵּל *m.* spy (√רגל)

מָרַד to rebel

מֹשֶׁה Moses

מָשַׁל to rule (over בְּ)
מִשְׁפָּט *m.* judgement, right (√שָׁפַט)
מִשְׁתֶּה *m.* feast, banquet: *cons.* מִשְׁתֵּה (√שָׁתָה)

נ

נָא I pray, we pray, now: *particle of entreaty*
נבא (*not used in Qal*) *Niph.* נִבָּא *and Hithp.* הִתְנַבֵּא to prophesy. *Cf.* p. 185 (*c*)
נָבִיא *m.* prophet: *f.* נְבִיאָה prophetess
נגד (*not used in Qal*) *Hiph.* הִגִּיד to tell, declare, announce: *Hoph.* הֻגַּד p. 258
נָגַע to touch: *imperf.* יִגַּע; *Hiph.* הִגִּיעַ to cause to touch, to reach; *Pi.* נִגַּע to plague: p. 276
נָגַף to plague, smite: *imperf.* יִגֹּף p. 258
נגשׁ *Qal* (*perf. not used*) *imperf.* יִגַּשׁ, *inf. cons.* גֶּשֶׁת to draw near: *Niph.* נִגַּשׁ to draw near; *Hiph.* הִגִּישׁ to bring near: p. 258
נָהָר *m.* river
נוּס to flee: *Qal perf.* נָס, *imperf.* יָנוּס p. 270
נָחַל to inherit, possess: *imperf.* יִנְחַל; *Hiph.* הִנְחִיל to give possession: p. 144
נָחָשׁ *m.* serpent
נָטָה to bend, incline, stretch: *imperf.* יִטֶּה, *with waw consec.* וַיֵּט; *Hiph.* הִטָּה p. 277
נָטַע to plant: *imperf.* יִטַּע p. 184
נכה *in Hiph.* to smite: *perf.* הִכָּה, *imperf.* יַכֶּה, *short. imperf.* יַךְ; *Hoph.* הֻכָּה to be smitten: p. 277
נָסַע to journey: *imperf.* יִסַּע p. 184
נָפַח to breathe: *imperf.* יִפַּח p. 184
נָפַל to fall: *imperf.* יִפֹּל; *Hiph.* הִפִּיל to cause to fall, cast: p. 258
נֶפֶשׁ *f.* soul, life, person (*segholate*): *pl.* נְפָשׁוֹת
נצל (*not used in Qal*) *Niph.* נִצַּל to be delivered, saved: *Hiph.* הִצִּיל to save, deliver: pp. 142, 258
נָשָׂא to lift up, bear, forgive: *imperf.* יִשָּׂא, *imper.* שָׂא p. 276
נָתַן to give, allow: *imperf.* יִתֵּן, *inf. cons.* תֵּת p. 258

ס

סָבַב to turn, go round: *imperf.* יָסֹב, *imper.* סֹב p. 274
סוּס *m.* horse
סוּר to turn aside, depart: *Qal perf.* סָר, *imperf.* יָסוּר; *Hiph.* הֵסִיר to remove: p. 270
סִינַי Sinai
סָפַר to count: *Pi.* סִפֵּר to recount, relate
סֹפֵר *m.* scribe
סֵפֶר *m.* book (*segholate*)
סתר *in Hiph.* to hide, conceal: *in Niph.* נִסְתַּר *and Hithp.* הִסְתַּתֵּר to hide oneself

ע

עָבַד to serve, labour: *imperf.* יַעֲבֹד p. 260

עֶ֫בֶד *m.* servant (*segholate*)

עֲבוֹדָה *f.* service, labour

עָבַר to pass over, cross, transgress: *imperf.* יַעֲבֹר p. 260

עִבְרִי *m.* a Hebrew

עַד *prep.* until, as far as

עֵדָה *f.* congregation: *cons.* עֲדַת

עֵ֫דֶן Eden

עוֹד *adv.* again, yet, still

עוֹלָם *m.* eternity: לְעוֹלָם, עַד־עוֹלָם for ever

עָזַב to leave, forsake: *imperf.* יַעֲזֹב p. 260

עָזַר to help: *imperf.* יַעֲזֹר p. 260

עַ֫יִן *f. cons.* עֵין (1) eye: *dual* עֵינַ֫יִם, *cons.* עֵינֵי

(2) spring: *pl.* עֲיָנוֹת, *cons.* עֵינוֹת

עִיר *f.* city: *pl.* עָרִים, *cons.* עָרֵי

עֵירֹם *m. adj.* naked: *pl.* עֵירֻמִּים

עַל *prep.* upon, over: *with suff.* עָלַי &c. p. 87

עָלָה to go up, ascend: *imperf.* יַעֲלֶה; *Hiph.* to bring up הֶעֱלָה pp. 225 f., 278

עֵלִי Eli

עִם *prep.* with, along with: *with suff.* עִמִּי &c.; *with 1st sg. suff. also* עִמָּדִי

עַם *m.* a people: *with art.* הָעָם, *with suff.* עַמִּי; *pl.* עַמִּים

עָמַד to stand: *imperf.* יַעֲמֹד; *Hiph.* הֶעֱמִיד to set up, place: p. 260

עָנָה (1) *Qal* to answer: *imperf.* יַעֲנֶה; (2) *Piel* עִנָּה to afflict: *imperf.* יְעַנֶּה *cf.* p. 278

עָפָר *m.* dust: *with art.* הֶעָפָר

עֵץ *m.* tree

עֵצָה *f.* counsel, advice (√יָעַץ): *cons.* עֲצַת

עֶ֫רֶב *m.* evening (*segholate*)

עָשָׂה to do, make: *imperf.* יַעֲשֶׂה, *short. imperf.* יַ֫עַשׂ p. 278

עֵשָׂו Esau

עֵת *f.* time, season: *with suff.* עִתִּי; *pl.* עִתִּים (עִתּוֹת)

עַתָּה *adv.* now

פ

פֶּה *m.* mouth: *cons.* פִּי; *pl.* פִּיּוֹת p. 288; לְפִי־חֶרֶב with the edge of the sword

פֹּה *adv.* here

פזר *usually Pi.* פִּזֵּר to scatter, disperse

פלל *in Hithp.* הִתְפַּלֵּל to pray

פְּלִשְׁתִּי *m.* Philistine

פֶּן־ *conj.* lest

פָּנִים *m. pl.* face: *cons.* לִפְנֵי before; *with suff.* לְפָנַי before me

פֶּ֫סַח Passover

פַּ֫עַם step, time: *dual* פַּעֲמַ֫יִם twice: *pl.* פְּעָמִים times

פָּקַח to open (eyes): *imperf.* יִפְקַח p. 264

פַּר *m.* ox: *with art.* הַפָּר, *pl.* פָּרִים

פרד *in Niph.* to be separated, to separate oneself

פָּרָה *f.* cow

פְּרִי *m.* fruit: *pausal* פֶּ֫רִי, *with suff.* פִּרְיוֹ

פַּרְעֹה Pharaoh

צ

צֹאן *c.* sheep, flock

צָבָא *m.* host: *pl.* צְבָאוֹת

צַדִּיק righteous, just: *pl.* צַדִּיקִים

צֶ֫דֶק *m.* righteousness: *with suff.* צִדְקִי (*segholate*)

צְדָקָה *f.* righteousness: *with suff.* צִדְקָתִי

צוה (*not used in Qal*) *Pi.* צִוָּה to command: *imperf.* יְצַוֶּה, *short. imperf.* יְצַו, *imper.* צַו, צַוֵּה p. 272

צָעַק to cry out: *imperf.* יִצְעַק p. 262

צְעָקָה *f.* a cry: *cons.* צַעֲקַת, *with suff.* צַעֲקָתִי

צֹר Tyre

צָרָה *f.* trouble, distress; *cons.* צָרַת, *with suff.* צָרָתִי

ק

קָבַץ to assemble, gather (*trans.*): *also Pi.* קִבֵּץ; to gather together (*intrans.*) *Niph.* נִקְבַּץ *or Hithp.* הִתְקַבֵּץ

קָבַר to bury

קֶ֫בֶר *m.* grave: *with suff.* קִבְרִי (*segholate*)

קָדַשׁ, קָדֵשׁ to be holy: *imperf.* יִקְדַּשׁ; *Pi.* קִדֵּשׁ to sanctify; *Niph.* נִקְדַּשׁ *and Hithp.* הִתְקַדֵּשׁ to sanctify oneself

קָדוֹשׁ *adj.* holy

קֹ֫דֶשׁ *m.* holiness: *with suff.* קָדְשִׁי (*segholate*)

קהל (*not used in Qal*) *Hiph.* to call together, assemble: *Niph.* to be gathered together, to assemble

קָהָל *m.* assembly, gathering

קוֹל *m.* voice: *pl.* קוֹלוֹת

קוּם to arise, stand up: *Qal perf.* קָם, *imperf.* יָקוּם; *Hiph.* הֵקִים to set up, establish: p. 270

קָטֹן *vb. stative* to be small: *imperf.* יִקְטַן p. 95

קָטֹן, קָטָן *adj. m.* small, young, younger: *f.* קְטַנָּה; *pl. m.* קְטַנִּים

קלל to be light, despised: *Qal perf.* קַל, *imperf.* יֵקַל; *Pi.* קִלֵּל to curse: p. 274

קָצַף to be angry

קָרָא to call, cry, read: *imperf.* יִקְרָא p. 266; *sometimes* = קָרָה, *e.g. inf. cons.* (לִ)קְרַאת to meet, towards

קָרַב, קָרֵב *vb. stative* to draw near: *imperf.* יִקְרַב p. 95

קָרָה to happen, befall

קָרַע to tear, rend: *imperf.* יִקְרַע p. 264

ר

רָאָה to see: *imperf.* יִרְאֶה, *short. imperf.* יֵרֶא, *with waw consec.* וַיַּרְא; *Niph.* נִרְאָה to be seen, to appear; *Hiph.* הֶרְאָה to show

רְאוּבֵן Reuben

רֹאשׁ *m.* head: *pl.* רָאשִׁים

רִאשׁוֹן *m.* first: *f.* רִאשׁוֹנָה p. 244

רַב *adj.* great, much: *pl.* רַבִּים many

רֶ֫גֶל *f.* foot: *dual* רַגְלַיִם (*segholate*)

רָדַף to pursue, persecute

ר֫וּחַ wind, spirit: *pl.* רוּחוֹת

רוּם to be high: *Qal perf.* רָם, *imperf.* יָרוּם; *Hiph.* הֵרִים to lift up: p. 270
רוּץ to run: *Qal perf.* רָץ, *imperf.* יָרוּץ p. 270
רָחֵל Rachel
רָחַץ to wash: *imperf.* יִרְחַץ p. 262
רְכוּשׁ *m.* wealth, substance
רַע *adj. m.* evil: *f.* רָעָה; *pl. m.* רָעִים
רֵעַ friend, companion: *with suff.* רֵעִי, רֵעֲךָ
רָעֵב *vb. stative* to be hungry: *imperf.* יִרְעַב p. 95
רָעֵב *adj.* hungry
רָעָב *m.* hunger, famine
רֹעֶה shepherd: *cons.* רֹעֵה; *pl.* רֹעִים
רַק *adv.* only, except
רָשָׁע *adj.* wicked

שׂ

שִׂים to place, set: *Qal perf.* שָׂם, *imperf.* יָשִׂים p. 270
שָׂפָה *f.* lip, bank, edge: *dual* שְׂפָתַיִם, *cons.* שִׂפְתֵי
שָׂרָה Sarah
שָׂרַף to burn

שׁ

שָׁאוּל Saul
שְׁאוֹל Sheol, Hades, the netherworld
שָׁאַל to ask, to inquire: *imperf.* יִשְׁאַל p. 262
שבח *in Pi.* שִׁבַּח to praise
שבע *in Niph.* נִשְׁבַּע to swear, take an oath
שֶׁבַע *f.*, שִׁבְעָה *m.* seven: שִׁבְעִים *c.* seventy: pp. 242 ff.
שָׁבַר to break: *Pi.* שִׁבֵּר to break in pieces
שַׁבָּת Sabbath
שָׁוְא *m.* vanity, falsehood
שׁוּב to return, come back: *Qal perf.* שָׁב, *imperf.* יָשׁוּב; *Hiph.* הֵשִׁיב to cause to return, *i.e.* to bring back, restore: p. 270
שׁוֹר *m.* ox: *pl.* שְׁוָרִים
שָׁחַט to slaughter: *imperf.* יִשְׁחַט p. 262
שַׁחַר *m.* dawn
שחת (*not used in Qal*) *Pi.* שִׁחֵת *and Hiph.* הִשְׁחִית to destroy, corrupt: *Niph.* נִשְׁחַת to be destroyed, corrupted
שָׁכַב *vb. stative* to lie down, sleep: *imperf.* יִשְׁכַּב p. 97
שָׁכַח to forget: *imperf.* יִשְׁכַּח p. 264
שְׁכֶם Shechem
שָׁלוֹם *m.* peace
שָׁלַח to send: *with* יָד to stretch out one's hand; *imperf.* יִשְׁלַח; *Pi.* שִׁלַּח to send away, let go: p. 264
שָׁלֵם *adj.* perfect, whole, complete
שְׁלֹמֹה Solomon
שָׁלֹשׁ *f.*, שְׁלֹשָׁה *m.* three: שְׁלֹשִׁים *c.* thirty: pp. 242 ff.
שֵׁם *m.* name: *with suff.* שְׁמִי; *pl.* שֵׁמוֹת
שָׁם *adv.* there: שָׁמָּה thither
שמד (*not used in Qal*) *Hiph.* הִשְׁמִיד to destroy: *Niph.* נִשְׁמַד to be destroyed

שְׁמוּאֵל Samuel

שָׁמַ֫יִם *pl.* heaven(s): *cons.* שְׁמֵי

שָׁמַע to hear, listen: *imperf.* יִשְׁמַע; שָׁמַע בְּקוֹל *or* שָׁמַע לְקוֹל to give heed, obey; *Hiph.* הִשְׁמִ֫יעַ to cause to hear, announce: p. 264

שָׁמַר to keep watch: *Niph.* נִשְׁמַר to take heed, beware

שֹׁמֵר *part. as noun* watchman

שֶׁ֫מֶשׁ sun: *with suff.* שִׁמְשִׁי (*segholate*)

שָׁנָה *f.* year: *dual* שְׁנָתַ֫יִם two years; *pl.* שָׁנִים

שֵׁנִי *adj. m.* second: *f.* שֵׁנִית p. 244

שָׁפַט to judge

שֹׁפֵט *part. as noun* a judge

שָׁפַךְ to pour out, shed

שקה *used in Hiph. as causative of* שָׁתָה; הִשְׁקָה to give to drink: *imperf.* יַשְׁקֶה, *short. imperf.* יַשְׁקְ (*defective*) pp. 238, 272

שָׁתָה to drink: *imperf.* יִשְׁתֶּה, *short. imperf.* יֵשְׁתְּ; *Hiph. from* √שקה pp. 238, 272

ת

תָּ֫וֶךְ *m.* midst: *cons.* תּוֹךְ in the midst of

תּוֹרָה *f.* instruction, law

תַּ֫חַת *prep.* under, beneath, instead of: *with suff.* תַּחְתַּי p. 87 f.

תְּפִלָּה *f.* prayer (√פלל)

ENGLISH — HEBREW

A

Aaron אַהֲרֹן
abide, to יָשַׁב (to sit): *imperf.* יֵשֵׁב p. 268
able, to be *perf.* יָכֹל: *imperf.* יוּכַל p. 238
Abraham אַבְרָהָם
according to, as כְּ *prep.*
advice עֵצָה: *cons.* עֲצַת
afraid, to be יָרֵא: *imperf.* יִירָא, *inf. cons.* יִרְאָה p. 211; *followed by* מִן, מִפְּנֵי, *or* אֶת־ p. 127 vocab.
after אַחַר, אַחֲרֵי: *with suff.* אַחֲרֵי p. 87
again עוֹד
against בְּ, עַל, נֶגֶד *prep.*
aged *adj.* זָקֵן: *vb. stative* זָקֵן; *imperf.* יִזְקַן
alive חַי
all כֹּל, כָּל־
allow, to נָתַן (to give)
alone לְבַד: *with suff.* לְבַדִּי I alone, &c.
also גַּם
among, amongst בְּתוֹךְ (in the midst of): *cons. of* תָּוֶךְ
angel (messenger) מַלְאָךְ: *cons.* מַלְאַךְ
angry, to be קָצַף
announce, to [*Hiph. of* נגד] הִגִּיד p. 258, *Hiph. of* שָׁמַע
another אַחֵר: *pl.* אֲחֵרִים other(s)
any כֹּל, כָּל־
appear, to [*Niph. of* ראה (to see)] נִרְאָה
approach, to (1) קָרַב, קָרֵב: *imperf.* יִקְרַב (*stative*)
(2) √נגשׁ: *perf. in Niph.* נִגַּשׁ; *imperf. in Qal* יִגַּשׁ; *imper. in Qal* גַּשׁ p. 258
arise, to קוּם: *Qal perf.* קָם, *imperf.* יָקוּם p. 270
ark (of the Lord) אָרוֹן
as כְּ *prep.*, כַּאֲשֶׁר
ascend, to עָלָה: *imperf.* יַעֲלֶה p. 278
ashamed, to be בּוֹשׁ: *imperf.* יֵבוֹשׁ pp. 205 f., 270
aside, to turn סוּר: *perf.* סָר, *imperf.* יָסוּר p. 270
ask שָׁאַל: *imperf.* יִשְׁאַל p. 262
assemble, to (*trans.*) קָבַץ (*Qal*) *and Pi.* קִבֵּץ: [*Hiph. of* קהל] הִקְהִיל
(*intrans.*) קבץ *in Niph.* נִקְבְּצוּ *and Hithp.* הִתְקַבְּצוּ: קהל *in Niph.* נִקְהֲלוּ
assembly קָהָל, עֵדָה

B

bad *m.* רַע: *f.* רָעָה; *m. pl.* רָעִים
bake, to אָפָה: *imperf.* יֹאפֶה p. 278
bank (of river) שָׂפָה: *cons.* שְׂפַת
battle, a מִלְחָמָה: *cons.* מִלְחֶמֶת
be, to; become, to הָיָה: *imperf.* יִהְיֶה, *short. imperf.* (*Juss.*) יְהִי p. 92
bear, to (carry) נָשָׂא: *imperf.* יִשָּׂא p. 276
bear, to (child) יָלַד, p. 268

beast חַיָּה
beautiful *m.* יָפֶה : *f.* יָפָה
because כִּי
befall, to קָרָה
before לִפְנֵי (to the face of): before me לְפָנַי (to my face) *&c.* *see* face [p. 268
beget, to [*Hiph. of* יָלַד] הוֹלִיד
behind אַחַר, אַחֲרֵי : *with suff.* אַחֲרַי p. 87
behold הִנֵּה, הֵן : *with suff.* הִנְנִי *&c.*
below, beneath תַּחַת : *with suff.* תַּחְתַּי p. 87
bespoil, to בָּזַז : *imperf.* יָבֹז p. 274
between בֵּין : *with suff.* בֵּינִי
beware, to [*Niph. of* שָׁמַר (to keep)] נִשְׁמַר : *imperf.* יִשָּׁמֵר
bless, to [*Pi. of* ברך] בֵּרַךְ : *imperf.* יְבָרֵךְ p. 262
blessing בְּרָכָה : *with suff.* בִּרְכָתִי
blood דָּם : *cons.* דַּם ; bloodshed דָּמִים (*pl.*), *cons.* דְּמֵי
book סֵפֶר : *with suff.* סִפְרִי ; *pl.* סְפָרִים, *cons.* סִפְרֵי (*segholate*)
border גְּבוּל
both . . . and גַּם . . . גַּם
boy (child) יֶלֶד (*segholate*) : (lad) נַעַר
bread לֶחֶם : *with suff.* לַחְמִי (*segholate*)
break, to שָׁבַר : to break in pieces *Pi.* שִׁבֵּר
breathe, to נָפַח : *imperf.* יִפַּח p. 184
bring, to *Hiph. of* בּוֹא (to come), *i.e.* to cause to come, *perf.* הֵבִיא, *imperf.* יָבִיא p. 279
bring back, to : *Hiph. of* שׁוּב (to return), *i.e.* to cause to return, *perf.* הֵשִׁיב, *imperf.* יָשִׁיב p. 270
bring down, to *Hiph. of* יָרַד (to descend), *i.e.* to cause to descend, *perf.* הוֹרִיד, *imperf.* יוֹרִיד p. 268
bring forth, bring out, to *Hiph. of* יָצָא (to go forth), *i.e.* to cause to go forth, *perf.* הוֹצִיא, *imperf.* יוֹצִיא p. 279
bring up, to *Hiph. of* עָלָה (to go up), *i.e.* to cause to go up הֶעֱלָה p. 278
brother אָח : *cons.* אֲחִי ; *pl.* אַחִים
build, to בָּנָה : *imperf.* יִבְנֶה, *short. imperf.* יִבֶן p. 272
bull שׁוֹר, פַּר
burn, to שָׂרַף
bury, to קָבַר
but כִּי : כִּי אִם *after negative clause*

C

call, to קָרָא : *imperf.* יִקְרָא p. 266
camel גָּמָל : *pl.* גְּמַלִּים
camp מַחֲנֶה : *cons.* מַחֲנֵה, *with suff.* מַחֲנֵהוּ
Canaan כְּנַעַן
Canaanite כְּנַעֲנִי
capture, to לָכַד
care, to take [*Niph. of* שָׁמַר] נִשְׁמַר
cattle (1) מִקְנֶה : *cons.* מִקְנֵה, *with suff.* מִקְנֵהוּ
(2) בְּהֵמָה
celebrate, to חָגַג : *imperf.* יָחֹג p. 274

child *m.* יֶלֶד: *f.* יַלְדָּה; children of Israel (sons of Israel) בְּנֵי־יִשְׂרָאֵל

choose, to בָּחַר: *followed by* בּ

city *f.* עִיר: *pl.* עָרִים

come, come in, to בּוֹא: *Qal perf.* בָּא, *imperf.* יָבֹא, *imper.* בֹּא p. 279

command, to [*Pi. of* צוה] *perf.* צִוָּה: *imperf.* יְצַוֶּה, *short. imperf.* יְצַו; *imper.* צַו, צַוֵּה p. 272

command, commandment מִצְוָה: *pl.* מִצְוֹת

companion רֵעַ: *with suff.* רֵעִי, רֵעֲךָ; *pl.* רֵעִים

complete (*adj.*) שָׁלֵם

conceal, to: (*trans.*) [*Hiph. of* חבא *or* סתר] הֶחְבִּיא, הִסְתִּיר: to conceal oneself [*Niph. of* סתר *or* חבא] נֶחְבָּא, נִסְתַּר; *Hithp.* הִתְחַבֵּא, הִסְתַּתֵּר

congregation עֵדָה, קָהָל

counsel עֵצָה: *cons.* עֲצַת, *with suff.* עֲצָתִי

count, to סָפַר (*number*)

country *f.* אֶרֶץ: *with art.* הָאָרֶץ; *pl.* אֲרָצוֹת, *cons.* אַרְצוֹת (*segholate*)

covenant בְּרִית: to make a covenant כָּרַת בְּרִית, *lit.* to cut a covenant

cow פָּרָה

create, to בָּרָא: *imperf.* יִבְרָא p. 266

cross, to עָבַר: *imperf.* יַעֲבֹר p. 260

cry, to (1) קָרָא: *imperf.* יִקְרָא p. 266

(2) צָעַק: *imperf.* יִצְעַק p. 262

cry *n.* צְעָקָה: *cons.* צַעֲקַת, *with suff.* צַעֲקָתִי

curse, to (1) [*Pi. of* קלל] קִלֵּל

(2) *Qal of* ארר: *imperf.* יָאֹר p. 274

cut, to כָּרַת

D

dark, to be חָשַׁךְ: *imperf.* יֶחְשַׁךְ

darkness חֹשֶׁךְ (*segholate*)

daughter בַּת: *with suff.* בִּתִּי; *pl.* בָּנוֹת, *cons.* בְּנוֹת

David דָּוִד

dawn שַׁחַר

day יוֹם: *dual* יוֹמַיִם; *pl.* יָמִים, *cons.* יְמֵי

death מָוֶת: *cons.* מוֹת, *with suff.* מוֹתִי

death, to put to: *Hiph. of* מות (to die), *i.e.* to cause to die הֵמִית: *imperf.* יָמִית p. 270

declare, to (1) [*Hiph. of* נגד] הִגִּיד p. 258

(2) [*Pi. of* ספר] סִפֵּר

deliver (save), to (1) [*Hiph. of* נצל] הִצִּיל p. 258

(2) [*Hiph. of* ישע] הוֹשִׁיעַ p. 211

deliver (hand over), to (1) נָתַן to give

(2) מָכַר to sell

deliverance יְשׁוּעָה

depart, to סוּר: *Qal perf.* סָר, *imperf.* יָסוּר p. 270

descend, to יָרַד: *imperf.* יֵרֵד, *imper.* רֵד, *inf. cons.* רֶדֶת p. 268

desert מִדְבָּר : *cons.* מִדְבַּר
desire, to חָמַד : *imperf.* יַחְמֹד
despised, to be קלל: *Qal perf.* קַל, *imperf.* יֵקַל p. 274
destroy, to (1) [*Pi. and Hiph. of* שחת] שִׁחֵת , הִשְׁחִית
(2) [*Hiph. of* שמד] הִשְׁמִיד
(3) *Hiph. of* אבד (to be lost), *i.e.* to cause to be lost הֶאֱבִיד
die, to מות : *Qal perf.* מֵת , *imperf.* יָמוּת p. 270
disperse, to [*Pi. of* פזר] פִּזַּר
distinguish, divide, to [*Hiph. of* בדל] הִבְדִּיל
distress צָרָה
divide, to *see* distinguish
do, to עָשָׂה : *imperf.* יַעֲשֶׂה, *short. imperf.* יַעַשׂ p. 278
door דֶּלֶת (*segholate*)
draw near, to (1) *vb. stative* קָרֵב, קָרַב : *imperf.* יִקְרַב
(2) נגשׁ *perf. in Niph.* נִגַּשׁ, *imperf. in Qal* יִגַּשׁ, *imper. in Qal* גַּשׁ p. 258 [p. 260
dream, to חָלַם : *imperf.* יַחֲלֹם
dream, a חֲלוֹם : *pl.* חֲלוֹמוֹת
dungeon בּוֹר
dust עָפָר : *with art.* הֶעָפָר, *cons.* עֲפַר
drink, to שָׁתָה : *imperf.* יִשְׁתֶּה ; *short. imperf.* יֵשְׁתְּ ; to give to drink [*Hiph. of* שקה] הִשְׁקָה ; *imperf.* יַשְׁקֶה *short. imperf.* יַשְׁקְ (*defective*) p. 238
dwell יָשַׁב : *imperf.* יֵשֵׁב ; *imper.* שֵׁב p. 268
dweller ישֵׁב (*part.*)

E

each כָּל־ , כֹּל
ear *f.* אֹזֶן : *with suff.* אָזְנִי ; *dual* אָזְנַיִם (*segholate*)
earth *f.* (1) אֶרֶץ : *with art.* הָאָרֶץ, *with old acc. case-ending* אַרְצָה
(2) אֲדָמָה : *cons.* אַדְמַת
eat, to אָכַל : *imperf.* יֹאכַל p. 260
Eden עֵדֶן
edge שָׂפָה (lip) : with the edge of the sword לְפִי־חֶרֶב (with the mouth of the sword)
Edom אֱדוֹם
Egypt מִצְרַיִם
Egyptian מִצְרִי
eight *m.* שְׁמֹנָה : *f.* שְׁמֹנֶה
eighth *m.* שְׁמִינִי : *f.* שְׁמִינִית
elder זָקֵן : *cons.* זְקַן ; *pl.* זְקֵנִים, *cons.* זִקְנֵי
Eli עֵלִי
Eliezer אֱלִיעֶזֶר
Elijah אֵלִיָּהוּ
enemy אֹיֵב : *with suff.* אֹיְבִי ; *pl.* אֹיְבִים
enter, to בּוֹא : *perf.* בָּא , *imperf.* יָבֹא p. 279
Esau עֵשָׂו
escape, to [*Niph. of* מלט] נִמְלַט
establish, to [*Hiph. of* קום] הֵקִים p. 270
eternity עוֹלָם
even גַּם
evening עֶרֶב
ever, for לְעוֹלָם : עַד־עוֹלָם (eternity)
every כָּל־ , כֹּל

evil *adj. m.* רַע : *f.* רָעָה ; *pl. m.* רָעִים

exceedingly מְאֹד

except (only) רַק : כִּי אִם (but)

exile, to go into (to be exiled) גָּלָה : *imperf.* יִגְלֶה p. 272

exile, to [*Hiph. of* גָּלָה] הִגְלָה (to cause to go into exile) p. 272

eye *f.* עַ֫יִן : *cons.* עֵין ; *dual.* עֵי֫נַיִם, *cons.* עֵינֵי

F

face פָּנִים : *pl. cons.* פְּנֵי

fair (beautiful) *m.* יָפֶה : *f.* יָפָה

fall, to נָפַל : *imperf.* יִפֹּל p. 258

falsehood (vanity) שָׁוְא

famine רָעָב

father אָב : *cons.* אֲבִי, *with suff.* אָבִי, אָבִ֫יךָ ; *pl.* אָבוֹת, *cons.* אֲבוֹת p. 288

fear, to יָרֵא (*followed by* מִן, מִפְּנֵי, *or* אֶת־ p. 127 vocab.): *imperf.* יִירָא, *inf. cons.* יִרְאָה p. 211

fear *n.* יִרְאָה

feast, to celebrate חָגַג : *imperf.* יָחֹג p. 274

feast *n.* מִשְׁתֶּה (√שָׁתָה to drink)

festival חַג : *with art.* הֶחָג ; *pl.* חַגִּים

field שָׂדֶה : *cons.* שְׂדֵה ; *pl.* שָׂדוֹת

fifth *m.* חֲמִשִׁי : *f.* חֲמִשִׁית

fight, to [*Niph. of* לחם] נִלְחַם : against בְּ

fill (be full with) מָלֵא : *imperf.* יִמְלָא p. 266; (*in the active sense*) *Pi.* מִלֵּא

find, to מָצָא : *imperf.* יִמְצָא p. 266

fire *f.* אֵשׁ

first *m.* רִאשׁוֹן, רִאשׁוֹנָה

firstborn *m.* בְּכוֹר

five *m.* חֲמִשָּׁה : *f.* חָמֵשׁ

flee, to (1) בָּרַח : *imperf.* יִבְרַח p. 264
(2) נוּס : *perf.* נָס, *imperf.* יָנוּס p. 270

flesh בָּשָׂר

flock (sheep) *c.* צֹאן

foot *f.* רֶ֫גֶל : *with suff.* רַגְלִי ; *dual* רַגְלַ֫יִם (*segholate*)

for *prep.* לְ, *conj.* (because) כִּי

forget, to שָׁכַח : *imperf.* יִשְׁכַּח p. 264

forsake עָזַב : *imperf.* יַעֲזֹב p. 260

four *m.* אַרְבָּעָה : *f.* אַרְבַּע

fourth *m.* רְבִיעִי : *f.* רְבִיעִית

friend רֵ֫עַ : *pl.* רֵעִים

from *prep.* מִן

fruit פְּרִי : *pausal* פֶּ֫רִי, *with suff.* פִּרְיִי

full *adj.* מָלֵא

G

garden גַּן : *with art.* הַגָּן ; *pl.* גַּנִּים

garment בֶּ֫גֶד : *with suff* בִּגְדִי ; *pl.* בְּגָדִים, *cons.* בִּגְדֵי (*segholate*)

gather together, to: (*trans.*) [*Hiph. of* קהל] הִקְהִיל : [*Pi. of* קבץ] קִבֵּץ
(*intrans.*) [*Niph. of* קהל] נִקְהֲלוּ : [*Niph. and Hithp. of* קבץ] נִקְבְּצוּ, הִתְקַבְּצוּ

gathering *n.* קָהָל

generation דּוֹר : *pl.* דּוֹרוֹת

gentile גּוֹי (nation) : *pl.* גּוֹיִם

Gilead גִּלְעָד

girl נַעֲרָה, יַלְדָּה

gift, offering מִנְחָה

give, to נָתַן: *imperf.* יִתֵּן, *imper.* תֵּן, *inf. cons.* תֵּת, *with suff.* תִּתִּי p. 258
glory כָּבוֹד
go, to *perf.* הָלַךְ: *imperf.* יֵלֵךְ (√ילך), *imper.* לֵךְ, *inf. cons.* לֶכֶת (*defective*) p. 237 f.
go down, to יָרַד: *imperf.* יֵרֵד, *imper.* רֵד p. 268
go forth, to יָצָא: *imperf.* יֵצֵא, *imper.* צֵא, *inf. cons.* צֵאת p. 279
go in, to בּוֹא: *perf.* בָּא, *imperf.* יָבֹא p. 279
go out *see* go forth
go round, to סָבַב: *imperf.* יָסֹב: *imper.* סֹב p. 274
go up, to עָלָה: *imperf.* יַעֲלֶה, *short. imperf.* יַעַל p. 278
go, to let [*Pi. of* שָׁלַח] שִׁלַּח, *imperf.* יְשַׁלַּח p. 264
God אֱלֹהִים: *with sg. vb. and adj.*
gods אֱלֹהִים: *with pl. vb. and adj.*
gold זָהָב
good, to be *perf.* טוֹב: *imperf.* יִיטַב (√יטב, *defective*) p. 238
good, to do [*Hiph. of* יטב] הֵיטִיב p. 268
good *adj.* טוֹב
grace חֵן: *with suff.* חִנִּי
grave קֶבֶר: *with suff.* קִבְרִי (*segholate*)
great, to be *vb. stative* גָּדַל: *imperf.* יִגְדַּל
great *adj.* גָּדוֹל
ground אֲדָמָה: *cons.* אַדְמַת
grow up, to גָּדַל

H

hand *f.* יָד: *cons.* יַד; *dual* יָדַיִם, *cons.* יְדֵי
handmaid אָמָה: *with suff.* אֲמָתִי
harden, to [*Pi.* of כבד] כִּבֵּד
he הוּא
head רֹאשׁ: *pl.* רָאשִׁים
hear, hearken שָׁמַע: *imperf.* יִשְׁמַע, p. 264
heart (1) לֵב: *cons.* לֶב־, לֵב, *with suff.* לִבִּי [לְבָבִי]
(2) לֵבָב: *cons.* לְבַב, *with suff.*
heaven(s): *pl.* שָׁמַיִם, *cons.* שְׁמֵי
heavy, to be *vb. stative* כָּבֵד: *imperf.* יִכְבַּד
heavy *adj.*: כָּבֵד: *f.* כְּבֵדָה
Hebrew עִבְרִי
heed, to give: שָׁמַע בְּקוֹל *or* שָׁמַע לְקוֹל (to hearken in *or* to the voice of)
heed, to take [*Niph. of* שָׁמַר] נִשְׁמַר (to keep oneself)
herd (cattle) בָּקָר
here פֹּה
hero (mighty man) גִּבּוֹר
hide, to: *trans.* [*Hiph. of* חבא *or* סתר] הֶחְבִּיא *or* הִסְתִּיר: *intrans.* [*Niph. and Hithp.*] נֶחְבָּא, הִתְחַבֵּא; נִסְתַּר, הִסְתַּתֵּר
high, to be רוּם: *perf.* רָם, *imperf.* יָרוּם p. 270
hill (mountain) הַר: *with art.* הָהָר; *pl.* הָרִים
holiness קֹדֶשׁ: *with suff.* קָדְשִׁי (*segholate*)
holy, to be *vb. stative* קָדַשׁ, קָדֹשׁ: *imperf.* יִקְדַּשׁ

holy, to make [*Pi. of* קדשׁ] קִדֵּשׁ
honour, to [*Pi. of* כבד] כִּבֵּד
horse סוּס
host צָבָא : *pl.* צְבָאוֹת
house בַּ֫יִת : *cons.* בֵּית ; *pl.* בָּתִּים (bātîm), *cons.* בָּתֵּי
hunger רָעָב
hungry, to be *vb. stative* רָעֵב: *imperf.* יִרְעַב
hungry *adj.* רָעֵב
husband אִישׁ, בַּ֫עַל

I

I אֲנִי , אָנֹכִי : *pausal* אָ֫נִי , אָנֹ֫כִי
if אִם
in בְּ (*insep.*)
incline, to נָטָה : *imperf.* יִטֶּה, *short. imperf.* יֵט p. 277
inhabit יָשַׁב : *imperf.* יֵשֵׁב, *imper.* שֵׁב, *inf. cons.* שֶׁ֫בֶת p. 268
inhabitant יֹשֵׁב (*part.*)
inherit, to (1) נָחַל : *imperf.* יִנְחַל p. 144
(2) יָרַשׁ : *imperf.* יִירַשׁ, *inf. cons.* רֶ֫שֶׁת p. 189
inquire, to שָׁאַל : *imperf.* יִשְׁאַל p. 262
instead of תַּ֫חַת : *with suff.* תַּחְתַּי p. 87 f.
is, there יֵשׁ
is not, there אֵין
Isaac יִצְחָק
Israel יִשְׂרָאֵל

J

Jacob יַעֲקֹב
Jericho יְרִיחוֹ
Jerusalem יְרוּשָׁלַ֫יִם : *usually found in the Bible as* יְרוּשָׁלַם
Jordan יַרְדֵּן
Joseph יוֹסֵף
Joshua יְהוֹשֻׁ֫עַ
journey, to נָסַע : *imperf.* יִסַּע p. 184
journey, a דֶּ֫רֶךְ (way)
Judah יְהוּדָה
judge, to שָׁפַט
judge, a שֹׁפֵט (*part.*)
judgement מִשְׁפָּט
just (righteous) צַדִּיק

K

keep, to (watch) שָׁמַר
keeper, (watchman) שֹׁמֵר (*part.*)
kill, to (1) הָרַג : *imperf.* יַהֲרֹג p. 260
(2) *Hiph. of* מוּת (to die), *i.e.* to cause to die הֵמִית, *imperf.* יָמִית p. 270
kindness חֶ֫סֶד : *with suff.* חַסְדִּי (*segholate*)
king, to be מָלַךְ
king, to make [*Hiph.*] הִמְלִיךְ
king, מֶ֫לֶךְ : *with suff.* מַלְכִּי (*segholate*)
kingdom מַמְלָכָה : *cons.* מַמְלֶ֫כֶת, *with suff.* מַמְלַכְתִּי
know, to יָדַע : *imperf.* יֵדַע, *imper.* דַּע, *inf. cons.* דַּ֫עַת p. 279
knowledge דַּ֫עַת

L

Laban לָבָן
lad נַ֫עַר

land אֶ֫רֶץ: *with art.* הָאָ֫רֶץ, *with old acc. case-ending* אַ֫רְצָה, *with suff.* אַרְצִי (*segholate*)
law תּוֹרָה
learn, to לָמַד: *imperf.* יִלְמַד
leave, to (forsake) עָזַב: *imperf.* יַעֲזֹב p. 260
lest פֶּן־ *with imperf.*
lie down, to שָׁכַב, *imperf.* יִשְׁכַּב, *imper.* שְׁכַב p. 97
life חַיִּים *pl.*, נֶ֫פֶשׁ (soul)
lift up, to (1) נָשָׂא: *imperf.* יִשָּׂא, *imper.* שָׂא p. 276
(2) *Hiph. of* רום (to be high), *i.e.* to cause to be high הֵרִים p. 270
light, to be (despised) קלל: *perf.* קַל, *imperf.* יֵקַל p. 274
light (brightness) אוֹר
lion אֲרִי
lip שָׂפָה: *dual* שְׂפָתַ֫יִם, *cons.* שִׂפְתֵי
little, to be *vb. stative* קָטֹן: *imperf.* יִקְטַן
little *adj. sg. m.* קָטֹן, קָטָן: *f.* קְטַנָּה; *pl. m.* קְטַנִּים
living *adj.* חַי
lord אָדוֹן
Lord (Yahweh) יהוה
lost, to be אָבַד: *imperf.* יֹאבַד pp. 161, 260
Lot לוֹט

M

magnify, to: *Hiph. of* גָּדַל (to be great), *i.e.* to cause to be great הִגְדִּיל
maidservant אָמָה: *with suff.* אֲמָתִי
make, to עָשָׂה: *imperf.* יַעֲשֶׂה; *short. imperf.* יַ֫עַשׂ p. 278
man אִישׁ: *pl.* אֲנָשִׁים, *cons.* אַנְשֵׁי
many: *pl. of* רַב (much) רַבִּים *&c.*
master אָדוֹן, בַּ֫עַל
matter דָּבָר
messenger מַלְאָךְ: *cons.* מַלְאַךְ
midst תָּ֫וֶךְ: *cons.* תּוֹךְ
mighty גִּבּוֹר: mighty warrior גִּבּוֹר־מִלְחָמָה
money (silver) כֶּ֫סֶף: *with suff.* כַּסְפִּי (*segholate*)
morning בֹּ֫קֶר
morrow, to-morrow מָחָר
Moses מֹשֶׁה
mother אֵם: *with suff.* אִמִּי; *pl.* אִמּוֹת
mountain הַר: *with art.* הָהָר; *pl.* הָרִים
mouth פֶּה: *cons.* פִּי; *pl.* פִּיּוֹת p. 288
much רַב: *pl.* many

N

naked עֵירֹם: *pl.* עֵירֻמִּים
name שֵׁם: *with suff.* שְׁמִי; *pl.* שֵׁמוֹת
nation גּוֹי: *pl.* גּוֹיִם
neighbour רֵ֫עַ
night *m.* לַ֫יְלָה (*longer form of* לַ֫יִל)
nine *m.* תִּשְׁעָה: *f.* תֵּ֫שַׁע
ninth *m.* תְּשִׁיעִי: *f.* תְּשִׁיעִית
no, not לֹא
now עַתָּה

O

offering (gift) מִנְחָה
old *adj.* זָקֵן
old, to be זָקֵן: *imperf.* יִזְקַן p. 95 f.

on (upon) עַל : *with suff.* עָלַי p. 87
one *m.* אֶחָד : *f.* אַחַת
one . . . another אִישׁ . . . רֵעֵהוּ (a man . . . his friend) : אִישׁ . . . אָחִיו (a man . . . his brother); זֶה . . . זֶה (this . . . this)
open, to פָּתַח : (the eyes) פָּקַח
opposite נֶגֶד
or אוֹ
other אַחֵר : *pl.* אֲחֵרִים
out of מִן
over עַל (on, upon)
ox (1) פַּר : *with art.* הַפָּר ; *pl.* פָּרִים ; (2) שׁוֹר ; *pl.* שְׁוָרִים

P

palace הֵיכָל
pass over, to (cross) עָבַר : *imperf.* יַעֲבֹר p. 260
Passover פֶּסַח
peace שָׁלוֹם
people, עַם : *with art.* הָעָם, *with suff.* עַמִּי ; *pl.* עַמִּים
perfect שָׁלֵם
perish, to אָבַד : *imperf.* יֹאבַד pp. 161, 260
permit, to נָתַן (give)
Pharaoh פַּרְעֹה
Philistine פְּלִשְׁתִּי
pit בּוֹר : *pl.* בּוֹרוֹת
pitcher כַּד : *with suff.* כַּדִּי
place, to שִׂים : *perf.* שָׂם, *imperf.* יָשִׂים, *imper.* שִׂים p. 270
place, a מָקוֹם : *pl.* מְקוֹמוֹת
plague, to נָגַף : *imperf.* יִגֹּף p. 258
plague, a מַגֵּפָה
plant, to נָטַע : *imperf.* יִטַּע p. 184
plunder, to בָּזַז : *imperf.* יָבֹז p. 274
pour out, to שָׁפַךְ
praise, to *Pi. of* (1) [הלל] הִלֵּל (2) [שבח] שִׁבַּח
pray, to [*Hithp. of* פלל] הִתְפַּלֵּל
prayer תְּפִלָּה
priest כֹּהֵן : high priest כֹּהֵן גָּדוֹל
prophesy, to [*Niph. and Hithp. of* נבא] נִבָּא *and* הִתְנַבֵּא
prophet נָבִיא
pursue, to רָדַף

Q

queen מַלְכָּה

R

raise, to *Hiph. of* (1) קוּם (to rise), *i.e.* to cause to rise הֵקִים (2) רוּם (to be high), *i.e.* to cause to be high הֵרִים p. 270
reach, to [*Hiph. of* נגע] הִגִּיעַ p. 276
read, to קָרָא : *imperf.* יִקְרָא p. 266
reign, to מָלַךְ
relate, to [*Pi. of* ספר] סִפֵּר
remember, to זָכַר
remove, to *Hiph. of* סוּר (to depart), *i.e.* to cause to depart הֵסִיר p. 270
rend, to קָרַע
restore, to *Hiph. of* שׁוּב (to return), *i.e.* to cause to return הֵשִׁיב p. 270
return, to (come back) שׁוּב : *perf.* שָׁב, *imperf.* יָשׁוּב, *imper.* שׁוּב p. 270

Reuben רְאוּבֵן
reveal, to גָּלָה: *imperf.* יִגְלֶה, *short. imperf.* יִגֶל p. 272
righteous צַדִּיק
righteousness (1) צֶדֶק: *with suff.* צִדְקִי
(2) צְדָקָה: *cons.* צִדְקַת, *with suff.* צִדְקָתִי
rise, to קוּם: *perf.* קָם, *imperf.* יָקוּם p. 270
river נָהָר: *cons.* נְהַר
rule (over), to (בְּ) מָשַׁל

S

Sabbath שַׁבָּת
sacrifice, to זָבַח
sacrifice, a זֶבַח: *with suff.* זִבְחִי (*segholate*)
sake of, for לְמַעַן: *with suff.* לְמַעֲנִי
salvation יְשׁוּעָה
Samuel שְׁמוּאֵל
sanctify, to [*Pi. of* קדשׁ] קִדֵּשׁ
Sarah שָׂרָה
Saul שָׁאוּל
save, to *Hiph. of* (1) [נצל] הִצִּיל: *imperf.* יַצִּיל p. 258
(2) [ישׁע] הוֹשִׁיעַ: *imperf.* יוֹשִׁיעַ p. 211
saved, to be *Niph. of* (1) [נצל] נִצַּל p. 258
(2) [ישׁע] נוֹשַׁע: *imperf.* יִוָּשַׁע p. 211
say, to אָמַר: *imperf.* יֹאמַר, *with waw consec.* וַיֹּאמֶר p. 162
scatter, to [*Pi. of* פזר] פִּזַּר
sea יָם: *cons.* יַם; *pl.* יַמִּים
season *f.* עֵת: *with suff.* עִתִּי; *pl.* עִתִּים
second *m.* שֵׁנִי: *f.* שֵׁנִית
see, to רָאָה: *imperf.* יִרְאֶה, *short. imperf.* יֵרֶא, *with waw consec.* וַיַּרְא
seed זֶרַע: *with suff.* זַרְעִי (*segholate*)
seek, to [*Pi. of* בקשׁ] בִּקֵּשׁ
seize, to אָחַז, *Hiph. of* חזק
sell, to מָכַר
send, to שָׁלַח: *imperf.* יִשְׁלַח p. 264
send away, to [*Pi. of* שׁלח] שִׁלַּח: *imperf.* יְשַׁלַּח p. 264
separated, to be *Niph. of* פרד
serpent נָחָשׁ
servant עֶבֶד: *with suff.* עַבְדִּי (*segholate*)
serve, to עָבַד: *imperf.* יַעֲבֹד p. 260
service עֲבוֹדָה
set, to שִׂים: *perf.* שָׂם, *imperf.* יָשִׂים p. 270
set up, to *Hiph. of* קוּם (to rise), *i.e.* to cause to rise הֵקִים: *imperf.* יָקִים p. 270
seven *m.* שִׁבְעָה: *f.* שֶׁבַע
Shechem שְׁכֶם
shed, to שָׁפַךְ
sheep *c.* צֹאן
Sheol (netherworld) שְׁאוֹל
shepherd רֹעֶה: *cons.* רֹעֵה; *pl.* רֹעִים
show, to *Hiph. of* רָאָה (to see), *i.e.* to cause to see הֶרְאָה: *imperf.* יַרְאֶה
sign אוֹת: *pl.* אֹתוֹת
silver כֶּסֶף: *with suff.* כַּסְפִּי (*segholate*)

sin, to חָטָא: *imperf.* יֶחֱטָא p. 277

sin, a חֵטְא, חַטָּאת

Sinai סִינַי

sister אָחוֹת: *cons.* אֲחוֹת, *with suff.* אֲחוֹתִי; *pl.* אֲחָיוֹת, *cons.* אַחְיוֹת, *with suff.* אַחְיוֹתַי

sit, to יָשַׁב: *imperf.* יֵשֵׁב, *imper.* שֵׁב *inf. cons.* שֶׁבֶת p. 268

slaughter, to שָׁחַט: *imperf.* יִשְׁחַט p. 262

slave (servant) עֶבֶד: *with suff.* עַבְדִּי (*segholate*)

slay, to (1) הָרַג: *imperf.* יַהֲרֹג p. 260

(2) [*Hiph. of* מוּת] הֵמִית: *imperf.* יָמִית p. 270

sleep, to *vb. stative* יָשֵׁן: *imperf.* יִישַׁן; שָׁכַב: *imperf.* יִשְׁכַּב

small, to be *vb. stative* קָטֹן: *imperf.* יִקְטַן

small *adj. sg. m.* קָטֹן, קָטָן: *f.* קְטַנָּה; *pl. m.* קְטַנִּים

smite, to (1) נָגַף: *imperf.* יִגֹּף p. 258

(2) [*Hiph. of* נָכָה] הִכָּה: *imperf.* יַכֶּה, *short. imperf.* יַךְ p. 276

so כֵּן

Solomon שְׁלֹמֹה

son בֵּן, *cons.* בֶּן, *pl.* בָּנִים

soul *f.* נֶפֶשׁ: *with suff.* נַפְשִׁי (*segholate*)

speak, to [*Pi. of* דבר] דִּבֶּר

spill (shed) שָׁפַךְ

spirit רוּחַ: *with suff.* רוּחִי

spring (fountain) (1) עַיִן: *cons.* עֵין

(2) מַעְיָן: *cons.* מַעְיַן

spy, a מְרַגֵּל

stand, to עָמַד: *imperf.* יַעֲמֹד p. 260

star כּוֹכָב

steal, to גָּנַב

still (yet) עוֹד

stone *f.* אֶבֶן: *with suff.* אַבְנִי (*segholate*); *pl.* אֲבָנִים, *cons.* אַבְנֵי

stretch (out), to נָטָה: *imperf.* יִטֶּה, *short. imperf.* יֵט p. 276

stretch out hand, to שָׁלַח יָד

strong חָזָק

substance (wealth) רְכוּשׁ

sun שֶׁמֶשׁ: *with suff.* שִׁמְשִׁי (*segholate*)

swear, to [*Niph. of* שבע] נִשְׁבַּע p. 264

sword *f.* חֶרֶב: *with suff.* חַרְבִּי (*segholate*)

T

tablet לוּחַ: *pl.* לוּחוֹת

take, to (1) לָקַח: *imperf.* יִקַּח, *imper.* קַח, *inf. cons.* קַחַת p. 258

(2) (to capture) לָכַד

take hold of, to אָחַז, *Hiph. of* חזק

teach, to *Pi. of* לָמַד

tear, to קָרַע: *imperf.* יִקְרַע p. 264

tell, to (1) [*Hiph. of* נגד] הִגִּיד: *imperf.* יַגִּיד p. 258

(2) [*Pi. of* ספר] סִפֵּר

temple הֵיכָל

ten *m.* עֲשָׂרָה: *f.* עֶשֶׂר

that *conj.* כִּי: in order that לְמַעַן

that *demonstr. adj. m.* הוּא: *f.* הִיא

then אָז

thence מִשָּׁם (from there)
there שָׁם
there is (are) יֵשׁ
there is (are) not אֵין
therefore עַל־כֵּן, לָכֵן
these *c.* אֵלֶּה
thing דָּבָר
this *m.* זֶה : *f.* זֹאת
thither שָׁמָּה (to there)
three *m.* שְׁלֹשָׁה : *f.* שָׁלֹשׁ
throne כִּסֵּא
thus כֹּה
till (until) עַד, עַד־אֲשֶׁר
time (season) *f.* עֵת : *with suff.* עִתִּי; *pl.* עִתִּים; a time פַּעַם; twice פַּעֲמַיִם *dual*
to, unto אֶל, לְ (*insep.*)
touch, to נָגַע : *imperf.* יִגַּע, *imper.* גַּע p. 276
towards לִקְרַאת : *with suff.* לִקְרָאתִי
tree עֵץ
trouble צָרָה, עָמָל
trust, to בָּטַח : *followed by* בְּ
truth אֱמֶת
turn aside, to סוּר : *perf.* סָר, *imperf.* יָסוּר p. 270
twice פַּעֲמַיִם : *dual of* פַּעַם (a time)
two *m.* שְׁנַיִם : *f.* שְׁתַּיִם

U

uncover, to גָּלָה : *imperf.* יִגְלֶה p. 272
under תַּחַת : *with suff.* תַּחְתַּי p. 87 f.
until עַד
unto אֶל : *with suff.* אֵלַי p. 87
upon עַל : *with suff.* עָלַי p. 87
upright יָשָׁר

V

vanity שָׁוְא
very מְאֹד : *follows adj.*
voice קוֹל

W

walk, to הָלַךְ : *and in Hithp.* הִתְהַלֵּךְ
wall (of a city) חוֹמָה
war מִלְחָמָה : *cons.* מִלְחֶמֶת
warrior גִּבּוֹר־מִלְחָמָה (mighty man of war)
wash, to (body) רָחַץ : *imperf.* יִרְחַץ p. 262; (clothes) [*Pi. of* כבס] כִּבֵּס
watch, to שָׁמַר
watchman שֹׁמֵר *part.*
water, to [*Hiph. of* שקה] הִשְׁקָה : *imperf.* יַשְׁקֶה, *short. imperf.* יַשְׁקְ (*defective*) pp. 238, 272
water מַיִם : *cons.* מֵי
way דֶּרֶךְ : *with suff.* דַּרְכִּי (*segholate*)
wealth רְכוּשׁ
when בְּ *or* כְּ *with inf. cons.* p. 132; כַּאֲשֶׁר *and* כִּי *with finite verb*
where ? אַיֵּה
wherefore ? (why) לָמָּה
which *relat.* אֲשֶׁר p. 135
who *relat.* אֲשֶׁר p. 135
who ? מִי
why ? (wherefore ?) לָמָּה
wicked רָשָׁע

wife (woman) אִשָּׁה : *cons.* אֵ֫שֶׁת ;
  pl. נָשִׁים

wilderness מִדְבָּר : *cons.* מִדְבַּר

wind רוּחַ

wine יַ֫יִן : *cons.* יֵין

wisdom חָכְמָה

wise חָכָם

with (1) *abl.* בְּ
  (2) (together with) אֵת, עִם

without בְּלִי

woe ! אוֹי

woman (wife) אִשָּׁה : *cons.* אֵ֫שֶׁת ;
  pl. נָשִׁים

word דָּבָר

work, to (serve) עָבַד : *imperf.* יַעֲבֹד
  p. 260

world עוֹלָם

write, to כָּתַב

Y

Yahweh יהוה (*usually read* אֲדֹנָי)

year שָׁנָה : *dual* שְׁנָתַ֫יִם ; *pl.* שָׁנִים

Z

Zion צִיּוֹן

INDEX OF SUBJECTS

The numbers refer to the pages